FORGING MEXICO, 1821–1835

Forging Mexico
1821-1835

Timothy E. Anna

University of Nebraska Press
Lincoln and London

© 1998 by the University of Nebraska Press
Manufactured in the United States of America
☉ The paper in this book meets the minimum requirements of American National Standard for Information Sciences—Permanence of Paper for Printed Library Materials, ANSI Z39.48-1984.
Library of Congress Cataloging-in-Publication Data
Anna, Timothy E., 1944–
Forging Mexico, 1821–1835 / Timothy E. Anna.
p. cm.
Includes bibliographical references and index.
ISBN 0-8032-1047-7 (cloth : alk. paper)
1. Mexico—History—1821–1861. 2. Federal government—Mexico—History—19th century. 3. Nationalism—Mexico—History—19th century.
I. Title.
F1232.A573 1998
972′.04—dc21
97-25062
CIP

México, de milenaria cultura
y multiple alma.

From an open letter signed by
sixteen Italian intellectuals,
film directors, and journalists,
La Jornada, 15 February 1995.

CONTENTS

PREFACE

My general purpose here is to identify and explain the process by which Mexico undertook its transition from colonial subservience to nationhood. The first response of anyone to such a proposal would be to say, "Naturally, it occurred with Mexican independence in September 1821." Indeed, the traditional periodization marks the achievement of independence in 1821 as the great divide separating the two major periods of Mexican history, colonial and national.

In more recent years, however, a number of scholars have suggested that 1821 did not constitute such a total break with the past, that there were as many continuities as discontinuities in independence. This idea was nicely summarized by Germán Carrera Damas and John V. Lombardi in recommended guidelines they wrote for contributors to volume 5 of UNESCO's *General History of Latin America*. They proposed the theme "Models of Continuity and Fracture." The real point of this era, they suggest, is not some assumed total break but a massive structural crisis in the transplanted societies of Spanish imperialism in America that provoked the emergence of a national project in each Latin American country.

I entirely endorse the approach suggested by Carrera Damas and Lombardi because it reflects Latin Americans' perceptions of their own national foundations and because it corresponds to my own findings. It constitutes a major step away from the old hagiography of an elite-oriented patriotic paradigm and toward a more sophisticated view of the birth of nations. In the case of Mexico, however, this perception remains more a generalization than a fully detailed historical argument. I think the reason that argument has yet to be elaborated is that one must study the issues of structural crisis and the coalescing of national identity by starting from the demands of the constituent parts and arriving at the whole, rather than by looking back from the whole to define the parts.

In Mexico, the "national project" took the form of a federal republic. One cannot understand federalism without starting with the provinces. I do not propose studying individually each of the Mexican provinces or states that emerged in the constitution of 1824; that would lead to repetition and squandered labor. My intent is to study the major themes that came from the provinces to the center and that culminated in an option for nationhood. I believe one cannot properly define what the nation is without starting with the constituent parts because they are what defined the nation. In Mexico, one such constituent part is the central core, the old heartland around Mexico City, but it is only one part. And I believe that nations are not so much imagined as they are forged; that is, they are the result of the political and social processes by which institutions of government and administration are established that conform with the existing identities, institutions, and history of a territorial space. They are processes of discovery and construction resulting from the pragmatic exercise of human will, not born fully formed from some mystical consanguinity.

Considerable revisionist scholarship in recent years has altered our views of what Mexican independence meant. But we have not yet bridged the transition from the breakdown of the Spanish Empire to the formulation of independent political entities. The transition was a subtle, complex, and difficult one because the Spanish regimen had resisted the gradual emergence of fully formed separate identities. The Mexicans had to invent Mexico after independence, not before as one might have anticipated. And the process of nationhood could not begin until it was expanded to include more than just the central core.

The transition to a federal republic was the real "revolution" because the old gave way to the new in Mexican history. It was during the brief period of March through August 1823, from the abdication of Agustín de Iturbide to the achievement of consensus on a federal republic, that the fundamental transition occurred. But why and how? Those now become the questions to be answered.

In the decision to create a federal republic in Mexico in 1823 and 1824, the emphasis was on the "federal" as much as the "republic." There was virtually no literature of republicanism in those days; but there was a huge and pervasive literature of federalism. The urge toward provincial home rule, born before the start of the movement for independence, was sidetracked by the mass insurrections that swept Mexico, but by 1821 it had reasserted itself as the dominant theme. The provincial elites wanted home rule to assure that they themselves would possess power at home and their provinces would develop as social and political entities in their own right. I believe, in fact, it is what the regions thought they were getting when they opted for Iturbide's Plan of Iguala because it recognized the political existence of provinces in every intendancy. But Iturbide's creation of the Mexican Empire did not complete the transition because it did not solve the problem of who was to rule at home in each province, nor did it address the critical issue of the course of future development. The achievement of the status of statehood with internal sovereignty for each state within a federal republic was both the termination of the process of independence and the beginning of the process of nationhood.

The first solution to the problem of how to organize a federal state was not the final one. In this, Mexico does not differ from Canada, the United States, or any other large American country in which the creation of a workable system that allowed competent national government and an effective regional voice was a delicate balancing act requiring frequent revision. The twentieth-century solution in Mexico was the creation of a very strong national executive in a federal republic in which the states have far less autonomy than they did in the first federal republic. This twentieth-century solution is now under massive attack by many Mexicans who feel it does not conform with present needs.

Nor do I interpret this process of devolution, as most of the historiography does, as the arbitrary breaking up by provincial strongmen of what had been a highly centralized viceroyalty. The creation of the intendancies, essentially provincial royal governments, by the Spanish Crown in 1786 had juridically weakened viceregal centralism, a fact that tended to be disguised because the last viceroys exercised exceptional powers during the struggle to resist independence. Most of all, the process of independence itself weakened the largely traditional concept of centralism, drastically reorienting relationships of political power. Provincialism was dispersionist and antihegemonic, but I believe the penchant of many historians to interpret it as dissolution results from a centralist bias that runs throughout the historiography.

The tendency in Mexico to think in terms of provinces dates from pre-Conquest days and derives from the sheer size of the colonial dominion, the Spanish creation of intendancies, and the reinforcement of provincial identity in the liberal Spanish constitution of 1812. This first written constitution of the Hispanic world was based on the assumption that provinces existed, which greatly enhanced Mexican regional aspirations. In 1821, the new Mexican Empire extended from the border of Oregon to the border of Panama, and devolutionist, even secessionist, tendencies were not un-natural.

The tendency to define the provinces and to grant power to them can be traced throughout the political history of the period. The core ideas were clear to Mexican deputies to the Spanish Cortes, the imperial parliament, in both 1812 and 1820. On instructions from their home provinces, these deputies focused on Spanish traditions to argue that political power was based on the privileges of cities and that the Spanish Empire itself was essentially a confederation of provinces or kingdoms. These same men were the authors of the Mexican constitution of 1824. In light of the long centuries of colonial control in Mexico, the creation of a federal republic of sovereign states can be seen not as a dissolution but as the attempt to define a nation out of many long-standing regional identities. The achievement of federalism did not, however, prevent the division of politics along ideological and interest-group lines.

Mexican federalism is not merely a slavish copy of U.S. federalism, as an ethnocentric historiography once argued, any more than Mexican nationhood is a slavish copy of anything else. Mexican federalism derived from its own needs and its own Spanish and national traditions. It was necessary because the provinces demanded self-government. Mexican federalism was the redress of deep historical grievances. The tensions between the forces of centralism and regionalism and between control of the few and a voice for the many are the dominant themes in Mexican history.

When approached in such broad terms as the creation of a nation, a study of the origins of the Mexican federal republic touches on the very heart of the Mexican being. That, in turn, opens up a vast historical and theoretical literature, fascinating in its diversity and enriching in its thoughtfulness, that sheds much light on early national history. In the past five or six years there has been a notable increase in the publication of historical research on the early independence period. This research reflects a natural continuity with the research that was conducted in the previous two decades on the late colonial period and the wars of independence as well as the relatively liberating impact of the end of a long period of excess theorizing stemming from the influence of competing Cold War ideological inspirations. Most of all, however, it reflects the fact that Mexicans are engaged in a general reconsideration of their country's political conventions and traditions, which naturally directs their attention, in part, toward the first years of their national existence.

Because several of the issues Mexicans are debating today are remarkably similar to those they discussed in the 1820s, I could not entirely resist linking the great questions of early national history with a few of today's. I have also chosen not to obscure my own preferences in the artificial pretense of objectivity, which in my view has no place in the scholarship of history. As the composer Maurice Ravel once said to a student who praised his new composition as a work of great inspiration, it had nothing to do with inspiration and everything to do with choices. The history of Mexico is the story of a free people making choices; that is the intrinsic splendor of it. There is nothing mystical or divine about nationhood. Recounting that history requires making choices too, choices openly arrived at and openly acknowledged. History is argument.

If history is argument, then having access to the elements of that discourse is fundamental. I could not have had full access to such a vast body of thought and writing without the assistance of the Benson Latin American Collection at the University of Texas, Austin, and the Archivo General de la Nación in Mexico City. I gratefully thank the directors and staffs of those institutions for their preservation and advancement of Mexican culture and history.

I could not have worked through such a vast body of thought and writing without financial resources and the incomparable gift of time. For the financial resources, I gratefully acknowledge a three-year Research Fellowship from the Social Sciences and Humanities Research Council of Canada. For the gift of time, I gratefully acknowledge a research/study leave from the University of Manitoba, as well as the many examples of meaningful support extended by my colleagues in the Department of History. With special warmth of gratitude, I acknowledge a Killam Research Fellowship for the years 1994–96 from the Killam Foundation Program of the Canada Council, which made it possible for me to find the form and content of a book that had long existed in the outer folds of my consciousness. I believe profoundly that Mexico and Canada have much to offer each other in their long encounters with the meanings of federalism and nationhood.

For the encouragement of a critical eye, I gratefully acknowledge Barbara Angel. For the support base of tolerance and affection without which no work would be possible, I gratefully thank Mary, Aaron, and Elizabeth.

FORGING MEXICO, 1821–1835

CHAPTER ONE

"Fragments Averse to Integration"

In researching and writing this book about the rise and fall of federalism in the first Mexican republic, I kept returning in my own mind to several fundamental dilemmas, not only about the nature of federalism and the meaning of nationhood, but also about the historical record. Late in the process I ran across an insight of Thomas C. Cochran, which, though drawn from the history of the United States, exactly summarizes my perception of the situation that faces Mexican historiography:

> By taking the written record that was easiest to use and most stirring from a sentimental or romantic standpoint, that is, the record of the federal government, the American historian prepared the way for one of the major misconceptions in American synthesis: the primary role of the central government in our historical development. While political scientists carefully pointed out that up to World War I, at least, most of the normal governmental contacts of the citizen were with his state, . . . historians, influenced perhaps by nineteenth century European training, persisted in writing a national history. . . . The realistic history of nineteenth and even early twentieth century politics, therefore, whether viewed from the standpoint of political parties or of the community, should be built around the states. This, of course, imposes an enormous burden on the historian. The situations in from 13 to 48 states cannot be adequately described in a unified narrative; to have meaning they need to be seen in an analytical structure.[1]

Because these are significant concerns, I start with a discussion of issues that have been clarified for me in undertaking this study.

Federalism is a form of government in which separate, self-governing, territorial entities join together to create a greater whole and in which power is distributed between the central authority and the constituent units. The Brazilian scholar Aspásia Camargo gives a suitably Latin American perspective to the definition of federalism: "We can define federalism as an extra-European model of state organization marked by the coexistence of two sovereignties: that of the union, which retains the control and the execution of some common functions, and that of the federated units that occupy themselves with the rest." It is characterized by "the existence of distinct and relatively autonomous powers, which can be identified by the distribution of constitutional competencies between the union and the states; by the existence of their own sources of revenue and of control over public order; and by political and juridical representation through executive, legislative, and judicial powers on the state and federal level."[2]

I say this is a Latin American perspective because neither in the United States nor, at least until recent times, in Canada would the scholar incorporate in the definition of federalism such an untroubled reference to the existence of dual sovereignties. The issue of whether federalism possesses such a thing as dual sovereignty, and if so what it comprises, is currently under hot debate in Canada because of the insistence of both Quebec and the aboriginal community that the issue be addressed. In the United States, the term *sovereignty* is not used in reference to the states, at least not since the end of the Civil War. Among Latin American federal systems, and certainly in the Mexican case, the idea both that the nation can be sovereign and that each state or province can be internally sovereign is accepted in theory, even if its precise meaning differs from time to time and place to place. The current constitution of Mexico (1917) encapsulates a vast and fascinating history when in Article 40 it declares, "It is the will of the Mexican people to constitute themselves in a representative, democratic, federal Republic, composed of free and sovereign States in that which concerns their internal administration [*régimen interior*]; but united in a Federation established according to the principles of this Fundamental Law."[3]

Federalism is an intimate element of our histories and identities in the three countries of North America. Although the United States was the first country to develop such a system, Mexico (in 1824) and Canada (in 1867), following their own traditions and for realistic geographical and political reasons, also formed federal unions (in the case of Canada the term *confederation* was used, suggesting the creation of a compact or league of provinces for mutual support or common action, but the resulting political system is always called federalism by Canadians). Neither Mexico nor Canada "copied" the United States. Despite surface similarities in form, the federal system in both countries derived from their own traditions, their own histories. Like the United States, Mexico and Canada adapted existing principles of political organization that derived from their colonial pasts, enlightened by the most advanced philosophies of the day and motivated by the need to create a functional government over the vast territories that European settlement had left them.

I make a point of emphasizing that both Canadian and Mexican federalism were born from home soil and adopted for consistently logical political reasons because in the United States the older literature on Mexican history often insisted that Mexican federalism was a copy of U.S. federalism inappropriately applied to a country where very different circumstances existed. The charge originated with early Mexican opponents of federalism, but nineteenth-century Anglo-Saxon ethnocentrism also found it appealing.

Federalism is such a fundamental part of our political structures that when it comes to articulating who and what we are as nations we sometimes forget to mention it. As Marcello Carmagnani comments, federalism is not just a base for the institutional organization of certain countries, "it is also a political culture capable of regulating through concrete political practices the rights and duties of the different actors" in that which involves their political participation, their citizenship, and their social interaction.[4] It is a political and philosophical way of harmonizing disparate identities. And although other countries in Latin America and other parts of the world maintain federal systems, or have done so in the past, federalism may well be the most important defining historical characteristic that Mexico, Canada, and the United States share. All three countries have historically faced and continue today to deal with issues of federalism.

As a system of national organization and a form of government in large countries of complex linguistic, ethnic, and regional makeup, federalism fulfills many purposes. It combines the contradictory impulses of unity and diversity, nationhood and regionalism, and oneness and pluralism, and it fulfills real political, ideological, organizational, and definitional needs. At the same time, it places priority on the rights of the constituent parts to their own self-determination, which is, of course, the key element. It seems a self-evident principle, though one that is sometimes forgotten, that nationhood is meaningless unless it is a voluntary association. All three North American countries have faced, or still face, the troubling issue of how to respond when one or more of the constituent units wishes to withdraw from the federation.

Some observers of the North American scene, including some who write history, overlook the most salient feature of the North American countries, a feature of which North Americans themselves are constantly, if not always consciously, aware—the sheer territorial immensity of our countries. The vastness of these three countries imposes both a different way of conceiving of space and time and the need for a different form of political organization. Geographic size is a cognitive and perceptual order that is simply fundamental to the history of an Ontario, a Texas, or a Chihuahua. The difficulties of political organization and establishing nationhood, great as they are in the late twentieth century, were even greater in a time before railroads, automobiles, airplanes, telephones, and telecommunications. To cope with geographical imperatives, to say nothing of many other imperatives, the generation of citizens who brought about the national organization of our countries had to come up with new ways of political organization and new forms of nationhood, among which the foremost was federalism. Great size is not, of course, the only historical characteristic that distinguishes most of the American countries from most of the European ones, but in the matter of choosing a form of political organization following national independence, it was fundamental.

Another great advantage of federalism, particularly in the early years of independence, is that in a setting where there are preexisting political and juridical entities it allows many voices to be heard in the always complex and difficult process of the development of nationhood. One of the most frequent mistakes many observers make is to assume that nationhood and independence are one and the same thing. The act of political separation from the colonial mother country, though an immense achievement in its own right, is not the same thing as the achievement of nationhood. This is a historical judgment that is universally accepted in the case of Canada (where, 130 years after Confederation, nationhood is still widely debated) and usually acknowledged to some degree in the case of the pre–Civil War United States (where, at any rate, the full modern nationhood that we know today was not in place until the settlement of the great constitutional issues that provoked the Civil War). But in Mexican history there continues to be a genuine gap in the literature, in that most authors assume nationhood at the moment of Mexican independence without actually demonstrating its existence.

In the formulation of nationhood independence is a necessary, but not sufficient, step. There are, of course, some cases in which we can agree that nations exist that are not politically independent, but in the case of the

American countries that derived from European colonial empires, the fact is that nationhood came after independence. Magnus Mörner, in a recent study, argues that in Latin America after independence the state came first, then the nation: "The newborn Spanish American states had to help in creating their own nations, rather than the other way around."[5] Simón Bolívar, liberator and president of Gran Colombia, believed that the creation of solid institutions and a functioning state was the basis for the construction of the nation. Alberto Filippi argues that this historical process in Latin America, where "the sequence goes from the state toward the nation," differs from the model seen in European history, "which moved from the nation toward the state."[6]

Ruggiero Romano raises the issue of the role played by Eurocentrism and ethnic bias in the conceptualizations of the nation of the late nineteenth and early twentieth centuries. He asks why nineteenth-century historians considered that only the "old" nations (those that organized the first national governments), such as France, Spain, and England, should merit "national histories," while others (nations formed in a "different mold" and which became independent and developed a civil state later), such as Germany, Poland, Greece, Italy, or Hungary, did not. For such other countries, Romano argues that it is possible to counterpose the concept of "a young nation" in "an old country."[7] It is in such a frame that I would place Mexico.

In addition, Francois-Xavier Guerra has argued that we should view the nation as a "new manner of conceiving of human communities" that erupted on the world scene at the end of the eighteenth century and whose implantation in different societies produced different modalities. He points out that diverse sectors of a society can hold distinct conceptions of the nation and that invocations to the concept of the nation may be stronger the further a society is from its realization. Guerra adds that not all the potentialities of a national model are revealed at the same time, and therefore to study the nation is "to examine its diverse and successive epiphanies."[8] Nationhood is not frozen in time; it is in constant flux, and it may assume different forms at different times.

In asserting that in Mexico the state came first, and then nationhood, I am fully aware that I contradict some general historical interpretation over the years that has suggested, or at least implied, that Mexican nationalism rose first and was the necessary precondition for independence. Horst Pietschmann, however, has pointed out how general is the tendency in colonial studies to refer to such terms as *the state* or *Mexican society* without defining them and without realizing that the use of such concepts might be "a projection backwards from a postindependence perspective."[9] Carlos Malamud has persuasively questioned whether there was such a thing as a "colonial state" when what one means is a regional government within the family of governments that made up the Spanish Empire.[10] Luis Alberto de la Garza has pointed out how misleading is the indistinct use by historians of terms such as *people*, *nation*, *country*, and *state*. Such use has led to the assumption, given twentieth-century concepts that the nation is "the fundamental thing and the supreme finality," that the Mexican nation existed, mystically and uninterrupted, since the time of the ancient civilizations, modified in the colonial period by the development of the mestizo nation (even though the creole, or Mexican-born white, minority of the population, was dominant in the nineteenth century).[11]

Eric Van Young makes the point that at the time of independence creole elites may have thought in terms of the aspiration to create a nation, but the popular masses did not: "Although the issue of state building was of considerable importance to the directorate of the independence movement, little if any evidence indicates that it mattered a fig to their followers. . . . For people even to conceive of a state, they must share a cognitive map that includes a view of a wider world beyond locality. . . . For much of the population of late colonial Mexico, such a vision did not exist, and to assume its presence is ahistorical."[12] In 1847 Mariano Otero declared with anguish, "In Mexico there is not nor could there have been that thing which is called a national spirit, because there is no nation."[13] D. A. Brading concludes his sweeping discussion of the development of Mexican culture with the thought that even after the Reforma the liberals had succeeded only in creating their own definition of a Mexican identity, which he calls "liberal patriotism" and "creole patriotism," but "they had yet to form a nation."[14] As late as 1861, *The Economist* of London summarized, "There is no power in Mexico. . . . It is not a nation. It is not a state. It is not a government at all."[15] Lorenzo Meyer argues that there was no state in Mexico, in the sense of an autonomous power, until the era of Porfirio Díaz, from the 1870s.[16]

The most recent and articulate statement of the view that Mexico was born in 1821 as a nation, Enrique Florescano's *Memory, Myth, and Time in Mexico*, is still a recognition of the developing, not yet fully formed, nature of that nationhood, phrased in terms of mythologized popular historical memory, of aspirations rather than practicalities. Florescano affirms that "during the viceroyalty, there was no precise idea or conception of the

Mexican nation, nor a national history or nationalist historiography, for the simple reason that the country was . . . a colony of Spain. This link of political submission impeded the appearance of the idea of nation." Thereafter Florescano writes in terms of an unfolding mentality, not yet fully fixed: "Beginning in 1808, the appearance of a political thought centered on the ideas of autonomy and sovereignty of the nation and the formation of a new political reality produced by the insurgent movement created the conditions that allowed the modern idea of nation and the conception of a historical national project to unfold vigorously." And Florescano concludes by declaring, "The elaboration of a history of their own by Mexicans would inextricably be united with the carrying out of the political project of the national state. . . . The appearance of a political entity that contained in itself all the parts of the nation was the new subject of history that unified the social and cultural diversity of the population in a joint search for national identity."[17]

Thus, although the founders of independence defined their nation as an old nation, Anáhuac, now freed from foreign domination—and which the Act of Independence referred to as having "recovered the exercise of its usurped sovereignty"—the fact is that the actualization of this nation, the forming of it as a working reality, was something that the founders of independence knew in 1821 still lay in the future. It is precisely the enterprise of creating "a political entity that contained in itself all the parts of the nation" that is the focus of this book.

The one condition, independence, is political and can be acquired in a moment of time. It can even be dated to a particular day, however artificial this may seem in certain ways. The other condition, nationhood, is a question of the creation and operation of institutions that bind a sometimes disparate and ethnically diverse people together within recognized territorial limits and with some degree of conscious perception or cognition of existence as a single nation amid observable differences. Nationhood may take many decades to develop, indeed, may not exist in the case of some countries that have been politically independent for years. We can agree, historically, that Mexico became independent on 27 September 1821, the day Agustín de Iturbide and the Army of the Three Guarantees made their triumphal formal entry into Mexico City at the completion of the struggle for independence. Yet the fact that as early as 1825 Mexicans were celebrating 16 September (the day in 1810 when Miguel Hidalgo proclaimed the first insurrection that launched the wars of independence) as their independence day suggests the way in which consciousness of symbols may differ from demonstrable history and how symbols may be manipulated to encourage a myth of national origins.[18]

When nationhood takes place, it is the fulfillment of a process of institutional construction, not the initiation of it. Thus, we may argue that Mexican identity, in some form, certainly existed prior to independence (it is a country whose cultural history dates back three thousand years), but modern nationhood did not. Mexican creolism, as an awareness of an identity different from that of the Spanish mother country, certainly existed before 1810 or 1821, but a Mexican nation that incorporated other regions did not.[19] Similarly, a Mexican nation may have existed by about 1857, but it is doubtful whether even then we can speak of the existence of a Mexican nation-state because to be a nation-state implies that at least a majority of its subjects, including the ethnic elements who made up the majority, were consciously incorporated (or co-opted) into it. Thus, I invite the reader to keep in mind the very subtle but practical distinctions that exist between formulation of a national government and consciousness of nationhood. Both are necessary, that is, there must be not only institutions but recognition of the legitimacy or authority of those institutions.

I believe that at independence Mexico was neither a nation nor a nation-state, that in the years after independence it gradually formulated a national government (no small matter in itself), and that in the decades between 1857 and the 1920s it became a nation-state. This formulation is not universally applicable to all nations, and I do not propose here an omnipresent "theory," but it corresponds to the history of many formerly colonial entities, especially many of the American countries. Mario Cerutti has phrased it as follows, "The construction of the nation-state in Latin America was made possible by relationships that linked regional power bases together. Either these regional power systems came together by agreement, or certain regionally dominant factions would emerge to force the other regions to integrate; . . . this is what occurred in countries that produced multiregional national states (particularly Brazil, Mexico, and Argentina)."[20]

The creation of nations is the work of human effort, not the consequence of the action of some mysterious blood-force, geographical determinism, or historical consanguinity, and, because it is the result of human labor, it is not instantaneous. It is a process, gradual by definition, in which a sufficient number of the population comes to feel that its own interests are served by belonging or adhering to the national entity. For our purposes, it does not particularly matter what portion of the population constitutes sufficiency or what the interests are that they perceive to be well served; the object is that they see some usefulness to it and, generally speaking, that they adhere to it. Nor does it particularly matter, for our present purposes, whether we see the existence of nationhood as an unequivocal good or an unalloyed evil. Nationhood, when it exists, is a measurable, though not immutable, actuality, and the historian may therefore trace it. It never stands still, however, and no historian can pretend that nationhood is an unchanging certainty. As Roger Bartra has put it, "The nation-state is the most traveled and at the same time the most impenetrable domain of modern society."[21] My own view is that nationhood, or at any rate nationalism, is at best only a mixed blessing; and Claudio Lomnitz-Adler makes great sense when he insists, "Mexico, like all the nation-states of the world, is a creature of modernity."[22] The first phase of this journey, of this process of the creation of nationhood—from independence to the first federal republic and its failure—is the subject of this book.

I believe the fundamental mistake of the historiography, when it confuses independence with nationhood, is a perceptual one. The historiography seems to assume that in 1821, with the achievement of independence, or in 1824, with the creation of a federal republic called the Estados Unidos Mexicanos, a nation had come into being. Then, Mexican historiography, in quite the opposite fashion of the triumphalism of both Canadian and United States historiography, proceeds with expressions of horror to trace the rapid "disintegration" of that nation.

Many historians confuse or slide together into one event the achievement of independence in 1821 and the proclamation of the federal republic in 1824. We shall see in the following chapters, however, that the creation of a federal republic that recognized the states of the union as "free, independent, and sovereign" was not an inevitable consequence of the gaining of independence but the result of a genuine revolution that occurred in the three years after independence and could not have happened until independence itself laid the essential foundation, which was the right to self-definition or self-determination. Furthermore, it was certainly not inevitable that Mexico should adopt a form of government that the Acta Constitutiva of 31 January 1824 declared would be a "representative, popular, federal republic."[23] Each one of the four words was critical. To choose to be a "republic" was in itself a gargantuan step, but to add that it should also be "representative," "popular," and "federal" implied obligations that contemporaries, to judge by their later actions, did not always recognize. Although it was logical and appropriate, it was not as simple a choice as much of the historiography suggests. Federalism is and always has been a very difficult form of national organization because it is complex and requires that many voices participate in the formulation of identity and policy. In essence, it requires power sharing. *Representative* meant that the national institutions would reflect the constituent parts, and *popular* meant that its rulers would be elected. Even some federal republics in our own day have difficulty assuring these three elements.

In addition, I believe that far too many English-speaking authors translate *Estados Unidos Mexicanos* as "the United States of Mexico," in unconscious imitation of "the United States of America" and thereby assume that *Estados Unidos Mexicanos*, a generic term in which *Mexican* is an adjective referring generally and quite loosely to the cultural identity of the hegemonic center of the country, is synonymous with the noun *Mexico*, establishing the certainty of nationhood. In fact, we can say that in 1824 there was a Mexican identity (in the sense of *mexicanidad* or Mexicanism) but not yet a Mexico (in the sense of national state). Furthermore, the mexicanidad that then existed did not apply to vast portions of the country. Mexicanism was only one of many identities. Many of the provinces had their own sustainable identity (or identities, because some provinces consisted of several regions and identifiably distinct ethnicities). Under the first regime following independence, the empire of Agustín de Iturbide, there were twenty-eight Mexican provinces, including the five in Central America, while in the constitution of 1824 there were nineteen states and four territories, not counting the five Central American provinces that had created their own federal republic.

Alan Knight has recently posited a useful distinction, drawn specifically from Mexican history, between cultural nationalism on the one hand and political nationalism and "nation-building" on the other. They are related but not coterminous, and, he believes, the first, at least in the form of sentiments of creole patriotism, neo-Aztecism, and the symbolism represented by the Virgin of Guadalupe, existed long before the last two. Thus, the "elaboration of a distinctive and valued Mexican cultural identity" is not in doubt, but political nationalism and nation building belong to the period after 1821. Mexico's struggle for independence provided a fund of heroic figures and myths to nurture this "polymorphous and incipient nationalism," but there was not yet any guarantee that it was strong enough to hold the country together.[24]

The tendency to assume that Mexico was one nation at independence is directly related to the assumption, nearly universal in the literature, that the colonial kingdom of New Spain was the same thing as Mexico. It was not. At the conclusion of the colonial era, territories that comprised the later "Mexico" belonged to three kingdoms—the Audiencia (high court) of Mexico (New Spain), the Audiencia of Guadalajara (Nueva Galicia), and the Audiencia of Guatemala (Central America)—as well as several vast regions on the peripheries that were subject to one or another of the audiencias but that, generally, were governed by military commandants or captains general—namely, the virtually self-governing region of Yucatán and the nearly uncharted vastness of the Interior Provinces of the East and the West (running from Sinaloa and California on the west to Tamaulipas and Texas on the east). The region then known as the "South"—comprising the modern state of Guerrero and parts of Morelos as well as the *tierra caliente* Pacific lowlands—was barely subject to organized government. With the adoption of the Ordinance of Intendants in 1786, the viceroy in Mexico City did not have direct control over day-to-day administration in most of this vast region, and under the Spanish constitution of 1812 his jurisdiction was further restricted to only the seven provinces of the Gobierno Superior of New Spain. Indeed, of the twenty-eight provinces in Iturbide's Mexican Empire, twenty-one had not been directly part of the late colonial entity of New Spain.[25] It is time that the general historiography started reflecting more carefully the precise differences in political jurisdictions that existed in late colonial times because calling the whole vast region "Mexico" has served to obscure the large variety of identities that existed in the late colonial era and had a great impact in the early independence era.

In 1821 the newly declared Mexican Empire extended from the southern border of Oregon to the northern border of Panama. It was, in fact, the largest of all the Hispanic American countries and, after Brazil, the largest country in the Americas (Canada and the United States had not yet attained their ultimate size). Even without counting Central America, Mexico in 1821 measured 4.5 million square kilometers and was twice the size of the United States at its independence. (By the mid-nineteenth century its size had been reduced by over a half, to 2 million square kilometers.) The geographical immensity of the region was so great that there is, strangely enough, a genuine difficulty in judging what terminology is correct when referring to it in the period just before and just after independence (in that, as already indicated, it cannot properly be called Mexico). At the end of the colonial period, the Spaniards tended as a general term to call this vast region América Septentrional (northerly America), as distinguished from América Meridional (southerly America, the continent of South America and much of the Caribbean). As general usage in the English language, I prefer the term Spanish North America. This conveniently distinguishes those territories that later became Mexico from those already comprising or that later comprised the United States and those already comprising or that later comprised British North America or Canada.

Iturbide dubbed this vast country el Imperio Mexicano, the Mexican Empire (not the Empire of Mexico), which roughly meant "the Empire of the Mexicans" and which in itself constituted an example of cultural appropriation on a vast scale in that many of its subjects did not equally share Mexican cultural influences. Other people called it América Septentrional, or Anáhuac, or, more sloppily, Mexico. The constitution of Apatzingán, written in 1814 by the rebel congress at the time of the Morelos movement and often considered the first Mexican constitution, had called the country la América Mexicana. This was not yet a nation. Carmagnani has argued that "at the beginning of the nineteenth century the Mexican geohistoric space was very far from constituting a unique or an integrated space."[26]

It is also significant to note that of the twenty-eight provinces that made up the short-lived Mexican Empire (which lasted only from September 1821 to March 1823), a total of ten of them either withdrew from the later Mexican republic or attempted to do so. The five Central American provinces (Guatemala, Nicaragua, El Salvador, Honduras, and Costa Rica) founded their own federal republic; one province (Chiapas) withdrew but later joined the Mexican republic; one (Yucatán) remained virtually outside the union and attempted several times to withdraw; and three (Texas, Nuevo Mexico, and Alta California) were taken by the United States along with substantial parts of seven other border provinces.

In short, to reiterate my point, if in using the term *Mexico* we mean to refer to the Mexican republic as it came to be after the 1847 war with the United States, we must remember that none of its three great predecessors was precisely coterminous. The colonial dominion that existed just before independence was not the same thing, the Mexican Empire of Iturbide was not the same thing, and the Estados Unidos Mexicanos during the first federal republic was not the same thing. Consciousness of jurisdictionality and territoriality is basic because effective jurisdiction is demonstrated by the exercise of power over territory.

Equally central to this historiographical problem of defining Mexico after independence is the confusion that often occurs over the chronology of the great issues. Up until the past decade or so, the historiography generally assumed that 1821 was the great break in Mexican history, that all Mexican history was divided into what came "before independence" and what came "after independence," and that if you had a picture of society before independence, the after-independence picture must be a new, and complete, whole. Thus, the fact that after independence Mexicans created a federal republic must mean that they arrived at such a choice before, or during, independence. Having studied the wars of independence closely, I have been impressed by the fact that this simply is not the case. It is, rather, a history of transition, of partial fragmentation and continuity, not of complete before-and-after scenarios. As Alicia Hernández Chávez put it, when the transition from the colonial period to the liberal republican period in Mexican history is seen only in terms of a profound break that affected the central government, the result is that the first phase of Mexico's independent history incorrectly appears to be characterized by nothing but disorder and disaster.[27] When approached from other perspectives, it takes on a different look.

The theme of continuity is widely recognized in recent historiography.[28] Indeed, concern has been voiced about whether historians, in emphasizing continuities, may not be underestimating the effects of independence.[29] I believe that to focus exclusively on either fragmentation or continuity to the exclusion of the other would be incorrect. Independence is perhaps the most significant single turning point in a country's history, but independence alone does not solve the various social or political issues confronting a society. The most significant value of the achievement of independence, perhaps, is that it may (but only may) permit a society to begin seeing social and political issues previously masked by the presence of the colonial power.

There were a whole host of critical issues, the most important of which was the form of government, that were not widely discussed during the process of the achievement of independence, or at least on which no consensus occurred, precisely because they could only be tackled after independence was attained. We must not lose sight of evolutionary processes by which developments, once inconceivable or only the object of dreams, become possible in the ongoing development of history. In his memoirs Iturbide, the man who completed the process of independence and led the first government, wrote, referring to Mexican political options during the wars of independence, "The Americans wished independence, but did not agree upon the method of acquiring it, nor upon the system of government that ought to be adopted. . . . There were votes for absolute monarchy modified with the Spanish constitution, for another constitution, for a federal republic, etc. Every system had its partisans."[30] This statement of Iturbide's has been largely ignored by historians, but the essential truism of which he wrote—that the struggle for political separation from Spain, by its very nature, had not brought about consensus on a new form of government—is of the greatest importance (as is his apparent recognition that he could not yet call the residents of this country "Mexicans").

Mexico was, and still is today, a country defined by its regions. Clearly then, the issue of a "national project" at independence automatically raised the issue of the regions, and it was not possible for it to be otherwise because the regions demanded to be heard. That was perhaps the most revolutionary consequence of independence because in the three hundred years of the colonial order the regions, though not entirely ignored, were rarely factored in to great political decisions, certainly never as equals with the center. In 1821 and after, attempts to define the identity of the whole automatically raised the issue of how the parts of the whole would relate to the sum of them.

"Mexican" was only one of those parts and, although it was certainly the most powerful part, there were others. In 1821 it must have come as the greatest surprise to a Oaxaqueño, a Jalisciense, or a Sonorense, much less to a Tejano or a Salvadoreño, to hear that they were Mexican given that they never had been before. Mexicans were the people of the center of the country, the region of the capital city and its hinterland, the people who resided in what had been the zone of greatest Aztec cultural sway before the Spanish Conquest. The term *Mexican* derived from the Culhúa-Mexica, the "Aztecs." Writing in the 1830s, the leading thinker of early Mexican liberalism, José María Luis Mora, expressed the truism that if independence had come forty years earlier, a person would not have understood the term *Mexican* because individuals in society thought in terms of their place within a corporate body rather than within a national identity.[31] The tension between the forces of centralism and regionalism is the dominant theme in Mexican history and can be traced back well before independence (indeed, before the Spanish Conquest); during all those centuries there had not been a Mexican nationality that included the noncentral regions.[32]

It is the fact, at once simple but also complex, that *tapatíos, sonorenses,* or *jarochos* would today unhesitatingly and proudly identify themselves as Mexicans that alerts us to two critical realities. First, sometime between 1821 and today a genuine Mexican national identity came into existence in those parts of Spanish North America that formed the Mexican republic. Second, the fact that they use as the word that identifies them the same term that at the time of independence almost exclusively meant "people of the center" suggests the extent to which the hegemony of the center has triumphed.

No student of twentieth-century Mexican history can doubt that Mexican nationalism exists. As Octavio Paz put it, from the early twentieth century on "Mexico dares to exist, to be." But when did this happen? When did Mexican national identity take on the cohesiveness and strength we know today? There is no easy answer. Mexican nationhood had begun to be formed in the years between independence and the fall of the first federal republic in 1835, which are the years covered in this book, but it had certainly not yet assumed its fully modern form. The full articulation of Mexican nationhood appears to have clustered around two epochal periods in Mexican history: in the 1860s during the Reforma and the struggle to throw off the Empire of Maximilian (Paz says, "Mexico was born during the epoch of the Reforma") and, again, in the shadow of the 1910 Revolution (Paz: "By means of the Revolution the Mexican people found itself").[33] Like all great processes, the formulation of Mexican national identity occurred over a long period of time. It began as a result of 1810 and 1824, but that was only the beginning; and by definition it has, as yet, no terminal point.

As a Canadian, surrounded by the ongoing constitutional debates of a large country where the issue of equality between the provinces is critical, where people are conscious of the distinct cultures of different provinces, and where some people view the "national identity" as an artificial construct that suppresses other identities, it seems obvious to me that the essence of Mexican history can be—needs to be—approached from a multiple, evolving, national-provincial-regional perspective. Provincialism— the aspiration for provincial equality and home rule, the desire for political devolution, the demand for juridical equality, the opposition to the absolute power exercised by Mexico City over the rest of the country— became the foremost driving force of the early period following independence, and one that the historiography rarely reflects. Indeed, Jorge Zepeda Patterson has gone so far as to assert the historical primacy of the provinces: "Independence, the Reform and the Revolution—the three constitutive moments of the Mexican nation—[all] had their origin in the province."[34] In a very suggestive, if perhaps overly optimistic, essay fifty years ago Harry Bernstein called for scholars to pay greater attention to the role of attempts at provincial integration in Mexican history, particularly for the early years after independence: "The history of Mexico is as much a movement of progress toward the assimilation of the legitimate claims and cultures of the different regions into a balanced harmony, as it is the history of revolution, labor, agrarianism, constitutional and land problems."[35]

The history of Mexico is a history of its states and regions; its identity is an identity based on states and regions. Luis González has long proclaimed the vital necessity of studying Mexico in its small parts, of focusing on what he calls *la matria* rather than *la patria*, "the small world that nurtures us," as he calls it—the *municipio*, parish, and *patriecita*. For González, one must remember the all-encompassing importance of "matriotism," love for the place or area where one was born, which does not, however, exclude patriotism, love for the nation. In a sentence that, among other things, brilliantly summarizes the primary weakness of Mexican national historiography, González insists that "our [Mexican] patriotism is a thing of the metropolis, and the inhabitants of the city that imposed its name over a country of 2 million square kilometers manage it as their own thing." González directs our attention mainly to the vibrant rural life of thousands of towns and villages and their "microhistories." Although I wish to focus our attention on the fact that Mexico is a country composed of provincial entities with many local regionalisms of their own, the fact remains that his perspective that Mexico is a "mosaic" composed of individual pieces characterized at times by a "minimal unity," a patchwork of very different matrias that may or may not add up to a single patria, is a valid and necessary perspective. González warns us that in Mexico the definition of patriotism comes from the city, that the city always operates to increase administrative centralization, and that we must not make the error of confusing unity with uniformity.[36]

Claudio Lomnitz-Adler has greatly clarified our sense of cultural-political structures in Mexico, a country, he insists, that is comprised of a myriad of "intimate cultures" defined by space (with varying degrees of coherence), which are linked in a complex variety of ways to make up the whole. The national culture, he argues, is the "fetish," an object to which autonomous and independent power has been imputed, when in fact it is the nexus of intimate cultures (and of caciques, the articulators of cultural region) that defines the country.[37] Mexico's history, in other words, must be written in a way that incorporates both provincialism and regionalism because they are the essence of a nation with a multiple soul, a society that is both one and many. As Jeffrey W. Rubin puts it, "Region as a political location and culture as a political force are central to Mexican politics because they form the place where life is experienced and characterized, where national initiatives are mediated and become practice."[38] To incorporate regionalism and provincialism into our historical approach means merely to recognize that much of Mexico's history has been driven by the provinces' demands for political devolution and power sharing, the demand for equality and home rule, made all the more acute by the understanding among provincials themselves that the provinces existed before the nation, that the nation is the work of the provinces. And although the meaning of *region* and *regionalism* has many variants, Eric Van Young helps to clarify our approach when he contends that incorporating regionalism into historical thought is nothing more than placing history in the context of the space in which it occurred. Van Young insists on the multiple definition of *region* and on the fact that, because the real object is to study history as expressed in geographic or spatial terms, regions should not be considered historically transcendent forms of social organization.[39] Neither the space nor the ways of perceiving it are eternal and unchanging, but events always happen in a spatial context, and that context sometimes plays a powerful role in the event.

However, the historiography of Mexico is so centralist in bias that this reality of plural identity, in which sometimes the provincial or local matria counts more than the national patria, is treated by the preponderance of the historiography as if it constituted disintegration. Could one study the history of the United States before 1860 without fully incorporating the regional demands of the blocs of states or of nineteenth-century Canada without recognizing the very different identities of Ontario and Quebec? Can we understand early-nineteenth-century Mexico without the political or economic agendas of Jalisco, Zacatecas, Yucatán, or the state of Mexico?

Why has the historical literature on Mexico not recognized the heterogeneity of the early independence period? Why does it continue to confuse unity with uniformity? Thomas Benjamin, in his bibliographical essay in *Provinces of the Revolution: Essays on Regional Mexican History,*

1910–1929, a book that considers the different roles of the states in the Revolution of 1910, puts it bluntly: "The consolidation of the postrevolutionary Mexican state by the 1940s, often referred to as the 'institutionalization of the revolution,' completed the centralization of politics, the economy, and, to a considerable extent, culture. . . . The [central] state institutionalized not only the Mexican Revolution but also provincialism, rendering both harmless and insignificant."[40] Unfortunately, the early independence period, unlike the twentieth-century Revolution, has not yet produced a literature based on detailed research into local and regional history.

Luis González makes the point that "the madness of Mexican intellectuals for the theme of their patria has scarcely been equaled in any other country," adding that "since the theft of half the national territory, . . . successive dominant groups in Mexico have done everything possible to create the image of an epic *patria*."[41] Indeed, it was in the half century after the loss of Texas and the other northern regions that Mexican governments defended the nation by creating nationalist myths, which in turn required the subordination of a multitude of peripheral identities into a single uniform nationalism. Although at the time of independence writers such as Carlos María de Bustamante and Servando Teresa de Mier linked Mexico's national identity to the ancient Mesoamerican civilizations, particularly the Aztecs, it was in the late nineteenth century that the center put forward the Aztecs as the progenitors of the entire Mexican nation and thereby co-opted or appropriated the national identity, subsuming a complex pluralism within a fictitious uniformity.[42]

Roger Bartra's interpretation is that late twentieth-century Mexico is currently experiencing a crisis in the political structures of mediation created by the 1910 Revolution.[43] Héctor Aguilar Camín and Lorenzo Meyer, perceiving that Mexican society in the mid-1980s showed "the signs of a great historical transition," attribute it to "the fact that the objective requirements of production, economic development, and social pluralism are now in conflict with the only formulas that the society and the state have to manage and organize themselves." They conclude, "Mexican society is witnessing the end of a fundamental agreement within itself, a true change of era," owing to the erosion of the fundamental pact of the Mexican Revolution.[44]

The great transition of the last two decades of the twentieth century, which is still underway and whose outcome cannot be predicted, is therefore not unlike the crisis of the early decades of the nineteenth century. It was in that period that the colonial system died, leaving all classes the unexpected, frightening, and only dimly perceived task of confronting the most profound transition since the Spanish Conquest, the daunting responsibility of redefining themselves. Such transitional episodes are always confused and messy, partly because the participants are not always fully aware that the canons of their society are undergoing fundamental transformation. It can be said, however, that they are not only crises, they are also periods of hope, for they only occur when people are convinced that existing official definitions of the national identity fail to reflect the reality they live.

Bartra has concluded, indeed, that in the late twentieth century Mexico has already moved into a profound cultural and political crisis. "A great number of Mexicans are starting to reject that old political culture which has, for more than sixty years, been the faithful companion of authoritarianism, corruption, inefficiency, and backwardness." If this is the case, and I believe it is, the link can be made back to the original shibboleths of independence and the first decades of national organization, "the dream of a thousand mythical heroes," "the archetypes and stereotypes of the national character," which form "a prolongation or transposition" of the reality of social and political dominance (all of these are Bartra's phrases) and which Mexicans in the 1990s are assessing critically.[45]

As the philosophers have implied, however, there is an exquisite, even painful, paradox at work here. An attempt to be present at the birth of Mexican nationhood in the nineteenth century—not just its gestation but the actual moment it attempted to take corporeal form as a complex of living institutions—has been, to some extent, confounded by the existence of the twentieth-century Mexican nationalism to which it helped lead. Bartra calls current Mexican nationalism "the odious, legitimating source of a dominant, exploitive system, which seeks to justify deep inequality and injustice through the imposition of uniformity on political culture" and notes that "this is shared by all varieties of nationalism."[46] Ultimately, modern Mexican identity became intimately linked to the efforts of the twentieth century's dominant political forces to absorb all elements into a united, singular, and centrally oriented sense of self. Thus, reconsidering the formative first years of the republic's existence is itself a way of revising its present identity; knowing what it set out to be sheds light on what it is now.

Based on his analysis of the history of Mexican regionality, Eric Van Young has formulated an argument that in Mexico it was the strong tradition of regional identity that the "modern" state had to break down.

"Most state projects, at least since the late Bourbon regime, have tried in the name of modernization to replace strong regional and weak class structures with weak regional and strong class structures. . . . Political and military struggles over the control and constitution of the Mexican state may be viewed as attempts to construct or capture an instrumentality to reduce the friction of distance and therefore increase the efficiency of energy extraction by the center." The net object is to achieve central control over both capital and labor by breaking down the protectionist walls of space, of vast territorial extent, which in an earlier time allowed the existence of a variety of regionally distinct social and economic modes of control and modes of life.[47]

One measure of the extent to which that hegemony of oneness has prevailed in the historiography is the literature's tendency to view the provincialist urge in the early independence period as nothing but a ruinous proclivity to suicide. Carlos Monsiváis has said of such twentieth-century thought, "The fatalistic faith in the omnipotence of the center (the peak of power in Mexico City) was such that to mention regionalism was most often to conjure up legends of the bewildered fringes and the feudal realities of backwardness." Speaking of the historical literature, Monsiváis continues:

> For more than a century a belief held sway that still has not completely dissipated: that in Mexico there are only two regions, the capital and the provinces. The capital concentrates the country's power and intellectual vitality, projects Mexico's national image, and controls the theoretical elements that make sense of what happens in the provinces: chaos, revolts, lawlessness, moral repression, few successes, and a culture of violence. According to this arrogant vision, which admitted no disagreement, the only purpose of the provinces was to suffer a linear history, an aborted history, a history that carried the imprint of the strongman. Within this schema, any idea of regionalism was declared insufficient, unfortunate, impoverished (the height of localism). Thus, *regional* and *local* were categories opposed in principle to *national*; they were fragments averse to integration.[48]

Carmagnani has said simply, "Nationalism interferes with the functioning of the federal principle" because it creates the image in people's minds of a very strong centralizing state that can do anything.[49] We need to remember Bartra's profound warning, "The nationalist metadiscourse is wont to impede or hamper the relation Mexicans have with their past and with world history: history is reduced to hieroglyphics, to static symbols destined to glorify national power and to tranquilize reason; when one awakes from this dream it is difficult to recognize one's own past or even one's presence in the world."[50]

It is that all-absorbing nationalist metadiscourse in twentieth-century Mexico that has led us to overlook what Josefina Zoraida Vázquez calls the "true miracle" of Mexican history—"that New Spain resisted the fragmentation that the other viceroyalties suffered, despite the fact that its territory came from two audiencias, two autonomous governments, twelve intendancies, and one captaincy general."[51] In short, contrary to the historiography's emphasis on the early nineteenth century as a period characterized by chaos, caudillos, and disintegration, the true characteristic of the period was a troubled but nonetheless distinct striving for integration and union.

The overwhelming dominance of definitions based on the largely unrecognized assumption that uniformity is desirable has led the historical literature to confuse the needful thing, unity, with the harmful thing, uniformity. But, Luis González asks, in what way does recognition of the legitimacy of the thousands of matrias that make up the patria threaten the whole?[52] Does recognition of heterogeneity endanger the survival of the nation? I believe not. I believe it constitutes a necessary awareness of the multiplicity of the mosaic without which the whole is weakened rather than strengthened. If modern Mexico faces a crisis of definition, perhaps some of its definitions have been false. The only way to make systems conform to the reality of Mexican existence is to recognize clearly the actuality of the past. Zepeda, carefully measuring the case for greater regional power as a source of democracy in the last decade of the twentieth century, states, "Against what the official ideology has argued, the creation and evolution of national culture does not annul but rather assimilates cultural expressions of the regional whole, whose union and interaction have made up the nation. From the perspective of democracy, each existing regional culture can be an element of ferment and stimulus in the development of a renovated and more plural national culture."[53] As Carmagnani points out, "the patria is not a sum of territorial units . . . but a feeling of belonging, of identity."[54]

In addition, and this is a point that readers may have great difficulty accepting because of all the prior conditioning, if we are to recognize and reflect the legitimacy of provincialism and regionalism in Mexican history, we shall also have to recognize the legitimacy of the first leaders of many of the regions or the evolving provinces or states—that group of provincial military strongmen traditionally dismissed by the historiography, with undisguised contempt, as "the caudillos." John H. Coatsworth, reflecting on the absence of research on the history of the states, writes, "One of the reasons for the lack of interest in the subnational political life of independent Mexico is the mistaken conception about the caudillo that permeates the literature of political history in Latin America."[55] Caudillism is intrinsic to a consideration of provincialism, and it originated with the combination of political and military power in the hands of local authorities (both royal and rebel) that occurred during the wars of independence. E. Bradford Burns's argument is that the caudillos, whether we like it or not and whether the leaders of central governments of the day liked it or not, were the legitimate and perhaps even natural leaders—the voices— of their home provinces.[56] Instead of condemning the caudillos in a chorus of unreflective criticism, the historiography should concentrate on trying to understand the origins of and distinctions between the caudillos, recognizing at least the theoretical possibility that many of them may have been not only legitimate but effective leaders.

It is necessary, then, to state clearly a major disclaimer of this book. What the period 1824 to 1835 comprises, and what constitutes the subject of this book, is not so much the rise of Mexican nationalism but of the slightly different, still very important, thing I shall call the "national project." Octavio Paz wrote of this period, "Spanish American thought begins as a justification of independence but transforms itself almost immediately into a project: America is not so much a tradition to be carried on as it is a future to be realized."[57] This book is about the origins and development of the formal, institutional, political forms of government and the national state in the first federal republic of the Estados Unidos Mexicanos and what became of them. This has greater relevance to the present than may first appear to be the case because of the uniquely enduring impact of the choice of federalism by a people aware of the primacy of provincial or territorial identity within the national identity.

I believe that the articulation of a "national project" in Mexico, that is, the creation of the national state and its forms and institutions, was not possible until the regions played their fair share in defining it. At the time of independence, the Mexicans had yet to create "Mexico." Viewed in this light, the creation of a federal republic of "sovereign" states in 1824 is not the beginning of dissolution, as some historians seem to feel, but the beginning of coalescence. Disintegration is in the eye of the beholder. Un-happily, the generation of 1824 did not quite master the task of creating political stability, and future generations would have to try again, but we, as students of history, must not so thoroughly ignore the voice of the provinces that we view their role as merely obstructionist.

We must stop defining the political developments after 1821 as the disin-tegration of a formerly cohesive political, social, or "national" unit. Such views are a holdover from nineteenth-century Positivism. What happened in Mexico after independence was disorderly and messy from the perspec-tive of those who, above all else, valued "order and progress," the late-nineteenth-century code words of Porfirian Positivism. But for those who encode their higher aspirations in terms such as self-determination, au-tonomy, home rule, or equality, what happened in early-nineteenth-century Mexico, though still messy, was a necessary expression of the striving of the regions for social, political, and economic progress in a country previously characterized by colonial centralism. We cannot allow the cultural and ethnic biases of the dominant elites of the late nineteenth century to determine our late-twentieth-century categories of analysis.

I emphasize that, in my view, disintegration is in the eye of the be-holder because an understanding of this precept is vital for the historian's understanding of what happened in Mexico, or any other newly indepen-dent country, following the termination of European colonial control. Al-though, of course, colonial traditions play a role in the ongoing process of identity, we must remember that the identity imposed by the European conqueror did not necessarily conform to the actual identity of the inhabi-tants of those territories. What Mexico experienced after independence was not a process of the "reconstruction" of nationhood following the de-struction of an earlier nationhood. The Spanish Empire in America was not a nation; that is to say, the "conquered and colonized America" was not. As Alberto Filippi has argued, following the achievement of indepen-dence from Spain, the new countries of Latin America were engaged in the construction of nationhood, a new and not previously formulated na-tionhood, not in the reconstruction of a lost nationhood.[58] This was, however, taking place in a context littered with so many continuing politi-cal-institutional influences left over from the Old Regime that the process was extraordinarily complex.

Donald F. Stevens has argued that, "seen from a local perspective, the events of these years constitute not a disintegration but a re-creation . . . the striving of the provinces not just to pull apart New Spain but to alter and reassemble the territorial pieces as something new."[59] If the process had been simply the rebuilding of a rather rickety old edifice that had collapsed, the subsequent nineteenth-century history of Mexico would not have been as complex, frustrating, and ultimately meaningful as it is. Jesús Reyes Heroles summarizes the role of federalism in Mexico's history as follows, "Federalism was the means of uniting the disunited. If it had not adopted the federal decision, Mexico would have been 'balkanized': various countries would have broken off from the common trunk."[60]

To adopt the interpretation that the early republic was primarily a period of disintegration is to assume, again, the prior existence of nationhood in the absence of its demonstration. Colonial New Spain was not "Mexico," and it was not a nation. What about Nueva Galicia, Yucatán, the Internal Provinces of the East and the West, and much of the south? Much less was it cohesive in social, political, or economic terms. What happened after 1821 merely appears to historians as disintegration because we have not fully registered the chaos, drift, administrative complexity, cultural and linguistic multiplicity, or ethnic and regional injustice of the colonial era; because we do not yet fully understand the relationship between provincialism and national identity; and because we do not even have a complete narrative of the decades between 1821 and 1857. I am not arguing that the early decades after independence were anything other than politically disorderly, but we must remember that one reason those decades saw such ideological and political division is that, when independence at last delivered political power into the hands of Mexicans themselves, they faced the task of building a nation from the ground up. And, as Stevens has also insisted, it is essential to note that the political history after independence is based on profound political and ideological disagreements and is not the product, as traditional historiography has it, of petty leaders absorbed in simple struggles for power.[61]

Even at its best, the colonial regime was based on conquest and provided a form of government that was astonishingly remote from the local needs of real people, with little or no connection to the community over which it ruled. Commenting on the arbitrary taxes and forced loans imposed on Mexico by a late Bourbon imperial system enmeshed in frequent European wars, Coatsworth states, "Nostalgia for a colonial era of peaceful productivity can only be sustained by failing to notice that the colony was part of a vast empire sustained only by war against increasingly powerful European competitors."[62] If we in the late twentieth century were to agree that the late colonial era in Mexico was chiefly characterized by peace, harmony, and enlightenment, we would simply repeat the error that, as Michael P. Costeloe has shown, was made by frustrated and self-serving nineteenth-century elites in Mexico when they, amid the turmoil of their day, looked with nostalgia (and selective hindsight) back to their colonial "good old days."[63] Colonialism and uplift are mutually exclusive, despite the fact that our culture continues uncritically to accept many of the rationalizations invented by European imperialism.

On the specific problem of federalism versus centralism in early republican Mexico, Nettie Lee Benson quite correctly turns the issue on its head and provides an insight into how we might break the dominance in Mexican historiography of centralist perspectives: "When historians awake to the fact that much is yet to be learned about what actually occurred during the period of 1810–1857, perhaps someone will investigate the overwhelming desire of Mexico City and its immediate area to control all of Mexico and will see this desire as a significant factor in the chaos of the period."[64] Alternatively, Mario Cerutti has pointed out that "a key question is whether Mexico City was indeed the hub of a nation-state that prior to the 1880s remained undefined, or whether it was the axis of a much more modest space, only a central strip of what would later become the nation-state."[65] Both scholars tend to cast doubt on unexamined assumptions that Mexico City should always be considered the one and only appropriate base for recounting Mexican postindependence history. In the nineteenth century the capital's absolute dominance was not as clear as it has been throughout the twentieth century, but the central elites nonetheless assumed they had a right to play dominant roles in the affairs of the republic.

On the basis of a comparison of the economic performance of the states with the much less positive performance of the Mexican federal government after independence, Pedro Pérez Herrero has argued that "the interpretation referring to the 'atomization' or 'regionalization' of territory in the first decades of the nineteenth century is a vision effected from the point of view of the capital" because such atomization was nothing more than the achievement by provincial elites of an autonomy for which they had fought since the sixteenth century.[66] In a similar vein, and based on economic data, Carmagnani has argued that, before the Porfiriato, regional elites prevented the central government from achieving financial autonomy and control over the national territory. Thus, independence did not create a power vacuum, local elites were in control of their home regions, and political chaos in the early republic was more apparent than real.[67] "If we could characterize Mexican life starting from the states and not, as in general has been done up to now, starting from Mexico City, we would be able to say that it was neither chaotic nor anarchic."[68] The historiography has not seen this localist perspective because the nineteenth-century sources either did not see it or, as in the case of Lucas Alamán (the most influential of the early-nineteenth-century interpreters) and others, consciously suppressed it, defining every attempt at an increase in provincial power as a disintegrative influence.

As the seminal era in the creation of a self-governing and self-defining Mexico, the first federal republic is fundamental to all that came after. As with other newly independent countries, in both the nineteenth and the twentieth centuries, many years of built-up political, social, and economic pressures exploded after independence, resulting in new formulations of identity that, though influenced by the past, were nonetheless impossible to foretell ahead of time. The result—as seen in some developments specific to the 1821–35 period such as the expulsions of the European Spaniards, the rise of leaders like Antonio López de Santa Anna and other caudillos, the intense struggle between competing visions of conservatives and liberals, the rise and fall of federalism—is not just some giant exercise in futility that left all the great questions to be settled all over again in the late nineteenth or the twentieth century. It is, for good or ill, the process, imperfect as always, of defining, creating, building nationhood.

My argument, indeed, is that there is a missing link in the historiography. The nineteenth-century writers, imbued with the legacy of colonial centralism, viewed attempts by the regions to secure a fair share of power and input in the process of nationhood as something akin to denying natural law and the undoubted right of the center to dominance. Moreover, provincial elites were, in fact, defeated in their massive struggle during the first federal republic to take away the center's dominance. For these reasons, late-twentieth-century thought, despite occasional glimmerings in the work of some recent authors, does not reflect a critical segment of the struggle to define a nation. Yet the critique, the dissent that is readily visible in today's Mexico, is remarkably similar to the critique that emerged just after independence. This segment or piece of Mexican history is critical because it offers historically based options that Mexicans in the twenty-first century can call upon in their daunting task of renewing and redefining a national identity that, in our own day, is in rapid transition. The first formulation of Mexican nationhood, in the first federal republic, was based on a principle of genuine power sharing between the center and the provinces or regions. Although it failed, it offers clues, as well as precedents and warnings, for possible alternative formulations of an enhanced federalism in what currently is an excessively centralized, authoritarian, and unequal late-twentieth-century Mexico.

Always there is a sense of great dissatisfaction with most of the historiography on the early republic. So much of it is impressionistic or anecdotal, sometimes characterized by lingering partisan denunciation or latter-day apologia, and usually informed by Positivistic assumptions. For example, although a few critical studies exist, most books on Mexico's first federalism are panegyrics published to mark some historical anniversary. Mexican historiography relating to the early nineteenth century in general is highly centralist in orientation, patriotic or nationalistic in inspiration, biased against political initiatives that reflected provincial as opposed to national objectives, and inclined to overstate the political harmony that supposedly prevailed in the days of the viceroys and to see the justified demands of the regional elites after independence as constituting disintegration. Enrique Florescano has said of the works produced in the nineteenth century, "From 1808 to 1867 the state lived through the worst crisis of its history and partisan historiography through one of its most brilliant moments." Twentieth-century scholars have sometimes uncritically depended on the classic eyewitness accounts of Mexican authors who were themselves partisan participants in early republican affairs—Mora, Mier, Bustamante, Zavala, Bocanegra, Alamán, Tornel, and a host of lesser lights—as well as the later nineteenth-century authors imbued with the ideas of the Reforma and of Positivism. Each of them, whether conservative or liberal, represents the ongoing struggle to establish mutually exclusive definitions of the national identity in what Florescano has called "a historiography of class, and more precisely, of the superior classes and groups who fought for power."[69]

The literature written by non-Mexicans must also be used with care. For the early nineteenth century, we are overly inclined to listen to the views of foreign travelers in Mexico, or perhaps under inclined to judge those foreign travelers when they fell back on cultural prejudice and racism to provide explanations for Mexican political and economic failures. Yet Alfred H. Siemens has demonstrated that the Victorian foreign visitors to Mexico should generally be considered unacceptable interpreters of historical reality: "Their accounts, indeed, are conjury—limited as sources of factual information, but most promising for an analysis of bias."[70]

Yet in regard to the historiography, there are significant signs of hope based on present-day developments. In very recent years, indeed since 1989, a new historical perspective on early republican Mexico has begun to emerge, undoubtedly stimulated, in part, by the growth of professional historical studies in the many important provincial universities but also reflecting the profound transition Mexico is now experiencing. Motivated by a powerful impulse to dissent, this provincially influenced historiography is beginning to counterbalance the overwhelming pessimism about the early nineteenth century that prevailed in the older centrally influenced literature. These new narrative and theoretical approaches question traditional views of the early national period, focusing on the role of the provinces in the defining of republican nationhood.

Reflecting on the historiography brings us to another great dilemma this book touches upon. Mexico continues in our own day to hold a variety of opinions about the potential risks that provincialism poses to national unity. Nineteenth-century Mexican history illustrates, or so many people suggest, the dangers of disunion. It is the more or less unanimous opinion of Mexican society today that the lack of political cohesion in the nineteenth century is what laid Mexico open to the greatest disasters of its national history—the loss of Texas in 1836, the loss of the northern provinces of the republic to the invading United States in 1847, waves of civil war, political chaos, and foreign intervention. The unspoken impression seems to be that the disunity that reigned in Mexico by the 1830s happened because of federalism. That is what the conservatives in Mexico during the period from the 1830s to the 1860s felt, the reason why by 1835 middle- and upper-class conservatives, after a decade of political turmoil, favored the abolition of the first federal republic and the adoption of centralism.[71] As justification for adopting centralism, in 1835 a commission of the Chamber of Deputies declared that federalism had destabilized national unity, provoking division and weakness.[72] Lucas Alamán coined the famous dictum by which centralists for decades attempted to bring the weight of historical judgment to the side of centralism: "Federalism divided that which was united and made separate nations out of that which was and ought to be only one."[73]

But they failed to recognize that the disunity and weakness that so blighted the first decades happened in spite of, rather than because of, federalism and that it is not provincialism that provoked such weakness. As Brian Hamnett reminds us, "Centralism between 1836 and 1846 similarly failed to build a lasting basis for the Mexican republic."[74] Alamán created the argument that the last decades of the colonial era were a nearly idyllic time of prosperity and enlightenment because, in Brading's words, as the "arch-reactionary of the epoch, . . . who sought to create a strong central government, based on a close alliance of the army, the church, and landed classes," Alamán wanted to place the privileged elites in undisturbed control.[75]

Issues of regionalism, power sharing, regional economic disparities, ideological and ethnic differences between certain states or regions, and regional demands for greater influence are still a part of Mexican life precisely because they are issues relating to the control and use of power. It is often said that Mexico solved the problem of the clash between centralism and federalism in the period after the 1910 Revolution by creating a system that is technically federalist but that functions like a centralist state, a republic adhering to the forms of federalism. But it is a centralist state in which the federal executive possesses such overwhelming power that the president of the republic can and does dictate amendments to the national constitution, can and does overturn governors' elections in the states, can and does control the largest portion of local and regional spending.[76] This modern presidentialist system, according to Carmagnani, has led Mexicans since the 1930s not only to the mistake of equating presidentialism with federalism. They have also united in the figure of the president the idea of both the federation and the nation.[77] Rubin, however, points out that the urge to autonomous regionalism is still very much alive in Mexico today and that the triumph of the centralized state in the 1930s "was actually a simultaneous forging of multiple regional arrangements . . . that together reinforced the power of the center. . . . What scholars traditionally label as 'national' occurs in and through what we call 'regional.'"[78]

Any observer of late-twentieth-century Mexico knows that the problem of federalism versus centralism is not dead, partly because in our own day the postrevolutionary "system" in Mexico is in a period of transition and possible breakdown and partly because regional identities do not disappear just because a federal government possesses the will, the tools, and the power to run roughshod over them. What is happening today in Mexico is that the great discourse between region and center has once again broken out, after over sixty years of quiescence, "a discourse whose intent is to recognize the need for identity in a population that without ceasing to be Mexican knows different, and that . . . rejects the official version of Mexicanness."[79] The crisis of the 1990s suggests, according to Carmagnani, that centralizing federalism is in crisis, but the federal pact itself may not be. The federal principle may simply be undergoing another of the re-formulations that it has experienced since 1824.[80]

It should be clear by now that my approach to Mexican federalism in the nineteenth century contains no hint of the sort of dismissive critique for the motives and objectives of the regions or provinces that so characterizes much of the existing literature. Recognizing that the provinces or states were certainly an instrument by which local forces chose to protect and enhance their interests, I would simply express the thought that all governments, to a greater or lesser extent, are the corporate voices of specific interests and would ask whether there were any other political entities that would speak for regional interests. Surely regions have a right to a voice, and it is not surprising that the regional notables would organize a political voice to look after their interests. Were centralist elites prepared to look after regional elites' interests? Nonetheless, it would do considerable violence to the facts to define early Mexican federalism as the same kind of "oligarchic neofeudalism" that early Venezuelan federalism is considered to have been.[81] Early Mexican federalism seems to have been too pluralist to be described as an instrument of neofeudalism as well as too dependent on electoral legitimization or military legitimization. Nineteenth-century Mexico was a far more fluid society, a far larger complex of social systems in which significant cities played too large a role, and a far more socially and economically heterogeneous country than nineteenth-century Venezuela.

In the end, then, I doubt the implications inherent in much of the historiography that regional fragmentation resulted from the wars of independence and the collapse of the colonial order and that federalism in Mexico institutionalized centrifugalism. My argument is that regional fragmentation did not result from the wars of independence and collapse of the colonial order; it had long existed, since pre-Columbian times, and continued to exist below the surface of an incomplete colonial centralism, as it still exists today, as an inherent characteristic of a large multiregional country. Neither did federalism institutionalize centrifugalism; rather, federalism attempted to create an operational union amid preexisting diversity.

I doubt the whole thrust of much of Mexican historiography, relating to either the nineteenth or the twentieth century, that *only* a powerful central state can lead to development or modernization precisely because we have in the Mexico of the last half of the twentieth century the evidence of what it can produce. As Jesús Reyes Heroles has attested, in Mexico centralism was, and still is, the tendency of the privileged. Centralism that ignores the regions' right to autonomy in a country of great size and ethnocultural complexity can lead, Reyes Heroles warns, to a situation in which "nationalism becomes the exclusive privilege of the strong."[82]

The unique strength of federalism, a strength that no other system of national organization can impart, is that it allows the creation of nationhood through voluntary association amid the continuation of a regional mosaic: the joining into one nation of all the disparate cultural, ethnic, linguistic, and geographical identities, a structure in which individual and provincial self-definition does not automatically have to surrender to the demands of national security or political cohesion. Self-definition and voluntary association are the two essential elements for a federal national state.

Although the Mexican constitution of 1824 was not permanent, it was the beginning of coalescence, an important stage in a process. As subsequent history indicated, it did not lead Mexicans to reject federalism as an objective because it was and is appropriate and essential for the organization of a Mexican nation. Reyes Heroles declares, "Thirty years of mortal war against the constitution of 1824 did not succeed in abolishing its essential principle, federalism. The legacy of the constitution of 1824 was its affirmation of the liberties of man and the establishment of the right of the distinct Mexican collectivities to self-government."[83] Mario Cerutti has shown how, in a later decade, the existence of autonomous state governments could actually become the means for survival of the nation-state.[84]

Carmagnani asks why federalism continued to survive in Mexico and answers, "The most simple reply is that [Mexicans] saw in the federal form of government a perfectible proposition and, as a result, considered the federal principle to be sufficiently ample and flexible that it could be revitalized and reelaborated."[85] The frequent resurgence and renewal of federalism in Mexico constitutes our primary evidence that it serves a useful purpose, that it is needed. The essence of federalism is self-government; self-government prevents nationalism from becoming the exclusive instrument of the few.

When it comes to the phrasing of my theoretical formula, Sergio Ortega Noriega put it best in a 1980 article.[86] Starting with the argument that the existing chronological stages perceived in Mexican historiography reflect primarily what was happening only in the central region of the country, he contended that the periodization of Mexican history needs to take into account the geographical space in which events developed (that the

Conquest did not occur everywhere in 1521, that identities were not the same everywhere, and that chronologies are not the same everywhere). And he went on to observe that "the historiography of the nineteenth century is the most lacking in internal coherence, because it presents us an invertebrate series of political events that far from explaining an evolving process only indicate the absence of profound knowledge of the period. The deficient explanations of the historiography of the nineteenth century are owing, in part, to the lack of knowledge of the regional reality of Mexico, in a period in which regions occupy first place." This leads to the overall judgment that Mexico's "national historical process" is "the history of the integration of diverse regional societies and that the explanatory key to this process is in the identification of the dynamic of interrelationships." Warranting special attention in Mexico's history, he says, is the period between 1786 and 1824, the period when internal territorial organization underwent the most rapid change, because it indicates the extent to which regions were aware of their particularity within the whole and acted to preserve their political autonomy through federalism.

But Ortega feels that microhistory, or concentration on the small rural locales advocated by Luis González, will not overcome these deficiencies because the relative small size of its objects of study "will make the dynamic of national integration indecipherable." Because each region must relate in some way, initially in terms of economics, to the other regions (and Ortega follows Angel Bassols Batalla in advocating that there are perhaps eight great economic regions that comprise the territory of Mexico), it is necessary, in articulating a regionalized history, to study simultaneously the integrative dynamic of general or national society.[87] Ortega's hypothesis, then, is that it is necessary to study the process of Mexican nationhood "through a double perspective, regional and general, particularizing and uniformizing, perspectives that are not opposed but complementary and that cannot be defined without obligatory mutual reference." The choice of the federal system for the organization of the nation at large, he says, is clear evidence that the effect of the earlier Bourbon reforms was an increase in regional strength and a weakening of the central power of Mexico City. Yet the regions, when finally able to make their own choices, chose to pursue both particularity and integration. Both regional differentiation and national integration occurred simultaneously; neither has meaning without the other. Provincehood and nationhood were not opposed but were two sides of the same coin.

We must rediscover what the first generation in our countries knew (or anticipated), that federalism is, or can be, one of the most effective forms of national organization. This is because in a nation of immense size and multiplicity of cultures, full nationhood lies in all regions playing a role in its definition and receiving a fair share of its benefits. Adherence to such first principles will result in diversity that, far from deserving the criticism of being disruptive, is more likely to lead to renewal and strength. In the Western cultural tradition, the ultimate, most meaningful heritage is the principle, not so much of responsible government, not so much of freedom from want, not so much of the citizens' participation in government, but of the right to self-definition, which incorporates and includes all the rest. The ultimate power is the power to define ourselves.

CHAPTER TWO

The Impulse to Provincehood

One of the least recognized aspects of Mexican independence is that it constitutes not only the moment of the creation of a self-governing country free from the political control of the former imperial mother country, it also represents a significant step in a long process by which the provinces achieved recognition of their existence as separate juridical entities with a primary claim to self-definition and self-government. Thus, when we speak of the achievement of home rule there is a double meaning. Mexico achieved home rule, which sparked a desire for the same among the constituent parts, the provinces. Though the process began well before the Spanish Conquest in some cases, its modern phase began in 1786 and was not completed until 1823 and 1824.

Outside of the overarching issue of whether or not to be independent, this was the other great issue of its day. To put it another way, it was the achievement of the full recognition of provincehood in 1823 and 1824, not the proclamation of a short-lived Mexican Empire in 1821, that brought the independence process to full closure. It was the first step in the creation of an authentic *Mexican* political culture. At the very least, it was a revolution equal to the revolution for independence.

Centrifugalism and economic localism were among the most marked features of colonial life.[1] As the long struggle for independence drew to a close, Mexicans realized that the effort was not completed simply by gaining political separation from Spain. The object of the conflict changed, or became clear, and the aspiration for home rule quickly came to mean provincial home rule. Political aspirations came to reflect the emergence of the peripheries, which, as John Tutino sketches it, was a tendency underway since at least 1760 and was characterized by population growth, commercial development, and land acquisition by elites in areas outside the traditional colonial center.[2] In Hamnett's memorable phrasing, from the late Bourbon period on the object of provincial elites "was to impose their own vision of political economy—doubly emancipated, in their perception, both from metropolitan Spain and from Mexico City."[3] The creation of the Mexican Empire by Agustín de Iturbide was an interim step characterized chiefly by continuity; the federalist revolution was the great break with the past.

For a number of reasons I do not want to call this impulse regionalism. As Francois-Xavier Guerra has pointed out, to call such a tendency regionalism or localism is to use inappropriate terminology because it is to assume the prior existence of a superior whole entity, a nation or kingdom, when in fact we are dealing here with human communities that preceded the construction of a superior entity. In the Hispanic tradition the city preceded all the other political entities, and the sway of its territorial influence defined a province or a kingdom. The Spanish monarchy was made up of kingdoms and provinces joined only in their sharing of a single monarch, and each territorial unit—city, province, kingdom—had as its constitutional base a direct personal and collective relationship with the king of Spain. Even in the Bourbon period the overseas dominions were not "possessions" of Spain. Indeed, there was no such thing as "Spain," only las Españas, for the peninsula itself was a congeries of kingdoms and provinces. Identities, even in the Spanish peninsula itself, were, as Guerra puts it, the identities "of a town, of a village or of a city; then, of a city-province; afterwards, of a kingdom; and in the end, 'Spanish.'" More than almost any system one could designate, the "Spanish empire" was a constructed community or, as Guerra calls it, "a pyramid of superimposed political communities." Even as late as 1810, contrary to the insistence of unitary absolutists, the Spanish monarchy, at home as well as overseas, remained a plural reality.[4]

In addition, the term *regionalism* is misleading because within each province there were often many regions and regional identities. When discussing specifically the question of identities that developed from the 1770s to 1820, Carmagnani insists "that each regional space developed a conjunction of values that had nothing to do with the modern idea of 'region.'"[5] Besides, in the hands of some authors, particularly the nineteenth-century elites who wrote the history of Mexico, the word *regionalism* carried a derogatory implication of rustic or insular. In the older historiography it also frequently implied some kind of groundless, practically inexplicable urge to chaos in the form of unwarranted resistance against the only proper authority, the authority of the center. This is the agenda of the later nineteenth century, of the Positivists, at work.

Mexican historiography, for example, has no school of thought (except, perhaps, among social anthropologists and folklorists) elevating the homespun virtues of the rural folk into the ultimate expression of the national values, as U.S. and Canadian historiography have, because in Mexico the hegemony of the metropolitan, urban center existed all through the colonial period. Even in the nineteenth century, in an atmosphere of intellectual exchange that was remarkably free and open, elites dominated the debate over what constituted the national identity and, with rare exceptions, ignored both the indigenous and the mestizo majority of the population. Meanwhile, in the twentieth century, through what Eric Van Young has called "the commodification of historical memory" by a "vampire state" that has "mummified the past to control the present and guarantee the future," the dominance of the Valley of Mexico over local and provincial realities and histories is almost complete, the appropriation of Mexican history by the center is nearly unquestioned.[6]

It is not easy to narrate in simple terms the origin of the urge to provincehood in Mexico because the Spanish colonial system of government, as just suggested, was multilayered, multi-jurisdictional, and prior to 1812 governed by tradition and compact but with no single written constitution. It was a structure that had developed organically and historically, that is, in response to the spread of Spanish conquest, and it was extremely pragmatic. The Spanish Empire in America began with a European mother country whose own history was also cumulative and which acquired vast territories in the New World before it, the conquering mother country, had coalesced into a nation-state. At the time of the conquest of Spanish North America, Spain itself was an aggregation of kingdoms and provinces (the two terms were used interchangeably) loosely gathered under the sovereignty of the monarch, which was itself the historical result of the marriage of Isabel of Castile and Ferdinand of Aragón, inherited as a personal patrimony by their grandson, the emperor Charles V. It is not until the time of the conquest of Mexico and Central America, in the 1520s, that the world began to think of Spain as a single unit (though Spaniards themselves did not), even though it had possessed a coordinated civil service and military, the key instruments of statecraft, since the time of Isabel and Ferdinand.

For our purposes, what is most important about this structure that we loosely call Spain is not that it was late medieval in its origins and not that it was unwieldy (it is misleading to dwell on the clumsiness of a system that proved efficient enough to conquer and administer the largest empire to exist in Western history until the second British empire of the mid-nineteenth century). What is important is that Spain was always, and indeed is still today, a state whose constitutional base is comprised of previously self-governing provinces or kingdoms, many (but not all) of which possessed specific written (or unwritten, traditional) guarantees of their separate identity and which had all been aggregated under a single throne. This was the origin of the long struggle in the twentieth century, during the dictatorship of Francisco Franco, over the restoration of provincial political autonomy and language rights to such regions as Catalonia, the Basque provinces, and even Andalusia, a struggle that culminated successfully in political devolution early in the reign of the present king, Juan Carlos. Spain itself, in short, has always been, though without full acknowledgment of the fact, a type of confederation.

This ancient tradition of thinking in terms of the existence of kingdoms or provinces, each of which was centered around a principal city, came to the New World with the Spanish conquerors and settlers. In the reigns of Charles V and his son, Philip II, the monarchy made extensive efforts to weaken or eliminate the autonomous political power of the conquerors, fearing they would take advantage of their control of vast territories in America to create satrapies and fiefdoms more enduring than any that had existed in the Spanish peninsula and which Isabel and Ferdinand had spent much of their reigns forcing to submit to regalist control. Even so, the far-flung provinces in America became home to powerful families that made up local oligarchies. In addition, there was the immensely complicating fact that the conquerors, especially in Mesoamerica, imposed Spanish political structures over the top of a huge indigenous American population that, at the moment of conquest, already lived in organized political states themselves. The Aztec empire, with its great capital at Tenochtitlan (Mexico City), was itself a vast confederation of separate cities and provinces that the Aztec rulers controlled by conquest, tribute, terror, and the frequent exertion of punitive military might. An indigenous tradition of separate political entities based on geographical territory met a Spanish tradition of separate political entities based on geographical territory, and although in both systems the central power (the Aztec authority, the Castilian throne) had acquired dominance, the separate identities endured, if no longer politically independent. More than merely the result of administrative convenience, provinces were a fundamental tradition in both Spain and Mexico.[7]

Yet as a simultaneous first fact, Mexico City, in the form of the Aztec capital of Tenochtitlan, had dominated most of the Mesoamerican center for a century prior to the Spanish Conquest, and the Spanish conquerors, being themselves from an urban society, chose the same physical place as the location for their capital. As Zepeda says of Mexican history, "In the beginning was the center." In order to use the existing tribute system of the indigenous rulers, Spain developed under the control of this hegemonic center a pyramidal structure of provincial urban centers capable of organizing, not only tribute collection, but also the rapid utilization of territory. As the sixteenth-century chronicler Motolinia put it, Mexico City was "the mother of provinces and kingdoms." Thus, both the center and the regions in Mexico grew up together, their elites characterized from the outset by differing views on the crucial questions of trade and regional autonomy.[8]

After completion of the conquests, the Spaniards continued to govern the new lands as provinces. This frequently happened because a particular group of conquerors spread Spanish power to new territories, always creating cities as the center of both settlement and administration while incorporating the hinterlands. The terms *province* and *kingdom* were often used interchangeably, as later were the terms *province* and *intendancy*. Sometimes a "kingdom" was a province (as, for example, Nuevo León, which properly was the Nuevo Reino de León), sometimes a kingdom was several provinces (as, for example, New Spain or Guatemala), and sometimes it was one very large province that would later be several provinces (as, for example, Nueva Galicia). Sometimes a "kingdom" corresponded to the territory of an audiencia (high court), as, for example, Nueva Galicia or Guatemala; but sometimes, as with Nuevo León, it did not. Most "provinces" consisted of many regions and different peoples. There were even some areas that, for various administrative and military reasons, were not considered to have the status of provinces but nonetheless were administered separately as "governments" (*gobiernos*, such as Tlaxcala, and much of the vast north, particularly Upper and Lower California). (There are also some states in modern Mexico that developed in the nineteenth or the twentieth centuries as entities that broke away or were separated from others, usually because they too had developed a sense of separate identity.) What all these entities had in common, however, was a tradition of thinking of themselves as a unit or as a province or as an identity corresponding to a geographical territory, which resulted both from being distinct administrative jurisdictions and from possessing their own cultural, ethnic, or linguistic characteristics. Some large territories, notably Nueva Galicia, Central America, and Yucatán, never thought of themselves as part of New Spain. Many differences in ethnicity, color, language, culture, and even traditions of landholding existed historically or developed in these far-flung territories in the three centuries of the colonial era.

Late in the colonial era as a result of the rise of a creole identity in the latter half of the eighteenth century, a considerable stirring of consciousness in many areas occurred. Although the historiography always emphasizes the importance of the *Historia antigua de México* (1780), written by the exiled Mexican Jesuit Francisco Javier de Clavijero, on the rediscovery of the glorious heritage of lost cultures and its impact on the rise of creole identity in central Mexico, the effect was also to emphasize the multiplicity of identity, the ways in which the peripheries of north, south, east, and west had identities that were also uniquely their own. The outlying areas, and their creole elites, began to perceive ways in which they were not Spaniards but not central Mexicans either.

Literate creoles began to formulate a definition of their own identity based on the belief that Mexican culture was a product of a unique blend of Indian and European. The heirs of this mixture were clearly identified by Clavijero as the mestizos. But the creole elites, whose intellectual tradition denigrated the indigenous elements, appropriated the identity for themselves.[9] In a multiple compounding of myth, the creoles of central Mexico came to see themselves as the heirs of the ancient Aztecs, who they defined as a highly cultured society with a recognizable political state that had been invaded and conquered by Spain in 1521. This is often called neo-Aztecism. Outside of the Aztec zone, in regions where other great Indian cultures had existed, similar identification with the lost glories of an indigenous past developed. The creoles came to feel that the European Spaniards who held the most important offices in the colonial regime were outsiders who had conquered what they began to think of as their land. Of course, it had been the Indians' land, but the creole middle and upper sectors ignored that fact. Similarly, the real heirs of the Aztecs (or whatever native civilization) were the Indian masses at the bottom of the social scale, and, besides, the creoles romanticized the original Aztecs, who had dominated the country through conquest no less than the Spaniards. And the real heirs of the mixed culture in Mexico were the mestizo masses who shared the lower rungs of the social scale with the Indians.

These contradictions, which would contribute an important part of the social conflict of later decades, were not immediately evident as the sense of creole identity, of mexicanidad or Mexicanism, began gradually to emerge. By the 1780s this creole identity had assumed recognizable form. A later generation of writers would further develop it, notably Servando Teresa de Mier, Carlos María de Bustamante, José María Luis Mora, and Lucas Alamán. They helped define the creoles' sense of self, distinct from the Spaniards and with differing political objectives. It cannot be said to have been fully formulated by 1821; indeed, political independence was a critical factor that this identity would require for further growth.

Yet although the development of neo-Aztecism was a critical step in the creation of a national cultural identity, it was also the beginning of a process by which the identity of the nation came to be vested in the Valley of Mexico, the capital city, the political center. As Barbara Tenenbaum points out, at the time of the Spanish Conquest "there were perhaps as many as two or three hundred different Indian groups living in the territory that became known as New Spain," and more Indians fought against the Aztecs than with them. Yet throughout the nineteenth century the nation became identified with only one of the country's many Indian cultures, the Aztec culture that ruled at Tenochtitlan, and this was simultaneously a process of the assertion of "the primacy of the central state as embodied in and ruled by Mexico City." Tenenbaum sees this process culminating in the work of the nineteenth-century "nationalist mythologizers," a tradition developed by Mier and Bustamante that led in the later nineteenth century to the myriad of identities that composed the country being permanently subsumed under the single identity of the center. In this same process of replacing the real past with an imagined one, the creole at last triumphed as the heir of the ancient civilizations of Mesoamerica, supplanting the living Indian and mestizo descendents of the ancient cultures.[10]

The last phase of the colonial era is particularly characterized by a series of fundamental political and economic structural changes decreed by the Bourbon kings of Spain in the latter part of the eighteenth century. The net effect of these so-called Bourbon Reforms, which were intended to strengthen the imperial system along regalist and absolutist lines, was to raise the expectations of the creole elites, weaken the political and administrative control of the viceroy, alter ecclesiastical structures, and implant a permanent army. Charles III, believing that the creoles' participation in government should be restricted, appointed peninsulars to most of the higher offices that became vacant in the colony. At the same time, however, a standing army in Mexico and various militia groups were created.

This restricted conventional political influence while opening the option of military influence to the creoles who could buy military commissions. The opening of foreign trade to Spanish merchants other than those in the great monopoly merchant guilds, the Consulados, in Spain and Mexico (a reform that is referred to in the literature as "free trade"), raised expectations and sparked new economic activity. At the same time, however, trade with the Spanish colonies remained closed to foreigners, and a mercantilist philosophy continued to prevail among imperial policymakers.

The most important Bourbon reform, for our purposes, was the creation of the intendant system of direct regional government, which was decreed for Mexico and Central America in 1786.[11] It established a system of royal administrators governing territorial districts, appointed by the king and answerable directly to the Spanish government in Madrid rather than to the viceroy in Mexico City. It was designed to increase governmental efficiency and to strengthen centralized royal power, but it had the effect of greatly enhancing provincial identity by giving some provinces their "own" government for the first time and by weakening the direct power of the viceroy over peripheral regions (because the viceroy did not appoint or control the intendants). Although the Ordinance of Intendants was specifically intended to break the links between local elites and local bureaucrats that were the power base of regional oligarchies (specifically, by prohibiting *repartimientos* and replacing the *alcaldes mayores* with intendants at the provincial level and subordinate *subdelegados* at the district level), much of the new law was never actually implemented. In addition, the new intendants and subdelegates could not function without arriving at some accommodation with existing elite interests in their jurisdictions, and thus the links between locally important merchants-financiers-landowners and district-level government bureaucracies (augmented now by the creation of local militias), though modified, continued to be the essential matrix of the political economy.[12]

Although the royal legislation did not establish the intendancies as provinces, the fact is that many of them were already thought of as provinces, and others aspired to be. The intendancy and the province were thought of by both the public and by officials as virtually identical and coterminous entities, which simply reflected reality. As with the peninsular terms *kingdom* and *province*, the terms *intendancy* and *province* were used so interchangeably, even in the highest state documents, that we have to remind ourselves that the Spanish Crown had never formally, fully granted the status of province to overseas imperial territorial units. It was a tradition, now seemingly further enhanced by the creation of intendancies. Besides having an impact on administrative institutions, the establishment of intendancies influenced the fundamental psychology of many colonial people, helping them to think of their home patria as distinct and separate.

Ortega summarizes the influence of the Bourbon reforms in general on regional identities: "They permitted the reinforcement of regional societies, by sponsoring local economic development and the appearance of strong regional oligarchies opposed to Mexico City. . . . The process . . . weakened the economic and political links of the regions with Mexico City."[13] Hamnett, though cautioning that "the impact of the Bourbon reforms at the pueblo level remains one of the least understood aspects of the period," sees the reforms as having weakened outside authority at the village level, inducing Indian community governments and local caciques to a new political activity, though they certainly did not eliminate local creole oligarchies.[14]

While the Enlightenment and the French Revolution were transforming thought in the Spanish Empire, the late colonial system itself was profoundly destabilizing in the realms of politics and economics. Spain would neither eliminate the old system inherited from the Hapsburgs, nor allow the new system of the Age of Enlightenment to be fully established. Meanwhile, as Spain plunged into wars with Britain or France, the great fear of Mexican creole elites, by about 1800, was Spanish peninsular instability. It is not so much that the Bourbon reforms either worked or failed. They implied promises to colonial elites of a revised and modernized commercial, political, and military regime but resisted the logical conclusion of the process, which would have been an increased degree of colonial autonomy. Meanwhile, the foreign policy of the Spanish Crown following the rise of the French Republic in the 1790s courted disaster.

In 1808 Spain suffered the ultimate catastrophe when the French armies of Napoleon Bonaparte overran and conquered much of the Iberian peninsula, taking captive the Spanish king, Ferdinand VII. Napoleon usurped the Spanish throne for his brother Joseph, and the Spanish motherland stumbled into its own war of national independence against the French conqueror.[15] With the loss of a recognized king and the disintegration of the royal government, the Spanish people responded to these stunning developments by falling back on the long tradition of municipal and provincial power. Beginning in May 1808, the cities and provinces of Spain, individually and without national direction, organized their own governing juntas to mobilize political and military resistance to the French armies. The first of the provincial juntas was organized in Oviedo, capital of Asturias, on 25 May and proclaimed itself the possessor of sovereign powers in the name of the captive Ferdinand VII. The Junta of Oviedo immediately embarked on a foreign policy by sending representatives to England to request, and receive, military and financial aid, and Great Britain became free Spain's chief ally. Other juntas quickly rose in Burgos, Galicia, Segovia, Castile, León and Zamora, Salamanca, Aragón, Valencia, Murcia, and Seville. Though some of these provincial juntas competed with each other in claiming to be the supreme government, and sent contradictory representations to the American colonies, by September 1808 they were forced by the continuing victory of French armies sweeping over the Spanish provinces to unite in a Junta Central composed of two deputies from each of the provincial juntas. Although the authority of the Junta Central to create a national government was openly doubted by many, including many American creoles, for a year and a half, until its collapse in Napoleon's final assault on the south of Spain, it provided Spain and the empire with its only recognized government in opposition to the usurper king, Joseph Bonaparte. This was a national government founded by and in the name of the provinces. When Madrid was finally taken, the Junta Central fled to Seville. Prodded by British pressure, the Junta Central issued an invitation for the Spanish provinces and the American territories to select deputies to meet in 1810 at an empirewide Cortes, or parliament. This was the first time a Spanish Cortes would contain representation from the American dominions.

Though the armies fielded by this government of the provinces won some significant victories against the French, aided both by British expeditionary troops and by Spanish guerrilla units that sprang up in many localities, Spanish resistance was shattered by a new French military assault on the southern provinces in early 1810. As the French took Seville, the Junta Central collapsed, and the last remnants of a free Spanish government fled to the most southerly point on the peninsula, the Isle of León and the port city of Cádiz.

The example of the creation of a Spanish government by act of the peninsular provinces themselves (and a government that did not hesitate to assume that its authority extended to the entire empire) was electrifying to many American creoles. It was a manifestation of the ancient tradition in political philosophy that the people, represented by their provincial or municipal entities, constituted in the absence of the monarch the locus of political legitimacy. The political and legal justification that the various peninsular juntas expressed in their statements, though almost entirely independent of each other, showed a remarkable coincidence of ideas. They affirmed the preexistence of the national community with a right to create a new form of government; they affirmed the concept that the authority of the king was based on the existence of a pact between him and the people, in other words, on the consent of the governed; and they asserted that such principles were strengthened by the old Spanish tradition of organizing resistance against tyranny city by city, province by province, with each acting independently of the other. In all cases the peninsular juntas also looked back to the historical precedent of the privileges conceded to the cities by medieval kings, and to the municipal-based laws and privileges of the kingdoms of Navarre and Aragón. There was, in short, a substantial Hispanic tradition that was not a result of French thought but that pointed toward sovereignty of the people, or at least toward sovereignty of the corporate entities, the city and the province, that spoke for the people. For its part, the Cortes tended always to favor restoration of traditional institutions that would serve to moderate the absolute monarchy. The argument was that, in the extraordinary circumstances of the captivity of the king, a new situation existed in which sovereignty had returned to, or been reassumed by, the people.[16]

One reason these ideas occurred simultaneously and spontaneously, not only among the various provinces of Spain, but also among the various American colonies, is that they were concepts deriving from traditional Hispanic political thought, not French, not English, not Anglo-American, not imported. Indeed, French ideas, implying as they did to Spanish Americans impious attacks on religion, regicide, the most extreme political radicalism that the age had to offer—in short, revolution—and by 1808 foreign military conquest, played a very minimal role. And in the period from 1808 to 1821, and possibly even a few years beyond that—from the captivity of Ferdinand VII to the achievement of independence in Mexico and to, I believe, the foundation of the first federal republic—there is little indication of influence deriving from the U.S. revolution for independence. If they looked for foreign precedents at all, the most advanced Mexican thinkers—and we could debate endlessly what impact such thinkers actually had on the process of independence—looked to either ancient Greek and Roman thought or to the ideas of the Age of Enlightenment (which were also Spanish ideas, not just French). The most educated Mexicans, if they read a foreign language, read

French; few read English. The most detailed book we have on the influence of Britons on what might be called the "inner workings" of Mexican independence—Guadalupe Jiménez Codinach's recent work—shows a growing British-Mexican contact by about the middle of the Mexican wars of independence, most of it motivated by British commercial interest or by highly secret interchange between supporters of Mexican independence and British political and business contacts, but no great flood of intellectual influence at the outset of the independence wars. Nor did the British reading public have much specific information about Mexico. Alexander von Humboldt's *Essay* was first published in English in 1811; the first book the English had about the wars in Mexico was Mier's *Historia de la revolución de Nueva España*, which appeared in London in 1813.[17] And though Jiménez Codinach has also found important contacts between exiles from Napoleonic France and Mexican conspirators, as well as many more commercial expeditions between British interests and Veracruz before 1808 than had been previously known, the influences came into play mainly after the Mexican independence wars had begun.[18]

Largely in order to assure the continued collection of revenues from the American colonies, in January 1809 the Junta Central invited the American territories to send delegates to join the junta, declaring "that the vast and precious dominions that Spain possesses in the Indies are not properly colonies or factories as are those of other nations, but an essential and integral part of the Spanish Monarchy, [therefore] the kingdoms, provinces, and islands that make up said Dominions should have national representation . . . and should constitute part of the Junta Central."[19]

Yet in a gesture typical of how the peninsula viewed the overseas territories, the Junta Central declared that each of the peninsular provinces that had founded its own provincial junta in 1808 would have two members on the Junta Central, for a total of twenty-six peninsulars, while there would be only ten members from the overseas territories. Thus, whereas there was to be one member from New Spain, Peru, Río de la Plata, New Granada, Cuba, Puerto Rico, Guatemala, Chile, Venezuela, and the Philippines, there would be two from each of the peninsular provinces of Aragón, Asturias, Old Castile, Catalonia, Córdoba, Extremadura, Granada, Jaén, the Baleares, Murcia, Seville, Toledo, and Valencia.

Equally significant, the fact that "the kingdoms, provinces, and islands" of the overseas empire came only to the number ten—four viceroyalties and six captaincies general—meant that the actual number of provinces and intendancies that existed was simply ignored and also that an area as vast as Mexico, with over six million inhabitants, was to have no more representation than one as small as Puerto Rico. Even so, the important principle is that the Junta Central had declared that not only were the overseas territories not colonies but they were to be represented in the government of metropolitan Spain and, moreover, represented, however inadequately, as provinces. In effect, it proclaimed that the overseas dominions, as juridical entities, were equal to the peninsular ones, which was a principle to which the American subjects had long aspired.

The impact of the calling of a Cortes, however, was even more important in the rise of the provinces in Mexico. When the Junta Central collapsed, a five-man regency was created to rule free Spain in the name of Ferdinand VII. Although it was far more conservative than the Junta Central had been, the Regency was located in Cádiz, the home of a thriving middle-class entrepreneurial population and the heartland of Spanish liberalism. After many months of delay, the Regency was effectively forced by the organized pressure of Cádiz to issue instructions for the convocation of the Cortes. In a decree of 14 February 1810 the Regency called on the American territories to elect deputies to the Cortes with the resounding declaration, "From this moment, Spanish Americans, you are elevated to the dignity of free men; your destinies no longer depend on ministers, or viceroys, or governors: they are in your hands."[20] It was yet a further step in the direction of declaring the equality of Spanish Americans, as citizens, with European Spaniards.[21] The letters of convocation for the Cortes decreed that the American territories were to elect deputies on the basis of provinces, at the ratio of one deputy for each one hundred thousand *white* inhabitants. This was grossly disproportional insofar as the American colonies had large nonwhite populations. In addition, the peninsular provinces were allowed one deputy for each peninsular city that had participated in the last Cortes of 1789 as well as one deputy for each peninsular provincial junta and one deputy for each fifty thousand inhabitants. For our purposes, however, the most important fact, even for the American deputies, is that they were to be chosen according to province and therefore presumably would speak for their provinces. It was yet a further step in the emerging recognition of provincial identities.

Simultaneously, the powerful merchants of Cádiz, who controlled the American trade and commerce of the empire, had erected their own Junta Superior de Cádiz, which controlled the local government of the last city in Spain free of French domination. The Cádiz junta sent a statement to all the American colonies urging them to follow the example of Cádiz and to elect "a representative government worthy of their confidence."[22]

The appearance in Cádiz of a quasi-governing junta made up of merchants from the Consulado of Cádiz alerts us to the critical role that organized commercial interest played in the impulse to provincialism. Amid the crisis of the Napoleonic invasion, the Spanish government depended on taxes raised in Cádiz on overseas trade and on the money sent to the port by Spanish America. Gabriel H. Lovett points out that "in view of this, the [Spanish] Regency abdicated the direction of the national treasury to the local governing body."[23] Given the lack of funds to pay for military expeditions to repress the rebellions in America, in 1811 these merchants convinced the Spanish government to allow the Consulado of Cádiz to finance the dispatch of ships and troops to America. Between 1811 and 1820 they funded, by their own count, thirty-two expeditions involving more than forty-seven thousand men.[24] It was the major military response that Spain made to the American rebellions, and although the expeditionary forces were under government command the merchants expected and received their compensation when every subsequent Spanish government, both liberal and absolutist, rejected the frequent American demands for free trade with foreign countries. Thus, the Consulado of Cádiz, at least until 1814, had immense power because it either controlled or was the dominant influence over municipal and territorial government and overseas military policy while traditionally controlling overseas commerce.

In the same time period, the Consulados in Mexico clearly aspired to emulate the influence of the Consulado of Cádiz. Merchants were "the traditional arbiters of Mexican economic life."[25] The Consulado of Mexico City was historically the controlling power in trade and commerce. This influence came not only from the dominance of the merchants' guild over the raising of tax revenues from trade but through its direct exercise of authority as the court of first instance over commercial suits arising within its jurisdiction. Competing demands from merchants in other major cities, angry at the capital's control of trade, led to the erection of two further Consulados, in Veracruz and Guadalajara, in 1795, though questions of economic policy and jurisdiction over appellate commercial suits still remained in the hands of the consular officials in Mexico City. Furthermore, merchant groups in other cities also demanded the creation of Consulados, most notably in Puebla, the country's second city. Robert S. Smith has explained that, in order to forestall such demands, the Consulado of Mexico allowed the establishment of commercial deputations in other locations. Although in 1807 it planned to set up a commercial deputation in the capital of each intendancy, in 1808 and 1809 the Mexico City

Consulado actually created deputations in Orizaba, Puebla, Valladolid, Oaxaca, Querétaro, and Guanajuato and, at a slightly later date, in Acapulco and Toluca. Meanwhile, the Veracruz Consulado created a deputation at Jalapa. Isolated Yucatán had created its own deputation in 1788 in Mérida, which functioned more or less independently of Mexico City, and later planned to establish a deputation in Campeche, but Spain refused to grant permission. At any rate, in the last years of Spanish control there were no fewer than three Consulados and ten regional deputations operating throughout Mexico, each of them an expression of local or regional commercial interests.

A further important role of the Consulados and deputations in the late colonial period is their control over the merchant militia units that were created in these centers. Thus, in Mexico, as in Spain, powerful merchants dominated trade, local commerce, some part of the militia establishment, and taxation revenues, and they were becoming increasingly articulated on the basis of provincial or regional location. When Agustín de Iturbide entered Puebla in August 1821, he authorized creation of a fourth Consulado there. Guy Thomson, however, notes that the Consulado in Puebla was unpopular with other elements of the local population and was quickly abolished in 1824 by the state congress because, being established at the moment of independence, such a closed corporation conflicted with the sudden spread of ideas of popular sovereignty and equality before the law.[26] In 1824 the federal Congress decreed the suspension of all Consulados in the republic.[27]

As far as the creoles in America could see, the imperial motherland was on the verge of falling irretrievably under French control, leaving free Spain nothing but a desperate and weak government hanging on to the last foothold of unconquered territory at Cádiz. Meanwhile, that same government was busily issuing calls for the Americans to replicate the provincially dominated actions of Spain, to create their own elected and representative governments, and to send provincial deputies to the Cortes. Even though there was as yet no formal declaration from Spain that the American territories were even made up of legal provinces, the word *province* was frequently used and the assumption seems to have been made that all Americans, like all Spaniards, would know what it meant. The actions of Spain, in regard to this matter, were simply inconsistent. But the fact is that when the first imperial parliament in Spain's history was formulated, theoretically representing all the empire, it was formulated on the basis of provincial representation. The empire itself was being ruled by a government formulated originally on the basis of provinces, and those provinces had acted independently on their own volition. The introduction, however narrow, of the principle of provincial primacy, though it does not appear anyone perceived it at the time, was the first glimmering of a fundamental revolution. If carried to its final conclusion, the source of legitimacy would shift from God and King to Province and People.

Reinforcing this tendency, the political culture of Spain and Spanish America had long possessed the principle, deriving from Roman tradition, that the city was the origin of political legitimacy. In Mexico this idea received its most outspoken restatement (which was quickly repressed) in Mexico City in 1808. A day after arrival of the news from Spain of the usurpation of the throne by Joseph Bonaparte and amid the uncertainty provoked by the captivity of Ferdinand VII, two members of the city council (*ayuntamiento*) of Mexico City, José Primo Verdad and Juan Francisco Azcárate, called for autonomy in the form of the creation of a Mexican provisional government to rule in the name of Ferdinand VII. Similar calls appeared in Caracas, Santiago, Buenos Aires, Bogotá, and many other centers throughout the empire, and they were generally the origin of the movements for Spanish American independence.

On 19 July 1808, the ayuntamiento of Mexico City met formally with the viceroy, José de Iturrigaray, and requested that he take over the government of New Spain "in the name of and representing the king and dynasty." The central argument was that in the Spanish tradition sovereignty devolved upon those existing corporate structures, chiefly the city councils, that represented the people. "In the absence or during the impediment [of the king], sovereignty lies represented in all the kingdom and the classes that form it; and more particularly, in those superior tribunals that govern it and administer justice, and in those corporations that represent the public." It is important to note, however, that this was not a claim that sovereignty belonged to the people directly, only to the whole of the community and those corporate bodies that spoke for it. The city council asked Iturrigaray to convoke a representative assembly, composed of delegates from all the cities, to formulate future policy in the crisis.[28]

Recognizing that this tradition, which Alberto Filippi calls "Hispanic American municipalism," is, in both the Spanish and the Roman tradition, the same thing as provincialism, because the provinces were historically the hinterland of a principal city, we can see that the urge to provincialism and the urge to municipalism were mutually reinforcing.[29] Indeed, the ayuntamiento's proposal is often interpreted as a request for a meeting of the provinces. On 1 September Iturrigaray asked the audiencia for its approval to call the general meeting of the cities, but the audiencia refused.[30]

The city's proposal was a call for the return of power to its origins in colonial Mexico. Historically, the ayuntamientos of Mexico City and Veracruz were the first legal governmental agencies created by the conquerors of Mexico and thus in the view of the creoles the original center of Mexican, as opposed to purely Spanish, legitimacy. Sovereignty would thus devolve to the functioning agents of the people, the city councils, during the absence of the monarch. The members of the city council conceived this formula in full recognition of the ultimate sovereignty of the king, which at the moment, however, was impeded. There existed an irrevocable pact between the people and the king; when the king was impeded from ruling, the nation assumed authority, but upon the king's return to power, the people's direct exercise of authority would cease automatically.[31] Brading points out that the city council's representation was simply the application of the conservative theory of natural law propounded by Samuel Pufendorf, as translated and popularized in early-nineteenth-century Spain by the Madrid professor Joaquín Marín Mendoza.[32] Nor was the proposal necessarily treasonous, as the members of the Mexico City audiencia and other Spanish conservatives interpreted it, for as long as the sovereignty of the king was recognized, independence, properly speaking, was not the aim.

Even so, conservatives and royalists moved swiftly to repress this thinking, which elsewhere in the Spanish Empire resulted in the first movements for independence. If the 1808 crisis in Mexico showed anything at all it is that the elites—both Spanish and creole—were badly divided at a moment of exceptional danger. On 16 September 1808 a conspiracy of Spanish merchants and bureaucrats overthrew Viceroy Iturrigaray in the first coup d'etat of modern Mexican history. He was replaced as viceroy by a puppet of the conservatives, and the coup was soon endorsed by the emerging government of free Spain, but it was not until 1810, after the rise of the Regency as the recognized imperial government, that Mexico got a new viceroy chosen by Spain. The urge to autonomy in Mexico was defeated, but only for the moment. Hamnett argues that "in the first decade of the 1800s the viceregal government had been losing control of political processes in the country." The overthrow of the viceroy "destroyed the legitimacy constructed by the Spanish crown during the previous three centuries."[33]

Soon the Spaniards in Mexico had more than the creole desire for autonomy to worry about. On 16 September 1810, Miguel Hidalgo issued his

Grito de Dolores and the country was swept by a mass rebellion that among other things was also a response to the crisis of the empire. Below the surface of this main event—the onset of the wars of independence—the urge to provincehood quickened its pace and strengthened. The impetus now came both from the Mexicans and from Spain.

In Spain, sweeping political changes were taking place. The Regency, desperate to strengthen the imperial loyalties of American territories where independence wars were occurring by 1810, reluctantly agreed that the imperial Cortes, earlier called by the dissolved Junta Central, would open in Cádiz on 24 September 1810, coincidentally only eight days after the initiation of the insurrection in Mexico. The first act of the Cortes was to declare that sovereignty resided in the nation rather than in the king, and it divided the government into the three branches of legislative (Cortes), executive (Regency, in the name of the king), and judiciary. It began the process that would lead to the completion in 1812 of Spain's first written constitution. All the American deputies in the Cortes had been chosen by the city councils of their respective provincial capitals (or from among the Spanish Americans living in Cádiz in the case of the very first deputies to the extraordinary Cortes), and therefore they represented the creole point of view. They immediately launched a campaign to raise the status of the imperial colonies to equal that of the peninsular provinces.

Though the American deputies were heavily outnumbered by those from the peninsula and therefore enjoyed little success, their parliamentary campaign provides a clear outline of the autonomist and provincialist urge that motivated creole elites.[34] The day after the Cortes opened, a group of American deputies submitted a draft decree providing that immediate steps be taken to raise the American representation to the same basis as the peninsular, that is, one for each fifty thousand inhabitants, and that the population figures for determining the number of deputies should include all free subjects, including all Indians, mestizos, and persons of African descent. The peninsular deputies rejected the proposal, which would have given Americans a majority.

The Americans next proposed that the overseas territories be granted a decree proclaiming the equality of "their natives and free inhabitants" with the peninsular population, arguing that the rebellions that now existed in most of the American colonies owed much of their force to their ability to attract the support of people of mixed heritage. There was no real difficulty with granting Indians and mestizos nominal equality, but the question quickly came to rest on whether the castes, or persons of African descent, should be equal and should be counted in apportionment of representation. On 15 October 1810 the Cortes accepted a compromise decree that declared that Spain recognized the "indisputable concept that the Spanish dominions of both hemispheres form a single monarchy, a single nation, and a single family" and that "natives derived from the said European and overseas dominions are equal in rights to those of this peninsula." The decree, therefore, excluded from equality those persons not "derived" from America or Europe, that is, the blacks and mulattoes deemed to have "derived" from Africa, and that exclusion would guarantee that American deputies could never outnumber peninsular ones. It did, however, constitute the formal declaration of the equality of all white, Indian, and mestizo Americans with peninsular Spaniards and of the overseas territories with metropolitan Spain.[35]

The issue of equality became the cutting edge that would demonstrate to moderate Americans the inherent contradiction of empire, for neither the Cortes nor the constitution of 1812 were able to deal satisfactorily with the problem of equality. The Americans threw themselves into the attempt to win implementation of the decree of equality, but Spain could not implement it fully without granting to the American provinces the same powers the Spanish provinces had exercised following the Napoleonic invasion.

The debate over equality of representation concluded in 1811 when the Cortes adopted a draft of the new constitution that differentiated between the status of "Spaniard" and the status of "citizen." This example of semantic gymnastics declared that "the Spanish Nation is the union of all Spaniards of both hemispheres" and that "Spaniards" were "free men born and domiciled in the domains of the Spains." By this decision, then, all American Indians, mestizos, and castes of African heritage were proclaimed "Spaniards," just like creoles. But another article declared that "citizens"—that is, persons able to exercise the vote and on whose numbers apportionment of representation would be based—were "Spaniards who on both sides trace their ancestry to the Spanish dominions of both hemispheres," which excluded those persons whose ancestry was African. Having dispossessed the blacks, the constitution was then able to proclaim that representation in the Cortes from both Spain and America was to be equal, one deputy for each seventy thousand persons apportioned on "the population composed of those native-born who from both lines are derived from the Spanish domains."[36]

Two significant problems resulted from choosing the principles that sovereignty resided in the nation rather than the people, that the Spanish

monarchy was a single nation, and that its people were equal. One problem was that the confusion created by this effort to compromise between
the political philosophy of Rousseau and the imperial needs of a mother
country facing colonial insurrections bedeviled the framers of the Mexican constitution of 1824. The underlying political theory that the framers
of a separate Mexican constitution had as precedent may have been a radical step forward in the Spanish context, but it was also somewhat confused—a mix of Rousseau and Burke, as Brading puts it.[37]

For the more immediate term, the second problem was that the declaration that all the vast territories of the Spanish monarchy constituted "a
single nation," though manifestly a myth, also had the effect of emphasizing the principle of national unity as a response to the provincialist spirit,
as David Pantoja Morán points out. If sovereignty resided in the nation,
and if the nation was the union of all Spaniards in both hemispheres, then
the national political representation was based on the citizen rather than
on intermediary corporate or territorial political structures. The peninsular majority in the Cortes insisted that a consequence of the principle of
national sovereignty, unlike the French or U.S. principle that sovereignty
resided in the people, was that Cortes deputies were representatives of the
nation and not of the province that had elected them. In clear response to
the independence movements in the American territories, the Cortes
adopted the point of view expressed by one peninsular deputy, "We call
ourselves deputies of the nation and not of such and such a province: there
are deputies 'for' Catalonia, 'for' Galicia, etc., but not 'of' Catalonia, 'of'
Galicia, etc.; [otherwise] we would fall into federalism or, to put it better,
provincialism, which would disturb the force and the harmony of the
union." Similarly, the adoption of the idea of national sovereignty, as a
specific rejection of Rousseau, meant that suffrage was not to be direct but
indirect and based on parish, district, and provincial levels in order to filter
and diffuse citizens' opinions.[38] Americans had no difficulty perceiving
the gaps in logic in a system that proclaimed that the right to vote belonged to the citizen but sovereignty did not; or that deputies, though
elected for a province, were not speaking on behalf of that province; and
that recognized the provincehood of peninsular territories but not overseas ones.

Francois-Xavier Guerra has defined the political philosophy that characterized Spain and the Hispanic world in the crisis of the Napoleonic invasion as constituting a midway point in the transition from the ancient
regime, in which the legitimacy of the state was based on corporate insti-

tutions and their pact with the king, and modernity, in which the legitimacy of the state is based on the individual and his contract with the nation. The sharp disparity between what peninsular liberals believed was necessary for the mother country and what they believed was good for the overseas possessions was brought into clear relief when the peninsular members of the Cortes defined the empire as a unitary state while the Americans were emphasizing its pluralism. When the Cortes defined the empire as a unitary state, it definitively closed the possibility that the American kingdoms would be maintained within the Spanish monarchy in a form that would be acceptable to the American subjects.[39]

In regard to other debates, the American deputies clearly set out the dominant creole demand for reforms that would lead to autonomy in the American colonies. The two most important expressions of American demands were those presented by the overseas deputies on 16 December 1810 and 1 August 1811. The presentation of 16 December 1810 consisted of eleven fundamental reforms that the overseas territories demanded, and it was submitted by the entire American caucus. The demands included free trade, freedom to plant and manufacture previously restricted commodities, suppression of all Crown monopolies, equal rights for Americans to appointments, and distribution of half the positions in each American kingdom to natives of that kingdom.[40] All the demands were either adopted in a form that made them inapplicable to real American needs or never acted upon.

The second of the two major statements of what the Americans wanted was a proposal for provincial autonomy that was submitted on 1 August 1811 and signed by all thirty-three of the American deputies then present in the Cortes. It was modeled on a proposal dated four months earlier from the deputy representing Mexico City, José Ignacio Beye de Cisneros, who had proposed that a system of provincial juntas, composed of subjects named by their own peoples, be established in America and be authorized to declare the independence of the Americas should Spain fall completely under French control. Beye's proposal had died after eight months on the table, but in August the American caucus at large rephrased the suggestions, declaring that only regional juntas of government would possess legitimacy to speak in the king's name, for in the king's absence sovereignty devolved upon the people. What Americans really wanted, they attested, was not independence but the right to form their own governments and to make their own decisions.[41] The Cortes, again, took no action on the proposal.

This emphasis on the necessity of autonomous government based on the regional level, which was making its second major appearance in 1810 and 1811 among the American deputies to the Cortes (over one-third of whom were from Mexico), continued to be the core political objective of Mexican creoles. Through all the buffeting and confusion of the struggle for independence it emerges as the one constant theme. Although the direct demand for regional autonomy was rejected, echoes of the demand appeared in the constitution of 1812.

The crowning achievement of the Cortes was the constitution, promulgated in March 1812. It swept away the absolute monarchy, decreeing that sovereignty resided in the nation and in the Cortes that represented it. It limited the king's powers and even put the royal family on a budget controlled by the Cortes. It abolished the viceroyalties and reduced the viceroy to the position of political chief (*jefe político*) of his province. He too was meant to be merely the chief executive, though the precise extent of his powers remained unspecified and the subject of extensive debate. The military captains general were also made political chiefs of their territories. Hence, those portions of Spanish North America that already had their own captains general—Nueva Galicia, Yucatán, the Eastern and Western Interior Provinces, Guatemala, and San Luis Potosí—were definitively separated from the control of Mexico City. The audiencias were reduced from their position as a semilegislative privy council to a mere court of law.[42]

The constitution created provincial deputations in keeping with the desire of its authors, especially the American deputies, to limit absolutism on the local level and as an echo of the demand for provincial devolution. Miguel Ramos Arizpe, a Mexican deputy, was the chief advocate of this type of local autonomy.[43] Another Mexican deputy, José Miguel Guridi y Alcocer, had advocated that the provincial deputations be local legislatures with powers derived from the people and representing the interests of its province. This was identical to the 1811 proposal for autonomous provincial juntas.

The constitution did not, however, go so far as to create provincial self-government. Although Mexican deputies argued that the provincial deputations should be legislative assemblies in autonomous control of each province, the Cortes was unwilling to accept the proposal and kept the provincial deputations as administrative councils only, with the capacity to advise the local political chief (who was appointed by the Crown). The provincial deputations were not designed to encourage devolution of power to the overseas provinces but rather to serve as agencies for the implementation of policies of the central government.

It is important to note that the provincial deputations, as Donald F. Stevens puts it, "demonstrate the creative power of ambiguity and confusion that characterized the birth of the Mexican republic." Because movements for independence existed in most of the Spanish American kingdoms, the Cortes had to compromise between its wish to reorganize the Spanish political system and the need to avoid encouraging outright colonial autonomy. Thus, the name *provincial deputation* was itself a compromise. Because the provincial juntas that existed in Spain between 1808 and 1810 were virtually autonomous, self-governing bodies, the term *junta* implied legislative power. Hence, the term *deputation* was substituted, on the suggestion of the Mexican deputy Ramos Arizpe, in order to imply subordination to and creation by a higher authority. Stevens points out that "once established, however, the . . . deputations proved themselves in their struggle with executive powers. The electoral and legislative practice they provided prepared Mexicans for life in a republic, indeed the provincial deputations were the vehicles that took the royal subjects of New Spain on a journey that transformed them into citizens in the Mexican republic."[44]

Members of the provincial deputations and Cortes deputies were chosen by a complicated formula of indirect election. First, the voters of each parish met to select a list of electors. These parish electors then met at a scheduled time in each province to select that province's junta of electors, one for each *partido* (district) of the province. The junta of electors then met to choose the Cortes deputies and members of the provincial deputation for each province.

A serious anomaly, however, was that the Cortes did not recognize as provinces all the regions in Mexico and Central America that already considered themselves provinces and were historically, or by usage, so considered. Article II of the constitution simply declared that there would be a new division of all the territory when "the political circumstances of the nation permits it," but in the meantime no new territorial limits of the provinces were stated. Between 1812 and 1814 only seven provincial deputations were recognized in all of Spanish North America—New Spain ("Mexico" proper), Nueva Galicia, Yucatán, San Luis Potosí, the Internal Provinces of the East, the Internal Provinces of the West, and (in what later became the separate Central America) Guatemala. Each had jurisdiction over between two and seven individual provinces.

Because of the existence of rebellions in many regions, the provincial deputation of San Luis Potosí never actually met. The one for New Spain (despite having elections in 1812) met for less than a month, in July 1814, before the arrival of the decree in which the restored Ferdinand VII nullified the constitution. Nevertheless, the map of a "Mexico" composed of provinces was beginning to be formulated. The precise legal and legislative details are complex; Benson has narrated them.[45] The constitution of 1812 declared that there were seven provincial deputations in Spanish North America: one at Mexico City (New Spain), with jurisdiction over the provinces or intendancies of Mexico, Veracruz, Puebla, Oaxaca, Michoacán, Querétaro, and Tlaxcala; one at San Luis Potosí over the provinces or intendancies of San Luis Potosí and Guanajuato; one at Guadalajara (Nueva Galicia) for Nueva Galicia and Zacatecas; one at Mérida (Yucatán) for Yucatán, Tabasco, and Campeche; one at Monterrey (Eastern Interior Provinces) for Nuevo León, Coahuila, Nuevo Santander, and Texas; one at Durango (Western Interior Provinces) for Nueva Vizcaya (Durango), Chihuahua, Sonora, Sinaloa, and the Californias; and one at Guatemala City (for Central America). Thus, the political chief, formerly the viceroy, of New Spain, presided over only seven provinces, while other political chiefs presided over San Luis Potosí, Nueva Galicia, Yucatán, the Eastern Interior Provinces, the Western Interior Provinces, and Guatemala.

Benson makes the point that in Spanish North America there were many more recognized provinces and intendancies besides the seven recognized that merited a provincial deputation, that many jurisdictions remained to be clarified, and that although in the first period of the constitution of 1812 the provincial deputation had only a brief existence, "it is also true that many Mexicans even at that date recognized it as a means to obtain more local and provincial autonomy."[46]

Carmagnani observes that the creation of provincial deputations in the Spanish constitution gave concrete form to the sense of provincehood that already existed. The intendancies gave way to formal provinces, and the provinces were endowed in the constitution with many functions, including management of taxes, investment of public funds, promotion of the economy, development of education, collection of scientific and statistical data about the territory, establishment of beneficent activities, and the right to report directly to the Cortes in matters relating to the implementation of the provisions of the constitution. By the 1820–21 period, when the constitution was restored, the provincial deputations were involved in approving new taxes, regulating municipal finances, resolving land-ownership disputes, establishing public works, and stimulating new agricultural production. The provincial deputations spoke for and represented the citizens within their jurisdiction, which by 1820 brought them into frequent dispute with agents of the Crown such as military commanders and subdelegates. Taking over many local governmental, judicial, and fiscal functions, the provincial deputations made more explicit the preexisting tendencies to self-government, making concrete a sense of territoriality and enhancing the existing distinction between royal authority, as represented in the agents of the Crown, and provincial authority. It was "the institutionalization of territoriality."[47] By 1821, it was the Crown and its imperial authority that had become distant and vague, while provincehood had become concrete and near.

The immense impact of the first local and provincial elections in 1812 and 1813, and the social and political anomalies they revealed, was also of the greatest significance. They not only for the first time permitted large sectors of the population a mode of political participation, however indirect, they also offered an alternative to armed insurrection and established an electoral model that continued after independence.[48] Furthermore, for the purpose of conducting the elections the Cortes ordered that preliminary electoral councils would be created in each of the seven greater provinces of Spanish North America in order to decide the number of Cortes deputies and members of provincial deputations these vast territories would have. These electoral councils began the process, based on historical precedent, population, and usage, of declaring how many provinces actually existed, what regions belonged to which province, what each province's population was, and how many Cortes deputies and provincial deputation members each should have. Although these electoral councils faced an immensely complex task, which meant they did not always arrive at clear or correct decisions regarding territorial jurisdiction, the main point is that Spain had no mechanism for implementing elections in the overseas colonies other than to allow those territories themselves to decide what was and what was not a province.

The royalist response to revolution reinforced the impact of the constitution, elections, and provincial deputations on the provincialist urge. As perhaps an equally important element in the process—particularly in military affairs—it also helped make provincehood concrete. In their effort to suppress the rebellions, the royalist authorities adopted a policy of conscription, forced contributions, and widespread militarization of the country. Francisco Javier Venegas and Félix María Calleja, viceroys (or, under the constitution, political chiefs of New Spain) during the period of the mass rebellions, created a network of semiautonomous royalist military forces in many parts of the country based on a policy of requiring the cities and towns to garrison royal troops at local expense. Calleja, both before becoming political chief in 1813 and while serving in that position, sought to construct what Christon I. Archer calls "a tiered system of counterinsurgent defense that would be based on . . . militias organized in cities, towns, and rural districts," with large haciendas and villages required to defend themselves.[49] In 1813 Calleja created a series of decentralized commands based on regions, provinces, and districts and frequently united both military and civilian administrative control in the hands of officers. Military officers moved quickly to establish military supremacy over the civil administration, sometimes retaining such powers until independence. José de la Cruz, royalist commander in chief of Nueva Galicia, president of the audiencia of Guadalajara from 1811 to 1821, and for a time intendant as well, provided perhaps the clearest example of the combination of civil and military authority. He launched a policy of terror designed to cut the rebels off from their sources of support. Commands of similar format were instituted (for New Spain) in Puebla, Guanajuato, Valladolid, Querétaro, Zacatecas, and Oaxaca, as well as in the constitutionally separate captaincies general of Guadalajara, San Luis Potosí, the Eastern and Western Interior Provinces, Yucatán, and Guatemala. Many commanders held their posts for most of the period of the struggle for independence, established business interests (even with the enemy), engaged in corrupt practices in the areas of their command, and became unwilling to surrender such powers. Given the need to support the royalist armies, local commandants usually had the power to tax populations, in the form of hated *contribuciones militares*, and to confiscate and sell property, at least until reestablishment of the Spanish constitution in 1820.

According to Archer, this system of regional *comandantes generales*, in control of nearly every aspect of society and the economy in specific regions and provinces, constituted a widespread example of the control military officers maintained over Mexican politics for much of the decade prior to independence. The struggle against the rebellions had led to "decentralizing the country into a series of semiautonomous and autonomous military satrapies," which provided "a prototype for the provincial caudillo."[50] The policy to create strong regional centers of royalist military power that could stop the insurgents left a legacy, quite simply, of strong regional centers of power in the hands of military commanders. Although restoration of the Spanish constitution in 1820 temporarily removed the officers from political power, the rapid rise of Iturbide reopened the door to military control of the regions.

In addition, the insurrections themselves were regional—that is, regionally based, regionally manned, regionally supported, and regionally commanded—and this diversification played a major role in creating or enhancing regional and provincial identities. As Hamnett has pointed out, after the defeat of Hidalgo in 1811 the insurgent camp experienced "early and irreversible fragmentation of command" under a host of chieftains whose control extended to large regions, often whole provinces, and the loyalties of these units frequently shifted from side to side. Military chieftains, both in the insurgent and in the royalist camp, became politicians with a clientele to satisfy. "Local chieftains and provincial commanders, whether royalist or insurgent, or oscillating between sides, represented, at the most blatant, the rule of force. . . . Royalist amnesty policies facilitated the transfer of insurgent bands into the government fighting forces, and thereby enabled the survival of these networks of personal allegiance."[51] Because the final achievement of independence under Iturbide brought together, under the guarantees of the Plan of Iguala, both former royalist officers and former rebel chieftains, the effect developed in the wars of independence was one of regionally based military commanders endowed with both military command and control of civil administration. Mexican militarism and caudillism predated independence, and it was through the urge to provincial autonomy that they would be institutionalized.

The insurgents, like other elements in Mexican society, were in the habit of thinking of political organization in terms of provinces. Thus, the constitution of Apatzingán, produced in 1814 by the rebel movement under the military protection of José María Morelos, recognized the existence of seventeen provinces—Mexico, Puebla, Tlaxcala, Veracruz, Yucatán, Oaxaca, Tecpan, Michoacán, Querétaro, Guadalajara, Guanajuato, San Luis Potosí, Zacatecas, Durango, Sonora, Coahuila, and Nuevo León. Each was to be represented in the supreme congress by one deputy. This was essentially the same approach to territoriality as the Cádiz constitution.[52] Interestingly, after independence the argument of the most radical federalist state, Jalisco, would be that each province should have only one vote in the federal congress so as to guarantee the equality of the provinces.

It can be said, indeed, that the most important legacy of the struggle for independence in Mexico was the tendency to territoriality combined with the intersection of civilian and military politics—in short, regionalism. The Hispanic traditions of municipalism and provincialism, reinforced by the Spanish constitution, were united with the fact that at the moment of independence military commanders, drawn from both sides of the conflict, were in control of many regions, sometimes with no effective interference from the central power. Both royalist and insurgent causes had come to depend on the regions. Both civilian and military elites owed their access to power to regional or provincial bases. Luis Alberto de la Garza summarizes the situation as follows, "The internal development of many provinces, their gradual decentralization with respect to the authorities of Mexico City, the notable growth in regional consciousness, the weakness shown during the revolutionary process by the same authorities in the capital, had all produced incipient forms of self-government."[53] With the coming of independence many great issues had yet to be settled—jurisdictional and territorial issues, chains of command, institutional infrastructure, trade and commerce and taxation, social policy— but the choices would always be affected by the extent to which power had begun to devolve to the dominant groups at the provincial and regional level.

Historians' emphasis should not be on some assumed vacuum in politics and institutions upon the severing of the imperial bonds but upon the wide spectrum of Hispanic cultural and institutional traditions, local interrelationships, and territorial linkages that were already in place or that quickly developed during the eleven years of the independence process. Participants in these events did not regret such developments; it is not clear why historians should. The reality was very different from what is reflected in the dominant, centralist-oriented historiography. Although this was not a coherent nation but rather a congeries of many patrias with many diverse sources of power, it was not a void either. Why should homogeneity or uniformity be the standard against which to measure such a development? It is largely our cultural bias in favor of the nation-state that leads to the assumption that the achievement of independence must normally be followed by, if not preceded by, nationhood. That was simply not the situation facing most Spanish American countries at independence. As the Spanish monarchy disintegrated, it was time to get on with the business of transferring of power from an artificial single center to the objects of that power in the regions where they lived. And independence was very much a process, a series of actions occurring in real space and time and leading toward a broadly sketched objective—independence—the details of which had yet to be worked out. As the Spanish Empire staggered, Mexican ideas, interrelationships, forces, and aspirations filled the newly opening spaces in a process of transition whose precise outcome was not yet in sight.

Spanish administrative centralism was a facade that had been severely weakened by the creation of intendancies, the impact of the constitution, and the wars of independence. The provinces were actually a collection of countries, too large to be controlled by a crumbling imperial center. Growing identities were compounded by anxieties about the status of the true patria (the local one) within the independent country. The tendency in these peripheral localities was uniformly antihegemonic. The urge to autonomy had only been suppressed in 1808, not eliminated. There is a clear continuum in terms of political thought and aspirations between 1808, with its early expression of autonomist sentiment; the period 1810–14, with the rising expectations provoked by American participation in the Cortes and by the massive changes decreed by the constitution; the period 1820–21, with the restoration of the constitution; and the final achievement of independence.

Pedro Pérez Herrero has suggested that the municipal level of government was the real thread of local identity and political action in late colonial Mexico. Because the ayuntamientos or *cabildos* "were, logically, the nucleus of power of the local oligarchy" in the face of the centralizing political tendencies of the Bourbon kings, "local oligarchies took refuge in the cabildos as bulwarks of defense against the centralizing attack." Because the cabildos also controlled the formation of provincial militias, creole elites did not fight to gain control of colonial governments; instead, they fell back on the level of political authority that Spanish regalism could never entirely dominate, that is, the municipal level. "Passivity was once again the most efficient arm of defense of local autonomy against the modernizing activity of Bourbon centralism." The Ordinance of Intendants of 1786 can thus be interpreted as an attempt by the Crown to overcome the political autonomy of the cabildos by placing a royal official directly answerable to Madrid in supreme control of government and administration. But the fact that in 1794 the cabildos regained the right to select "honorary" members from among local notables meant that the purpose of creating intendancies was frustrated.[54]

The Spanish constitution of 1812 greatly broadened the role played by municipalism. In the Bourbon reform era of the 1780s and 1790s, cabildos existed only in the more substantial cities, so that they were the instrument of a regional or provincial oligarchy and thus something of a counterbalance to the regalist power of the intendant. The Cádiz constitution, however, decreed that ayuntamientos were to be created in every town or village with a population of more than one thousand, which would effectively counterbalance the oligarchic power of the larger cabildos. As indigenous communities rushed to create their own ayuntamientos, the effect was to encourage the reconstitution of indigenous territoriality, fragmented since the sixteenth century. Nearly nine hundred new ayuntamientos were created by 1814, most of them in indigenous and mestizo communities.[55] It was a gigantic step in the direction of local self-government, for as Hernández Chávez points out, recognition of an ayuntamiento not only constituted recognition of the self-governing status of a community of residents (*vecinos*) but recognition as well of their control over the land, water, and woods in their territories.[56] As Terry Rugeley shows for Yucatán, the many new ayuntamientos, authorized by constitutional decrees in the period from 1812 to 1813, moved "to draw up *arbitrios* or plans of incorporation designating community assets, necessary expenses, and proposed revenues—that is, taxes."[57] Though repressed between 1814 and 1820, the constitutional experience held out at least the promise of a massive devolution of power through the creation of hundreds of local ayuntamientos.[58]

Until 1812 the struggle for local dominance had been between the local oligarchy and the Crown. Under the 1812 constitution the local notables were no longer forced to fight the Crown; instead, they had to gain control of regional electorates in the complicated multilevel voting system decreed by the constitution. Thus, Pérez Herrero adds a necessary refinement to our understanding of the meaning of "local autonomy." Within each province the urge to local autonomy would be expressed through both cabildos and provincial deputations. In some provinces, the two levels of local expression complemented each other and spoke for the same interests, but in others a political divide would exist between the provincial deputation and the cabildo of the major city or cities, on the one hand, and the cabildos of smaller, less powerful towns and communities, particularly indigenous ones, on the other.

Indeed, Antonio Annino argues that the creation of large numbers of municipalities under the constitution of Cádiz was not only important but of fundamental significance. It constituted the beginning of self-government in hundreds of Indian pueblos, transferring to their hands control of both fiscal and justice matters. It was, he says, "a form of complete self-government of the new organisms over their territories, to such a point that the towns began to define themselves as 'sovereign.'" This was the birth of "a new syncretism" out of the crisis of the Old Regime, a silent revolution at the local level, "a massive transference of the powers of the state to the new elective municipalities." Hispanic traditions of political action were based on the existence of corporative bodies speaking for individuals. For rural Indian communities, the corporate body that represented them was the local municipality, elected by local residents under provisions of the Cádiz constitution, and inheriting from the former *repúblicas de indios* the control of local common lands and other assets. In the local communities, liberal constitutionalism linked the ancient community rights to the new rights provided by the charter, and it was read by local citizens as a new form of pact between the king and his subjects.[59]

Federalism, then, could be both a response by regional oligarchies to assure that their economic power would be complemented by political power and a response by groups lower down the social scale to implement their objectives in the face of the rise of those same oligarchies. The important point is that both the Ordinance of Intendants and the constitution of 1812 were important steps forward in the definition of provincehood and the growth of incipient political autonomy at the community level, and both were necessarily implemented through the refracted lenses of local circumstances. Particularly in a country like Mexico, where vast differences in geography and local development prevailed, there were always lapses of time or consciousness between one location and others. That is the very essence of the mosaic. Thus, we would not expect that all regions of the country would move with monolithic intent and at precisely the same time toward both the perception and the achievement of a particular set of goals. Human agency was the determining factor, particularly because it seems to me that the story of the spread of federalism in Mexico is an excellent example of the way in which ideas occur because of a set of circumstances that spark them and because of conditions that allow or encourage their spread. My argument is that federalism was an idea that emerged and rapidly spread because it was a solution to perceived needs.

Alicia Hernández Chávez argues that the collapse of the imperial colonial system and the constitution of 1812 gave rise to a new legitimacy in the form of a newly strengthened but long-standing regional autonomy. Both the political and the military arms of government came under the control of local "notables" who "kept the country afloat" by the way in which they

formed various alliances between themselves and with the various caudillos (liberal, conservative, and royalist) who sometimes gained dominance in their regions. These constantly changing local relationships were
sustained by the power of local notables, by the existing community organization of towns and villages possessing their own juridical identities,
and by ancient social structures defined by extended family units, links of
compadrazgo, loyalties, and common interests. Moreover, in the context
of this new form of legitimacy, which European and urban elite modes of
thought dismissed simply as chaos, "the regions or territories functioned
with singular efficacy."[60] Hernández Chávez is sketching a legitimacy
based on multiple diversification of power and in which the first principle
is local autonomy. The greater part of Mexico's nineteenth-century history remains incomprehensible without at once recognizing this first
principle and granting it a degree of legitimacy at least equal to that which
the historiography traditionally grants to the contrary European-derived
organizing principle of the nation-state.

Indeed, Antonio Annino has made the fundamental point that Mexican creoles, and indeed Latin American creoles in general, had rejected
the new French idea of nation, a product largely of the French Revolution
and an idea that had captivated the Spanish liberals in the Cortes of Cádiz.
Spanish America believed in a contractual conception of sovereignty that
was fundamentally different from the emerging European idea of sovereignty based on nationhood. In Spanish America, the nation, when it was
identified, was made up of "provinces," "territories," and "cities." As
Annino writes,

> Hence, contrary to conventional opinion, the *Grande Révolution*
> was not the centerpiece of American thinking. This was apparent
> when it came to the decisive question of the future imperial arrange-
> ment: the fount of sovereignty. During one entire day (28 August
> 1811), both Spanish liberals and American representatives debated on
> the use of a single adverb. The former defended the formula coined
> by Sieyés, that sovereignty reposed *essentially* in the nation; the lat-
> ter sustained the seventeenth-century contractualist theory that
> sovereignty reposed *originally* in the nation.

The early-nineteenth-century Spanish American idea of sovereignty, then,
was based in the intermediate corporate bodies, the cities and provinces,
which were the political base of creole identity. The "originary" creole
sovereignty was divided among the intermediate bodies; it was contrac-

tualist in its values and, above all, in its practice. Spanish American federalism was heavily indebted to this contractual conception of sovereignty.[61]

Overall, by 1820 and 1821 there was a greatly enhanced urge to autonomy, based in the provinces and intendancies, that was further strengthened by the brief experience with elected city councils and provincial deputations as well as by regional rebellions and regionally based royalist
resistance to the rebellions. Mexican caudillism was being born in the military struggle of rebellion and counterinsurgency, but at the same time
Mexican federalism was being born through the precedent of the Spanish
constitution of 1812 and the Hispanic traditions that dated back hundreds
of years. Both caudillism and federalism sprang from the ground they in-
habited, and their roots were Mexican and Hispanic. Mexican federalism
was not copied from the example of the United States. Hamnett has written that "it is fundamental that we comprehend that the concept of region
did not originate simply with the ideology of federalism, but that, on the
contrary, it was a natural product of the Mexican soil. Its significance was
not merely territorial, but also cultural and psychological."[62]

Many scholars perceive the caudillism and the disputatious federalism
of Mexico after independence as a kind of disintegration or atomization.
This perception is based on a false understanding of the process of independence. Independence was the product of regional social tensions and
regional aspirations to home rule. The regions were themselves large ag-
gregations of hinterland areas; many provinces were larger than some European countries. How would it benefit Mérida, or Guadalajara, or Veracruz, or Guatemala City if power were simply transferred from Madrid
to Mexico City? There was no disintegration. There were, rather, attempts at aggregation of an already disaggregated entity, but it is not as if
a single thing was created and then broken down into its constituent
parts.

In January 1820 a large expeditionary force of Spanish troops that had
been gathered in Cádiz to launch an attempted reconquest of Río de la
Plata revolted against the restored absolutism of the king. Motivated by
military grievances against the royal government, the revolt was soon
joined by the liberals, Masons, supporters of the 1812 constitution, former
collaborators of the French, radicals, and other sectors hostile to the despotic absolutism of Ferdinand VII. The movement coalesced behind the
idea of restoring the constitution of 1812, and the king had no choice but to
submit. From 1820 to 1823 a liberal regime again governed Spain, while
Ferdinand VII secretly conspired with the French king, Louis XVIII, to
overthrow the constitutional government that, he insisted, was holding

him captive. The example of the restoration of constitutional liberalism in Spain soon spread to Portugal and Naples, two kingdoms closely linked to Spain by dynastic relations. For America, the impact was even greater, in that it virtually guaranteed the independence of the Río de la Plata and Chile, while in Peru the independence movement took renewed vigor.

The Spanish revolution of 1820 had important political consequences in Mexico as well. The constitution, which had not been fully implemented between 1812 and 1814 because of resistance by colonial governments, was now fully implemented. By August 1820 the city councils, provincial deputations, and deputies to the Cortes had all been elected in Mexico. One immediate consequence is that the restored or newly created elected city councils in many localities moved rapidly to terminate the heavy tax burdens imposed on them for the maintenance of local militias, and in many districts the royalist militia system simply ceased to exist. Thus, exhaustion from a long and intense war combined with the developing spirit of regionalism to spell the end of royalist power. "The rejection of the counterinsurgency militia system," Christon I. Archer states, "marked a new awareness in provinces, towns, and rural districts that Mexican regions need no longer bow to the superior authority of the central regime and its military governors."[63]

In the 1820–21 session of the Cortes, deputies from that part of Spanish North America designated the "province" of New Spain composed the largest bloc of overseas deputies, with forty-four deputies and seven alternates taking their seats. From early in the session of the new Cortes, Mexican deputies focused their demands on one main issue: that the Cortes implement the constitution's Article 325, which declared simply that "in each province there will be a provincial deputation," and that it order that each existing province or intendancy have its own provincial deputation.[64] Thus far, only six provincial deputations had been created in Mexico and one in Central America. By 1821 almost all the powerful peripheral areas had gone on record demanding such a development. Most significantly, many of the intendancies within the one great "province" of New Spain— such as Puebla, Valladolid, Veracruz, and Oaxaca—demanded recognition of their provincehood. In short, the provinces were demanding that they be recognized as provinces, as political units entitled to function apart from Crown sufferance, independent of each other, and with the right to be self-governing in provincial affairs.

As a result of the efforts of Mexican deputies, the Cortes began debate on a bill proposing that, because each intendancy overseas had the character and was in fact a real province, a provincial deputation should be installed in each intendancy that did not currently have one. In May 1821 the Cortes passed the bill. News of this act quickly spread overseas by unofficial means, and by the time the official decree arrived, carried by the new captain general, Juan O'Donojú, Mexico was nearly independent.

In the months following the appearance in February 1821 of the Plan of Iguala, many of the provinces moved to implement the status of provincehood that they had long sought. In August 1821 Iturbide granted the request of Puebla for establishment of its provincial deputation (at the same time that he acceded to the demand of its merchants for creation of a Consulado of Puebla). Meanwhile, Michoacán (Valladolid) moved in March to establish its deputation. At the same time, several Mexican deputies presented to the Cortes a proposal for dominion autonomy. The proposal was to create separate American monarchies by establishing three separate Cortes, in Mexico City, in Bogotá and in Lima, each with its own executive, cabinet, and supreme court. It was presented in June 1821 by the Mexican Cortes deputies Mariano Michelena and Miguel Ramos Arizpe. Lucas Alamán, Francisco Fagoaga, and Lorenzo de Zavala, all Mexican deputies who played major roles in politics after independence, were also members of the Cortes committee that discussed the proposal. Some fifty American deputies, most of them from Mexico, signed this proposal, but the Cortes took no further action.

The Plan of Iguala swept Spanish North America because it encapsulated what by 1821 had become the leading-edge view of most elites—the demand for monarchy, the constitution of 1812, and home rule. The constitution gave each province its own provincial deputation; it conceded to the ayuntamientos the internal government of their cities; and it gave each province its own jefe político. It thus created a political structure that both confirmed and further intensified the identity of the regions and that made autonomy real. As Iturbide spread his control in the last months of the independence process, he indicated his full support for these principles, indeed, in order to win he had no other choice. The Plan of Iguala provided for separation from Spain in a setting that would guarantee stability, protect vested interests, and preserve the promise of enhanced provincial identity. Throughout the country, the provinces rushed to independence because the Plan of Iguala not only encouraged the rapid recognition of their provincehood, it also promised protection and development for groups in control of local power.[65]

In this headlong race to provincehood and independence, a rarely noticed fact of the greatest significance was that the provinces subscribed to the Plan of Iguala, that is, they accepted independence, by acts of their own volition. It came about usually by a vote of the provincial deputation and the cabildos of the chief cities or in a decision of the regional armed forces and commandants, or both. That is, the provinces entered independence as provinces and in the full understanding that their provincial identity would prevail. Independence was, in the end, a political act rather than the result of military victory. It guaranteed provincial identity, and it was relatively bloodless. Each province had to respond to the fait accompli of independence, and they did so on a province-by-province basis. Although the historiography of the independence era has been dominated by a focus on military affairs, civilians as well as military officers made important contributions to independence.[66]

Within two weeks, the major rebel leader in the south, Vicente Guerrero, adhered to the Plan of Iguala. With notable speed, most provinces and most royalist armies came over, and there emerged a fundamental consensus in support of the proposal of political independence as outlined in the Plan of Iguala. In March the ambitious creole lieutenant Antonio López de Santa Anna, in command of the coast of Veracruz province, joined the plan. In the Bajío region, center of the original Hidalgo rebellion, royalist Colonels Luis de Cortázar and Anastasio Bustamante came over. At Zitácuaro Captain Vicente Filisola proclaimed his adherence to the plan. Much of the provinces of Nueva Galicia, Zacatecas, and San Luis Potosí came over. Iturbide's newly created army, the Army of the Three Guarantees, won the support of important towns in Puebla and Veracruz provinces. General Pedro Celestino Negrete, second in command of the royalist armies in Nueva Galicia, came over. Colonel Luis Quintanar, in command of Valladolid, joined the independence cause in May. In June the city of Guadalajara joined, and Colonel Domingo Luaces surrendered Querétaro. In May Viceroy Juan Ruíz de Apodaca (now superior political chief of New Spain) reported to Spain that "the major part of the troops of this kingdom with many of their officers, subalterns and some commanders, have been seduced, and passing to the rebels have left me in the greatest conflict and the kingdom on the verge of being lost."[67] So divided were the Spanish forces that on 5 July the vestiges of the royal army located in Mexico City overthrew Apodaca (the second coup in modern Mexican history) in an effort to mount a final resistance against the rebel juggernaut.[68] On 3 August the city of Puebla came on side, and its second in command, José Morán, the marqués de Vivanco, joined the cause; then Oaxaca joined too. In the strategic geography of Mexico, Puebla is always the final bastion before Mexico City itself. As of August 1821 the Army of the Three Guarantees controlled almost all the country except Mexico City, the port of Veracruz, and the centers of Acapulco and Perote.

Thus, within a month of the achievement of independence, nine provincial deputations were functioning in Mexico and Central America and another six were authorized. The nine that were functioning were Mexico (the center of what had formerly been called the "province" of New Spain), Guadalajara (Nueva Galicia), the Eastern Interior Provinces, the Western Interior Provinces, San Luis Potosí, Yucatán, Puebla, Chiapas, and Guatemala. Six others—Sinaloa and Sonora, Guanajuato, Michoacán, Oaxaca, Veracruz, and Zacatecas—were in the midst of creating their deputations.[69] That made a total of fifteen. By November 1822 the imperial government of Iturbide recognized the existence of twenty-three provinces in the Mexican Empire (eighteen in Mexico, five in Central America). Although for centrally located regions independence from Spain might be the goal in itself, for the majority of areas, not centrally located and struggling for identity, it now became chiefly a means to the actual goal, which was self-government. The Plan of Iguala succeeded in winning independence because it was not only what elites and old rebels wanted, it was a giant step forward for the regions.

This rush to provincehood continued throughout the short period of the Mexican Empire and just beyond. Indeed, it was clearly a response to the empire that, though it may not have encouraged the further devolution of power to provinces, at least did not discourage it. Changes occurring both before and after the fall of Iturbide, chiefly in the Eastern and Western Interior Provinces, brought the total number of provinces authorized and established in Mexico by December 1823 to twenty-three, and by that time the five provinces of Central America had withdrawn.

This rush to provincehood was most significant in jurisdictions like Tlaxcala, Guanajuato, Chiapas, Durango, Tabasco, Sonora, Sinaloa, Texas, Nuevo Mexico, Chihuahua, Coahuila, Nuevo Santander, Nuevo León, and the Californias, where full provincial status, separate from the hegemony of a larger neighbor, had not fully existed before. Indeed, three politically peripheral regions—Tlaxcala, Nuevo Santander, and Nuevo Mexico—simply elected and installed their own provincial deputations without authorization. The "big" provinces—particularly Mexico, Guadalajara, and Veracruz, but also Oaxaca, Michoacán, San Luis Potosí, Puebla, Zacatecas, Querétaro, and Yucatán—had a greater claim on their status as distinct provinces but still needed to have it guaranteed.

When we approach the Plan of Iguala as an act extending provincial status and guaranteeing the constitution of 1812, it becomes clear what its attraction was to such peripheral areas as Central America and Yucatán. They saw in the plan the same things central Mexico saw, and their response was the same. Acting as provinces, they also adopted the plan.

Yucatán had never been integrated into Mexican administration and had no desire to retain Spanish political control. Its most important trading partners were Cuba and England, not Mexico. After the habilitation of its port at Sisal in 1814 and Spain's recognition of Yucatán's right to sell its logwood directly to England, it had enjoyed rapidly expanding exports, a virtual free trade of its own. Consequently, the friendly attitude toward Spain reflected in the Plan of Iguala, which promised the continuation of existing trade links, was favorably received by Yucatán. When the Plan of Iguala won the support of neighboring Tabasco, Yucatán had to make its choice. On 15 September 1821 a meeting of leading figures took place in Mérida, called by the captain general, and it proclaimed Yucatán's independence from Spain while simultaneously recognizing European Spaniards "as brothers and friends" and expressing the desire to continue "peacefully the business and transactions of civil life." For Yucatán, liberty meant free trade, but its merchants recognized that it lacked both a sufficient internal market for rapid development and the resources to be an independent country.[70] With Mexico's promise in the Plan of Iguala that it would abide by the Spanish constitution, in November Yucatán joined the independent Mexican Empire.

In Central America the constitution and the promise of provincial status were also popular, and they were the keys to the success of the Plan of Iguala. The decision of Spain to create provincial deputations in each intendancy reawakened aspirations for home rule in such provinces as Honduras, Chiapas, and El Salvador. When Chiapas decided in late August 1821 to subscribe to the Plan of Iguala, and by so doing transferred its allegiance from Guatemala to Mexico, a decision had to be made. The captain general, Gabino Gaínza, called a meeting of notables for 15 September in Guatemala City, and this meeting adopted a declaration of independence. The other provinces of Central America held their own meetings to determine what course to follow. In San Salvador, where fear of annexation by either Mexico or Guatemala was strong, a meeting proclaimed the independence of El Salvador on 29 September. In Nicaragua, the provincial deputation proclaimed independence on 28 September and assumed its declaration applied to Costa Rica. The Costa Rican town councils met on their own and proclaimed independence, deposing the Spanish governor on 1 November. In Honduras, independence was also declared, but a split occurred over whether to join Guatemala or Mexico. As in Mexico, Central America moved to a final decision on a provincial basis; for it the main appeal was the Plan of Iguala's support for constitutionalism and provincial identity.[71]

Gaínza, who had earlier opposed the annexation of Central America by Mexico, now invited the Central American towns to hold open town council meetings (*cabildos abiertos*) to decide upon the incorporation of the entire former kingdom of Guatemala into the Mexican Empire. In a series of irregular meetings, considerable support for unification with Mexico was expressed. On 29 December Guatemala City and Quezaltenango joined Mexico, and on 9 January 1822 Gaínza announced the union of all Central America with the Mexican Empire. Some Central Americans opposed the union, particularly the Salvadorans, but in June 1822 a small Mexican army under the command of Brigadier General Vicente Filisola arrived in Central America and subdued El Salvador by force. On 11 July 1822 the Mexican congress formally ratified the union of Central America with the empire.

The pursuit of provincial identity had brought independence from Spain for all of Spanish North America, but the logical conclusion to the process was not yet reached in September 1821. If we look at independence as a process in which each aspiration, once it was achieved, opened new possibilities, then it becomes clear that September 1821 was not the last phase of the process but the next to the last. In 1821 the Plan of Iguala provided such a significant guarantee of provincial interests that it made independence possible. By 1823 it was not enough.

CHAPTER THREE

"Without Tears and without Lamentations": Unfinished Beginnings

América Septentrional, the northern part of the vast Spanish Empire in America, became independent from Spain in September 1821. The first ruler of the new country was Agustín de Iturbide, who led the final and successful phase of the struggle for independence and then founded and became emperor of its first state, the Mexican Empire.[1] Only two years later, in September 1823, he was in exile in the Italian port city of Livorno where he wrote a short memoir defending his record as liberator-emperor. The *Memoria de Livorno* is a remarkably telling commentary not only on the brief eighteen months of Iturbide's rule but also on the attitudes of Mexicans in general at the time of independence.

There are many important thoughts in Iturbide's memoir, but perhaps the most meaningful occurs when he reflects on why he opposed the revolutionary insurrections led by Miguel Hidalgo, José María Morelos, and others, and why between 1820 and 1821 he converted to the side of independence. In so doing, Iturbide was commenting not only on himself but on most of the other white elites, both Spaniards and creoles, who during the eleven years of warfare had chosen to oppose the mass insurrections. "Hidalgo, and those who came after him, and who followed his example, desolated the country, . . . sacrificed a great number of citizens, obstructed the sources of riches, . . . destroyed all kinds of industry, rendered the conditions of the Americans still more wretched . . . and far from obtaining independence increased the obstacles that opposed it." Reflecting the view that the mass insurrections threatened anarchy, Iturbide explained that as a consequence "I sallied out then to be useful to the Mexicans, to the King of Spain, and to the Spaniards."[2] Elsewhere, in the letter in which Iturbide sent Viceroy Juan Ruiz de Apodaca the first announcement of the Plan of Iguala, he declared of the Hidalgo insurrection, "The night of 15–16 September 1810 the cry of independence was given amid the shadows of horror, with a system, if it can be called that, [that was] cruel, barbarous, sanguinary, coarse, and unjust as a consequence."[3]

Thus, he became one of the leading creole commanders in the royalist army, a "rebel-killer" as some of the survivors of the earlier rebellions later called him, because for him, and for most other members of the elites, defeating the mass rebellions was necessary to preserve their fortunes and their religion and to avoid the possibility of being preempted when the political power passed to new hands. Conscious of the imminent disintegration of the existing order, when old ways were breaking up and new ones were not yet formed, the one thing the elites could not do was court their own suicide. The danger of social revolution was brought home to elites by the mass rebellions that constituted much of the struggle for independence. At the dawn of Mexico's existence as an independent country the social struggle was already paramount.

According to the testimony of his memoirs, the reason Iturbide converted to the side of independence between 1820 and 1821, advocating the Plan of Iguala that led to the achievement of independence, was to save the country, not from the radical decrees of the restored Spanish Cortes, but from the factionalism and strife that political events in Spain unleashed in Mexico. Still embodying the triumphalism that swept up the supporters of independence in 1821, Iturbide concluded his discussion of winning independence by discussing how his phase of the struggle had cost the lives of only a few people, unlike the earlier insurrections: "Without bloodshed, without incendiaries, without murders, without robberies, in short, without tears and without lamentations, my country became free."[4]

It would be highly misleading to suggest that independence came easily to Mexico. The statement by Iturbide that the Hidalgo insurrection "sacrificed a great number of citizens" may have been vague, but it expressed the relative horror the elites saw in the Hidalgo insurrection. It is not possible to arrive at a precise estimate of the death toll in the insurgencies, but Carlos María de Bustamante, in an 1823 statement to Congress, suggested that two hundred thousand died in the struggle, out of a total population of slightly over six million. Joel R. Poinsett, in a report in 1822 for the U.S. secretary of state on his observations as a special agent in Mexico, guessed that four hundred to five hundred thousand had died.[5] José María Luis Mora estimated six hundred thousand, nearly 10 percent of New Spain's population. These are estimates only; there are no reliable statistics.

As to economic and infrastructural damage, no historian has entirely succeeded in quantifying this either. Although some sectors of mining or agriculture began to recover even before independence was completed, most historians agree that Mexico's economy was paralyzed as a result of the property damage, collapse of the export sector, and capital flight caused by the struggle for independence.[6] Between 1806 and 1823 government revenue fell from 39 million pesos to 5.4 million; between 1809 and 1821 coinage of silver fell from 24.7 million pesos to 7.6 million; and exports fell from 20 million pesos in 1800 to 5 million in 1825. During the years of the most intense fighting, 1810 to 1816, it is estimated that agriculture lost 70 million pesos, mining 20 million, and manufacturing nearly 12 million. The loss in currency was a staggering 786 million. Mexico, the world's largest producer of silver, had been hemorrhaging capital for a decade before the outbreak of the insurrections and continued to do so during and after the war. The output of gold and silver from the mines fell by 50 percent from 1810 to 1820; agricultural production dropped by half, and craft output by more than half.[7] Not all the decline was attributable to the insurrections or the royalist resistance to them, and the statistics are very tenuous. Yet there can be no doubt that the years of warfare took a terrible toll. This, in itself, played a major role in determining how independence, when it finally came, would be achieved.

John H. Coatsworth points out that the economic decline of Mexico began well before the war of independence: "It has become commonplace to contrast the 'harmony and prosperity' of the colonial era to the conflict and depression of independent Mexico. This contrast is essentially inaccurate. The research of the past two decades points clearly to a sustained economic decline in the last decades of the colonial era. Indeed, nearly all of the factors cited by historians to explain postindependence economic trends were powerfully at work decades before the Grito de Dolores." Even so, he points out that an especially sharp short-term decline occurred during the independence wars, particularly in mining and government revenue. The overall economic decline was inexorable over the first six decades of the nineteenth century—Mexico's gross domestic product per capita fell from roughly half that of the United States in 1800 to less than one-seventh by 1860. The country's loss of natural resources was especially staggering; its national territory, which stood at nearly 4.5 million square kilometers at independence, not counting Central America, fell to 2 million square kilometers by 1853, entirely from the loss of Texas and U.S. territorial aggrandizement.[8]

Perhaps most ominous was the fact that Mexico had become independent as a consequence of a wide variety of wars and insurgencies that had been profoundly colored by class conflict, ethnic conflict, and regional conflict. Josefina Vázquez has emphasized that, contrary to the assumption of much of the historiography, at independence Mexico possessed no group naturally destined to govern.[9] The previous ruling class, the Spaniards, was defeated, but the independence process had simultaneously raised to positions of influence some individuals drawn from the lower orders and people of color while leaving in place the vestiges of the colonial corporatist tradition, particularly in the army and the church. This virtually guaranteed continuing struggles for power. Although the social and political contexts were fluid and changing, there continued to be strong ethnic barriers and class structures.

The elites perceived the mass insurrections as terrifically destructive. The most important leaders after independence, both liberals and conservatives, were deeply traumatized by the legacy of mass violence. Lucas Alamán, the ideologue of Mexican conservatism, was an eyewitness of the massacre of Spaniards and creoles by Hidalgo's forces at the Alhóndiga of Guanajuato in 1810, and many years later, in 1849, he wrote that the "shout of death and destruction . . . still resounds in my ears with a terrible echo."[10] José María Luis Mora, the leading liberal thinker, was also deeply affected by the social violence represented by Hidalgo's attack on Guanajuato and by the confiscation of his father's fortune by Hidalgo's troops. As Charles A. Hale sketches it, the inner contradictions of the independence process, the dichotomy between Hidalgo's failed social revolution and Iturbide's elitist but nondestructive achievement of independence, continued to pose a profound dilemma for Mexican liberals in the following decades, while it motivated conservative leaders in their resistance to popular movements.[11]

For elites, the menace of a mobilized lower class was a constant threat in the first decades after independence. Increasingly, new historical research is suggesting that creole elites at the beginning of the nineteenth century perceived a general state of crisis involving not only the rupture of the colonial pact between Spain and America but also the rupture of the social order.[12] Moisés González Navarro, for example, has evoked the primacy of class and color tensions as a leading element in the ongoing political-military struggle between the Mexican federal government, notably during the dominance of Lucas Alamán, and the regional caudillos of the south. In the early republic, the "south" began at Cuautla and Cuernavaca, not far from Mexico City and at that time still part of the state of Mexico but under the control of Vicente Guerrero and, after his death, of Juan Alvarez (both of whom were of mixed color). Alamán feared the Indians of the south and thought a race war was coming. In response, he adopted paternalistic and racist views toward the peasants. Even Antonio López de Santa Anna, a creole, hated and feared Alvarez, a mulatto.[13] The stakes were so high because, as Peter F. Guardino succinctly phrases it, "Mexico's peasantry entered the national political stage in 1810 and was not even temporarily excluded until after 1876."[14]

In another highly suggestive essay, González Navarro discussed the typology of Mexican conservatism, from Lucas Alamán to Justo Sierra to the governing Institutional Revolutionary Party of our times. He posits the development of a unique Mexican tradition of conservatism among those who had the most to lose. It is a tendency, at once both subtle and proactive, that is characterized by consistent use of techniques of co-optation and by the development of an argument that gradualism is the same thing as revolution, thereby both mobilizing the masses and also restraining them.[15]

Torcuato S. Di Tella posits the struggle of the elites both to co-opt and to control mass action as the dominant characteristic of Mexican political life for the first forty years of independence. He says that consciousness of "the high level of popular menace pending over the heads of the upper classes" was present in Mexico in the first part of the nineteenth century "to a much higher degree than in practically any other part of Latin America." At the same time, however, intense political factionalism sometimes made elites "blind to the dangers of agitating the masses. Involved, against better counsels, in this risky business, the elites eventually acquired some expertise in the art of channelling and controlling a crowd."[16] Michael P. Costeloe states that the fear of a class war, of "social dissolution," was the greatest fear of the decent folk, the *gente decente* as they were called in colonial times or the *hombres de bien* as they were called by the late 1820s. He also emphasizes that the ruling elites in the early republic were not great landowners or "aristocrats" but educated, professional men of middle incomes derived from property, business, professional activities (including military service as officers), and investments.[17] Hamnett argues that popular unrest was endemic throughout both the eighteenth and nineteenth centuries, motivated by administrative abuse and fiscal pressures, conditions on the land, changes in customary rights, and pressure on the food supply, and that the war of independence itself was but another stage "in a protracted series of conflicts that appear to have neither a beginning nor an end."[18]

Set against the picture of the massive disruption and damage caused by the Hidalgo and Morelos insurrections and the years of guerrilla warfare that followed, the successful Iturbide phase of the wars of independence stands in stark contrast. Iturbide issued the Plan of Iguala on 24 February 1821. The plan was the culmination of the thinking of a number of individuals from Mexico's urban elites, including both liberals and conservatives as well as several clergymen and Mexican deputies to the Spanish Cortes.[19] It was an accommodation based on a broadly shared sense among creoles that the Spanish royal regime in Mexico had decayed beyond repair, particularly because with the reestablishment of the constitution commanders of the regional militias were no longer able to continue levying the local war taxes upon which a military response depended. Short of supplies, unable to pay their units, and facing the desertion of their troops, many commanders searched for a political solution.[20]

The speed with which the Plan of Iguala gained the support of local military commanders, provincial deputations, and city councils, even extending into the far geographical peripheries in Central America, Yucatán, and the north, is its most important characteristic. Many of the foremost royalist officers joined, not only the Mexicans, but also the Spaniards, and in a startling paradox that tells much about the nature of independence the men who won Mexican independence were, to a very great extent, the same men who previously fought it. The essence of the plan's appeal was that it guaranteed no reprisals against the defeated Spaniards or royalists and it incorporated both creole and Spaniard in a proposal for independence that protected a remarkably broad array of existing vested interests. The royal army went over in such numbers that when the remaining loyal troops left Mexico, there were only two thousand of them.[21] In only five months Iturbide controlled most of the country, and only a month later the newly arrived Spanish captain general and political chief of New Spain, Juan O'Donojú, had accepted the Plan of Iguala and on 24 August 1821 signed with Iturbide the Treaty of Córdoba, by which O'Donojú recognized the political autonomy of Mexico. Within another month after the signing of the treaty, Iturbide and the Army of the Three Guarantees made their triumphal entry into Mexico City.

No wonder triumphalism was the order of the day. Compared to ten years of civil war, the Iturbide phase took only seven months to displace the Spanish colonial regime. As the municipal council of Mexico City told the last Spanish military commander when it urged him on 3 September to capitulate, "The will of the nation cannot be more decisive, and no legitimate opposition to it can be made."[22] No one had foreseen that victory would come so quickly. The regency created to head the new government declared that fewer than two hundred persons had died in the Iturbide phase, and Iturbide himself reported the deaths to be fewer than one hundred fifty.[23]

Thus, though it would be incorrect to say that independence came by surprise, the fact is that when it came, it came so rapidly that both supporters and opponents of independence seem to have been momentarily stunned. From his refuge in Cuba Apodaca wrote the Spanish government, "I had a presentiment of this disgrace in the middle of last year, 1820, but not of the terms in which it happened nor of the means by which it was effected, because they are so extraordinary that it was not possible for anyone to imagine them."[24] The joy of almost all sectors of the population was unrestrained, whether they had supported the cause of independence for a long time or had just converted to it (as was the case with the many royalists who immediately became leading figures in the new government). There was at first almost no detailed consideration of what was to come next.[25]

Just as the Plan of Iguala was the first of the many so-called pronunciamientos (revolutionary pronouncements) that would characterize Mexican history, so the achievement of independence was itself the first great act of political co-optation in Mexico's independent existence. Eleven years of rural insurrection and guerrilla warfare were preempted by a movement created and led by urban creoles and Spanish elites that, though not a counterrevolution, represented nonetheless a distinct moderation of the goals of the revolution. The thoroughness of the victory is beyond dispute. But under the surface of this joyful unanimity many differences of political opinion and of goals and aspirations soon emerged. There were as many different reasons for supporting independence, from the most base and self-serving to the most exalted and patriotic, as there were people.

One of the most impressive aspects of the recent historical literature on the Mexican wars of independence is the extent to which scholarship is beginning to provide a better sense of what it was like for individual men and women who lived through this epochal event. Christon I. Archer, for example, has provided us with a variety of images drawn from his studies of the royalist armies that reveal something of the impact on ordinary people of conscription and military procurement procedures as well as special war taxes. It is an image that reveals a high level of brute force, particularly on the part of royalist military commanders, and of real terror in those regions of the country that were the scene of military campaigns. But the economic and social effects were felt in many other areas too.[26] Virginia Guedea's study of the Guadalupes, a Mexico City secret society of supporters of the insurrections between 1812 and 1814, emphasizes the consequences of human choice amid the terror the viceregal government was able to marshal in its counterinsurgency activities among the elite civilian population.[27] It was a society in which for three hundred years most people in most localities had not had to face the possibility of subversion of the existing order, military assault, or economic sabotage. We now see that in this revolutionary civil war, amid the context of a collapsing world empire, few if any levels of society were free of danger and intense anxiety, making all the clearer how great was the relief when it was over.

The struggle that swept Mexico from 1808 to 1821 was an evolving process in which the creole elites were searching for a new political power, a new political culture.[28] What the members of the elite wanted was to rule at home. Gradually, independence emerged as the means to that end. As Jaime E. Rodríguez puts it, "That it had ultimately required independence was merely an accident. . . . In the end [creole elites] accepted independence because it was the only way they could control their own government."[29] But there was as yet no agreement on an alternative form of government. Except for the consensus of Iguala, no concordance on fundamental principles had yet developed. An important part of the universal rejoicing was the feeling that anything was possible. Not only were the old Spanish colonial impediments to political power and foreign trade expected to disappear but also the restrictions on thought, publication, and outside influences. One reason the historical literature ever since 1821 has tended to view independence as the single great dividing line in Mexican history—a view that tends to overlook the many significant continuities that linked late colonial and early independence eras—is that the contemporaries of the day themselves believed it was. To participants it was a revolution, and contemporary writers used that word to describe the process of independence. Political separation from Spain may have come without tears and without lamentations, but the organization of all the fundamental political and social structures that independence entailed would not be accomplished so easily. Richard J. Salvucci, for example, notes that "as Mariano Otero . . . observed. . . , Mexico's gaining independence was not all that difficult. But staying independent—in essence, governing well—was *'la parte más difícil.'"*[30]

Continuity and fragmentation were one and the same process. The first formulation for the political organization of the country, the creation of a limited constitutional monarchy under provisions sketched in the Plan of Iguala and Treaty of Córdoba, was relatively noninnovative. It was designed as an instrument to co-opt a divided elite to the side of independence and as a means, essentially, for preserving the continuity of the dominant classes. It was a brilliant political compromise, and it accomplished its primary goal, marshaling consent for independence. But it ultimately satisfied too small a minority of the politically active elements in the country.

In the Iturbide phase of independence the army was the guarantor of the Plan of Iguala and of independence itself. As a result, as Josefina Vázquez emphasizes, the military and leading civilian politicians essentially formed a "pact" in which the army was given the all-important job of moderating political and social extremism wherever it appeared. For their part, the civilian political leaders would finance and maintain the armed forces. It was a symbiotic military/civilian relationship that continued for many decades. And although this pact with the military soon took on a life of its own, becoming self-sustaining and irresistible, it was motivated, ultimately, by fear of the masses. The symbol of this pact, as Vázquez puts it, is that though the coups d'etat that occurred in the first federal republic (in 1823, 1828, 1830, 1834, and 1835) were led by officers, they were always decided by Congress.[31] Iturbide founded the politics of pronunciamiento.

Elsewhere, I have discussed both the strengths and the anomalies in the Plan of Iguala and Treaty of Córdoba.[32] Immensely complex in its implications but deceptively simple in its wording, the Plan of Iguala held something for everyone and thereby brought together liberals and conservatives, rebels and royalists, creoles and Spaniards. It declared Roman Catholicism as the official religion of the country, called for the independence of the country from Spain, and called for creation of a monarchy tempered by a written constitution. It invited the king of Spain, Ferdinand VII, or a member of his family to become the monarch. It called for a Mexican Cortes, or Congress, to meet and declared that in the meantime a "Sovereign Provisional Governing Junta" would be formed and a regency would be chosen to await the arrival of the monarch. The plan further stipulated that all persons and property would be respected and protected, the secular and regular clergies would retain their special juridical exemptions and privileges, and all political and military officeholders would be guaranteed their positions unless they refused to accept the plan. The plan declared that all the inhabitants of the country were citizens (which therefore included the majority of the population, who were Indians and persons of mixed ancestry), while the preamble to the plan endorsed the "general union between Europeans and Americans, Indians and indigenous."[33]

In Iturbide's view, the three basic points of the Plan of Iguala were the creation of a moderate constitutional monarchy, the protection of the church, and the protection of Spaniards left behind in an independent Mexico. Each of these principles was critical to the victory of independence because each protected existing interest groups while opening the door to creole elites who fully expected to augment their long-standing economic and social dominance with a newfound political dominance after September 1821. Other persons, however, could interpret the plan to include their dearest aspirations. The emphasis on the general union of all ethnic elements and the citizenship of people of color met one major demand of such longtime rebels as Vicente Guerrero, Guadalupe Victoria, and Nicolás Bravo, and because the old rebels lacked their own agreed upon proposal for the political organization of the country or were unable to resist the Iturbide juggernaut, they enrolled themselves under the banner of Iguala. Servando Teresa de Mier, an outspoken later opponent of Iturbide and monarchy but at that time in exile in the United States, recognized that the Plan of Iguala was an instrument of consensus. He wrote, "Absolute independence was the object and the base of the Plan, and the rest is a political stratagem imposed by circumstances to incorporate all parties into the network."[34] Elsewhere Mier affirmed of the Plan of Iguala, "The object [of the plan] is independence, the rest is calculated to avoid the scoffing of rebels and to make all parties enter in it, conciliating their interests."[35] Mier provided an accurate assessment of the major effect of Iguala. It united the vast majority of interests and social levels behind the attainment of independence, something the earlier insurrections had been unable to accomplish.

The Plan of Iguala also appealed to the masses, as did the charismatic image of Iturbide. Eric Van Young has concluded that during the movement for independence the masses identified Spain's King Ferdinand VII with their messianic hopes, and these same hopes sustained the struggle for independence. It is important to remember that the first insurrections were also uprisings in support of the return of Ferdinand VII to the throne from which the French invaders had precipitately toppled him.[36] This messianic veneration instantly transferred to Iturbide, upon whom the mantle of savior, king, and ruler descended. Conscious of his appeal, Iturbide frequently addressed himself directly to the masses and came to personify their messianic inclinations. Although he was himself, like all elites, frightened of unrestrained mass political action, Iturbide was a product of a provincial landholding elite whose members bridged both the urban and rural contexts. This was an important element in Iturbide's appeal.

Iturbide's father was a Basque immigrant landowner of noble ancestry and a member of the city council of Valladolid (Morelia). His father-in-law, Isidro Huarte, was the wealthiest and most powerful man in Valladolid and holder of the office of Alcalde Provincial Mayor, and in dowry and gifts he contributed no less than thirty thousand pesos to his daughter and her husband over the years.[37] A brother-in-law, Ramón Huarte, was jefe político of Valladolid (governor of Michoacán) from 1821 to 1825. Iturbide was the product of a prosperous and powerful regional elite of landowners, agricultural producers, merchant suppliers of local and regional markets, and holders of local or regional appointive or elective political or military office—an elite that revolved around his father-in-law. In 1805, for example, the city council of Valladolid included Iturbide's father, his father-in-law, his brother-in-law, and three of the business partners of his father-in-law. Iturbide thus nicely represents a whole class, a class that was rooted in a provincial setting and whose members believed the time had come to exert their role as the rulers of their home provinces.

Iturbide's social and regional origins help account for his success, but they also help to explain both the cause of his fall from power and the enduring influence his image exercised on those men who would take his place as the rulers of Mexico. Though Iturbide was a product of the provincial elite, once in power, particularly as emperor, he essentially betrayed the provincial elite or at least pursued objectives they increasingly came to feel were inimical to their primary interests. Yet despite all the emphasis that the historiography places on such other figures of early-nineteenth-century Mexico as Antonio López de Santa Anna—who is often said to represent the first generation of rulers—the fact remains that Iturbide was the most powerfully influential figure. Some of the later leaders, in their heart of hearts, adored him; others openly despised and reviled him; but they all remembered him even when it was not wise to speak of him publicly.

Why was Iturbide so influential? It is not only that he led the achievement of independence, important though that is. It is also because he accomplished something that his immediate successors (all of whom were roughly the same age, members of the same generation that dominated Mexican politics for thirty years between independence and the Reforma) were not able to accomplish. Torcuato Di Tella explains that the Iturbide period, often seen in the old historiography as a mere interlude, was the first and for many decades the only successful example in Mexico of a popular dictatorship, a government that combined both the political aspirations of the elites and the consciously manipulated affection and loyalty of the masses.[38] Josefina Vázquez argues that Iturbide was not a dictator and that, in fact, prior to the dictatorship of Porfirio Díaz in the last decades of the nineteenth century there were only three actual dictatorships in Mexico (Santa Anna between 1841 and 1843; Mariano Paredes y Arrillaga in 1846; and Santa Anna again between 1853 and 1855). Vázquez attributes the importance of Iturbide to a different factor, closely related to Di Tella's explanation: "In reality, between 1821 and 1855 the only leader who had a national character was Agustín de Iturbide, thanks to the ample alliance of social groups [that supported him]."[39] Ocampo neatly characterizes how Iturbide's phase of the independence struggle differed, in the minds of elites, from the earlier phase: "The [phase] of Hidalgo and the first insurgents [was] distinguished by a violent revolution with the support of the inferior classes; the [phase] of Iturbide and the Trigarante Army [was] a peaceful revolution with the support of the clergy, the army and other groups from the superior classes and the consent of the inferior classes."[40] It was Iturbide's achievement of a truly national following across class lines that explains both his fundamental importance as a symbol to the leaders who came after him and the special mixture of loathing and profound admiration that many of them had for him. As the officer who was also the protector of religion, independence, and union, he was Mexico's unique figure of Napoleonic dimensions, very much what Santa Anna later aspired to be.

The main reason the historiography has had so much difficulty interpreting the first decade of independence is that it has not understood fully what contemporaries thought they were getting in the consensus of Iguala and consequently why the consensus of Iguala so quickly broke down. What was the real meaning of independence to those persons who expected to take the reins of power from the faltering grasp of Spain? The Plan of Iguala and Treaty of Córdoba, the founding documents of independence, constituted a political consensus on the great issue of whether to be independent, on the question of the survival of interests that were prominent in the Old Regime, and on the status of the church and other institutions inherited from Spanish rule. Iguala and Córdoba represent a remarkably tolerant, even magnanimous foundation for a break with the mother country, serving as they did the interests of Mexicans (though not evenly) while firmly but almost politely closing the door on the Old Regime. Although there had been eleven years of frequently fierce internal warfare, when independence finally came it was a remarkable expression of political compromise. In the letter in which he dispatched a copy of the Plan of Iguala to Apodaca in February 1821, Iturbide had declared simply that "any country is free that wants to be."[41]

Showing himself to be, indeed, one of the few really skilled political mobilizers of early independence, Iturbide provided an easily remembered motto for the program in the preamble he wrote for the published Plan of Iguala. He phrased it as the Three Guarantees—Independence, Religion, Union—and underlined the offer by naming his army the "Three Guarantee Army," *ejército trigarante.* He chose the tricolor flag—green, white, and red—to represent the Three Guarantees. Though subsequently modified several times, it is still the flag of Mexico. But if we put these symbols at arm's length and ask what meaning they really encoded, we see that they represented principles already agreed upon but not a program for future development. Even after Iturbide fell from power and the Plan of Iguala and Treaty of Córdoba were nullified by Congress, the Three Guarantees were retained for a short time.

In a country like Mexico, devastated by internal war, independence was no longer the issue. Iturbide himself wrote that the Americans wanted independence, they just did not agree on the method for acquiring it or on the form of government to be adopted. The few official testimonies we have from Spanish loyalists also agree that independence was universally supported. One Spanish officer reported that Iturbide and his army entered Mexico City "amid the acclamations of the numberless people who in that manner made known the general opinion of themselves and of the rest of the kingdom."[42] In explaining to the Spanish government why he signed the Treaty of Córdoba, Juan O'Donojú wrote, "Independence was now unavoidable; no force in the world would be capable of arresting it."[43] Religion, that is, the guaranteed status of the Roman Catholic Church, was also not under debate in the process of independence. The first declaration of independence, produced in 1813 by the rebel congress of Chilpancingo, not only determined that the Catholic religion would be maintained and the religious orders protected, but it prohibited the practice of any other religion. The constitution of Apatzingán, promulgated by the same congress in 1814, repeated that principle and declared that the right of citizenship was to be forfeited for the heretic or apostate.[44] Union represented the hope that social revolution could be avoided by creating unity between all ethnic groups (and probably between the regions as well).

But if the Three Guarantees represented elements for which there was already broad agreement, what was the program for the future contained in Iguala? The real appeal of the Plan of Iguala was what might be called the "Three Ps"—Prince, Privilege, Province. They express the core content of Iguala in a way that both clarifies its attraction and its weakness. *Prince* means the promise of a monarchy. Spanish North America had known no other form of government for three centuries, and politically conservative elements could not, at this point, have endorsed a republic. The monarch, as it happened, turned out to be Iturbide, the only man who combined in one person both the popular support of a wide spectrum of Mexicans and the right to be monarch through his incomparable achievement of independence.

In calling for the creation of a monarchy—one that would be tempered by the existing Spanish constitution of 1812 and would in turn be replaced by a Mexican constitution to be written by the future Congress—the Plan of Iguala called on both the long-standing prestige of monarchy and the popularity among all Mexicans of the Cádiz constitution. It was indeed the rejection of the radical social revolution represented in the mass insurrections, but it was not counterrevolution, for the whole Spanish Empire had spent the last twelve years closely following the struggle to throw off the French conquerors in Spain and to implant parliamentary constitutionalism throughout the empire. Between 1820 and 1821 Mexico sent the largest contingent of deputies to the imperial Cortes in Madrid of any part of the empire other than Spain itself. For the Mexican elites, moderated constitutional monarchy was the ultimate word in systems of government. The choice of moderated constitutional monarchy was a profound but nonrevolutionary change. It meant Mexicans were expressing their clear preference in the great political debate between absolutism and constitutionalism that swept the Spanish Empire in the decade of the 1810s and for many decades thereafter. In a public statement in October 1821 Iturbide argued that at the time of Iguala the political base of the new country was fixed as a constitutionally moderated monarchy, not because monarchy was necessarily the best form of government, but because a monarchy modified by a constitution was.[45] The important thing is that in opting for a constitutional monarchy he voiced the political convictions of the majority of Mexican elites in 1821.

Iturbide exercised statesmanship (not always understood as such among radicals) by standing for conciliation with Spaniards. The separation was to be an example of evolution, not revolution; it must be good for both Spaniards and Mexicans, and throughout his writings he emphasized that it came about through peaceful means. This is consistent with Iturbide's class and education, but, again, it is also consistent with the leading-edge liberal (but not revolutionary) viewpoint of the elites who supported three political principals—monarchy, the constitution of 1812, and home rule. Iturbide's formula was preventive and prescriptive but neither radical nor original. As the child left its father's home it would be both something new in the world and also the essential continuation of its parents. As Luis Villoro has said, the real revolution was yet to come.[46]

The term *empire* was chosen, not to signify monarchy (the two words are not synonymous), but because the new state would be an aggregation of distinct jurisdictions, in this case including the territories formerly comprising New Spain, Nueva Galicia, the Eastern and Western Interior Provinces, Yucatán, and even perhaps the kingdom of Guatemala. Room was left for the enrollment of Central America in the Mexican Empire, and it is clear that Iturbide, at least, wanted such a union.[47] It was to be an empire because it was to consist of many regions, many peoples, many language groups. Contemporaries knew that this was not a single nation, and they adopted the term *empire* because it was the appropriate term of their day. (In standard usage, an empire is a state comprised of various kingdoms, provinces, or peoples.) It also resonated with the historical grandeur of the lost Aztec empire. It was to be an aggregation of provinces, some central and well integrated, some peripheral and scarcely populated. Any territory that chose to join could become part of it. Iturbide made the mistake of attempting to govern as if the Mexican Empire were a centralized unitary political system.

Ocampo explains that the choice of the term *Mexican Empire* was itself an act of wholesale compromise in that liberals and traditionalists would later come to have very different definitions of what independence, and the nation itself, represented. Liberals, following the tenets of neo-Aztecism, would later perceive independence as the restoration of the ancient conquered and colonized nation, now freed of the weight of Spain and able to resume an authentic nationhood. Traditionalists would come to argue that independence was not the reestablishment of the ancient Mexican nation but the emancipation of New Spain, a nation formed by Spanish culture and identity. They would also argue that the Conquest represented only the final termination of the ancient Mexican empire. But this ideological dichotomy lay in the future, in the clash of liberal and conservative thought that enveloped most of nineteenth-century Mexican history. In the euphoria of the consummation of independence, both liberals and traditionalists defended the concept of an autochthonous identity.[48]

Privilege, the second "P" of the Plan of Iguala, means that the Plan of Iguala guaranteed all existing privileges for both creoles and Spaniards living in Mexico. Although this was certainly not social revolution, it was politically necessary and also wise. The possibility of social revolution had already been ruled out when the mass insurrections were effectively stalemated by a multiclass counterinsurgency. Hidalgo and Morelos were not defeated by "Spaniards," or even by "royalists," but by "Mexicans" fighting not so much on Spain's behalf but on their own. At one stroke the Plan of Iguala wiped out the objections of both old-time rebels and supporters of the royal regime by guaranteeing economic and political stability and the preservation of vested corporate interests. At the same time, it promised the abolition of caste distinctions. The elites immediately recognized that Iguala fulfilled the aspirations of 1808. The clergy and military were able to support it because it guaranteed no loss of their status. Meantime, dedicated rebels could now find common cause with their former opponents. The plan forged a new, if temporary, alliance of political forces. Even if limited, it was for the moment sufficient.

Province means that the Plan of Iguala was predicated on the continued development of the provinces as entities in their own right. This part of the program would ultimately be seen as contradicting the nonradical promises of a monarchy retaining traditional privileges for certain groups. The impulse to provincehood was fundamental in the achievement of independence. The Plan of Iguala furthered this impulse, and that was a critical element in the consensus of Iguala. We saw in the previous chapter that the emerging provinces, from the far north to the far south, chose of their own volition to support the Plan of Iguala because it represented not only the compromise that would bring independence but the pact by which the existence of the provinces was recognized.

The effort to define what the new Mexican Empire was, and to do it quickly, led to a false sense of homogeneity (to say nothing of optimism).

What creole elites thought Mexico was turned out to be wishful thinking. At best, their first steps toward self-awareness can only be called protonationalism because the sense of the nation's identity that characterized the writings of contemporary thinkers was highly personal, sometimes idiosyncratic, and frequently motivated mainly by anti-Spanish sentiment. There may have existed a sense of creolism, even perhaps of Mexicanism, and certainly there are strong signals of what Brading called neo-Aztecism.[49] But at this critical historical moment, it is too early to see a fully developed sense of nation. *Mexico*, in the sense in which we normally use that term today, did not yet exist.

Even if we concede that in some spiritual sense the nation (or nations) already existed, the nation-state did not. Iturbide, more than anyone else in the independence process, attempted to create the nation-state, and he did it by fiat. That is, he declared it to exist. This was an important effort that his successors in office (who faced the same task of forging the nation-state) recognized. He declared its characteristics to be religion, independence, and union. He declared it a moderated constitutional monarchy. And perhaps most important, he declared it to include any territory that wanted to be a part of it. In a sense, these definitions of Iturbide were acts of faith (though some of them survived his brief time in power), but in proclaiming the existence of a nation, Iturbide and his cohorts, who at the time included both conservatives and liberals, were trying to create something that was beyond their powers to devise.

What happened is that Iturbide's empire was destroyed by the same force of regional autonomy and aspirations to regional power that brought independence in the first place. Just because he declared the creation of a unified nation-state does not mean it was one. Running from Upper California to Costa Rica, the Mexican Empire, on paper at least, was the second-largest country in the New World. Although Iturbide thought he had created a centralist regime, he actually had very limited control over much of the territory of the empire. In the guise of a centralized empire, the regime over which Iturbide presided, though it never recognized provincial self-government, could not prevent and actually helped encourage the ongoing dispersion of separate political identities.

During the existence of the empire many provinces began to experience real local self-government for the first time, largely because the end of Spanish control left a space that local elites immediately moved to occupy. To assume that the end of Spanish dominion meant there was a vacuum is to assume that only Spain could provide leadership, ideology, and purpose. Just as the struggle for independence was a war between Mexicans themselves, so the inhabitants of the former colony were themselves ready, willing, and able to assume political power. That is what they were doing when they opted for the Plan of Iguala. Networks of power linkages between local elites were already centuries old. Nothing had happened to displace them; quite the contrary, the final impediment to their undeterred exercise of political power disappeared when the colonial regime ended. Often this led them to resist the agents of the central government in making decisions concerning provincial affairs. While the general government of the empire was being organized, regional oligarchies, as well as the former royal commanders of the regions, began to formulate alliances for control in their home areas. They probably assumed that Iturbide would be true to his own class and regional origins and would, through the creation of a system of pluralism, be their ally at the top of the pyramid. In another book I have recounted the formative first eighteen months of the independent country.[50] Here I will only recapitulate it briefly.

In the historically unparalleled effort to create a first independent government there was a period of transition that consisted of two distinguishable parts. The first phase, from September 1821 to May 1822, was, to paraphrase Javier Ocampo, the "day of independence," the triumph.[51] Iturbide presided over this phase, as the "Immortal Liberator," the "Undefeated Hero," and the "new Moses." As president of the regency he was chief of state; he was also commander in chief of the army, an army he himself had created; and, most of all, he was endowed with an authority that comes only once in a country's history, the authority of the liberator. A time of joy and unrestrained hope, this phase need not detain us here, although we should remember that it happened because at perhaps no other time in the nineteenth century would such unanimity reign again.

The second phase of the transition was the period from May 1822, when Iturbide was elected as emperor by the first Constituent Congress, to March 1823, when he abdicated. This fall from grace, from the artificially dizzying height of a throne no less, is what the historiography remembers. It was Iturbide's peculiar fate that the thinking of Mexicans moved beyond his own, rendering him an object of scorn, a nonperson, ever since.

What was Iturbide's great sin, his unforgivable error? It was not that he had once been a leading royalist officer responsible for repressing insurgencies in several regions of the country; the vast majority of the first leadership after independence had a similar background, indeed most of the presidents of the republic until 1855 had fought for the royalists in the wars of independence.[52] It was not that he suffered from the sin of hubris, of overweening pride; that was the norm, not the exception. And it was not that he was elected emperor; Mexicans had not yet decided they wanted a republic, in the Plan of Iguala a monarchy had been created, and when it came to selecting the emperor no one had anything like the right to it, the claim on it, that Iturbide had. The transgression was that Iturbide forgot where independence came from, what caused it. He turned his back on the provinces.

The event that destroyed Iturbide was his dissolution of the first Constituent Congress on 31 October 1822. It posed the first real threat to the rapid development of provincial autonomy that had been gathering steam for the past several years because it led provincial leaders to perceive Iturbide as opposing a provincial voice in central government affairs. The interests of the central government and the interests of the provinces collided head on and at a moment when the provinces saw that they might soon be supreme.

The first Constituent Congress of Mexico has been largely ignored by historians, probably because the whole Iturbide period is usually ignored. Yet this legislature and its actions were critical to understanding what happened to the Iturbide government. Although it was assumed that the Congress would be chosen by proportional representation, as the Spanish Cortes had been, the lack of an up-to-date census for Mexico (the most recent general census dated from 1792) and the fact that some outlying provinces in the far south and the far north had not yet decided if they were part of the Mexican Empire meant that some alternate method of selecting a congress was necessary. There were several proposals. The commission appointed by the Sovereign Provisional Governing Junta recommended one deputy for each fifty thousand inhabitants, chosen by an electorate consisting of all adult males without exclusion of any class (such as domestic servants and people of African origin, both of whom had been excluded from voting under the Spanish constitution). The regency recommended a congress of two houses, the upper house or senate representing the clergy, the military, the cities, and the audiencias and the lower house based on proportional representation and excluding those represented in the upper house. Iturbide himself recommended a unicameral congress based strictly on social class or estates, *estamentos* as they were known in Spain, which would be divided between members representing public officials, clergy and intelligentsia, merchants and miners, officers, titled nobles, and the remainder of the population. It is not clear why the junta arrived at its final decision for the convocation of the Congress, but it chose to combine the three proposals, resulting in a disastrous amalgamation of ideas.

On 17 November 1821, the junta decreed that the Congress would consist of deputies based on the number of partidos in each intendancy or province rather than on proportional representation. Because the total number of deputies would amount to 242, the formula that was decreed was that the number of deputies from each intendancy or province would be equal to two-thirds of the number of partidos in each province or intendancy, for a total of 162 deputies. This was highly disproportional to population because the former colonial regime had created partidos based on territorial extent and defense needs rather than population. Thus, the intendancy of Mexico, with forty-three partidos, got twenty-eight deputies; Guadalajara, with twenty-eight partidos, got seventeen deputies, and so on. Some of the most peripheral and least populated provinces, however, had a larger number of partidos than some of the more populous provinces. Thus, the Internal Provinces of the East (Nuevo León, Nuevo Santander, Coahuila, Texas) got one deputy each because they had one partido each; but among the Internal Provinces of the West, Durango had thirty-four partidos, hence twenty-three deputies; Arizpe had twelve partidos, thus eight deputies; and Nuevo Mexico had one deputy for its one partido. Durango, with two hundred thousand inhabitants, got twenty-three deputies; whereas Guanajuato, with more than four hundred thousand inhabitants, got only seven deputies.[53]

In addition, it was decreed that each province or intendancy with more than three deputies (there were twelve of these) must have among its representatives an ecclesiastic from the secular clergy, a member of the army, and a magistrate or lawyer. After these three deputies were chosen, the other members elected could not be from any of those professions. Furthermore, the province of Mexico was also required to select one miner, one titled noble, and one *mayorazgo*; Guadalajara and Veracruz were to choose one merchant; Puebla and Sonora, one artisan; Nueva Vizcaya (Durango) and Valladolid, one manufacturer; San Luis Potosí and Yucatán, one employee; and Guanajuato, one miner.[54]

This meant the first Constituent Congress was based neither on population nor on estates or class but on a rather clumsy combination of professions and regional jurisdictions. Furthermore, the proposal for an upper house got lost. The convocation declared that the Congress, once it started meeting, would divide itself into two chambers of equal size, but when Congress convened this matter was dropped because it served no identifiable purpose to have two houses when all the members were selected in the same way.[55] In addition, because the convocation was issued before Guatemala, Chiapas, and Yucatán had yet decided whether they would join the empire and because of the distance and time constraints involved in sending deputies from the far north, when the Congress opened on 24 February 1822, Guatemala, Yucatán, Tabasco, the Californias, and the Eastern and Western Interior Provinces were all represented on an interim basis by deputies chosen by and from citizens of those territories who happened at that moment to reside in Mexico City. Though this was a technique used by the Cortes of Cádiz to select deputies from areas that would otherwise be unrepresented because of the length of time required for communications, it meant a significant portion of the country started out with deputies chosen by and from a handful of men.[56]

No one was satisfied with the makeup of the Constituent Congress, a particularly troubling issue given that this Congress was supposed to write the constitution. Iturbide blamed the anomalies of the Congress for producing what he called "monstrous inequality" between the provinces. Lorenzo de Zavala said that the Congress was based on "the most monstrous amalgam of heterogeneous elements" that sowed the "seed of the destruction of the Congress and of civil war."[57] As a member of the Congress himself, Zavala proposed that it should be dissolved and a new, more representative one, consisting of two chambers, should be elected.[58]

Although Iturbide's enemies blamed him for the anomalies of the Congress, the lack of proportionality actually gave a substantial majority to deputies who would oppose him. The deputies would represent regional elites because they were to be chosen by the same indirect elections that the Spanish constitution had originally created, meaning that the elections were held in three stages, at the parish, district, and provincial levels, with the municipal councils decisively intervening in most localities.[59] This opened the door to the demands for political power of the periphery, until now suppressed by the dominance of the core areas.

The first Constituent Congress quickly emerged as the representative of the provincial elites and the foremost opponent of the executive. Congress moved to shore up its powers, beginning on the day of its installation when, following the example of the Cortes of Cádiz, it declared that the national sovereignty resided in itself and that it possessed not only constituent power but also ordinary legislative power in all its extent. It also declared immunity for its members.[60] According to Zavala, initially there were republicans in the Congress, but they were a small minority.[61] José María Bocanegra, a deputy and another major chronicler, said that he was surprised to see how much division existed in Congress between the "old patriots, called insurgents" and "those patriots who decided and worked for independence in 1821"—in other words, between the former insurgents and the former royalists.[62]

Congress's election of Iturbide as emperor on the night of 19 May 1822, following noisy street demonstrations by army enlisted men and other working-class segments, is usually pointed to as the major single event that led Congress to become an open enemy of Iturbide. Although that is certainly what Iturbide's opponents, most notably Carlos María de Bustamante, deputy and foremost anti-Iturbide writer, wanted posterity to believe, the causes of the enmity between Congress and the emperor were more complex. Contrary to the argument that Bustamante and other contemporary writers inserted in the historical record, Iturbide's election as emperor was not, as the Congress itself later declared, an illegal act imposed upon it by a tyrannical army chief in the absence of a legal quorum. The provisions of the Spanish constitution still prevailed, specifying that a quorum was one-half plus one of the members. There were 90 members present on that evening out of a total membership that by then was set at 178, and thus there was a quorum present. It required only a plurality of votes to pass a major measure, and 67 deputies voted for the immediate proclamation of Iturbide as emperor, while 15 voted to refer the matter to their provinces for advice.[63] No substantial opposition to the choice of Iturbide as emperor was raised in other parts of the country. Thus, although the election of Iturbide was certainly a major cause for complaint by his enemies, it was a legal election, and even after the Plan of Casa Mata in February 1823 many of the highest officers and also a few of the provincial deputations continued to think so. In a telling admission, Zavala scoffed that Iturbide was the choice of "the clergy, the miserable nobility of the country, the army in its greater part, and the common people," to which Francisco Bulnes later commented, "That is to say, the immense majority."[64]

The real source of the enmity between Iturbide and Congress was their dispute over division of powers and, indeed, the exercise of sovereignty itself. As the champion of the Plan of Iguala and signer of the Treaty of Córdoba, Iturbide believed that he embodied the wishes of all citizens, that as he himself put it, "I was the depository of the will of the Mexicans."[65] The growing view of Congress, on the other hand, was fittingly summarized in a letter that an unnamed deputy sent to Servando Teresa de Mier: "We [Congress] have the powers of the nation that normally are distributed into a legislative, an executive, and a judicial power; we have them all."[66] As José Bravo Ugarte has said, the dispute was, fundamentally, a dispute over the possession of sovereignty.[67]

What the provinces cared about by 1822 was the principle that the Congress, being constituent, was to speak for them. Their deputies to the Constituent Congress insisted that Iturbide, though emperor, did not possess the right to exercise sovereignty. Congress insisted that, in keeping with the interpretation of the Spanish Cortes, the exercise of sovereignty belonged to it, whereas Iturbide believed that the Plan of Iguala, as the only fundamental consensus that existed, granted him the right to interpret the national will. In addition, Congress denied Iturbide the powers that the king possessed under the Spanish constitution of 1812 to exercise the veto, to appoint the Supreme Court, and to create rural military tribunals. These three issues were the main points of contention in mid-1822, with Iturbide's opponents seeing them as examples of his attempt to usurp the powers that belonged to Congress. By August 1822 some members of Congress were involved in a conspiracy to overthrow Iturbide. For the next several months there was an increasingly bitter struggle over the immunity of those deputies who were arrested for their involvement in the conspiracy, until most members of Congress had turned against the emperor.

In October Iturbide held two important meetings with leading members of Congress, military officers, and councillors of state to discuss what should be done about the recalcitrant and paralyzed Congress. Though a majority of persons participating in these meetings were members of Congress, the meetings could only agree that there was an impasse between the executive and legislative branches. Iturbide received large numbers of requests from various provincial deputations, municipalities, corporations, army officers, and military units asking for the dissolution of Congress.[68] Ultimately, he informed Congress that he expected that his power of veto would be extended even over the constitution that the Congress was to write.[69] Congress refused this demand, and Iturbide's response was to dissolve Congress on 31 October 1822. In his memoirs he railed against a Congress "which while it inveighed against despotism was endeavoring to collect in itself all power, reducing the monarch to the condition of a phantom."[70] He soon found that he had committed his greatest error, for the dissolution of Congress was used as proof of Iturbide's tyranny by the opposition, which now burst forth from many regions of the country.

Iturbide thus represented the continuity of the principles of Bourbon unitarism, and Congress represented the voice of provincial power. In this they symbolized the first clash between the old centralism and the new dispersionism that would be the main theme in Mexican history for the next century. They both represented constitutionalism, only they interpreted the constitution in starkly different ways.

The political battle that broke out during the Iturbide monarchy was a struggle over the division of powers between the general and the regional levels. As we look back on it today, it appears the conflict began within a few weeks of Iturbide's triumphal entry into Mexico City in September 1821, and it clearly outranks in importance any issues relating to individual personalities. It should not be surprising that this was the case because no decision on what form the state should take would survive very long without settlement of the issue of division of powers.

Iturbide's regime failed to acquire the legitimacy it needed to stay in power because the creole elites, unlike the masses, were immune to the persuasion of his charisma. What did the elites stand to gain from Iturbide's empire? Nothing, not when compared with what they could gain by governing their own regions in their own right. Because he was the only really effective block to their achievement of power he threatened all those networks of provincial and regional power that begot independence and were begotten by it and whose ultimate spokesmen were the deputies in the first Congress. Once it became clear that Iturbide chose a centralized form of government, and that was not clear until he became emperor, the elites who favored a dispersion of power to the regions had no reason to be loyal to him, in spite of the fact that he was extremely liberal in his granting of offices and honors (the first appearance of another characteristic of nineteenth-century Mexican governments). He could have accommodated himself to the legitimate demands of provincial elites, if he had recognized the need, because federalism and monarchy, contrary to the unanimous view of his enemies at the time and as the Canadian example later in the nineteenth century would show, need not be contradictory.

Devoted as he was to the principles of Iguala and Córdoba, Iturbide was attempting to preserve the best features of the social and administrative structure of the Bourbon monarchy, which was the political system he had grown up with. But he insisted that it be modified by the constitution of 1812. He believed national unity required uniformity and attempted to create what his opponents saw as essentially a new form of Bourbon centralism with a new name and a new center. He was catapulted by events, and without adequate preparation, to the peak of power and then struggled to create a state and the apparatus of government. The fact that in the last weeks of his reign he gave in to the Casa Mata rebellion and agreed to restore the Constituent Congress he had just dissolved suggests that he was beginning to learn the need to accommodate. His greatest fear was that the provinces would fly away in all directions, leading to the atomization of what he believed was the nation. That fear is what ultimately brought him back from exile in 1824 to his death in a small Tamaulipas town, vainly protesting to the firing squad and to future centuries, "Mexicans, I die with honor and not as a traitor; . . . I am not a traitor, no." His image haunted his generation; they knew he represented both their best and their worst at the same time, both their most successful rebel and their first conservative, both the first Mexican and the one to whom other Mexicans have refused the name. The fall of Iturbide represented the final collapse of the Bourbon state.

CHAPTER FOUR

"The Mexican Nation Is Composed of the Provinces"

The title of this chapter encapsulates the essential core of Mexican federalism as it emerged in 1823 and as it was formulated in the founding document of the federal republic, the Acta Constitutiva of 1824. In the view of the elites who took over as the rulers of their home provinces and municipalities, the Plan of Iguala, and with it the moderated constitutional monarchy of Iturbide, proved deficient by not granting home rule to the provinces. Only after the Iturbide regime was in place did they see that it constituted Bourbonism with a Mexican accent. That was a surprise to them, and it took some time to rally around the minimal principles of a genuinely independent national legislature and a limited executive.

The historiography has not fully recognized how tremendously difficult were the problems of political organization facing Mexico after independence and after the end of the Iturbide monarchy and how innovative the solutions were. As Guerra sketches it, the newly independent Latin American countries faced two gigantic political challenges: to create a structure that would allow them to be independent, republican, and Catholic, something not even the French Revolution had succeeded in doing, and to found a political system that was representative in the absence of a tradition and a practice of representation, something the United States had not had to do because it possessed a tradition of representative institutions.[1]

Most of all, there was the challenge of creating nationhood. In the period of March to July 1823 there emerged in Mexico an overwhelming consensus in support of provincial self-government and political autonomy from the city that had exercised uninterrupted hegemony for three hundred years (and more) over the provinces. With growing certainty of their purpose, the provinces chose self-reliance, self-government, self-sufficiency, "liberty" (as many of them phrased it), and in the first and one of the most profound "revolutions" in the history of independent Mexico, they formulated their own political agenda. This urge to particularity, this thirst to be masters in their own house, was natural, organic, and legitimate. The provincial deputation of Guadalajara, after proclamation of the state of Jalisco, asked, "Would Jaliscienses believe it more advantageous to commend to Mother Tenochtitlan the right to rule them with laws at times repugnant to them but sanctioned by the predominant majority of another province, or to govern themselves?"[2]

Yet with a unanimity that was truly remarkable and deserves the close attention of historians, the provinces (or at least most of them) made no attempt to propose secession or withdrawal from the polity composed of their sister provinces, whatever that polity might turn out to be. They knew they had to create the kind of nation in which they could voluntarily participate. Their desire to seize the moment and obtain the long-sought home rule and internal autonomy, a desire so pressing that it caught the center by surprise and forced its grudging acquiescence, did not go so far as to assume, in most cases, that each province could stand alone. If there is any message that emerged clearly from the many demands that the American deputies in the Spanish Cortes recorded in the periods 1812–14 and 1820–21, it is that they were acutely aware of the infrastructural underdevelopment of their home regions. The chief legacy of three centuries of colonialism was underdevelopment, and it created an ever-present consciousness of the need for joint action with other regions.[3] Thus, even as the provinces moved to proclaim themselves free and sovereign states they simultaneously sought links that would make a nation of the whole. Even as they sought independence from Mexico City they also sought federation with Mexico, that is, an end to central control and the creation of a nation. Though they no longer wanted to be controlled by the country's strongest and most developed region, they knew they needed that region and had to form some sort of political arrangement with it. There is nothing mysterious or mystical about such a clearheaded assessment of reality. Nationhood is only real when it is voluntary, only voluntary when it is based on a thoughtful assessment of both tradition and need.

Our sense of self, our way of knowing and designating ourselves, is today so intimately linked with our citizenship of an organized nation-state that it is hard to conceive of political identities existing apart from and predating the nation-state. But, just as we have seen that in the period immediately after independence the word *Mexico* did not automatically or necessarily refer to the country but, more likely, to the province of Mexico, so too, as we begin to address the issue of the role of the provinces in the formation of nationhood, we need to go one step further and consider the meaning of words in specific times and specific places.

In an insightful essay, Victor M. González Esparza has demonstrated that in Mexico in the early nineteenth century there was a different order of consciousness from that of today regarding one's identification within a specific territorial entity. The Mexican "national" territory, he argues, "was drawn and 'imagined' late." The first maps drawn up following Mexican independence were maps of the sovereign states rather than of the sovereign nation. The first map of Jalisco, for example, dated from 1824; of Zacatecas from 1833; and of Jalisco, Zacatecas, and Colima together from 1840. Yet even though there were plans to create a general map of the republic from the time of the first president, Guadalupe Victoria, it was not completed until 1850, and it was not until 1863 that the first reliable new map, Antonio García Cubas's "Carta General de la República Mexicana," was terminated. Until that time, the only representation of the "national" territory as a whole was Humboldt's map of New Spain and those that derived from it. This suggests the difficulties encountered in the early republic in "imagining" a national community, to say nothing of the weakness of the central state.[4] Similarly, Sergio de la Peña, pointing out that the right to count is a sign of authority, shows that the first full national census in Mexico was not taken until 1895.[5]

González Esparza also shows that in the Spanish language, well into the nineteenth century, the idea of "nation" was not connected with the concept of a political state exercising control of a specific territory. In the official dictionary that governed usage in the Spanish language, the Spanish Academy's *Diccionario de la Lengua Castellana*, in both the eighteenth and the nineteenth centuries and specifically in 1826 *nación* was defined as "The act of birth . . . the place of birth. The collection of the inhabitants of some province, country or kingdom." It was not until the 1884 *Diccionario* that the concept of "nation" appeared for the first time linked with a "state or political body that recognizes a common supreme center of government." In addition, in 1826 the *Diccionario* defined the word *federation* as "an alliance, league or union . . . made between princes or republics," while *to confederate* was commonly used as "to reciprocate." Thus, "to federate or confederate implied in those years, in the Spanish context, an equal treatment among different sovereigns."[6]

In the context of the Americas as a whole Mónica Quijada shows that the concept of nation, which in its traditional mode referred to an ethnic community (such as the indigenous nation), was beginning to take on its modern meaning in some Spanish dictionaries by the 1780s, although the word was mainly used either in the sense in which it appeared in the Spanish constitution of 1812 (in which the "nation" was all the people of the empire, the "Spanish nation") or in the 1814 constitution of Apatzingán (in which it was the "American nation" as opposed to the "Spanish nation"). But it was still not the Mexican nation. The constitution of Apatzingán, for example, was issued in the name of the "Supreme Mexican Government," but when it defined citizenship it did not speak of "Mexicans" but of "Americans." After the consummation of independence, the American projection and the local projection of the nation (in its double sense of kingdom or province and birth city) continued to interact for many decades. By the time of independence, there was in place what Quijada calls "a substrate of collective, but segmented, identification."[7]

What this means is that political leaders in 1823 and 1824 were fully aware of the innovative nature of their actions when they proclaimed a republic based on a federative union between the existing sovereign provinces and when the Acta Constitutiva (Article 1) declared, "The Mexican nation is composed of the provinces comprehended in the territory of the old viceroyalty called New Spain, in that of the captaincy general of Yucatán and in the general commandancies of the internal provinces of the east and of the west." The authors of the Acta Constitutiva literally meant that they were creating a political entity based on dual sovereignty, a union of provinces that were themselves the patrias and naciones of their inhabitants. Shortening the phrase in the Acta Constitutiva makes the position of the provinces clear: "The Mexican nation is composed of the provinces. . . ."[8] It was a union of sovereign provinces reciprocally joined into a federation of equals. Nation and province were the same thing, two sides of one coin. It was a perfectly appropriate early-nineteenth-century reading of terminologies that later in the nineteenth century under the influence of European thought shifted substantially in nuance.[9]

In the 1820s, the massive weight of the state and city of Mexico within the first federal republic was an inescapable fact. The state of Mexico, not including Mexico City, had a population of just under a million, while Mexico City had a population of 188,793 (according to the *Memoria* of the state of Mexico in 1826). The city and the state of Mexico together accounted for nearly 20 percent of the country's entire population of roughly 6.2 million people in the 1820s. The capital city by itself had a larger population than eight of the original nineteen states. The next largest state, Yucatán, with 600,000 people in 1827, had only half the population of Mexico state and city, and that population was spread out over a vast territory, with two important cities (Mérida and Campeche) contesting for primacy. Among the provinces in the 1820s, the third and fourth most populous were the states of Puebla (584,000 in 1825) and Jalisco (547,000 in 1822).[10] All population figures were actually estimates, and other sources provide significantly different figures. For example, a report of the finance committee of Congress, dated 5 March 1824, had the population of the state of Mexico at 1,300,000, Puebla second at 750,000, Jalisco third at 650,000, and Oaxaca fourth at 600,000.[11]

The misfortune for the republic, perhaps, is that the center was large enough to be dominant but not so large as to be overwhelming in its dominance. In 1822 and again in 1824, national treasury officials estimated that one-third of the country's entire wealth was located within the state and city of Mexico.[12] With 20 percent of the country's whole population, the center was the historical powerhouse of the country but not big enough simply to dictate policy to all the regions. Yucatán weighed in at 10 percent of the whole, Puebla and Jalisco at about 9 percent each, Oaxaca and Michoacán at about 7 percent each, Guanajuato at 6 percent, and Zacatecas at 5 percent. Simply put, if the province and city of Mexico did not voluntarily accede to a drastic change in their historical and traditional primacy, there would be a contest for power. In addition, at times during the early nineteenth century groupings or alliances between neighboring provinces would form—Mexico and Puebla, for example, or Jalisco and Zacatecas—and although these were never permanent they would alter the relative weighting of regional power.

It is necessary to treat the city and state of Mexico as two separate legal entities given that in late 1824 the capital city was separated from the political jurisdiction of the state of Mexico and made into the Federal District (with the status of a territory governed by the federal Congress). But the fact is that people in other regions of the country continued to think of them as one, and throughout the first federal republic they referred to an ill-defined, but real, "center." What they were describing is a network of accumulated economic, political, financial, and intellectual power located in the Valley of Mexico. The inhabitants of this area were characterized by their assumption that the nation was themselves—their worldview, their culture, their way of life, their business and finance, their government. Though partly a habit of thought, the assumption reflected the historical reality of political and economic dominance.

During the period of the Iturbide empire, the newly emerging provinces had the Constituent Congress as their only forum for pursuing their objective of greater provincial autonomy. Iturbide's decision to close the Congress convinced the provinces that his regime was inimical to their goal. The opposition's response came in the form of the rebellion led by Antonio López de Santa Anna in Veracruz in December 1822, followed by the revolt of the imperial army at Casa Mata on 1 February 1823. The Casa Mata rebellion led to Iturbide's abdication as emperor in March 1823.

The chief factor at work in the uprisings was a rapid radicalization of political objectives. Emilio Rabasa writes that one of the fundamental causes of federalism was the desire that existed by 1824 to procure a truly radical change regarding the traditional political structures, the wholesale abandonment of Hispanic monarchism and the establishment of what in its day was the exact opposite, a federal republic.[13] In explaining why Gordiano Guzmán, one of the leading caudillos after independence in the south of Jalisco and Michoacán, supported federalism, Jaime Olveda has said, "He believed that federalism was the type of organization that most suited the nation because it had the least similarity with the colonial order, and because it was also the one that would best protect regional interests."[14]

To a great extent, the uprisings used Iturbide's dissolution of the Constituent Congress as an excuse to launch this fundamental change. The uprising in Veracruz was provoked initially by Iturbide's removal of Santa Anna from the command of the port of Veracruz following a report from the commandant general of Veracruz and Puebla provinces, General José Antonio Echávarri, that Santa Anna was conspiring with the commander of the Spanish forces that still controlled the fort of San Juan de Ulúa in Veracruz harbor. Santa Anna had long demanded to be promoted to commandant general and governor of his home province of Veracruz, and because he was already well along the path to becoming the regional caudillo, Iturbide knew that removing him from command would require great delicacy. As a result, in November 1822 Iturbide made his only official visit to the provinces as emperor, traveling to Jalapa to interview Santa Anna in person and to request that he return to Mexico City where his presence, he argued, was needed. When Santa Anna excused himself by saying he had no money for the trip, Iturbide offered to lend him the money from his own pocket. Santa Anna asked for a few days to arrange his personal affairs in Veracruz, and racing back to the port before word of his removal from command had arrived there, on the afternoon of 2 December he raised a rebellion against Iturbide.[15]

The precise object of Santa Anna's uprising was not as clear as some historians assume. On 2 December 1822, Santa Anna issued two proclamations, one addressed to the citizens of Veracruz and the other to the soldiers under his command. They were so confused that the Iturbide government actually published them in Mexico City as part of its campaign to discredit Santa Anna. In his proclamation to the citizens, Santa Anna declared that the dissolution of the Constituent Congress had led public sentiment to opt for the republican system of government, by virtue of which fact he declared that he had proclaimed a republic. He also promised to uphold the Three Guarantees and to open trade with Spain. This support for free trade was the first appearance of what would be perhaps the major principle of Santa Anna's early political career and naturally reflected his home base in the province of Veracruz. In his proclamation to the soldiers, however, Santa Anna did not mention republicanism.

There were also two separate statements of principles, an initial one drawn up on 2 December and a longer set of "clarifications" dated 6 December. Both of them were written, according to most sources, by the former minister of Colombia, Miguel Santa María, an avowed opponent of monarchy who, having been ordered to leave the country by the Iturbide government, was in Veracruz at the time awaiting a ship to carry him home.[16] Both statements make up the "Plan of Veracruz," and were issued jointly under the signatures of Santa Anna and Guadalupe Victoria, the former leader of a Veracruz guerrilla force during the wars of independence and a longtime enemy of Iturbide who had dodged capture by imperial forces by hiding out in the bush of Veracruz during most of Iturbide's period in power. Neither of the two statements of the uprising's program called for creating a republic. They focused instead on the need to restore the Sovereign Constituent Congress that Iturbide had dissolved, which would determine what form of government the country should adopt. They declared, however, that Iturbide's act of dissolving the Congress meant that he should no longer be recognized as emperor. The 6 December program also called for the creation of provincial militias whose members would possess the military *fuero* (exemption from prosecution by civil courts) and insisted that debts incurred to finance this rebellion be recognized as national debts.[17]

In many ways the real key to the Plan of Veracruz was its reference to the creation of provincial militias. Iturbide had already ordered the establishment of provincial militias in Mexico City, Puebla, Michoacán, and Guanajuato, but they were not autonomous. And the government initiated a very effective campaign to impugn the honor and motives of Santa Anna, pointing out that he had been a strong supporter of Iturbide and a persecutor of republicans and citing letters from him as late as October in which he declared his dedication to capturing Guadalupe Victoria.[18] Despite these efforts, however, the uprising's chief attraction was its call for autonomous provincial militias. This appealed to the emerging regional caudillos who were themselves one of the most significant legacies of the struggle for independence. They were highly politicized, they were grounded in local and regional interests, they believed it was their efforts that had brought independence, and they chafed under the control of Iturbide. Santa Anna was only one among several regional caudillos who were emerging in 1822.

Nevertheless, during the first months of the rebellion the imperial army in Veracruz and Puebla, under the command of Echávarri, drove back Santa Anna's attempt to take Jalapa. Santa Anna believed his rebellion was defeated and proposed to Victoria that they flee to the United States. Only Victoria's stalwart refusal to do so and his insistence that Santa Anna fortify himself in the city of Veracruz prevented their complete destruction.

On 5 January 1823, Iturbide's cause suffered another setback when the two most distinguished surviving military leaders of the movements for independence, Generals Vicente Guerrero and Nicolás Bravo, left the capital and raised a rebellion in their home region in the south. Both were motivated by discontent over what they felt was Iturbide's failure to advance their careers.[19] But in the proclamation of their objectives dated 13 January, they declared that although they refused obedience to Iturbide and demanded restitution of the Constituent Congress, they did not oppose the established system of government.[20] At any rate, the imperial army defeated Guerrero and Bravo on 25 January at Almolonga. Guerrero, seriously wounded, was believed to have died in the battle. The fact that he had survived was not widely known for some months.

It was the rebellion of the imperial army at Casa Mata that destroyed Iturbide and provoked the onset of the federalist revolution. Echávarri, commanding the imperial army besieging Santa Anna at the port of Veracruz, decided to end his unsuccessful siege of the city and to seek a face-saving device that would both ensure Iturbide's security on the throne and meet Santa Anna's major demand for reestablishment of a national representation in Congress. On 1 February 1822 the commanders of the imperial army outside Veracruz signed an act, called the Plan of Casa Mata after the place where they were headquartered, in which they called for the convocation of a new Constituent Congress (rather than restoration of the dissolved one, as Santa Anna had proclaimed). The two principal points of the Plan of Casa Mata were, first, that sovereignty resided essentially in the nation, which required the immediate installation of a new Congress, and, second, that "The army will never make any attempt against the person of the emperor." The plan not only did not call for creation of a republic but, as Echávarri wrote to Ramón Rayón the same day, "Upon pronouncing our votes for the installation of the Congress we have considered as a sacred duty the conservation of the emperor, and as a result these armies attempt no act against his august person, which they respect as inviolable."[21] A critical part of the plan, scarcely noted at first, was that in order to resolve the political crisis in Veracruz, the government of the province of Veracruz was to be given over to the provincial deputation of Veracruz until such time as the new Congress could meet.[22]

As Nettie Lee Benson has pointed out, the Plan of Casa Mata, although it did not call for the creation of a republic, had the effect of destroying the central government. When the plan declared that the government of the province of Veracruz would be vested in the provincial deputation of Veracruz, it induced the provincial deputations throughout the country to adopt the plan almost immediately, for it assured each deputation that it could have what it most wanted, administrative control of its own territory. Thus, the plan quickly gained the adherence of most of the major cities and provincial deputations. In February the Plan of Casa Mata was accepted by Veracruz (on the first), Oaxaca (the eighth), Puebla (the eleventh), Toluca (the eighteenth), Querétaro and Guanajuato (the twenty-third), and Guadalajara and Mexico City (the twenty-sixth). In March it was accepted by Zacatecas (on the first), San Luis Potosí (the second), Valladolid (the third), Yucatán and Campeche (the fourth), Durango (the fifth), Saltillo (the ninth), and Nuevo Santander (the tenth).[23] When the provincial deputation of Puebla asked Echávarri whether Article 10 of the Plan of Casa Mata, which gave the provincial deputation of Veracruz control of the province independently of the central government, applied to Puebla as well, Echávarri replied that it did.[24]

There is no indication that the leaders of the imperial army at Casa Mata consciously aimed to create federalism. Quite the contrary, neither they nor Iturbide seem to have foreseen that a federal republic would be the outcome of the movement sparked by Casa Mata. The high-ranking officers who led the movement of Casa Mata—Echávarri, Pedro Celestino Negrete (both of whom were Spaniards), and the creole José Morán (the marqués de Vivanco)—were not republicans.[25] The army of Casa Mata, as Hamnett notes, was "a very complex aggregation of autonomous bands directed by ambitious military politicians who frequently had a clientele to satisfy."[26] As usual, the eyewitness historical accounts were primarily written by centralists, and they did not initially recognize the full meaning of Casa Mata.

When the provincial deputations, major cities, and leading local military commanders accepted the Plan of Casa Mata they were not necessarily declaring for the end of the monarchy, the fall of Iturbide, the creation of a republic, or the founding of a federal system. All of those elements were perhaps inherent, or they would rapidly develop, but the Plan of Casa Mata said absolutely nothing about any of them. It merely called for the election of a new Constituent Congress to replace the dissolved first Constituent Congress (and on the basis of the same highly defective formula). Moreover, by granting the deputations control over their provinces, it opened the ultimate door to the onset of provincial autonomy. Thus, in the view of the provinces, whether Casa Mata meant retention of the monarchy or not it undoubtedly meant the beginning of effective provincial self-government.

Each province had a slightly different agenda or set of circumstances in adopting Casa Mata. For example, Alamán pointed out that when the city council and commanders of the port of Veracruz declared for Casa Mata on 2 February, superseding Santa Anna's Plan of Veracruz, they were actually "desisting from the proclamation of a republic that they had made and from the idea of reestablishing the dissolved Congress."[27] When they adhered to the Plan of Casa Mata, two provincial deputations, Valladolid and Yucatán, indicated that in their view the plan did not mean the abolition of the monarchy. Indeed, Valladolid, where Ramón Huarte, a brother-in-law of Iturbide, was jefe político and presided over the provincial deputation, announced that its acceptance of Casa Mata was merely "ratifying anew the inviolability of the emperor." And Yucatán did not adhere until it was assured that Casa Mata did not proclaim the abolition of the monarchy.[28] When it accepted Casa Mata, the provincial deputation of Mexico City did so entirely to support the reunion of a Congress. It wrote Iturbide, asking him to save the country.[29] However, both the provincial deputation of Mexico and the city council of Mexico City feared that the move to provincial autonomy threatened the capital's hegemony, and as a result they were divided and compromised. On the whole, both the jefe político and the provincial deputation of Mexico City supported Iturbide until his abdication on 19 March.[30]

For Yucatán, maintaining contact with Spain and Cuba was the most important object because they were its major trading partners, and it saw provincial autonomy as the major defense of its free trade. Campeche, on the other hand, was deeply enmeshed in a struggle to free itself from the political and economic hegemony of Yucatán and thus saw Casa Mata and later federalism with Mexico as the way to provide access for its goods to the markets of interior Mexico.[31] Zacatecas, which would soon become one of the strongest supporters of federalism, was initially troubled by the fact that Casa Mata was a serious political intervention by the military. When the military garrison of the city of Zacatecas adhered to Casa Mata, it was with the opposition of the provincial deputation, which argued that the plan was an act of violence similar to the one Iturbide had committed when he used the army to dissolve Congress. It announced its support of negotiations between the government and the rebellious officers.[32]

It was the province of Nueva Galicia or Guadalajara, however, that voiced most clearly the element within the response to Casa Mata that would become the dominant theme. When the provincial deputation of Guadalajara adhered to Casa Mata it published a manifesto, dated 12 March 1823, that declared its rejection of Mexico City's "universal domination over the provinces." In a foretaste of things to come, it warned that if "the new Tenochtitlan" wished to impose its will over the provinces, it should know that "from now on the free State of Xalisco" was prepared to pursue the objectives of its people "to be independent, free and happy."[33]

The net effect of Casa Mata, then, was not that it produced federalism. Its actual effect was that it forced Iturbide to restore the dissolved Constituent Congress. By the end of February 1822, even Iturbide's own Council of State was clamoring for the return of Congress. Iturbide had no choice but to reestablish the old Congress, which he did on 4 March.[34] Although the restored Congress did not have a quorum for some time, Iturbide had already decided to abdicate rather than create civil war.[35] He no longer controlled the imperial armies and at the beginning of March had only part of the garrison of Mexico City at his command. On 19 March 1823, Iturbide presented Congress with a handwritten message abdicating the throne.[36]

In truth, however, the survival of the Iturbide government had become irrelevant. The Veracruz rebellion and the Casa Mata rebellion together called for self-government by the provinces and for the devolution of some degree of military power to the provincial militias under the command of provincial leaders. A vast new enterprise, soon to bear the name of federalism, had supplanted the Iturbide enterprise. The Plan of Iguala had merely recognized the existence of provinces; this new program gave them their own self-government and, potentially, the military strength to defend it.

A fundamental idea that accompanied these views, and that was now universal, was the rejection of a strong executive. The prevailing view was that Mexico had now defeated two "tyrants," Ferdinand VII of Spain and Agustín I of Mexico, and that the exercise of sovereignty could only rest in the hands of a representative body. In keeping with the precedent of the Cortes of Cádiz and the views expressed by the deputies in the Constituent Congress throughout 1822, the principle that now triumphed was that the exercise of national sovereignty belonged to Congress in its role as the elected representation of the people rather than to the executive. Of course, the swelling demand for provincial autonomy would soon propose that sovereignty was not unitary and undivided.

Among the victorious supporters of Casa Mata, however, there was a serious split between those who favored the restored Constituent Congress and those who adhered to Casa Mata's call for the election of a new Congress. Those who favored provincial autonomy did not trust the old Congress because it had been elected on the basis of partidos rather than population. The leaders of Casa Mata had formed what was called the Junta of Puebla, and they invited two representatives from each province to participate in it. As the "liberating army" of Casa Mata and its political branch, the Junta of Puebla, prepared to enter Mexico City, the legitimacy of the restored old Congress was under debate. Throughout the middle of March offers arrived from several provincial capitals, including Valladolid and Guanajuato, for Congress to meet in their cities, and a discussion ensued in which the possible transfer of the central government to Puebla was considered. On 27 March 1823 the "liberating army" entered Mexico City. On 29 March, and for the first time, the restored Congress had a quorum and was able to make legislative decisions again.[37]

It was Iturbide's abdication that converted the idea of a republic from a principle held by relatively few among the leadership into the only logical way to organize the country. There was little discussion in Congress or in the very active pamphlet and periodical press about republicanism itself. The assumption appeared to be automatic that, once the monarchy fell, the only choice was a republic. The great issue on which discussion was clearly beginning to focus was whether this republic would be federalist or centralist, whether the general government would share power with the provinces. Although there was little sign of debate over republicanism, March 1823 marked the beginning of a massive debate over federalism. Rabasa points out that "the Republic was adopted as a result of its being the indispensable complement of the Federation for which the provinces clamored, and not because of the inverse procedure that once the Republic was accepted it had the federated form ascribed to it."[38]

Indeed, Benson contends, first, that the Plan of Casa Mata was so quickly accepted throughout the country because of the careful planning and skillful organization of republican conspirators working through a network of Masonic lodges and, second, that Echávarri and his officers served chiefly as their mouthpiece. The speed with which the Plan of Casa Mata was accepted, she argues, suggests "that the groundwork had been well laid."[39] It is in the nature of conspiracies, of course, that they do not leave documentary evidence of their operation, but we know that conspiracies abounded, and by the mid-1820s political life in Mexico City revolved primarily around the Scots Rite and York Rite Masonic lodges. Even if there were no conspiracies, however, it is certain that the real prime objective of Casa Mata, provincial autonomy, struck an immediate chord throughout the regions. The provinces were becoming enthusiastically federalist.

In this great issue, the more conservative, or centralist, elements were caught at a significant disadvantage. This was particularly true of those elements representing the interests of the traditional hegemonic region of Mexico City and environs who had the most to lose if federalism were established. The conservative elements were still reeling from the effects of the wars of independence; the flight of many of the peninsulars (though by no means all of them); the infrastructural and economic destruction caused by the fighting; the massive outflow of capital; and, indeed, the loss of an organizing principle for society with the separation from the Spanish monarchy. But they suffered a nearly shattering blow with the collapse of the Iturbide monarchy and the withdrawal from power of the man who had been the hero-liberator and indispensable figure in organizing a government. Bravo Ugarte points out that Iturbide himself must bear some of the blame for the disorganization of the more conservative forces in society because by his abdication he nullified "the immense national force of Iturbidism," ordering it to remain inactive.[40]

An important part of the explanation of the victory of federalism in the next few months, in other words, was the disarray among the forces of traditional conservatism. It was a conservatism that had not yet begun to perceive itself as a school of thought because it had previously been the universal standard of political, social, and cultural organization, and it did not even use the word *conservative* to describe itself until the 1840s. It was not gone, not destroyed, but it was disorganized, and in the next several months as the conservatives sought direction in the new order implicit in the transition to a republic the federalists seized the moment.

The soon-to-emerge federalists did not have a name for their school of thought either. But in the next three months, between Iturbide's abdication in March and the proclamation of the first "free and sovereign state" in Jalisco in June, their objectives came together rapidly, spurred by the opportunity presented to them by the end of Iturbide's empire to achieve the long-desired provincial autonomy. Their philosophy was that power should be exercised where it could best serve the needs of the people, which is to say, at the provincial and local levels.

As Benson characterizes it, the disintegration of the Iturbide regime, leaving the provinces to act on their own volition, reveals that as early as March 1823 Mexico was divided into independent provinces, each one of which was taking over administration in its own region. The jefe político was becoming the provincial executive, and the provincial deputation was assuming the legislative function in each province. No central government actually existed, and even after the restored Congress regained its quorum, the provinces obeyed it only when they chose to do so.[41] Yet what most surprises the historian is that these independent provinces, rather than going their own way and passively observing the disintegration of the old colonial linkages that bound them together, actually turned their active attention to formulating a system by which nationhood could be established, as long as it did not ignore their demand to be masters in their own houses.

When Congress declared itself in session on 29 March, it decreed that there now existed no recognized executive power and proceeded to establish a provisional executive in the form of a triumvirate called the Supreme Executive Power, whose members would alternate the signing authority between themselves on a monthly basis. In what Rodríguez considers an effort to control the nearly independent military, Congress appointed three generals—Nicolás Bravo, Guadalupe Victoria, and Pedro Celestino Negrete—to make up the triumvirate. Because those three officers were in the field commanding their troops, Congress later chose substitute members for the triumvirate—José Mariano Michelena, José Miguel Domínguez, and Vicente Guerrero. Because Guerrero was also normally in the field and Domínguez was elderly, Michelena exercised most of the executive power. Congress established a single cabinet member, José Ignacio García Illueca, but the work was too great for a single person, and so within two weeks it began to name other members until the cabinet consisted of four men, the most powerful of whom was Lucas Alamán as the minister of Interior and Exterior Relations. The leadership was thus mixed, for Michelena was a champion of provincial rights, and Alamán quickly emerged as the most capable and articulate conservative opposed to provincial power.[42] The creation of a weak executive whose members operated almost independently of each other, combined with the existence of a Congress that lacked credibility in the minds of many people, meant that in the contest for provincial power the central authority was unusually frail.

Although the creation of a republic appeared logical, Zavala wrote of the period immediately following the abdication, "Everyone spoke of a republic; but no one understood it. . . . Neither the army, nor the Congress, nor the parties themselves knew what had happened, much less what should follow."[43] Nonetheless, in order to leave the country free to constitute a new government as it saw fit, Congress nullified the Plan of Iguala and the Treaty of Córdoba as well as its own earlier vote by which on the day of its original installation it had declared its allegiance to the principle of constitutional monarchy. Alamán has pointed out that, in so doing, Congress declared that it had not legally represented the nation, even though now it claimed somehow that it did represent the country, and Zavala wrote that the Constituent Congress, having been elected on the premise that it would create a monarchy, did not now have the power to create a republic.[44] Many believed that in nullifying the Plan of Iguala, the basis on which Congress itself had been convoked, Congress had declared itself illegitimate.

On 12 April 1823 a commission of Congress created to discuss whether the present Congress should be dissolved and a new one convoked rendered a report recommending continuation, and Congress accepted the recommendation. Of the members of the commission, only Valentín Gómez Farías, the man who would later become the leading voice of early Mexican radicalism, dissented strongly.[45] This provoked a statement from the provincial commissioners who had gathered in Mexico City representing the provinces of Guadalajara, Michoacán, Oaxaca, Zacatecas, Guanajuato, Querétaro, and San Luis Potosí in which they insisted that the provision of the Plan of Casa Mata that called for the convocation of a new Congress must be implemented. The argument of the provincial commissioners revolved around four points: the restored Congress was elected on the basis of the number of partidos and not population, thus denying citizens equal representation; the Congress was chosen for the purpose of creating the monarchy and was therefore unfit to proceed to the creation of a more suitable system; too many of the members of Congress had lost public confidence; and as a result the Congress lacked the moral influence necessary to create a new government that could be supported by the majority.[46] Many provinces also issued statements declaring that because the restored Congress had not been elected on the basis of proportionality it could not represent them. With this, the revolt of the provinces began.

The province of Nueva Galicia took the lead. After hearing of Congress's decision not to call new elections, on 9 May 1823 the provincial deputation of Guadalajara decided, with the full support of Guadalajara's captain general and political chief, Luis Quintanar, to rescind its earlier recognition of Congress on the grounds that the province had recognized Congress only on the expectation that it would convene a new legislature.[47] On 12 May the provincial deputation and the ayuntamiento of Guadalajara met jointly and resolved to support the creation of a federal republic, declaring that they would no longer obey Congress and the Supreme Executive Power. They also declared that the provincial deputation was the highest authority in the province and that they would send copies of these decisions to all the other provincial deputations in the country, inviting them to join in the declaration of federalism.[48] When Guadalajara dispatched these enactments to the other provinces it initiated a new type of independent direct communication between the provinces, itself a revolutionary development. The central government responded on 26 May by ordering the removal of Quintanar as jefe político of Nueva Galicia, replacing him with José Joaquín Herrera. But when Herrera arrived near Guadalajara to take possession of his office, a large troop of local militia blocked his passage, obliging him to abandon the effort.

These actions by the province of Guadalajara, when replicated elsewhere in the country, set the tone for federalism's challenge of traditional centralism. Its final outcome would be the decision of the second Constituent Congress on 16 December 1823 to endorse Article 5 of the proposed Acta Constitutiva, which declared, "The Nation adopts for its government the form of a representative popular federal republic." Pursuing this determination, the second Constituent Congress would then write the federal constitution in 1824. That was the outcome of the federalist revolt. Mexico was in the process of creating one of the world's most original republics.

The full content of the principles of Mexican federalism that the provinces were proclaiming would take several months to emerge, but in the early summer of 1823 there were three major elements already evident. First, federalism would be based on provincial self-determination, the provincial exercise of sovereignty. That is, each province would determine its own future and would jointly participate in constructing the nation. Second, the legislative branch would be clearly and undeniably superior to the executive branch, a universal tenet that continued to be a critical foundation of nineteenth-century Mexican federalism. This form of legislative supremacy was drawn from the Cádiz model and bore no sign of influence from the U.S. model in that the latter was based on a system of checks and balances between executive and legislative branches roughly equal, or at least balanced, in their powers. And, third, the fundamental historical imperative of Mexican federalism, its historical argument, and a concept fundamental to the Plan of Casa Mata and clearly outlined by Jalisco in many of its enactments was that the disappearance of the Iturbide regime meant that existing civil society had been dissolved. Under those circumstances all previous legitimacy vanished, leaving society, as in a state of nature, free to reconstitute itself as it saw fit. It could only formulate itself anew by "constituting the nation," that is, through the enactments of a legally elected and representative Constituent Congress. This concept, of course, was a natural link to the idea that prevailed in Spain following the capture of Ferdinand VII: that the exercise of legitimacy had devolved to those institutions that represented the nation. It had been clearly stated in its Mexican form in the Plan of Veracruz of December 1822: "The nation is free, and in addition, it finds itself in a natural state. Being independent, and sovereign, and free, it has full faculties to constitute itself in conformity with what seems most suitable to its happiness, by means of the Sovereign Constituent Congress."[49] These would be the bedrock principles of Mexican federalism throughout the nineteenth century. They were startling in their originality and were examples of sui generis Mexican thinking.

The full response of the general government in Mexico City to the provincial revolts, however, and particularly the responses of the first Constituent Congress, will forever remain clouded. This is because the records documenting in detail the thinking and many of the orders of the cabinet and even Congress were not preserved. Jaime E. Rodríguez, for example, points out that it is necessary to reconstruct the events from June to about October 1823 from such sources as Carlos María de Bustamante's *Diario histórico*, an idiosyncratic diary that was not intended for publication, because the classic histories written by eyewitness participants in these events—such as José María Bocanegra, Lorenzo de Zavala, Lucas Alamán—and even Bustamante's own historical writings, do not discuss these months in detail. In addition, the minutes of the Supreme Executive Power (the "Resoluciones del Supremo Executivo" published in the *Diario del Congreso Constituyente*) do not discuss the provincial revolts. Minutes of closed meetings of Congress (issues as delicate as the refusal of the provinces to recognize the general government were considered in "secret," or closed, sessions) do not appear in the normal sources (such as volume 2 of *Historia parlamentaria de los Congresos Mexicanos de 1821–1857*, edited by Juan A. Mateos). Even the *Sesiones Secretas* of the *Historia parlamentaria*, which were published between 1982 and 1984 (compiled by Luis Muro, two volumes), does not have the minutes of these sessions. Even the lively periodical press, which normally published the parliamentary minutes in their entirety, did not reproduce congressional discussions on the provincial revolts. Meanwhile, in the executive branch, Alamán was minister of interior relations, the dominant cabinet post, from 16 April 1823 to 23 April 1824 and again from 15 May to 21 September 1824. These were the critical moments during which the provincial demands and the formative discussions on the constitution occurred, and Alamán was the leading opponent of provincial power. Rodríguez concludes that "it is as though there was a general agreement to eliminate these events from the national record."[50]

This helps explain why the revolt of the provinces has not been a focus of the historiography, and why we have not recognized the extent to which the creation of a republican nation was primarily the work of the provinces. Political power was passing to the provinces, each of which assumed control over affairs in its own territory, and Mexico entered a period characterized by "decentered simultaneous action in multiple locations," as Stevens nicely phrases it. Reflecting on this "dialectical business of disintegration and re-creation," Stevens continues, "It was almost like a magician's trick, a sleight of hand. While we have been watching and wondering at the bewildering flourish of events at the national level, the important work was being done largely out of sight in the provinces. It was provincial leaders who had the clarity and the determination to articulate what Mexico would be."[51]

And here, too, is the explanation for why the guardians of the center's hegemony either ignored or failed to emphasize the significance of the provincial revolts. The movement toward federalism meant Mexico would constitute itself as a republic of many independent centers; the unbroken power of the central hegemonic city and province would be gone; and the business of ruling would be much more complicated, especially for those who preferred not to consult with the ruled. This was a mortal threat to the traditional national elites, and a cause of genuine confusion and alarm for centralists who witnessed the end not only of rule from Spain but the threatened end of rule by themselves. Federalism questioned the traditionalists' view of what constituted the nation, where it came from. Alamán, for example, believed that the nation was created by the Spanish Conquest and the colonial experience and could not be the product of federalism, which he called "this beautiful invention of modern politics."[52] In June 1823, referring to Mexican nationhood, he scolded the authorities of Oaxaca by declaring, "It would be the greatest absurdity to destroy that which is already built in order to rebuild it afterward."[53] The debate that was underway, in other words, was about much more than merely the form of government; it was about the definition of nationhood and who had the right to define it. Centralists believed the nation was an organic whole born of three centuries of colonial history; federalists believed the nation was a pluralistic union that was still to be constructed.

Supporters of a strong central power found it both convenient and necessary to overlook the fact that the first federal republic was the result of independent provincial action that imposed a political solution upon the center. Many governments since the 1820s have overlooked this as well because the implications are clear: the Mexican republic was first constituted as a nation-state in which legitimacy flowed from the provinces to the center, not the other way around.

The movement in favor of autonomous provincial self-government extended to the Central American provinces too and makes it clear that this was a generalized Mesoamerican response. In Central America, the fall of Iturbide and nullification of the Plan of Iguala ended the link of constitutional monarchy that had joined those provinces with Mexico for slightly more than a year. As he prepared to withdraw his troops from Guatemala in March 1823, the captain general, Vicente Filisola, who Iturbide had sent the year before to encourage the Central American provinces to join the Mexican Empire, called for the provinces to send deputies to a Central American congress. On 1 July 1823 the provinces proclaimed absolute Central American independence under a provisional junta. On that same day the Mexican Congress confirmed the order to withdraw Filisola's troops from Central America, Minister of Relations Alamán having made the argument that Guatemala should be free to create the government it found most suitable.[54] These events were occurring during the same critical months that the provinces in Mexico were in revolt against Mexico City. Liberals, representing the provinces, controlled the government in Guatemala City. They then proceeded to create the United Provinces of Central America, and responding very much to the same need as in Mexico to combine provincial self-government with the strength of others, in 1824 they wrote a liberal constitution for a federal republic in which the five states had home rule and considerable autonomy. The state of Guatemala had over half the total population of the new Central American republic. Meanwhile, in June 1823 Chiapas proclaimed itself independent of both Guatemala and Mexico. In 1824 it joined the Mexican federal republic.

The fact that the political life of Mexico in 1823 became a scene of simultaneous action in multiple locations has also meant a great hardship for historians. Multiple, vociferous subnational units voicing their opinions at once, even if those opinions tended to point in the same direction, make for an overly complex narrative. I have simplified these events, employing Benson's pioneering research on the rise of the states, in the chronology of provincial action presented in table 1. Table 1 lists the most important developments in the process running from March to November 1823 by which the provincial demands for self-government, linked with their desire to forge a national union, forced the adoption of the federal republic. Vázquez points out that this process constituted, after Iguala and Casa Mata, the third great national consensus in Mexico's independent history.[55]

That it was a consensus there can be no doubt. In April and May the provinces, acting independently of each other and by their own volition, rejected the decision of the restored first Constituent Congress to remain in power, declaring that under the provisions of the Plan of Casa Mata they had recognized the restored Congress only for the purpose of determining the basis on which a new, more representative Congress was to be

Table 1   Chronology of Provincial Action

Date (all 1823)	Event
27 March	Army of Casa Mata enters Mexico City
29 March	First Constituent Congress regains quorum
8 April	Congress annuls Plan of Iguala and Treaty of Córdoba
12 April	Congress commission recommends against convoking new Congress
18 April	Commissioners of Seven provinces demand new Congress (Guadalajara, Michoacán, Oaxaca, Zacatecas, Guanajuato, Querétaro, San Luis Potosí)
23 April	Provincial deputation of Puebla demands new Congress
25 April	Provincial deputation of Yucatán demands new Congress, begins to organize a government
30 April	Provincial deputation of Guanajuato demands new Congress; municipal councils affirm demand
7 May	Provincial deputation of Michoacán demands new Congress
9 May	Provincial deputation of Guadalajara rescinds recognition of Congress
12 May	Guadalajara calls for federal republic, declares provincial deputation highest authority in province, refuses to obey Congress, suspends remission of funds to Mexico City
14 May	Committee picked by Mier to produce "Bases for a Federative Republic"
16 May	Provincial deputation of Querétaro polls municipal councils, which call for new Congress
20 May	Congress agrees to convene new Congress soon
27 May	A provisional junta in the Eastern Interior Provinces demands federal republic
30 May	Alamán informs Congress it must act to prevent disintegration of country
30 May	Yucatán installs elected provisional junta that sets elections for the provincial congress for June-July
1 June	Oaxaca declares separation from national government in Mexico City, installs a provisional government and governing junta
3 June	Santa Anna and army, in San Luis Potosí, call for federal republic; province of San Luis Potosí refuses to accept Santa Anna's leadership
4 June	Saltillo calls for self-government for the Eastern Interior Provinces
4 June	Chiapas installs an elected provincial junta
5 June	Provincial deputation of Eastern Interior Provinces calls for federal republic; Eastern Interior Provinces are to form one or more free, sovereign states

5 June	Santa Anna, in San Luis Potosí, declares himself "protector of the federation"
7, 9 June	Chiapas provincial junta becomes supreme provisional junta and declares Chiapas independent of both Guatemala and Mexico
11, 12 June	Provincial deputation of Querétaro repeats demand for new Congress and for federalism
12 June	Congress votes in favor of principle of a federated republic
mid-June	Central government attempts to replace Quintanar as captain general of Guadalajara but fails
16 June	Guadalajara declares creation of the "free, independent, and sovereign state of Jalisco," linked to other provinces by "brotherhood and confederation," issues a plan of provisional government of the state
17 June	Electoral law for new Congress
18 June	Provincial deputation of Zacatecas withdraws recognition of Congress, agrees to create provisional government
20 June	Provincial deputation of Veracruz agrees with the general demand of the provinces for a federal republic
25 June	In a secret session of Congress, Pablo de la Llave, minister of justice, proposes Congress adopt a provisional federal pact; Congress decides to make each of the four Eastern Interior Provinces a separate province
1 July	Santa Anna, in San Luis Potosí, agrees to give up his separate federalist revolt
1 July	Oaxaca installs state congress
1–10 July	Celaya meeting of Michoacán, Querétaro, Guanajuato, and San Luis Potosí demands a federal republic and elections for new Congress
July	Guadalajara and Zacatecas refuse to reelect provincial deputations as required by 17 June electoral law
5 July	Army leaves Mexico City to invade Jalisco, commanded by Bravo and Negrete
12 July	Zacatecas provincial deputation issues plan for government of the free state of Zacatecas
18 July	Bravo halts advance on Jalisco
19 July	Provincial deputation of Nuevo Santander votes for a federal republic
19 July	Provincial deputation of Mexico states its support for federalism but objects to Jalisco's methods, preferring the national Congress create federalism
8–18 August	Lagos conference between central government and Guadalajara and Zacatecas
16 August	Congress recommends settlement and amnesty for revolted provinces
20 August	Yucatán installs state congress

14 September	Jalisco installs state congress
19 October	Zacatecas installs state congress
31 October	Second Constituent Congress seated
20 November	Ramos Arizpe presents his committee's draft of the Acta Constitutiva

Sources: Benson, *The Provincial Deputation*, 82–129; Rodríguez, "Formation of the Federal Republic," 316–28.

chosen. The decision was virtually unanimous; only the province of Mexico resisted, and its resistance was relatively muted. The difference in timing of these provincial pronouncements depended primarily on the speed of communication within the country and on the degree of internal organization in the provinces. Some, such as the Western Interior Provinces and the Californias, were too sparsely populated, too distant, and too unorganized to play a role, and there are some provinces in which detailed documents have not been located.

Four provinces, Guadalajara, Zacatecas, Oaxaca, and Yucatán, took the lead in initiating this revolt, but others, such as Michoacán, Guanajuato, Querétaro, and San Luis Potosí, took council with each other in order to present unified action. By May, Guadalajara, Yucatán, and Oaxaca, the most populous noncentral provinces with the strongest grievances against inherited centralism, began transforming their provincial deputations into provisional governments with the announced intent of forming a confederation with Mexico City. These actions were taken, moreover, with the fullest support of local military authorities, such as the captains general and garrison commanders, and in consultation with the city councils of the provincial capitals. Usually the provincial deputation invited the city council to participate directly in its deliberations, a clear continuation of the colonial tradition of open town council meetings, or cabildos abiertos, involving the foremost local residents. Several provinces, such as Guadalajara and Querétaro, formally polled their municipalities and found effectively unanimous support for federalism.[56] The link between provincialism and municipalism was very close.

By June, the movement was well advanced in even the most peripheral provinces. Chiapas installed a provincial junta formally elected by all the districts. In the vast Eastern Interior Provinces (Coahuila, Nuevo León, Nuevo Santander, Texas), Miguel Ramos Arizpe, former deputy to the Spanish Cortes and key member of the national Congress, headed a provisional governing junta in Coahuila that by the end of May declared for self-government and federation and in the next few days began to organize a government in a permanent form (it was not yet determined if they would form one or more free sovereign states). Nuevo León and Nuevo Santander also formally called for federalism.

The response of the Congress and the cabinet was largely reactive. In an attempt to forestall the establishment of state sovereignty and federalism, Servando Teresa de Mier handpicked a group of deputies in Congress to work on a proposed constitution that would create a federal republic without full autonomy for the states, in effect a centralized republic. Andrés Lira states that Mier was motivated by the impending dissolution of the first Constituent Congress, the fear that it would give way to a much more radical revolutionary convention, and the desire to try to set the agenda for the next Congress.[57] The "Bases for a Federative Republic" produced by this committee on 16 May was not discussed in Congress, however, because the provinces were making it clear that they rejected the right of the restored Congress to produce a constitution. It called for creation of a federal republic but one in which sovereignty would be national and unitary, not shared by the provinces, with prefects appointed by the central government to rule the provinces and with a national Congress that was all powerful. Coining a concept that would come into its own in the twentieth century, Mier admitted that the object was to create a republic that would be "federal in name and central in reality."[58]

On 30 May, Minister of Interior Affairs Alamán encapsulated the fear of centralists when he informed Congress that if it did not act soon the country would disintegrate. When Iturbide heard of these events in his European exile, he also concluded that the country was disintegrating. Convinced of the consensus against continuation of the existing Congress, on 20 May Congress promised it would issue a call for new elections as quickly as possible (in a vote in which seventy-one members voted in favor of calling a new congress and thirty-three voted against, a third of all the negative votes coming from the province of Mexico). On 17 June Congress issued the convocation or electoral law for the new Congress.

By mid-June, the most radical states were prepared to proclaim their sovereignty. Nueva Galicia (Guadalajara) took the lead. When its municipalities met in late May to consider whether they supported the provincial deputation's proposal for a federal republic, they presented a remarkable example of a province whose people knew what they wanted and where their best interests lay. At least one authority, the commander of Tepic, de-

clared that there were still too many among the common people who favored the empire, while only the most enlightened knew anything about
federalism. But after what appeared to be extensive discussion and genuine lessons in the principles and practice of self-government, the vast majority of towns and corporations declared their fervent support of federalism. There was, for example, the enthusiasm of such locations as San Blas,
where naval officers and enlisted men gave federalism their resounding
support, and the town of Colotlán, where the predominantly Indian community, declaring itself "convinced of the advantages that would redound
to us as docile people," warmly embraced the federal republic. And in the
town of Amatitán an open town council meeting heard citizens make a resounding declaration of their willingness to leave their home territory to
fight those who opposed the adoption of federalism. The city council of
Tepic actually discussed the way in which the independence of Jalisco
within the federal republic duplicated the independence of the two subordinate ayuntamientos of Jalisco and Huaynamota within the partido of
Tepic—each determining their own internal affairs while simultaneously
expecting that the head town, Tepic, would speak for the others on general or external matters. A first-instance judge in the city of Guadalajara
put it well when he declared, "It being incontrovertible that concord, fraternity and equality are the bases of a republican government, so much the
better when it is reduced to is own sphere, as in federalism." The town of
Ejutla, having earlier sent a proposal for a federal government to the provincial deputation, declared, "Now that we have begun to work against
despotism, let us throw down that work of despotism and of the militia,
that weak, traitorous, despotic Congress." Although not every town in
the province replied, towns in every one of the twenty-eight partidos of
the province did, as did the twenty-eight *cabeceras*, or head towns. The
feeling of the towns of Nueva Galicia was perhaps best summed up by the
statement of the pueblo of Autlán de la Grana: "The glorious struggle of
the provinces to acquire our greatly desired liberty would serve for nothing if, on beginning to possess it, the towns suffered the cruelty of being
unable to use it."[59]

What all these responses suggest is that there was a clear understanding
of the infrastructures of self-government in a federalist system—namely,
that each municipality, as the basic organized political structure, was internally self-governing but looked to the cabecera, the chief town of the
partido, to represent it externally. Similarly, each cabecera was internally
autonomous but reported to the state authorities in Guadalajara. The

state, in turn, was internally sovereign (with the hierarchy of authority being the elected representative state legislature first and the executive, or governor, second), but for external questions it looked to the general government of the federation (where the hierarchy would be similar: an elected representative federal congress first and an executive power, or president, second). Although the constitution of 1824 referred specifically to the example of the United States in the functioning of this model, there were hardly any references to the United States in the consensus in favor of its adoption that derived from the autonomous action of the provinces in 1823. This reinforced the argument that Mexican federalism, deriving from the Spanish 1812 constitution, the Hispanic traditions of provincialism and municipalism, and indeed even from pre-Cortesian indigenous political entities, was overwhelmingly self-generated. Simply put, Mexican federalism was unabashedly Mexican. If it had not been it would not have been as remarkably enduring in the face of the many subsequent challenges it faced.

Furthermore, Peter Guardino has shown, in a study of the south of the province of Mexico (the region that later became the state of Guerrero), that indigenous peasants fully recognized the significance of the elected municipal councils that had been decreed in the Spanish constitution of 1812 for all towns with a population of a thousand persons. In the period 1823–35, indigenous municipalities, continuing the traditional function of the colonial repúblicas de indios, "became the crucial agents of government in rural Mexico, actually implementing most state and federal laws and orders." In many localities Indian peasants and village elders maintained much of the power and autonomy they had enjoyed under the *república* system. Throughout the first federal republic, particularly because of the universal male suffrage that existed during that time, indigenous peasants often retained local political power or at least had a mechanism for obtaining concessions in exchange for their electoral support. They were thus able to protect their community's interests, particularly access to land and water, from the encroachments of wealthier local white and mestizo landowners. This happened even though most of the states reduced the number of municipalities when they wrote their state constitutions in 1824 and 1825. During the first republic peasants developed a popular version of federalism that emphasized local political autonomy as a means of protecting their resources. In Guerrero, it was only the establishment of the central republic in 1835 that gave local white and mestizo elites unchallenged control of local political power.[60]

Nueva Galicia, the first state to be erected, declared itself on 16 June 1823 as "the free, independent, and sovereign state of Jalisco." By doing so, its provincial deputation defined it—in words symbolic both of the transition of thought that had now occurred and of the simultaneous processes of regional differentiation and national integration that were under way—as "a sovereign State federated with the others of the great Mexican nation."[61] Jalisco declared in its *Plan de gobierno provisional* that "the State of Jalisco is free, independent, and sovereign within itself and it shall recognize no relations with the other states or provinces except those of fraternity and confederation."[62] When Jalisco's first state congress took office on 14 September, its members took an oath that asked them, "Do you recognize the sovereign and independent State of Jalisco, as one of the federated States of the Mexican Nation?"[63] Zacatecas followed soon after, declaring in its *Reglamento para el gobierno provisional del estado libre de Zacatecas* of 12 July 1823, "The state of Zacatecas is sovereign in itself, and does not depend on the others that compose the great Mexican Nation except in that which relates to the general well-being of all."[64] Nationhood, in short, was being defined, and it was the equal union of the several free, independent, and sovereign states.

Two fascinating phenomena need to be emphasized here. First, the process by which the individual provinces created and elected their state governments represented a significant expansion of political participation in Mexico, whether measured by the standards then prevailing within the Spanish-speaking world or by those then prevailing within the North Atlantic world. Although the exercise of state sovereignty meant that each province might proceed in slightly different ways to the election of its first government, the route generally followed was to transform the existing provincial deputation into the state legislature (congress), which would then declare the incumbent jefe político or commandant general (the positions had often been combined under Iturbide) as the state governor. By early 1824, every state proceeded to new elections to choose the first ordinary state congress, usually a constituent congress whose main duty was to write the state constitution. (By general agreement, however, the state constitutions were not written until the national Congress completed the federal constitution.)

The provincial deputations, of course, had been chosen in elections under the provisions of the Spanish constitution, which meant that although the elections had been indirect—direct voting occurred at the parish level only—the voters, nonetheless, did include a genuinely broad spectrum of the population. It was a far wider franchise than existed in the United States, Britain, or France, the countries usually cited as examples of the maximum achievement of liberal democracy in the early nineteenth century.[65] Although there were, in effect, property qualifications for holding electoral office, there were no property qualifications for voting, and the provision of the Spanish constitution barring servants from voting was simply unenforced in many locations in the period 1820–23. There was as yet no movement in Mexico to bar clergy from voting or holding elective office. Although there is no doubt that military officers played a disproportionate role in electoral politics as well as in society, in Mexico enlisted men voted too. And though there was provision in the Spanish constitution that would bar illiterates from voting, it was scheduled to go into effect only in 1830. Indeed, in Mexico the majority of voters were Indians, blacks, and mestizos. When the provinces demanded federalism they insisted that it come in the form of a popular, representative federal republic.

Di Tella has emphasized how unusual Mexico's widespread right to participate in elections actually was in the third decade of the nineteenth century. This growth in suffrage was a result of the way in which Spain had resisted the Napoleonic conquest through mass mobilization, institutionalized and transmitted to America in the Cádiz constitution. It would have an exceptional impact in Spain and some of its former colonies, notably in Mexico where "after the insurgency the phenomenon of popular participation could not be ignored by anyone who wanted to participate in politics." In Mexico the war period had also given rise to caudillos whose power base lay in their ability to mobilize people. The militia, based on the civil population of the regions and primarily charged with maintenance of internal order, constituted a means of social advancement and of creating a clientele for aspiring individuals of modest social origin.[66]

In addition, there was then in Mexico a genuinely free popular press, characterized by regular periodicals speaking for all major political persuasions, and not merely limited to Mexico City but occurring on a wide scale throughout the country.[67] There was also a massive output of pamphlets, dating from the struggle for independence and continuing thereafter for many decades. There can be little doubt about the accuracy of Guerra's contention that the mass press was the major diffuser of modernity in Mexico after 1810.[68] The production of pamphlets reached its peak in the early 1820s, and because the cost of printing a pamphlet was small compared to the cost of producing a regular periodical, those who aspired to political influence found pamphlets an accessible medium for expressing their views. Costeloe, for example, argues that "above all, independence brought freedom of the press, and polemical journalism became one of the most decisive factors in political life."[69]

It is possible to debate how extensive the influence of the mass press was in this period given that Mexico in the 1820s had a level of literacy estimated to be as low as 1 percent of the total population.[70] Even so, the mass press was the most effective means yet found of reaching an expanded audience, and from 1823 to 1830 it was completely unfettered by official controls, though the press itself often voiced complaints about the pressures of partisan groups. Costeloe insists that newspapers "became the main organs of political debate, and they had, or were certainly believed to have, significant influence on public opinion."[71] In a society where political activity revolved around the café and *pulquería*, the *tertulia* (home social gathering) and the Masonic lodge, the impact of the mass press cannot be accurately gauged by the extent of literacy alone because many people would have heard the periodicals read aloud at gatherings and meals. On the other hand, the extremely partisan nature of the press suggests that we cannot assume it accurately reflected "public opinion" on any specific issue. If used with care, the periodicals and pamphlets may provide historians with their most ample original evidence for what contending elements within society in this period thought.[72]

Mexico in 1823 and for the first few years of the federal republic was characterized by a great degree of political mobilization, even if much of it undoubtedly occurred in noninstitutionalized forms such as the pronunciamiento. Perhaps this explains why much of the historiography professes to find this period of Mexican history a time of disintegration; many of the early-nineteenth-century authors did not consider expanded political participation to be a good thing. It is essential to know that such wide participation occurred, however, because it helps account, not only for the frequency with which governments fell in the early republic, but also for the conservative response that set in by 1830. No doubt Mexican popular political participation was characterized by vulnerability to demagoguery and clientelism, but the evidence contradicts those modern historians who have argued that the people played little or no political role in the early decades.

Di Tella concludes that "in the first decades of independence, in the countryside as in the cities, the presence of socially mobilized masses was a central factor in creating the political system of the epoch."[73] The provincial deputation of Jalisco, having polled the municipalities in 1823, was thus able to speak with some authority and only some overstatement when it declared, "There is not a single person in all the state of Jalisco who is not convinced of the advantages of republics united in federation."[74]

The second major phenomenon that merits emphasis is the question of sovereignty of the states. It is what Rabasa calls "the problem of problems, the crucial point of dispute of the two great ideological currents that have sustained our political life and that have, with brief intervals, characterized our constitutional system."[75] To a Canadian, from a country currently debating the meaning and consequences of Quebec's sovereigntist movement, this is a particularly fascinating issue. In Mexico, as in Quebec in the 1980s and 1990s, sovereignty meant supremacy within a specific territorial sphere, autonomous, independent, possessing undisputed ascendancy. It should not be confused with the more frequent twentieth-century use of the word, which refers to national sovereignty, or supremacy on the national level. Opponents of federalism tried, in fact, to confuse the two ideas of sovereignty during debates over the constitution of 1824. The Mexican use of the word in the 1820s is in no way inappropriate, particularly given that, as we have seen, not only one's patria but even one's nación was the city-province where one lived.

When Jalisco led the way in proclaiming itself a "free, independent, and sovereign" state, followed immediately by the others, no implication was intended or implied that Jalisco was sovereign over the Mexican republic. It only meant that Jalisco would be sovereign over Jalisco, Zacatecas over Zacatecas, and so on. In Mexico in 1823 when the states variously proclaimed themselves both "independent" and "sovereign" they meant autonomous, self-governing in all matters within their own borders. Jaime Olveda points out that in 1823 in Jalisco there were some references to the state as a "country," a "new republic," or even as a "nation," but Muría thinks that the use of such terms merely demonstrated an understandable vagueness about federalist categories at such an early date in the process.[76] My interpretation is that the concept of the state or province as a "country" within a greater country is not necessarily inconsistent. Such terminologies, for example, are universally used in late-twentieth-century Quebec where the provincial legislature is called the National Assembly and the provincial premier is called the prime minister.

In general, when the states called themselves "sovereign" the meaning was that each state was independent from each other and from Mexico City in all matters involving internal government, but also that each of them recognized the national sovereignty of the republic, that is, that each surrendered to the republic or endowed the national state with certain powers, primarily to conduct interstate and foreign affairs. The states were, thus, supreme. Indeed, the constitution of 1824 and related legislation recognized that the states were autonomous in taxation and fiscal affairs, that they volunteered a yearly grant of money to the federal government for its expenses, and that the state legislatures elected the federal president and vice president and the members of the federal Supreme Court. Among the American countries, in fact, the closest equivalent to the Mexican constitution of 1824 was perhaps the constitution of the Confederate States of America (the Southern states in the U.S. Civil War).

When considering the objectives of the provinces in 1823, it is important, however, not to confuse the issue of internal and external sovereignty. The principle of restricting provincial sovereignty to internal administration came from the provinces themselves because they fully recognized the impracticality of one state claiming to exercise sovereignty over any other. That Jalisco clearly understood the limits of state sovereignty, for example, is reflected in the wording of its declaration of 16 June—"the State of Jalisco is free, independent, and sovereign within itself"—and in the oath the elected members of its legislature took to recognize "the sovereign and independent State of Jalisco, as one of the federated States of the Mexican Nation." Thus, the concept of state sovereignty was radical, but it was not unlimited.

It is Rabasa's argument, indeed, that the provinces demanded sovereignty because federalism provided the ultimate bulwark against centralized autocracy, whether in the form of a monarchy or a republic. Having already tried two forms of centralized constitutional autocracy—the Spanish constitution of 1812 and Iturbide's moderated monarchy—liberals realized that a much more radical alternative was needed. "Whatever were the evils that the introduction of federalism brought, in all cases, it tended to avoid the greatest evil, the true one: falling into republican absolutism." Miguel Ramos Arizpe, the principal author of the Mexican constitution of 1824, had a long experience as a deputy in the Spanish Cortes, and it had convinced him that the major cause of complaint under Spanish imperial rule was not so much submission to peninsular domination as the fact that Spanish rule had ignored the various provinces of New Spain. Thus, political self-sufficiency for the provinces formed the final defense against the political philosophy of the Old Regime: centralism in the hands of an autocracy. The object of federalism was to "create a linkage among all the entities so that they could protect themselves without the help that the central government would not provide them."[77] In its manifesto of 12 March 1823, the provincial deputation of Guadalajara had defined the province of Nueva Galicia as "a reunion of men who want to be independent, free, and happy, and who will be, despite the efforts of a central aristocracy."[78] Because a centralist republic would be a republican autocracy, the best defense was to shift the balance of power sharply toward regional and local government, thereby guaranteeing political protection to the greatest number of people and, particularly, to peripheral regions. This was a truly revolutionary objective, the value of which is not lessened today, and it explains the peculiarly enduring nature of Mexican federalism despite the many attempts to eliminate it.

Some authors have argued that what Mexico created between 1823 and 1824 was actually more a confederation than a federation. In his *Derecho constitucional mexicano*, however, Felipe Tena Ramírez explains that a confederation is a system in which the member states continue to possess both interior and exterior sovereignty to such an extent that the decisions adopted by the organisms of the confederation do not directly oblige the subjects of the states unless previously accepted and endorsed by the states. In contrast, in a federation the member states give up their exterior sovereignty and certain interior faculties in favor of the central government, but they conserve for their own government the faculties not granted to the central government. Thus, Tena Ramírez reminds us, a major characteristic of federalism is "a division of powers between the general and the regional authorities, each one of which, in its respective sphere, is coordinated with the others and independent of them. . . . Our constitution was based on the supposition that the Mexican federation was born of a pact between preexisting states, which delegated certain faculties to the central power and reserved the rest." He points out, furthermore, that this key ingredient of a division of jurisdiction characterizes federalism "whatever the historical origin of the federation may be, whether it was in a pact of preexisting states or in the adoption of the federal form for a State that was previously centralized."[79] In the federalist revolt of 1823, even the most radical federalist states did not propose that they would take on the responsibility for external defense, foreign affairs, or the foreign debt.

The famous *Pacto Federal de Anáhuac*, written by the future governor of Jalisco, Prisciliano Sánchez, provides perhaps the clearest indication that the radical federalists did not aspire to create a confederation of independent powers. This publication, dated 28 July 1823, is usually described as one of the most influential documents leading to the formulation of the Acta Constitutiva and the constitution of 1824. Although it was one of several proposals circulating in late 1823 about how to construct a federal republic and although it seems to have been in broad outline and terminology the most influential of them, the real point of Sánchez's statement was to explain to central Mexicans what provincial Mexicans wanted in the federalist revolt. The provinces, he said, did not want to be absolutely independent nations; what they wanted was "to remain always integral parts of the great whole of the nation of which they are members, united by the indissoluble link of federation, under a central authority." To those who worried about the threat of possible invasion by an aggressive Holy Alliance of European monarchies, Sánchez countered that the greatest danger was that the provinces would be denied self-government and would thus give in to endless internal rivalry and dispute, which would make the country vulnerable to even a modest foreign invasion. The country would be well defended, he said, when its citizens were certain of their rights and content with the government and laws that guaranteed them. The demand of Guadalajara, Yucatán, Oaxaca, Zacatecas, and the Internal Provinces of the East as well as of Querétaro, Valladolid, Guanajuato, and San Luis Potosí was, quite simply, "to remain united with the fraternal links of a just federation that guarantees them their mutual tranquility and external security." Coining a term that established the future liberal terminology, Sánchez insisted that federalism was a *pact* between equal participants but not a treaty between separate powers. Finally, Sánchez gave perhaps the clearest statement of the federalist view of the dual sovereignty of the nation and the state: "The nation remains one, indivisible, independent, and absolutely sovereign in all senses. . . . Each state is independent of the others in everything concerning its interior government, in which respect it is said to be sovereign in itself."[80]

In November 1823, the military commander of Jalisco, General Anastasio Bustamante, wrote to the military commander of the four neighboring provinces, Miguel Barragán. "Only union can save the Patria," he said. "For me to say 'union' means to say peace, independence, liberty, enlightenment, and ultimately, complete happiness, and according to the present state of things I believe that only the august National Assembly can unite us."[81] This was one of the men Mexico City accused of plotting secession for Jalisco or the restoration of Iturbide.

In the provincialist revolt for federalism in the period from March to September 1823, the dominant image is never one of the abandoned baby chicks of the provinces randomly scratching about the barnyard in search of a substitute mother hen of federation. Neither is it an image of self-serving local caudillos or oligarchs grabbing power where they found it. And, most importantly, it is not an image of the nation or the Congress granting to the provinces a political role either as a gift or as a concession to regional pressure. When historians adopt such imagery or terminology it may sometimes indicate, if even unconsciously, a centralist bias. Quite the contrary, the appropriate image is one of a predominantly civil society in which the several provinces moved toward the construction of a union between them all with judicious forethought and growing resolve, and always in search of the *dual* objectives of provincial autonomy and national unification. Without the pact formed between the provinces there was no nation. Thus, the provinces created the nation, the nation did not create the provinces.

It was a foregone conclusion, however, that the Supreme Executive Power would resist the movement toward state sovereignty that was so clearly stated by Jalisco and Zacatecas. With Nicolás Bravo functioning as the effective head of the executive triumvirate by this point and Lucas Alamán as chief minister, the national government was centralist in orientation and preference. In June 1823, as an initial response to Jalisco, the Supreme Executive Power drafted, but did not publish, a manifesto arguing against the idea of state sovereignty in a federal system. It gives a clear sense of what Mexico City was thinking and what motivated its responses in the face of the federalist revolt. Acknowledging that Jalisco was motivated by patriotism and the desire to assure its citizens their independence and liberty, the government nonetheless suggested that Jalisco could not operate on its own until it received approval from the new Constituent Congress that had just been convoked. "But this pact of union," continued the executive, "is inconceivable on the hypothesis that isolated fractions of the state will be separating themselves before agreeing on the terms under which they are to remain united, joined but at the same time independent in themselves. An arrangement of such interest to all the members of the nation must indisputably come from a common center, and that can be none other than the Congress." Until the new Congress could meet, continued the government, "the Supreme Executive Power will conserve the unity of the provinces." The executive insisted that "its motives are no other than the supreme necessity of conserving the union and the integrity of the provinces so that the legitimately installed Congress can fix the bases of the federation, declare those rights and obligations of the states that are to compose it, and assure by means of good laws the privileges of all citizens." It concluded, "the slightest deviation from this path will visibly compromise the existence of the Nation itself," laying it open to conquest and tyranny. "May the enemies of liberty have no pretext to ridicule our efforts, painting us as consumed by anarchy. . . . Union and concord must be our device; love of the Patria our dominant passion, and the exercise of public virtue the invulnerable shield of our rights."[82]

Though this particular statement was not published, probably because it expressed much too frankly what the executive's strategy was, none of the states opting for federalism in the summer of 1823 could have been under any illusion about how Mexico City would respond to their demand for self-determination. The Supreme Executive Power was suggesting, of course, that it was not the provinces that were to be the creators of the republic but rather the center, that the future Congress would "fix the bases of the federation," thereby preempting the provinces from doing so. The conflict was thus clear: which power would forge the republican nation, the provinces or the central government?

The clearest evidence that the birth of federalism was not simply a power grab by military caudillos is the rejection of Santa Anna's proposed leadership of federalism by the province of San Luis Potosí and its neighbors. When the Plan of Casa Mata swept Veracruz province in February 1823 it superseded the rebellion Santa Anna had launched, essentially bypassing his personal control. In an effort to regain a prominent voice on the national scene, Santa Anna embarked his forces in Veracruz and landed in Tampico. From there he marched to San Luis Potosí, threatening to occupy the provincial capital city. He proclaimed himself the "protector of the federation" and tried to impose himself as leader of the federalist movement. The local authorities, including the provincial deputation, the San Luis Potosí city council, and the new political chief recently chosen by the deputation, resoundingly rejected Santa Anna's pretension to command them. When the authorities met in late May to consider how they would respond to Guadalajara's call for a federal republic, Santa Anna insisted he was ready to protect the province with his division. At the same time, San Luis Potosí planned to join the conference called at Celaya, where the four north-central provinces, Michoacán, Querétaro, Guanajuato, and San Luis Potosí, would discuss their response to the proposal for federalism. On 5 June Santa Anna issued a proclamation creating a military leadership of the federalist cause, guaranteeing that his forces would protect Guadalajara and any other province attempting to become self-governing. He attempted, in other words, to co-opt the movement, the first of many examples in his long career where he placed himself at the head of a generalized movement so it would become an instrument of his advancement.

When Santa Anna called upon the garrison of San Luis Potosí to join him, however, the entire garrison refused, declaring it would resist any aggression on Santa Anna's part. Meanwhile, the central government dispatched an army under the command of Brigadier Gabriel de Armijo to foil Santa Anna's efforts. When Santa Anna requested the support of the provincial deputation and city council on 19 June, they requested that he leave the province. The provincial deputation attempted to mediate between Armijo and Santa Anna, but when Santa Anna refused the mediation and occupied the city, the provincial deputation fled. When the four provinces began their Celaya meeting on 1 July, agreeing to recognize Miguel Barragán as commander-in-chief of the troops of the four provinces, Santa Anna had no choice but to withdraw. On 10 July he did, claiming to the central government that his duty was done once the four provinces arrived at a joint plan of action to attain federalism. The four provinces of Michoacán, Querétaro, Guanajuato, and San Luis Potosí met a second time in Celaya on 10 July, where in order to restore political order they agreed to recognize the Supreme Executive Power in Mexico City but also to approve the establishment of a federal republic.[83]

Clearly, in this his second attempt to become a dominant force in national affairs, Santa Anna had made two critical mistakes that he would not repeat in subsequent ventures. He had left his home base in Veracruz province and had attempted to have as his field of action a province where he possessed neither a following nor any prior experience, and he had attempted to use military force to interfere in an undertaking that was already well advanced as a predominantly civil process and that had rejected militarization. His moment had not yet arrived. More important, the failure of Santa Anna in San Luis Potosí meant that the federalist revolts remained civilian and did not fall under the arbitrary direction of a willful and erratic officer.

The critical moment for the federalist cause, however, came in July when the central government decided to send an army to subdue the most outspoken and radical of the federalist provinces, Jalisco. Four things motivated Mexico City to adopt an aggressive policy toward the self-proclaimed state of Jalisco in an open challenge to the federalist movement, something the central government had attempted to disguise when it dispatched military force against Santa Anna in San Luis Potosí. The first cause was that Jalisco, soon supported by Zacatecas, had declared actual freedom from the center in specific terms, declaring that it would not obey Congress and refusing to remit funds to Mexico City. The second cause was Jalisco's refusal to implement the congressional law of 17 June, which called not only for new congressional elections but also for new elections for provincial deputations. Jalisco, seconded by Zacatecas, considered the electoral law an undue interference in its internal affairs and refused to replace the provincial deputation that had the population's confidence. A third cause was the fear of many in Mexico City that Guadalajara's two leading generals, Luis Quintanar and his second in command, Anastasio Bustamante—both of whom had been close to Iturbide during the empire—were engaged in secret efforts to restore Iturbide to power. The charge of Iturbidism aimed at Jalisco's leaders may have been nothing but an unfounded notion disseminated by the central government because of Guadalajara's refusal to recognize and obey it, but it is repeated by almost all subsequent historians. The fourth reason for sending a national army to Guadalajara, as Rodríguez has pointed out, was the extent to which Guadalajara threatened to emerge "as an alternative national center to Mexico City."[84] In June and July 1823, Guadalajara seemed not only ready but able to become the new national capital of a federal republic, if it did not, indeed, become the center of a rival union.

Disguising its intention to invade Jalisco, the central government ordered an army of two thousand men under the command of Generals Bravo and Negrete (two members of the triumvirate of the Supreme Executive Power) to aid Armijo in San Luis Potosí. Departing on 5 July, before Jalisco had formally proclaimed statehood, the army had secret orders to move toward Jalisco. Bravo, who was universally considered a man of honor because of his humane treatment of royalist prisoners during the wars of independence, was then emerging as perhaps the most distinguished military advocate of a central republic. He issued a public statement declaring that his intention was to go to the provinces that were in turmoil, "not to attack them as enemies, but to persuade them . . . like brothers." Guadalajara and Zacatecas mobilized their militia forces, making it clear they were prepared to defend their sovereignty. At a moment of great tension, the centralists became aware of how strong the support for provincial sovereignty had become. In Congress there were alarmed calls, led by deputies from Guadalajara and Zacatecas, to avoid civil war. It became clear that the conflict could be ended only by war or by compromise on the part of the national government.[85] Thus, Bravo halted his advance on 18 July, and both sides agreed to confer at the town of Lagos in Jalisco.

The talks at Lagos between commissioners of Bravo on the one hand and Quintanar and commissioners of Jalisco and Zacatecas on the other began on 8 August 1823 and ended on 18 August. The states insisted that, though they recognized the supreme government and Congress in Mexico City "as the center of union of all the States of Anáhuac," they possessed sovereignty in all matters internal to their states. Bravo, insisting that the two states could not dictate terms to the new Congress, whose members were about to be elected, argued that the future Congress would possess the authority to limit the powers of the states. The two states, however, were able to declare that they would recognize the Congress and Supreme Executive Power as long as they did not oppose the creation of a federal republic. Bravo did not have the power to agree to a treaty in the name of the central government (even though Jalisco historians nearly always report the outcome of the talks as if they had resulted in a treaty), but the discussions at Lagos were reported to the national Congress, which in turn authorized the government to settle the dispute with Guadalajara.[86] Rather than withdrawing its troops from Jalisco, the central government sent another division to the south of the state.[87] The real point of the Lagos talks is that it now became clear that the central government could not govern without consent of the states and that the two states of Jalisco and Zacatecas were willing to concede national authority to the central government as long as it did not prevent the creation of a federal republic.

Although the Lagos conference produced no clear settlement, it nonetheless marks the moment that federalism became victorious. That is, on the one hand, the conference induced Congress on 16 August to authorize the executive to negotiate a settlement that included amnesty for the rebellious provinces, and, on the other hand, it crystallized for the provinces, through the stance taken by Guadalajara and Zacatecas, the central issue of the nature of provincial sovereignty.

But before the Lagos meetings were terminated, the central government succeeded in striking Jalisco with one major blow. In collaboration with the military commander of Colima, Anastasio Brizuela, who had been sent out in June to help organize the separation of the partido of Colima from the state of Jalisco, Bravo accepted the decision of the city council and residents of Colima on 20 June to remove their district from the jurisdiction of Jalisco. Deeply hurt by what he saw as a betrayal, Quintanar wrote Brizuela on 2 July, "Guadalajara does not need Colima to form its State," and his government declared that, in keeping with its liberal principles, it recognized the right of Colima to separate.[88] Although Colima had requested to join the state of Michoacán, in July Michoacán refused to accept it, having promised in the Celaya meetings to preserve the territorial integrity of all the provinces.[89] Over the loud protests of the state congress of Jalisco, the Supreme Executive Power authorized the separation of Colima on 12 August, provisionally converting it into a territory directly administered by the central government. With the separation of Colima, Jalisco lost not only about a quarter of its Pacific coastline but also the growing port of Manzanillo. Bravo also communicated with the military commander of Tepic, urging him to oppose the federalist objectives of Quintanar and Jalisco, but in this case did not receive a favorable response. Soon after, Negrete attempted to maneuver the separation of the partido of Zapotlán el Grande from Jalisco, but Quintanar's dispatch of a military force under Anastasio Bustamante in October prevented that region from being separated.[90]

The attempts to whittle down the size of Jalisco's territory do not suggest, to say the least, good faith on the part of the central government. Because Alamán, as minister of Internal and External Affairs, had as his prime responsibility the management of the central government's relations with the provinces, he emerged as the most active and talented opponent of federalism. Given the disorganization among conservative sectors that then prevailed, Alamán was perhaps the most skilled of the conservative antifederalists, but Bravo was emerging as the public figure at the head of centralism (though his political acumen would turn out to be distinctly limited).

At about the same time, the central government had also launched a military intervention against the federalist government of Oaxaca. Under the leadership of the provincial commandant, Antonio de León, Oaxaca had declared itself a free and sovereign state on 1 June 1823, created a provisional governing junta that served as its executive power until December, installed its provincial congress on 6 July, and issued the *Bases Provisionales* of its statehood on 28 July. The *Bases* declared that Oaxaca would recognize with Mexico only "relations of Fraternity, Friendship, and Confederation" and would recognize the Supreme Executive Power and Congress in Mexico City only in order to convoke a new Congress. As a result, in June Mexico City ordered General Manuel Rincón to march from Tehuacán to Oaxaca to force the province to submit and also ordered General Vicente Filisola, recently returned from Guatemala, to aid Rincón.[91] Carlos María de Bustamante, a congressional deputy for Oaxaca but a central-ist, scoffed that Oaxaca was "delirious, and the same prudence was neces-sary to deal with it as would be used to deal with a crazy person, a child."[92] Bustamante's older brother, Manuel, was a member of the Provisional Governing Junta in Oaxaca and a strong supporter of federalism. Part of the clergy in Oaxaca refused to endorse federalism. Meanwhile, part of Tehuantepec rose up to resist the state government, installing a provi-sional government on 15 August and requesting assistance from Mexico City. Nonetheless, León, with a force of about a thousand men, moved to close the road to Oaxaca to the advancing forces of General Rincón. With a far superior force, Rincón, in what would become the usual format, of-fered to negotiate with the sovereigntists. Representatives of both armies met on 21 September at El Carrizal, where they agreed that Oaxaca would submit to the newly convoked Constituent Congress and await its deter-minations on the creation of a federal system. León's forces were incorpo-rated into Rincón's, which meant León was, at least for a while, separated from military command of Oaxaca.[93] In October the Congress decreed the establishment of a separate province of the Isthmus, made up of the ju-risdictions of Acayucan and Tehuantepec, but by the time the Acta Con-stitutiva was completed this idea had been dropped.[94]

Nor were these the only examples of the attempt by the center to re-press federalism or to punish those provinces that pursued radical federal-ism. On 3 September 1823 the Congress passed an act authorizing the gov-ernment to transfer the partido of Isla de Términos (Isla del Carmen) from Yucatán to Tabasco, and the Supreme Executive Power immediately made the transfer. Isla de Términos, source of Yucatán's major export, logwood, was at the time the richest region of Yucatán. Manuel Crecencio Rejón, a deputy for Yucatán, argued that the intention of the transfer was to muti-late his state for having embraced the cause of federalism. When the sec-ond Constituent Congress came to power, however—and with a re-markably skilled group of Yucatán deputies, including Rejón, Lorenzo de Zavala, and José María Alpuche—Yucatán's pleas were answered. At the request of the Yucatán deputies, the phrase "The Laguna de Términos be-longs to Yucatán" was added to Article 7 (the article that specified which states existed) of the Acta Constitutiva. Although some deputies pro-tested that the deputy for Tabasco was not yet present, Congress accepted the phrase on the last day of debate on the Acta.[95]

One thing was clear: the country had rejected the right of the restored Constituent Congress to form the republic without consulting the aspira-tions of the regions. The revolt of the provinces made it unavoidable that a new constituent congress would be convoked. The electoral law for the election was issued on 17 June, and on 31 October 1823 the second Constituent Congress was seated. Bocanegra wrote that by giving in to the provincial rebellions and agreeing to call a new Constituent Congress the first Congress committed suicide and declared itself unworthy of the confidence of its constituents and the great struggle it had waged against Iturbide.[96]

David M. Quinlan has shown some of the characteristics of the 144 identified deputies and alternates who made up the new Congress. Not all of them were active. For example, the Acta Constitutiva was signed by 107 deputies whereas the constitution was signed by 98. The deputies' mean age was 40.9. By background or education, the largest group of the deputies were lawyers (39.1 percent), 29.8 percent were clerics, 16.9 percent were military officers, and 12.5 percent were *hacendados*. Quinlan found that two-thirds of the deputies had previously held elected public office in the Spanish Cortes or Mexican Congress or in provincial deputations and ayuntamientos, and 35 of them had been members of the first Constituent Congress. Approximately 70 percent of the deputies favored federalism in one form or another—there were a variety of formats the federal republic could take.[97]

Though it was only five months after the abdication of Iturbide and fourteen months before completion of the federal constitution of 1824 federalism had effectively won. When it proclaimed the federal constitution on 4 October 1824, the second Constituent Congress declared simply, "the fact is that, once the State was dissolved with the fall of [Iturbide], nothing could contain the cry of the provinces."[98]

CHAPTER FIVE

Moderated Federalism

The clash of views that existed by late 1823 between the supporters of a dominant central state and the supporters of provincial autonomy remains the perennial point of contention in Mexican national life. By the middle of 1823, Chiapas, Oaxaca, Yucatán, Querétaro, San Luis Potosí, Michoacán, Guanajuato, Zacatecas, Coahuila, and, most clearly, Jalisco, as well as the five provinces of Central America, had all proclaimed themselves either sovereign or at least self-governing. At least fifteen of the twenty-eight provinces that had made up the Iturbide monarchy—or, to put it another way, at least ten of the nineteen states that made up the United Mexican States—had broken away from the control of Mexico City. For the traditionally dominant elites in the capital, no greater threat could be imagined. The central power was not strong enough to suppress federalism, to eliminate it utterly. What response, then, could it make? Centralists decided, in effect, to let the provinces have federalism because it could not be prevented in any case but to make certain that it was a federalism that was modified and interpreted by the center. The center's strategy was to subject the federalist concept to a governmental interpretation, to take it out of the hands of the autonomous states and centralize it. It was a plan of assault that was so subtle that many participants at the time, and many historians subsequently, failed to notice it.

As it swirled back and forth, the political debate over the formation of the new nation encompassed many strands of thought, but overall there was one very stark reality, summarized by one of the few historians to note it, Brian R. Hamnett:

> The reply of the central power to the federal movement was "intervention" against the free and sovereign states by means of the

armed forces, which could count on the help of the military officers opposed to the ambitions of the provincial commandants. In fact, blood did not flow in rivers: but the federal concept was subjected to a governmental interpretation. The central power despoiled the free states of their aspiration to be effectively sovereign entities. . . . As a result of these interventions, the radicalism of 1823 ceded to the compromise accepted by the central power: a moderated federalism, encapsulated in the Acta Constitutiva of 31 January 1824, and expressed in the first Federal Constitution in October. Both documents delimited the sovereignty of the states to internal matters.[1]

I would amend Hamnett's interpretation only in two slight respects. First, the intervention of the centralists was not only in the form of military attacks on the leading provinces that supported radical federalism, it also occurred in the civilian political forum of the second Constituent Congress, which had begun meeting on 31 October 1823 with the primary task of writing the constitution. Second, as we have seen, the most radical federalist states never opposed the principle that state sovereignty related exclusively to internal administration. The victory of the centralists was not so much in their imposing the principle that state sovereignty was internal, because the states themselves accepted that, but in their watering down of the concept of the sovereignty of the states and their frequent ability to intervene in the internal affairs of the states.

From the perspective of many members of the new Constituent Congress, the country presented a scene of widespread political decomposition. The province of Nueva Galicia had proclaimed since June that it was a free and sovereign state, and its own constituent congress began meeting well before the general Congress in Mexico City. Other self-proclaimed states existed in Zacatecas, Yucatán, and Oaxaca. In the center of the country, the intention of Michoacán, Querétaro, Guanajuato, and San Luis Potosí to form a coalition was on hold only because of the military threat from the central government. José Joaquín Herrera, named to replace Luis Quintanar in Guadalajara, had been prevented from entering Jalisco. Nicolás Bravo's forces had been unable to force Jalisco and Zacatecas to give up their demand for sovereignty at the conferences in Lagos. In the north, Felipe de la Garza was leading a federalist movement in the eastern internal provinces. In the south, the Central American provinces were breaking away to form their own republic or to pursue their own path, in the case of Chiapas. The central government's only real achievement against the regions had been the successful intrigue to separate Colima from Jalisco.[2]

One of the first acts of the new Congress when it began its regular sessions in November was to select a committee to propose a constitution. Miguel Ramos Arizpe, chairman of the committee, is usually said to have been the dominant member of the committee, but members of the national cabinet frequently attended the meetings as well. In only fifteen days, on 20 November 1823, the committee read to Congress its projected Acta Constitutiva, or constitutive act. Composed (in its final form) of thirty-six articles, the Acta Constitutiva, formally proclaimed on 31 January 1824, was the fundamental founding legislation of the first federal republic.

José Barragán has argued that Alamán and the other centralists who represented the cabinet and the Supreme Executive Power as well as the centralist deputies in Congress, particularly from the provinces of Mexico and Puebla, played a disproportionate role in formulating the Acta Constitutiva. He points out that the terms of reference of the committee, as expressed in the Preliminary Discourse and the first eight articles of the Acta (which were the most fundamental ones), appeared to have ignored or sidestepped "the phenomenon of the moment . . . the phenomenon of . . . the autonomist and sovereign movement of many of the provinces."[3] In other words, it was in Congress during its debates over the Acta Constitutiva and later over the constitution that the principle of sovereignty of the states was moderated, or watered down, to the point that it gave equal or perhaps greater weight to the principle of national sovereignty. This process was accompanied by the central government's extensive use of military force throughout late 1823 and early 1824, particularly against Jalisco and Puebla.

Debates over the most basic of all issues, sovereignty, brought about a clear division in Congress. Barragán states there were three schools of thought: those who believed sovereignty was one and indivisible "and that it resided essentially in the Mexican nation and not in the states"; those who believed the states were primarily sovereign, "that sovereignty is one and indivisible, but that it corresponds exclusively to each one of the states"; and those who believed sovereignty was shared, those in other words who were "in favor of the federation and at the same time in favor of the states."[4] Basing his assessments on a quantification of congressional voting, David M. Quinlan sees those same three schools of thought and adds a fourth, if relatively weaker, group: deputies who opposed both the federal form of government and a strong national government.[5]

That the central government in Mexico City did not let the victory of federalism stand uncontested was indicated by a statement issued on 31 October 1823 by the Jalisco state congress, which constituted "a formal and energetic protest of the central government's subversive action against the federalist movement."[6] Though overstated in regard to some specifics, Jalisco's indictment of the central government was impressive. It accused the government of the Supreme Executive Power despite declaring its adherence to the consensus in favor of federalism of opposing the implementation of state sovereignty at every opportunity. It charged that the central government had intervened in the first Congress's discussions on the convocation of the new Congress, that it had intervened in some of the provinces in an attempt to install new provincial deputations that would oppose federalism, and that it had intervened politically in the Celaya meetings in an attempt to prevent Querétaro, Michoacán, Guanajuato, and San Luis Potosí from forming the state governments they wanted to form. Moreover, Jalisco also accused the central government of sending troops against Oaxaca and Zacatecas when they declared their intention of creating their own governments and sending an army against Jalisco, meanwhile separating it from Colima. Finally, it charged that the central government had failed to fulfill the agreement at Lagos to withdraw troops from Jalisco and had arranged for Colima to name its own deputy to the new Congress even though Jalisco did not recognize the breakaway partido's right to have its own deputy and despite the fact that Colima had only twenty-six thousand inhabitants. The state congress insisted that the national consensus that now prevailed was for "federation or death" and that the objective of Jalisco and the other states was the creation of a federal republican form of government "in which each state is sovereign and independent in everything respecting its interior government, reserving to the congress and government of Mexico, as the center of union of all of them, decisions on subjects that lead only to the general well-being of the nation." It concluded resoundingly, "Jalisco does not want to be independent."

When the new Constituent Congress received the draft wording of the Acta Constitutiva in November, it was clear that it proposed a compromise between the opposing theories of exclusive state sovereignty and exclusive national sovereignty. The three fundamental articles of the Acta Constitutiva declared the following:

Article 3. Sovereignty resides radically and essentially in the nation, and to it exclusively belongs the right to adopt and establish, by means of its representatives, the form of government and other fundamental laws.

Article 5. The nation adopts for its government the form of a representative, popular, federal republic.

Article 6. Its integral parts are independent, free, and sovereign states in that which exclusively concerns their interior administration and government.[7]

This compromise reflects the resurgent influence of the center. Barragán points out, for example, that in the votes on the most critical clauses of the Acta Constitutiva in December 1823, the two central provinces of Mexico and Puebla were disproportionately represented because it was easier for their deputies to be present owing to their physical proximity to Mexico City. In the key voting in December, for example, there were 29 deputies from Mexico and Puebla states, 6 from Jalisco, 5 from Guanajuato, 2 from Zacatecas, and 2 from Yucatán. Thus, the radical federalist states were not as yet fully represented. This meant that the "unionists," those who favored a strong union and who opposed full state sovereignty, had substantial influence.[8] Quinlan confirms that at first the antifederalists played a disproportionate role, although their initial advantage faded as more deputies from the provinces arrived.[9] However, among the 107 congressional members who signed the Acta Constitutiva, 39 of them, nearly 36 percent, were from Mexico and Puebla alone. When all the deputies to Congress took their seats, Mexico had 21 members and Puebla had 17; the next largest contingents were Jalisco and Oaxaca with 9 each.[10] It was in the early moments of the new Congress, during the first six weeks of working sessions, that Articles 3, 5, and 6 were debated and passed.

Although Articles 5 and 6 of the draft Acta Constitutiva established a federal republic, Article 3 denied the full exercise of state sovereignty that Jalisco and others demanded. And although the Spanish constitution of 1812 had declared that sovereignty resided "essentially" in the nation, it was José Miguel Guridi y Alcocer, the deputy for Tlaxcala and like Ramos Arizpe a participant in the writing of the Spanish constitution, who inserted the word *radically* into Article 3. He explained that he believed that sovereignty resided radically in the nation, by which he meant that it was inalienable and imprescriptible and that the nation conserved the roots of sovereignty even when it did not have the exercise of it.[11] Article 3 also declared that the right to adopt and establish the form of government belonged exclusively to the nation. This meant that neither the Acta Constitutiva nor the constitution would be referred to the states for their approval. They would be adopted by the national Congress alone and, unlike the United States, where two-thirds of the states had to accept the Constitution before it was adopted, the Acta Constitutiva and the constitution would be in effect as soon as Congress approved them. This was the essence of the compromise, for in order to have federalism the radical states had to settle for something less than full state sovereignty.

In this development, the thinking of Servando Teresa de Mier was fundamental. He argued that Mexico needed a "very compact" union, a union in which the balance of political weight was on the side of the national over the provincial. It was Mier's argument that the deputies in the new federal Congress were not to represent their home state, but that, in keeping with the theoretical definition that the Cortes of Cádiz had established, they were to speak as representatives of the nation. The Mier argument, which was what Barragán calls the "classic Hispanic, Cádiz notion of traditional sovereignty," was that sovereignty was one and indivisible, that it resided essentially in the nation, and that it was exercised by delegation to the federal Congress and the state congresses in their function as representatives of the nation. The insistence of the provincial congresses of Jalisco, Oaxaca, and Yucatán that the deputies from those provinces could only act as representatives of their home province in the national congress—virtually as diplomatic agents whose ability to vote depended on direct prior instructions from their state legislatures—was rejected by the committee that drafted the Acta Constitutiva. Similarly rejected was a proposal that Jalisco and San Luis Potosí made, that each state should have only one vote in the federal Congress, an idea that would have guaranteed the absolute equality of each state regardless of size or population but that would have meant a profound weakening of the heavily populated center.

After several days of general discussion, it was determined that the Acta Constitutiva should be debated and voted on article by article, and those debates occupied the months of December 1823 and January 1824. Together with the debates later in 1824 over the draft constitution, this was the critical process that gave final form to the first federal republic. Among the issues that were directly addressed in the debate over the Acta Constitutiva were the questions of dual sovereignty and whether federalism was the path to unity or disunity. The level of the debate was very high, and reports of the public sessions were published in *El Sol*. The important closed sessions, however, were not published.

Mier's famous statement on Article 5 encapsulated the fears of centralists concerning national unity.[12] It was Mier who made famous the arguments that federalism was a foreign idea imported into Mexico by provincial demagogues who aspired to political power, that it would disunite a country that was formerly united, and that nature had determined that Mexico should be a centralized country. These phrases were not, in fact, original with Mier, each thought had already been expressed in one form or another by other centralist deputies, but it is significant how enduring these ideas have been. Nonetheless, federalists in the second Constituent Congress countered each argument, as have a number of modern historians. Among the latter was Jesús Reyes Heroles who in his sweeping study of Mexican liberalism replied to each of Mier's objections. He pointed out, for example, that the regional demand for federalism was very real and that the provincial deputations were not motivated by demagoguery or mere aspiration for employment. He also noted that Mexico in 1823 was not a united country but that federalism was the only means to unite a previously disparate group of territories. Finally, he pointed out that geography proved that Mexico was not centralized by nature because it was a country that lacked great navigable rivers, flat lands to facilitate communications, or unity of climate and ethnic makeup and language. Reyes Heroles concluded, "Fray Servando threw out . . . opinions that have endured and circulated despite the fact that when they were said they must have sounded false."[13]

Mier identified federalism with the French Jacobinism that he so despised. He averred that the committee that drafted the Acta Constitutiva had "condescended too much to the anarchical principles of the Jacobins, the supposed general numerical will . . . of the provinces, and the ambition of their demagogues" and that "the federation has converted our provinces into leagues of powers." In his references to Jalisco and the other federalist provinces, Mier was nothing short of dismissive. He raised again the rumor that Jalisco was controlled by secret Iturbidists, keeping open the door for a later invasion of Jalisco. He declared that the provinces lacked sufficient numbers of educated leaders to be self-governing. He scoffed at the argument of the congressional deputies from Oaxaca and Jalisco that they were representatives or plenipotentiaries of sovereign provinces and bound by their pledge not to exceed the authority their home legislatures had granted them. "There are four dissident provinces," he declared in chilling terms, referring to Jalisco, Zacatecas, Oaxaca, and Yucatán (which together accounted for 30 percent of the national population), "and if they want to separate, let them separate, a small evil and a little lawsuit." He continued, "We need union and the federation tends to division; we need force and every federation is weak by its nature." And Mier had powerful words of dismissal for the common people: "This numerical general will of the people . . . with which the poor politicians of the provinces are pounding our heads, is nothing but the rank, worm-eaten, detested principle with which the Jacobins lost France. . . . How many great, wise, and excellent men expired on the guillotine raised by the French people, after having been their chiefs and their idols?" Mier reiterated his call for a republic along the lines of his earlier proposed constitution, which he admitted had projected "a government federal in name and central in reality." He rejected the principle that the states were sovereign and independent.

Barragán argues that Mier was incorrect in alleging that Jacobinism lay behind the self-proclaimed status of Jalisco, Zacatecas, Oaxaca, and Yucatán as free and sovereign states in that their reasons for taking such an action were well known. As Jalisco had explained, they were based on their view that with the fall of the Iturbide empire the state had ceased to exist, the country had reverted to a state of nature, and the state had to be constructed anew.[14] The radical federalists believed, indeed, that the contractual origin of the federation was the basis for constituting the nation, that the states came first and the federalist pact—that is, the Acta Constitutiva and the constitution still to be written—came second. Their argument, as several deputies put it, was that the constitution would be nothing more than "the pact in which the sovereign states express by means of their representatives the rights that they cede to the confederation for its general well-being and those that each one reserves to itself."[15] Valentín Gómez Farías, exhibiting considerable historical insight, urged the Congress to recognize the reality that "the provinces are separated and going to unite, and not the contrary, because lacking a fundamental pact there is certainly no such union."[16]

The idea that nationhood was a pact arrived at between the various constitutive parts alerts us to the essence of the federalist view of Mexican nationhood in the early decades of the nineteenth century, the view that prevailed in the long run: that the crisis of the Spanish Empire in 1808 had terminated the essential social compact of the Hispanic world, the contract that existed between the king and his subjects, which in turn had necessitated that each country should arrive at a new social compact for its governance. When the existing state disintegrated, sovereignty reverted in a state of nature to the corporate bodies that represented the people, and they, in turn, reconstituted it by means of a constituent congress. The fundamental path of legitimacy was manifested by the "pactedness" of the "constituted nation." This is why, for example, after the Plan of Casa Mata the province of Jalisco was so precise about its argument that the end of Iturbide's empire had been a return to the state of nature, that the new nationhood created thereafter must be the work of a constituent congress representing the provinces, that the provinces spoke for the ayuntamientos, and that the ayuntamientos spoke for the people. This is the concept of contractual sovereignty rooted in the exercise of power by intermediate bodies. Nationhood was a pact, and it possessed the fullest legitimacy precisely because it was a pact. This is why, according to Annino, most major pronunciamientos in Mexico during the nineteenth century would call for the establishment not of a new government but of a new representative constituent congress in order to write a new constitution. This was the source of legitimacy.[17]

Although the federalists of 1823 thought they had settled the issue of the origin of nationhood once and for all, there was a dissenting view of the origin of nationhood and legitimacy. It was formulated chiefly by the thought of Lucas Alamán, and it took on greater influence in later years whenever Mexicans became disenchanted with the instability of the federal republic. This dissenting view held that the nation was the product of the Spanish Conquest, the joining of Hispanic and Mesoamerican cultures under the dominance of the Hispanic one and its creole heirs. The nation was primordial, not pacted; rather more divinely than humanly sanctioned; and rather more mystical than political. This is the concept of national sovereignty that, like Bolivarian thought, denied the existence of the sovereignty of the intermediate bodies.[18] This view, which in the Mexican context was generally conservative and centralist, at least in the nineteenth century, so easily corresponded to the ideas of romantic nationalism and race that arose in Europe in the later nineteenth century that it would enjoy periods of dominance, particularly during the Porfiriato.[19] The contest of these two opposing views still drives much of Mexico's political thought.

The response of Jalisco to the draft Acta Constitutiva illustrates how far it fell short of fulfilling the objectives of the most radical federalist states. Although it endorsed what it saw as the two chief principles of the

Acta, sovereignty of the states and its refusal to delegate to the supreme powers of the nation any greater faculties than were absolutely necessary to uphold the federation, Jalisco's state congress pointed to a number of articles that it believed would destroy those two fundamental principles. Most important, Jalisco still insisted as it had all along that each state, regardless of how many deputies it had in the general Congress, should have only one vote. In all other issues Jalisco held out for the states' freedom of action—including their right to approve the future constitution, stringent limits on the ability of the federal legislative and executive branches to interfere in the affairs of the states, and the right of the states to name the commanders of the troops that each would contribute to the national armed forces. It cited the U.S. Articles of Confederation (the first constitution of the United States, which had been replaced by the 1787 constitution) as the model that Mexico should adopt. It concluded with three major recommendations pointing to significant future issues: the seat of the new federal government should be located in Querétaro, the future federation should have a president and vice president elected by the states, and the patronage over the church, previously exercised by the king of Spain, should now be exercised by each state within its own territory.[20]

The final vote to approve the word *federal* in Article 5 passed by a margin of seventy-two to ten. However, the vote on Article 6—declaring the states free, sovereign, and independent—produced greater division. In order to get it passed, its supporters brought Article 6 to the vote in two parts. The first part of the clause—establishing that the states were "free and independent" to manage their own affairs—passed sixty-two to seven; the second part—that the states were "sovereign"—passed with forty-one in favor and twenty-eight against, with Mier and his proponents of national sovereignty joining the centralists in the vote against.[21]

It is important to note, as Barragán points out, that even some of those who supported state sovereignty did not agree precisely over which sovereignty—state or national—was to be supreme. Some argued that the states were sovereign entirely in their own right and had ceded some degree of sovereignty to the collective whole; others believed that the nation and the states shared a dual sovereignty.[22] Based on his statistical analysis of voting patterns in the second Constituent Congress, Quinlan concludes that those who favored a federal form of government and a weak national government (the group he dubs "confederals") held the voting majority in the Congress but that those who favored a federal form of government and a strong national government (those he dubs "federals") controlled the committee on the constitution and set the agenda by proposing the draft Acta Constitutiva and the draft constitution. This helps explain why the system adopted was a mixture of both tendencies.[23]

Thus, Barragán concludes that the Constituent Congress ended up adopting "flexible sovereignty" because the center actually dominated in Congress but was forced to make concessions to the states in order to calm the spirits of those who advocated federalism along the lines of Jalisco.[24] Quinlan, similarly, concludes that the Acta Constitutiva and constitution of 1824 were "a mixture of confederal and federal." And he argues that, after the constitution was adopted, the high level of political struggle in the Constituent Congress between centralists and federalists indicated that neither side was entirely happy with the outcome, in that each struggled to shift the balance of power that had been struck in the founding enactments. He found that the level of conflict in the Congress was very high, greater than in the Constitutional Congress of 1856 and 1857, which produced the next great Mexican constitution; that it had actually increased after the constitution was in place; and that the two dominant issues over which the deputies grappled were the conflicts of the center versus the periphery and centralism versus federalism. In short, the great issues at stake in creating a new nation were not laid to rest but continued to be the focus of profound conflict throughout the lifetime of the first federal republic and throughout most of nineteenth-century Mexican history. Indeed, it can be said that the most profound issues a society can face were only beginning to be formulated.

Two other important issues in which we can see tension between federalists and centralists during the debates over the Acta Constitutiva were the issue of whether to create a constituent senate and whether to create a single or plural executive. In the original committee proposal for the legislative branch, it was suggested that the Constituent Congress should also convoke a "constituent senate" composed of two senators named by each state, whose task would be to speak for the states in revising and sanctioning the general constitution. Its role, in other words, would be to act as a voice for the interests of the states in the constitution that was to be written by the proportionally elected Constituent Congress and as a symbol of the autonomy and real sovereignty of the states. When this article was about to be submitted for discussion, however, it was deleted, and no further commentary or explanation exists.[25] Some of the congressional debate over both the Acta Constitutiva and the constitution occurred in closed sessions, which were not reported in the Actas and for which no detailed information was published in the press.[26] The act, as finally adopted, called for the creation of a bicameral ordinary legislative power to be composed of a chamber of deputies, elected on the basis of population, and a senate with each state represented by two senators chosen by the state legislatures, thus retaining as in the U.S. constitution a clear distinction in origin and purpose of the two houses of Congress. But this bicameral legislative power would not exist until after the constitution was written and adopted by the Constituent Congress.

In the Acta Constitutiva, many details were left to be determined by the future constitution. Thus, it was, as Quinlan describes it, "a sketch of a constitution that served as a guarantee of federalism."[27] Perhaps the most important matter left open for later determination by the Congress was whether the executive would be single or plural. Barragán feels that the deputies in Congress did not divide on this issue according to whether they were centralist or federalist but according to a genuine disagreement over whether the efficiency and speed of action of a single executive was to be preferred over the safeguard against tyranny provided by a plural executive. Quinlan, however, shows that by the time Congress turned to discussion of the draft constitution, the issue of a single or plural executive had become a major point of division between centralists and federalists, except that the sides shifted during the debate. In the original proposal of the Acta Constitutiva, a clear choice was made for a single executive: "The federal constitution will deposit . . . the executive power in an individual with the title of President of the Mexican Federation." But in the vote on this article that took place on 2 January 1824 the proposal was rejected. Ramos Arizpe's constitutional committee brought a reformed article to Congress two weeks later, which continued to call for a single executive but added the creation of a Council of Government. This proposal, too, was rejected by those in Congress who favored a collegiate executive.[28] Other proposals for a two-, three-, or four-member executive failed to gain sufficient votes. Unable to decide the issue, the Constituent Congress simply declared that the executive power would be deposited in the individual or individuals to be determined in the constitution, in other words, it tabled the matter for future discussion when it turned to writing the constitution.[29]

When the Acta Constitutiva was promulgated on 31 January 1824 we may say that the decision in favor of creating a federal republic was in place. Yet the extent to which the Acta was a political compromise and how successful the centralists had been in diluting the principle of a federation of fully autonomous states in the name of national unity are indicated by the long preamble that accompanied the Acta, in the form of a statement from Congress to the nation.[30] Emphasizing that the Acta Constitutiva was the culmination of fourteen years of revolution—counted from the Hidalgo uprising in 1810—the preamble was an eloquent argument that the revolution was now terminated, a sweeping call for order. Recapitulating the history of the independence movement, it adopted the view that the early rebellions had led to anarchy. The nation had preferred the more peaceful path of Iguala, but the "hero of Iguala" (Iturbide, whose name was not used) had plotted to subject the people to servitude, with only the first Constituent Congress standing in his way. Congress was thus declared to be the representative of nationhood, and Iturbide's attack on it was "a war to the death against the national representation." This made Congress the expression of the will of the nation, and it was Congress that saved the nation from tyranny. A federalist, of course, would have said it was Casa Mata or the action of the states that saved the nation. In discussing the uprisings and the end of the Iturbide monarchy, the preamble did not mention Casa Mata specifically and made no reference to the initiative of the provinces in the Casa Mata rebellion.

After the tyrant was overthrown, a more mature nation realized "that a central republic could not be established among a people so numerous, spread over such a great extension of land; the Nation thus had to pronounce for federation." The preamble then moved on to insist that the revolution was now terminated and, furthermore, that if the revolution went on it "could only be to precipitate us into dissolution, which would cause the ruin and death of the State." The most astute of "the enemies of our liberty," Congress declared, "cover themselves with the cape of federalism, and say to [the people] that the Acta is very imperfect, demanding the rights of the states." Congress argued that when the state legislatures were fully established they would equalize the balance between central and provincial power, and public opinion would force the central government not to interfere in the internal affairs of the states. "Once the [state] legislatures are established, the hydra of centralism cannot appear." This, of course, directly ignored the fact that fully functioning legislatures already existed in the radical federalist states, and it also staked out the principle that the only legal state legislatures were those the general Congress recognized, a major breach of the principle of self-determination. The Congress made it perfectly clear that the Acta Constitutiva was a balancing act designed largely to prevent one state from achieving dominance over the others. It specifically referred to the evil of uncontrolled local interests, which must, it declared, defer and sacrifice themselves to the public good. "The nation now has a form of government that it asked for . . . and as a result it cannot be attacked without committing a crime; all men who love the patria and liberty should unite under this national standard, and form a compact and homogeneous mass."

In several passages the preamble pleaded for the revolution to stop, urging the people to cease asking for more, to settle for what was now achieved. It was necessary to understand, Congress said, that protecting the Mexican federation would be difficult because the Mexican republic was born from discord. "And it is necessary to be aware that as long as the revolution lasts, not only can the desired guarantees [of legal protection for the person] not be provided, but they will be more frequently violated." "The people are tired of agitations that have produced no good for them." The great object to which all should now turn, said Congress, was to make the promises of the new system actually work, to implement what had been sketched out.

A critical reading of the preamble makes it clear that Congress was trying either to ignore or to co-opt the radicalism of the provinces. In the same way that Mexican conservatives throughout the nineteenth and twentieth centuries have advocated gradualism in order to preempt revolutionary objectives, Congress was literally saying that the revolutionary objectives of 1823 would be achieved but only through gradualism. To put it in the modern idiom, Congress was, in effect, declaring to the provinces, "We agree with your goals, and we will certainly do our best to achieve them, but in the meantime order is the primary need, and you will have to trust us." It was a remarkable example of the appropriation by a more conservative tendency of objectives that radicals thought they had won.

Similarly, the statement of the Supreme Executive Power (then consisting of José Mariano Michelena, Miguel Domínguez, and Vicente Guerrero) that accompanied the Acta Constitutiva repeated the theme, declaring that the Acta "is the work not of one or another particular person, but of the entire Nation. . . . The votes of the states have been fulfilled: we have an Acta Constitutiva; and if we love order, if we want to have a patria, if we long to be a nation, the moment has arrived to make it so. . . . To want to deviate from the tone [of the Acta], or to work in a contrary way, would be to dispute the independence and sovereignty of the Nation." The founding act of sovereignty for the states was thus interpreted in a way that upheld the uniformity of the whole. The Supreme Executive Power, as it did throughout its existence, emphasized the primacy of the sovereignty and dominance of the nation.

The Acta Constitutiva was thus a work of profound anomalies. Even as it created the federal republic for which the states clamored it was not the document that the states themselves would have written. Perhaps most important, although it recognized the existence of certain preexisting states, it also established the power of the central government to create other states and territories that did not yet exist, which was, again, a contradiction of the principle of self-determination. Can a sovereign entity be created by the fiat of another sovereign entity? (During the lifetime of the first federal republic, new states and territories were created. These were the territory of Colima in 1823; the Federal District and the territory of Tlaxcala in November 1824; the separate states of Sonora and Sinaloa, formed out of the state of Occidente in October 1830; and the territory of Aguascalientes in May 1835.)[31] Although it declared the existence of federalism, it gave the greater weight to the union rather than to the states. Nor, as Barragán says, was it written by those provinces and states already preexisting and recognized as such.[32]

The Acta Constitutiva cannot be said to be a full expression of the will of the founding states. Rather, it was an expression of the will of the center. While trying to create a pact of free, independent, and sovereign states it also tried to establish a single center that was declared to represent the nation. It thus reflected the partially developed political thought of its day, and it built in the potential for future conflict between the states and the center. It was a subtly but profoundly flawed document, and the rest of the history of the first federal republic would make those flaws manifest. Although the centralists conceded to the states only as much as they were forced to concede, the federalists, who appeared to have won the war, actually lost the peace.

Even as the Acta Constitutiva was being adopted, and later as the constitution was being debated, the central government did not abandon its policy of military intervention in the states. The late Bourbon era had seen the creation of regionally based military commands as part of the process of modernizing and centralizing the Spanish imperial system. The wars of independence, in turn, left a legacy of a militarized country, laying the foundations for both regional military caudillos and a greatly enhanced military role in national affairs. Iturbide had created provincial general commandancies in order to guarantee his political control of the regions and to assure the defense of the new country from threatened European intervention. On 10 September 1823, Congress reorganized the provincial and regional military commandancies that Iturbide had created, establishing twenty-four regional commandancies, comandantes generales, roughly one for each state and territory.[33]

Since 1762, a variety of military units had been created in Mexico: urban militias, provincial militias, mobile squadrons, semiautonomous frontier commandancies. These forces were grouped into the regular army and the active militia and constituted the standing forces. The overall size of these military units had grown mightily during the struggle for independence. In the period from 1824 to 1829 the official size of the regular forces—those under the command of the central government—was listed at about fifty-nine thousand men, of which twenty-two to twenty-three thousand were in the permanent army and about thirty-six thousand were in the active militia, although among the latter only ten to fifteen thousand were regularly in active service.[34] According to the constitution, when it was completed, this standing army constituted the force that the central government could use on the authority of the executive power and, except in the event of the formal declaration of war, without the consent of Congress. The cities and provinces, meanwhile, had also created militia units, raised and equipped by landowners, miners, merchants, city councils, and major regional interest groups. Some of these units were counted among the active militia, and some of them came to form state and urban militia corps. These were the units that the cities and states considered their own, and they could usually be organized under the command of the state governor.[35]

The existence of armed forces at the command of the central government, of other armed forces at the command of the state governments, and of federal military commanders in every state meant that even at the best of times the military would play a disproportionate role in national affairs. In general, however, it should be emphasized that, as Hamnett has put it, the military was "an aggregation of rival armed bands" and that until the decade of the 1840s the intervention of officers in politics "was not motivated in order to promote the objectives of the army, rather it was determined by the nature of the constitutional conflict among the civilians."[36]

The fact that there was a federal commandant in every state meant that in the provinces the army commandants became the embodiment of the central state. The budgets at their disposal often exceeded those controlled by the state governors. They could function quite separately from the local authorities, whether the governor, the legislature, or the municipal council.[37] The constitution required the consent of Congress to declare war, but it also gave the president the authority "to dispose of the permanent armed forces on sea and land and the active militia, for the interior security and exterior defense of the federation," meaning the federal executive did not require congressional consent to use the armed forces in a situation short of war. Protected by the *fuero militar*, the regular armed forces were free of the danger of legal judgment by civil judicial authorities. Receiving their orders by direct courier from Mexico City, they possessed their own network of communications. Because they were not dependent on the tax base or civil society that existed in their regions of operation, the federal commandants-general and the federal armed presence that they constituted became the fundamental threat to the exercise of provincial sovereignty.

Did the state governors and the framers of the 1824 constitution perceive the commandants-general as an unwarranted federal presence inside the states? There was some recognition of the possibility of danger in a letter the governor of Yucatán sent Congress in July 1824 complaining that Antonio López de Santa Anna, when he arrived to be commandant general of Yucatán, had begun to exercise his authority without presenting his letters of appointment to the governor and without taking an oath to obey the laws of the state. Manuel Crecencio Rejón, deputy from Yucatán, demanded that Santa Anna and all other commandants-general and federal military officers operating in the states be required to recognize "the superior authorities of the states and the laws of their legislatures in everything which did not oppose the legislation of the Union." There was no other way, he said, to prevent federal military officers from attempting to assert their absolute independence from the particular laws of the states in which they served and thereby operating arbitrarily.[38] In 1824 and 1825 the state of Michoacán requested that the federal Congress determine what the relationship between the governors and the military commandants should be.[39]

Clearly, federalists realized that the federal army could exercise an arbitrary power that could nullify state sovereignty. With insight born of his experience as a state governor, Benito Juárez, the mid-nineteenth-century president who was the ultimate symbol of Mexican liberalism, reflected on the first federal republic, "In effect, a commandant-general entrusted with the exclusive control of the army and independent of the local authority completely nullified the sovereignty of the states because their governors lacked sufficient power to implement their policies."[40] As Vázquez put it, the commandancies general became a new way of organizing

space and the poles of power; paradoxical as it may seem, they could operate as centers of centralization under federalism and of decentralization
under centralism.[41] In 1823 and 1824, even as the federalist principle swept
the country and the federal republic was created, some of the fatal flaws
that would bring about the failure of the federal republic were already
evident.

The long-term response of the states to the threat they perceived in the
federal commandants general, however, was to bring pressure on the federal government to allow them to gain state control over militia units
raised in each state. In 1823 a level of militia, called the civic militia (*milicia
cívica*), was authorized under control of the municipalities and states to
operate side by side with the active militia controlled by the general government. The principal purposes of the civic militias were to defend their
homes and towns and to escort prisoners and treasury shipments when
the permanent army was not available. Until 1827 the ayuntamientos were
charged with organizing and maintaining the corps in each locality. The
primary difference between the permanent army/active militia on the one
hand and the civic militia on the other is that in the civic militias the officers were chosen by and from their own participants, thus making them
instruments of local interests. The officers of the civic militias were citizens who commanded other citizens at the behest of the local civil authority; they were independent of the army and the active militias.

It was only in 1827, however, that the civic militias became the bulwark
of state sovereignty when a new regulation was produced that resulted
from the pressure applied by the state governments. The 1827 regulation
declared that the civic militias had the obligation not only to defend their
homes but also to defend national independence, the federal constitution,
and the constitution of their respective states. Each state was authorized
to raise the militia forces it deemed necessary and regulate them in accord
with its interests. The governors were the chief commanders of such
forces. This law permitted the states to fortify themselves and, if necessary,
oppose the orders of the federal government.[42] By 1827, of course, all states
already had significant civic militias, and they were the power base of the
caudillos.

In addition, there is the fundamental problem of the precedent set by
the central government's frequent recourse to the use of force against the
states. In 1823 and 1824, before the constitution was proclaimed and before
Guadalupe Victoria took office as the first president—both of which occurred in October 1824—the center had frequently used military action

against the states. Examples in 1823 alone included the separation of Colima from Jalisco, the attempt to separate Zapotlán el Grande and Tepic from Jalisco, the military expedition against Jalisco in July 1823, and the mission led by General Bravo to Querétaro in December 1823 to protect local Spaniards in response to the demands of the garrison of Querétaro that measures be taken to proscribe European Spaniards. In addition, on 27 September 1823 Congress accomplished something that Iturbide had been prevented from doing by the previous Congress in 1822 when it passed a law declaring that civilians as well as soldiers could be given summary courts-martial. In this case, however, unlike Iturbide's proposal, persons could be court-martialed even before committing a crime against the nation if four witnesses stated that such individuals posed a danger to the established system.

In 1823 and 1824, the Acta Constitutiva and the constitution that would give final existence to a republic of free, independent, and sovereign states was being debated and completed. In this same period, there were further military incursions by the central government that our narrative has not yet touched upon. These included the December 1823 intervention in Puebla; the May 1824 expedition led by Bravo against Jalisco; the forced surrender in August 1824 of Antonio de León, commander of Oaxaca and leader of Oaxaca federalism, for his anti-Spanish campaign in Oaxaca; and an expedition against Tabasco over a dispute there between the commandant and the governor over who should control revenues.

The point of these examples is that it was the center that first used force against various expressions of the political will of individual states, and its purpose was to counteract the unrestricted exercise of state sovereignty, even in matters involving internal administration only. The precedent thus established—that the use of military force, the resort to violence, was an acceptable strategy in the pursuit of political goals—was immensely powerful and harmful. The representatives of provincial demands, particularly the caudillos, would soon adopt the same methods. By 1825, even those federalists at the state level most dedicated to the preservation of civilian power, such as Governors Prisciliano Sánchez of Jalisco and Francisco García of Zacatecas, would consider the creation, supply, and financing of state-controlled militias as among their foremost priorities. Leaders less dedicated to the rule of law in a civil society, such as Santa Anna of Veracruz, found the use of force to be an automatic choice. The symbiotic military/civilian relationship that continued for many decades was becoming self-sustaining.[43]

In addition, the historian needs to be aware of how quickly this precedent was set—during the same period in which federalism appeared to be victorious and the federal constitution was being formulated. If U.S. federalism had been born with the same degree of centralist intervention that existed in Mexico in 1824, it probably would not have been called federalism. Between the time that federalism won the revolt in July 1823 and the federal constitution was completed in October 1824 much of the essence of federalism slipped away.

There was no universal outcry from federalists against the military interventions in Jalisco, Zacatecas, Puebla, Oaxaca, and Tabasco, although future efforts to organize coalitions between various states were motivated by the need to defend state sovereignty from assault by the general government. Perhaps centralist intervention in the affairs of the regions was too much a part of Mexican history, or perhaps the federalists were too stunned at the historically unprecedented victory of the provinces in the achievement of federalism. Perhaps, as we know from a substantial historical literature, federalists themselves could not overcome their preference for order and their fear of the masses. Perhaps federalists were not adequately organized at the national level or were overly absorbed in the mighty task, for which there were no domestic precedents, of creating state governments and state congresses, writing state laws, developing state sources of revenue, and making statehood operational. At any rate, by definition the federalists were the representatives of individual provincial interests and were spread throughout the entire vast territory of the republic, lacking a single leadership, diverted by the priority of local regional needs, and not yet having formulated effective coalitions between the states. It is even possible that many federalists, never having lived under a federalist system, were not entirely convinced of its efficacy, that they adopted a school of thought that promised them greatly increased local power without considering that it would cost constant effort and vigilance.

Lucas Alamán, the chief minister of the central government in 1823 and 1824—in the words of Arturo Arnáiz y Freg, "a Metternich in a land of Indians"—clearly understood that the great weakness of federalism was that it lacked a single guiding hand that could prevent its advocates from dissipating their energies in the pursuit of a myriad of different and often conflicting agendas.[44] Amid their initial disorientation, opponents of federalism gradually learned that it was not necessary to divide in order to rule, that the divisions were ancient, while the union was new and untested. Alamán was not opposed to all forms of administrative decentralization because it was clearly more efficient for purely local issues to be handled by local authorities. However, he was convinced that only juridical and political centralization would guarantee national unity. Alamán's preferred form of national organization would be, as he wrote, "a central republic with a certain amplitude of faculties in the provinces, which would themselves be divided into smaller territories, in order to be able to deal with local issues without the inconveniences of the states being sovereign."[45]

The operative principle of Alamán's political activity in these early moments of his thirty years as the "soul," as Hale called him, of nineteenth-century Mexican conservatism, was to prevent the formation of coalitions between the states that might have been powerful enough to impose their will on the central government.[46] Thus, on 10 January 1824 he made an initial effort to limit political coalitions between the states by issuing a decree prohibiting the spontaneous formation of "all juntas or reunions of whatever kind that are not authorized by law" and prohibiting any corporation or authority from taking decisions that were outside its respective faculties.[47]

Even as the Constituent Congress was in the final weeks of debating the Acta Constitutiva, the clearest indication that the central government had not abandoned its traditional assumption of the right to dominate the states was the military intervention in Puebla. The city and province of Puebla was controlled by General José Antonio Echávarri, who had remained as the commandant of Puebla after Casa Mata. It had pursued a distinctly nonradical course during the period of the provincial rebellions in 1823. Although the Puebla provincial deputation had received in June and July the decrees of Oaxaca, Santa Anna in San Luis Potosí, and Jalisco declaring themselves free of the rule of the center and urging creation of a federal republic, it did not act decisively to declare federalism until December. This was six months after the more radical provinces had done so and after the congressional approval of Article 5 of the Acta Constitutiva, which declared the representative, popular, federal republic. The provincial deputation of Puebla, which shortly before had been renovated by the election of new members, called a general junta of all the authorities of the province to discuss whether to implement Article 5. On 23 December 1823 at this meeting, Puebla's jefe político, provincial deputation, ayuntamiento, and civil, military, and religious authorities heard of the congressional passage of Article 6 of the Acta Constitutiva recognizing the sovereignty of the states. They therefore decided to put Articles 5 and 6 into effect and proceeded to declare the provincial deputation as the state congress (to which each partido would also send a deputy) and to choose a three-man provisional executive.

Aware that this was a revolution, but also that it was by no means the first province to make this "difficult but necessary change," Puebla's new executive declared, "Fortunately Puebla does not find itself, like Guadalajara, in the difficult and painful necessity of being the first to announce the new form of federal republic." Puebla did, however, declare that although it recognized the existing central government and Congress it would take military action to defend itself if the Congress of the Union did not proceed with the institution of state sovereignty.[48]

Receiving confused information on these events, particularly from some officers of the local garrison who did not accept Puebla's statehood and fled to Mexico City, the central government decided it was necessary to suppress what it viewed as an uprising in Puebla. A force of eight hundred soldiers under the command of Manuel Gómez Pedraza was dispatched from Mexico City, Vicente Guerrero and his units were ordered to move from Cuautla to Puebla, and General Vicente Filisola was ordered to leave Oaxaca and march with his troops to Puebla. Emboldened, the Puebla cathedral chapter declared itself opposed to the action taken by the civil authorities to establish their own government.

Gómez Pedraza called on Puebla to submit to the Constituent Congress and the Supreme Executive Power or face military attack. After arriving in the province, Guerrero took over negotiations, pressing General Echávarri to dissolve the state legislature and executive triumvirate.[49] Adopting a rather more conciliatory line, Guerrero told Mexico City that he thought the majority of Poblanos favored "the sovereignty of the nation."[50] On 6 January 1824, the city of Puebla surrendered, submitting to the central government. The authorities of the province were removed, and Echávarri, who since early 1823 had attempted to make his military command in Puebla the base for his political aspirations, was replaced as civil and military chief by Gómez Pedraza. The Puebla federalists were granted amnesty, and on 5 January the Constituent Congress issued its own convocation for installation of the state legislatures, including Puebla.

Puebla's effort to create a government free of the control of the center coincided closely in time with the congressional decisions on the Acta Constitutiva and convoking elections of state legislatures. It is clear from this sequence of events that what was wrong with Puebla's conduct was not that it was federalist, but that it acted independently of Mexico City. Guerrero said as much in his statement to the inhabitants of Puebla on 6 January, declaring that only the sovereign Congress had the power to sanction the federalist system.[51] As the country's second largest city, whose proximity to Mexico City made it of unusual strategic importance, Puebla was unable to duplicate the actions of more distant Jalisco. When in March the state legislature elected under provisions of the congressional convocation was seated, it chose Gómez Pedraza as Puebla's first governor. Though Gómez Pedraza is considered in the literature to have been a devoted and austere republican, his administration in Puebla constituted the military suppression of Poblano self-determination in the name of national unity.

In the long debates in Congress over the proposed constitution, which went on until October 1824, the federalist concept—that the nation was a pact formed between sovereign states—was the principle at the heart of federalist thinking. For example, in a debate over whether the federal territories should be represented in the Chamber of Deputies by "delegates" who would not possess the right to vote, Manuel Crecencio Rejón of Yucatán reiterated that the right to have voting deputies in the Chamber did not derive solely from a region's population. Rather, it derived from the characteristic of sovereign statehood because it was sovereign states that formed the federation. Gómez Farías reiterated that the issue of representation in the Chamber of Deputies was not a question of the rights of the individual but the rights of "the moral persons of which the federation is composed." The deputy from Baja California protested that the territories ought to have the same right as states to vote in the Chamber because they participated in the social pact as equals. Another leading federalist, Juan de Dios Cañedo of Jalisco, responded that the principle was sovereignty and that the sovereign states alone composed the federation.[52]

It is all the more notable, therefore, that this essential expression of the role of the states as creators of the union was not specifically stated in the Mexican constitution when it was completed. Nonetheless, Reyes Heroles insists that the principle that a pact between the states formed the origin of nationhood, which was expressed so clearly by Montesquieu, formed the essence of the constitution. Montesquieu had defined federal government as "a convention, by which various political bodies consent to become citizens of a state larger than they were willing to form. . . . It is a society of societies, which forms a new one, which can be enlarged by new associates who join it."[53] This was the principle that the federalists referred to in the debate over the territories, reinforced for them by the writings of the U.S. Federalists, which were widely translated and published in Mexico.

Nonetheless, the completed constitution continued the subtle process of shifting the balance toward emphasizing the rights and powers of the nation, what the constitution called the "federal union of the states." To some extent, of course, this was natural because the federal constitution was the codification of a national entity and did not necessarily need to focus at any great length on the constituent parts. Nonetheless, in the entire constitution of 171 articles, the word *federation* appeared forty-nine times and the word *nation* fourteen times, but the words *sovereign* or *sovereignty*, whether in relation to the nation or the states, did not appear at all. This is because the solution to the problem of sovereignty, which as we have seen was the choice of a flexible dual sovereignty that put the greater weight on the nation, was already set out in the Acta Constitutiva. In addition, the Acta had also declared that the right to adopt and establish the form of government belonged exclusively to the nation.

In fact, it is inappropriate for historians to focus exclusively on the discussion and approval of the constitution, as some of the historical literature does because the fundamental decisions about the organization of the nation-state appeared in the Acta Constitutiva, not the constitution. As Quinlan puts it, the purpose of the constitution was to codify and clarify a de facto political system, "institutionalizing the then prevailing political reality."[54] Clearly, in the minds of the members of the Constituent Congress, the Acta Constitutiva and the constitution—both of which were drafted by the same constitutional committee—were perceived as being the two founding documents of the republic, and the Acta Constitutiva created federalism, while the constitution codified the political and administrative details for the federal system. The Acta was thus of greater significance, for as Ramos Arizpe himself said, the Acta was the basis for national formation and not only the basis for the formation of the constitution.[55] Juan Cayetano Portugal, a leading federalist deputy, said, "By the Acta the people have covenanted to govern themselves with a federal system, and they have recognized the independence and the sovereignty of the states that make up the grand federation; by the constitution essentially nothing has been done but to divide up the general powers and detail their attributions."[56] A further argument for the greater importance of the Acta Constitutiva over the constitution might well be that although the constitution was being ignored on a wide scale as early as 1828, four years after its promulgation, the Acta Constitutiva set forth the essential formulation of nationhood to which Mexicans have continued to adhere, with interruptions, to the present day.

Indeed, if a person totally unacquainted with the history of the first Mexican federal republic sat down and read the 1824 "Constitución Federal de los Estados-Unidos Mexicanos" from beginning to end, he or she would not notice that the states had previously been recognized as sovereign. Although the power of the states to exercise control over their internal administration and government was indirectly alluded to—in Article 161, which gave the states the obligation to organize their internal government and administration "without opposing this constitution nor the Acta Constitutiva"—clarification of the powers of the states was left up to the state constitutions themselves. Those state constitutions were to be written only after the federal constitution was in place. The states were also required to contribute to paying the national debt and to submit an annual report to Congress on their incomes and expenses, the condition of their industrial and agricultural production, and their population. The states were specifically prohibited from maintaining permanent military forces without the consent of the general Congress and from negotiating territorial limits with other states without approval or prior consent of Congress. They were also prohibited from imposing their own import or export duties, having transactions with a foreign power, or declaring war against a foreign power (though they could respond to invasion). The constitution contained only six articles relating directly to the states.

One aspect of what the constitution said about restrictions on the powers of the states has been misunderstood in some of the modern literature. Several authors have said that Article 162, Section 5, prohibited the states from arriving at accords or agreements between themselves. There is no doubt that what most alarmed Alamán and other centralists was the tendency of the states, particularly in 1823, to consult between themselves and bypass Mexico City. As secretary of relations, Alamán established the precedent of asserting the power of the central government over state autonomy. Indeed, it was probably the fundamental bedrock of his policy and one that future administrations, notably under Anastasio Bustamante from 1830 to 1832, would pursue with vigor. The text of the constitution, however, did not actually prohibit agreements between the states. Article 162, Section 5, only declared that the states could not enter into transactions or contracts with each other, if those transactions concerned the setting of territorial limits between the states, without the previous consent or later approval of the general Congress. It was not a universal prohibition on all forms of compact between the states. At any rate, there were several later occasions on which they did arrive at agreements between themselves.[57]

Three other provisions of the constitution directly acknowledged the agreement expressed in the Acta Constitutiva. The general Congress was obliged "to maintain the independence of the states within themselves with respect to their interior government"; to form regulations for the organization, arming, and control of local militias belonging to the states, reserving to each state the right to name the officers of such local militias; and to dictate laws and decrees without becoming involved in the internal administration of the states. But as commander in chief of the armed forces the president was given the power to make use of the local militias, although if he wanted to use them outside their home states or territories he was required to obtain the approval of the general Congress.[58] A total of ninety-eight members of Congress signed the constitution, and of that number thirty-nine (nearly 40 percent) were from the states of Mexico and Puebla alone; over half the states (ten of them) had four or fewer signers, and six had only one or two signers each.

The historical problem, then, is that although constitutional theory and exegesis might indeed be considered a concrete reality in itself, the constitution actually did not say that Mexican nationhood was a compact of states making up distinct constituent parts of the whole. Rather, because it was meant to actualize the decision already taken to create "the Mexican nation," the constitution emphasized just that. The written evidence of the constitution, in other words, suggests that the defense of the prerogatives and principles of statehood, of the concept of the federal republic as a society of societies, would have to be up to the states themselves.

The federalist principle might have been greatly strengthened in later years if there had been an assertive and genuinely independent judiciary to play the role that the Supreme Court played in U.S. history, but the 1824 constitution reserved for Congress the right to interpret the law. In addition, as Linda Arnold has shown, the Mexican Supreme Court was frequently disrupted and in the early years unable to deal clearly with such contested issues as limited government, the division of powers, and sovereignty.[59]

It may be true, as Reyes Heroles, following Mora, affirms, that when the word *federal* was added to the word *republic* "this then began to become something." But the emphasis was correct, for this thing called the Mexican federal republic or the United Mexican States throughout the lifetime of the first republic was only just beginning to become something. "The forces of the old society," continues Reyes Heroles,

> were by their nature and interests intrinsically centralized and centralist, and the forces of the new society—the localities, the embryonic middle class—were themselves decentralized and decentralizing. The federalist forces were geographically decentralized, and their interests were based in political and juridical decentralization. This, and no theoretical dogmatism or slavery to political theories, was what made the struggle so polarized for so many years between the alternatives of centralism and federalism. . . . Federalism constituted the legal instrument of the [new] forces.[60]

In other words, the early republic was the scene of a clash of interests that differed so radically from each other, not only in their goals and objectives but even in their definition of the nation, that the failure of the first federal republic owed less to any flaw in federalism or its basic principles than to the sheer immensity of the task. The ongoing social struggle was manifested in the conflict between federalism and centralism.

The constitution when finally completed and published specified the nineteen states and four territories defined as "the parts of this federation." The states were Chiapas, Chihuahua, Coahuila and Texas, Durango, Guanajuato, Mexico, Michoacán, Nuevo León, Oaxaca, Puebla, Querétaro, San Luis Potosí, Sonora and Sinaloa, Tabasco, Tamaulipas, Veracruz, Xalisco (Jalisco), Yucatán, and Zacatecas. In September 1824, Chiapas, which had broken from Mexico in June 1823, held a statewide referendum and in a vote of 96,829 to 60,400 freely chose to join the Mexican federal republic.[61] Particularly in the north, there were several states that were recognized as consisting of two or more of the old colonial provinces (such as Coahuila and Texas, Sonora and Sinaloa), and it was understood that in the future such large but underpopulated states might divide up into two or more separate states.

After intermittent debate that went on for ten months, the decision to join Texas to Coahuila (contrary to the wishes of the Texans, who wanted territorial status) resulted from a divided vote taken only two days before the constitution was published. Ramos Arizpe, chief author of the Acta Constitutiva and constitution, was the deputy for Coahuila; he had worked since the time of the Spanish Cortes to unite all four of the Eastern

Interior Provinces but had given way to the strong sentiment for state-hood in Nuevo León and Tamaulipas. Thereafter, in order to avoid the possibility that Coahuila, with roughly 65,000 inhabitants, might be re-duced to the status of a territory, he had agreed to statehood for it in which it was joined with Texas but shorn of the two other regions that had previously made up the Interior Provinces of the East. "The Deputy of Texas and I have agreed to the union," he reported.[62] The secession of Texas from the Mexican republic eleven years later was motivated, in part at least, by the Texans' resentment at being governed from Coahuila. A census of 1828 listed Coahuila with 66,131 inhabitants and Texas with 4,824.[63]

The four federal territories were Upper California, Lower California, Colima, and Nuevo Mexico. The exact status of Tlaxcala, then caught up in a debate over whether it should be a state, a part of Puebla, or a terri-tory, was left to be decided later. In January 1824 Congress had approved making Tlaxcala a state, and it was so listed in the Acta Constitutiva. But by the middle of 1824 its status was in doubt; on 24 November 1824 Con-gress made it a territory.[64] The most disputed question, exactly where the seat of the general government would be located, was also left until later. Two months after publication of the constitution and following heated debate, Mexico City was made into the Federal District with the status of a territory governed by the general Congress, and the federal capital was located there. In addition, in 1830 Sonora and Sinaloa were divided into separate states. Thus, by the end of the first federal republic in 1835, the nineteen states and four territories had grown to twenty states and six territories.[65] In May 1835, Aguascalientes was separated from Zacatecas and made into a territory, but this occurred as the federal republic was collapsing.

The constitution determined that deputies to the lower house of the general Congress were to be apportioned at the rate of one for every eighty thousand persons in the population and each state would have at least one deputy regardless of population. Moreover, territories with more than forty thousand inhabitants would name one deputy in Con-gress who would have both a voice and a vote, while territories with fewer than forty thousand people would have one deputy with voice but no vote. That solved the problem of representation for the least populated entities, such as Colima and the Californias. In keeping with the prece-dent of the Spanish constitution of 1812, deputies were elected indirectly and served a two-year term. The Senate, meanwhile, was to consist of two members from each state chosen by the respective state legislatures for four-year terms.

There was one school of thought involving the establishment of a senate that is worth noting. Some federalists, notably Francisco García, deputy for Zacatecas and future governor of that state, advocated the creation of a federal senate that would be, in effect, a multiple national executive. In discussions of the 1824 constitution, for example, García advocated that the executive power should be deposited in a senate composed of one deputy from each state (thereby equalizing the influence of each province over the national executive). The general Congress would elect the president of the Senate, who would then serve as the signing authority of the executive branch, while the Senate would be the deliberating authority of the executive branch.[66] Although this proposal was not accepted, the idea that the proper role of a senate was as a part of the executive branch, rather than of the legislature as in most federal systems, apparently explains why Jalisco in its first state constitution made the state senate part of the executive, as a kind of privy council to the governor with the power to propose candidates whom the governor would appoint to office. It was a distinctly minority view, however, because most of the states, including Zacatecas, had no state senate at all.

In the course of debating the constitutional foundations of the republic, the issue that took the longest to resolve was whether to create a single or a plural presidency. This question was discussed intermittently in Congress from March 1823 to July 1824. Motivated by fears of another Iturbide, Congress twice rejected the constitutional committee's proposal for a one-man executive. Nonetheless, on 14 July 1824, Congress reversed itself and voted in favor of what became Article 74 of the constitution: "The Supreme Executive Power of the federation is deposited in a single individual, who will be called president of the United Mexican States." The sources, both published and archival, do not explain what motivated Congress to change its mind. But Quinlan provides a plausible explanation that is closely linked to our theme of the erosion of state sovereignty.

The immediate concern, says Quinlan, was that by January 1824 Nicolás Bravo was the dominant force in the triumvirate of the Supreme Executive Power, Mariano Michelena having resigned and agreed to become minister to Great Britain. Throughout 1823 and 1824 Bravo was at the center of the most highly organized and most important political tendency in Mexico City. He was Grand Master of the Scots Rite order of Masons, which had been founded in Mexico in 1821 by Spanish liberals who came in the entourage of the last Spanish political chief, Juan O'Donojú. The Scots Rite Masonic group (the Escoceses) became the secret hub of aristocratic, centralist, and Spanish elements in the postindependence period. Until the creation in 1825 of the opposing York Rite Masonic lodges (the Yorkinos), which represented the democratic, nativist, popular tendency, the Escoceses were the major organized political movement or faction. Given the clear preference of the members of the executive for centralism, radical federal deputies introduced a bill in Congress to select new members of the executive from among individuals who had given "clear and positive proof of their singular adhesion to the federal system," but the bill did not pass.

At the end of March 1824 Bravo attempted to force Congress to accept the idea of a single executive. A special committee of Congress proposed the creation of a supreme director with dictatorial powers to serve until the constitution was in place. The object, according to Quinlan, was to block implementation of federalism. Mier wrote to a friend, "We are [engaged] in the great question of centralizing the government, because the coach of the sovereign Federation cannot roll. . . . Everything will go to the devil if the remedy proposed by the committee is not adopted."[67] Centralists supporting the proposal cited the presumed existence of a pro-Iturbide conspiracy in radical Jalisco, which meant that, again, the radicalism of Governor Luis Quintanar of Jalisco and his commanding general Anastasio Bustamante was the real target.

The proposed powers of the supreme director would have created a virtual dictator. Under the proposal, the supreme director, who was to be chosen by the members of the Supreme Executive Power from among themselves (meaning Bravo would probably be the person selected), would have an absolute veto over legislation passed by either the Constituent Congress or the state legislatures. He would also receive extensive military powers, and he would consult at his own discretion with a council of the states, to be composed of one representative of each state.[68] The proposal was a blatant attempt by Bravo and the cabinet to restore the balance of power to the central government and was met with strong resistance by the deputies from Jalisco and Zacatecas. The federalist majority rejected the concept of a supreme director, but enough of them saw a possible return of Iturbide from his European exile as a threat that a coalition of centralists and anti-Iturbide federalists formed to support the establishment of a single executive, though with powers greatly reduced from those proposed by advocates of a supreme director. On 21 April Congress approved a bill to create a provisional president, without the power to veto, who was to be elected by the Congress voting by states.[69] Those radical federalists from the west who had previously favored a single executive now opposed it, while the majority of deputies from other parts of the country, many of whom had opposed it, now supported it. This enactment, however, was never implemented because its opponents exploited the developing rivalry between the two leading candidates, Bravo and Guadalupe Victoria, to prevent either of them from being elected.

Ultimately, when Congress again debated the issue of a single executive, in July as part of the debates over the constitution, it approved creation of a single president on 14 July. In discussing the length of the president's term of office, Mier proposed that the presidential term be five or six years with a prohibition on reelection in order to prevent a president from manipulating his own reelection.[70] The majority, however, favored a four-year term and permitted reelection four years after a president left office. The president was to be chosen by the votes of the state legislatures, and that election was set for 1 September 1824 so the new president would be in a position to take office as soon as the constitution was published.

Bravo and the centralists now made their boldest attempt yet to eliminate what they argued was a unique link between advocates of the return of the former emperor, Iturbide, and radical federalism. For months, central elites had been charging that Jalisco's federalism was motivated by the desire to restore Iturbide to power. Despite the repetition of these charges by many contemporary sources, there is no hard evidence to prove that the Jalisco federalists were Iturbidists and certainly none that Jalisco federalism was motivated primarily by the objective of restoring the ex-emperor. Although it is true that Governor Luis Quintanar of Jalisco and his military commandant Anastasio Bustamante had been close to Iturbide when he was emperor, the same may be said of countless other civil and military leaders and hardly constitutes adequate proof that Quintanar and Bustamante pursued federalism in Guadalajara in order to provide a base for Iturbide's restoration. In fact, of all the early leaders of the republic, only Guadalupe Victoria had stalwartly resisted the blandishments, appointments, and honors dispensed by Iturbide while he was in power, having remained a rebel hiding out in the hills of Veracruz province and occasionally sought by Iturbide's forces. Quintanar only became jefe político and captain general of Guadalajara in November 1822. In late February 1823 he joined the other officers and civilian political leaders of Guadalajara to proclaim the Plan of Casa Mata, and on 16 April he published a decree prohibiting public manifestations of support for Iturbide in the province.

In addition, we need to remember that the charges against Quintanar and Bustamante came from such opponents of federalism as Carlos María de Bustamante and Lucas Alamán. The late-nineteenth-century Jalisco historian Luis Pérez Verdía argued that Jalisco was not Iturbidist and that the charge was never proved. "The attitude of the state [of Jalisco] was in truth hostile to the Supreme Executive Power, but not to national unity nor to the republican form; far from it, it was precisely the love for the federation and a perhaps exaggerated zeal for liberty that moved the local government. That neither the governor, nor the [state] congress, nor the ayuntamiento were for the return of Agustín I is a constant fact that only those who ignore a whole series of official acts can fail to recognize."[71] It was, after all, the actions of Jalisco that had essentially forced the creation of a federal republic.

Eyewitnesses in Guadalajara in early 1824 wrote frequently to confirm this same argument. For example, Prisciliano Sánchez wrote Gómez Farías on 22 May 1824 urging him to do something to counteract the charge being made by Jalisco's opponents that it was Iturbidist. "If something has been done here that contradicts what is ordered by [the central] Government, it is not because of affection for Iturbide but for just cause because of the lack of confidence that they have here in that [government]."[72] The day before, Sánchez had written Gómez Farías about the "false and alarming" articles in *El Sol*, the Mexico City newspaper that pursued the antifederalist line and spoke for Lucas Alamán: "If there is Iturbidism [here] it is in the desire of four idlers who count for nothing, but in the mass of the state and in its authorities there is only a just impatience for those who want to command us with the dictatorial whip. . . . Stop in Mexico [City] those efforts and stop those writers' outcries about Jalisco, otherwise I believe that we are approaching a break that I fear will have bloody anarchy as a result."[73] Gómez Farías appears to have responded to such pleas with a statement to Congress, the draft of which remains among his papers, in which he argued that Jalisco and Zacatecas were being falsely accused of Iturbidism. He insisted that the essence of the problem was that Jalisco and Zacatecas had led the fight for a federal republic. He pointed out that the two states had pursued the federalist objective openly and kept all other states fully informed of what they were doing, a laudable effort that should be copied by the national government in its operations. He then asked if those two states would have worked so diligently and so publicly to convince other states of the need for federalism if all they wanted was to restore Iturbide.[74]

A leading modern historian of Jalisco, José María Muría, adds the interesting thought that in 1823 and 1824 Quintanar was the best-known provincial political leader in the country, his manifestos and reports filled the pages of the local and central press, and he had the general support of Jalisco and was not threatened by internal opposition. In short, he was perceived by the "great men of the Mexican metropolis" as the greatest possible danger.[75]

Jaime Olveda, another modern *tapatío* scholar, points out that it is difficult to be precise about the accuracy of the charges against Quintanar but that there was a series of issues that angered the Supreme Executive Power concerning Guadalajara's politics. The state congress of Jalisco, for example, had not expedited the decree of the national Congress declaring as traitors those who attempted to support Iturbide. The reason for this was that the Jalisco congress, under provisions of the Acta Constitutiva, did not recognize the right of the national Congress to impose legislation relating to internal issues. The Jalisco congress had given Quintanar authority to make military appointments, and he had appointed Bustamante to be general commandant even though the Supreme Executive Power renewed its previous appointment of José Joaquín Herrera to that office. Secretary of Affairs Alamán and the new Secretary of War Manuel Mier y Terán informed the general Congress on 8 June 1824 that the state of Jalisco was responsible for the troubles the republic was suffering; that it had exceeded the faculties granted state governments in the Acta Constitutiva; and that Quintanar and Bustamante plotted the secession of Jalisco, refused to obey the supreme government, and plotted the overthrow of the existing government by granting protection to fugitives from the other states responsible for disobeying the central government.[76] The charges against Jalisco were particularly spread by Carlos María de Bustamante and Miguel Beruete, both avid anti-Iturbidists.[77]

Another reason Bravo and the Scottish Rite lodge had for wanting to destroy Jalisco's radicalism is that Jalisco was showing some of the earliest examples of the appeal to nativism and anti-Spanish sentiment that was rapidly growing in the most profederalist locations and within a year or two would intensify throughout Mexico to become the driving political force in the country. As early as February 1824, Anastasio Bustamante had informed Gómez Farías that the two things Jalisco demanded and the national Congress needed to act on quickly were the replacement of the current members of the Supreme Executive Power and the removal of Spanish peninsulars from public office.[78]

The evidence, then, is strong that what was actually at work is that centralists decided to use the charge of Iturbidism directed at the leaders of Jalisco and carefully reiterated by figures of such stature as Mier to break the back of Jalisco's resistance to central domination. Members of the Scottish Rite lodge of Freemasonry, led by Bravo, were in control of the government in Mexico City, and they opposed the idea of state sovereignty. They accused Jalisco of being in favor of restoring Iturbide because in 1824 there was no more damning charge that could be made.

At any rate, the general Congress on 3 April passed a bill to declare Iturbide "outside the law" and a traitor if he returned to Mexican soil and those who called for or supported his return traitors as well. Carlos María de Bustamante and Bocanegra both say that on 12 May the government broke up and arrested a group of twenty-five conspirators in Mexico City who were plotting the return of Iturbide. Alamán and Mier y Terán told Congress that these arrests revealed links between the conspirators and Quintanar and Bustamante, though again that evidence comes from the two cabinet members who were even then ordering the expedition that would overthrow Quintanar and Bustamante.[79]

With a justifying explanation in place, on 12 May 1824 Secretary of War Mier y Terán gave Bravo, still a member of the Supreme Executive Power, command of a military expedition to intervene against Jalisco. Generals Pedro Celestino Negrete and José Joaquín de Herrera, who like Bravo were leaders of the 1823 intervention in Jalisco, were also appointed commanders of the expedition. They left the capital that same day with a large contingent of troops. The Supreme Executive Power appointed General Francisco Moctezuma to replace Bustamante as commanding general of Jalisco. The government informed the Congress of Bravo's departure on 18 May but did not reveal the nature of his mission. Bravo arrived at the border between Michoacán and Jalisco, while, simultaneously, General Gabriel Armijo moved his forces from the Bajío to positions along the border of Guanajuato and Jalisco. In all, about eight thousand federal troops were poised to attack Jalisco, representing the most massive military threat thus far against a state, while Bravo, following what was now a well-worn pattern, offered to negotiate with the Jalisco government.[80]

When it became clear that the Bravo expedition was aimed at invading Jalisco, congressional deputies from that state attempted unsuccessfully to have the troops recalled. After denying the charge that the state favored

Iturbide, the Jalisco state congress demanded that the central government explain its motives for the invasion, and Governor Quintanar asked the central government to explain why it had sent hostile troops against Jalisco. Bravo and Quintanar each accused the other of violating the Acta Constitutiva. Quintanar understood, nonetheless, that both the state government and his personal position were in grave danger. He created a special fund from public monies to pay for mobilizing defense, he obtained a loan of one hundred thousand pesos from the church in Guadalajara, and he created a platoon of street people to defend himself.[81]

Given the extent to which Bravo's large force outnumbered the local forces, Jalisco had no choice but to accept Bravo's offer of negotiations. Jalisco's main fear at the moment related to the discussions in Congress on the proposed creation of a supreme director, a national dictator. On 11 June Bravo and the Jalisco legislature reached an accord in which Bravo promised on behalf of the national government that the nation would not be forced to obey an executive power contrary to the existing law or a dictatorship of the sort the Congress had been considering. In turn, the Jalisco state congress promised to obey the Acta Constitutiva and other laws that the national Congress might adopt. Article 6 of the agreement guaranteed the personal security of those who had defended Jalisco.[82] With this, Bravo, who had arrayed a total of 4,361 troops outside the city of Guadalajara, entered the city without firing a shot.

Once established in Guadalajara, however, Bravo began operating on the secret instructions he had received from Mexico City and proceeded to break the accord by seizing both Quintanar and General Bustamante as they slept. Taken prisoner, they were immediately conducted to Colima and from there to the port of Acapulco. Bravo informed the state congress that Quintanar and Bustamante were removed because of their "deviations and obstinacy."[83] Protesting that no specific charges had been laid against him and that only the Jalisco legislature had authority to hear any case against him, Bustamante asked the state congress to intervene in his behalf. With their city under military occupation, the state legislature declined to act.[84] Some of the few Iturbidists who lived in Jalisco took refuge in the port of San Blas, then commanded by Eduardo García. General Francisco Moctezuma, the new military commander of Jalisco, sent a small expedition against them, took them prisoner, and executed a number of them.[85]

With Quintanar captive, Jalisco was at the mercy of occupying forces. Although Bravo himself returned to Mexico City, Guadalajara was occupied from 17 June 1824 to 24 January 1825, during which, as Muría puts it, "the political binding of Jalisco to the Supreme Executive was complete." In that interval there were three provisional governors, the second and most important of whom, Rafael Dávila—though immensely unpopular with Jalisco merchants and other citizens—insisted that the invasion had freed Jalisco from the enemies of the federal system and from a corrupt and delinquent governor. Exulting in the establishment of a "moderated freedom" in Jalisco, he informed the residents that their best interests rested with an indissoluble union of the states and subordination to the supreme authorities in Mexico City.[86] In Muría's words, "The imposition of Rafael Dávila as governor and, more than anything, his servility, limited the exercise of full autonomy" in Jalisco.[87] In January 1825 the newly written state constitution came into effect and under its provisions Prisciliano Sánchez, a devoted federalist and author of the *Pacto Federal de Anáhuac*, was elected Jalisco's first constitutional governor. On the day Sánchez was installed as governor, the Jalisco legislature showed its dedication to federalism by voting Luis Quintanar a lifetime pension for his services as the state's first governor and the principal caudillo of the federal system.[88] Nonetheless, it was in the period during which Jalisco was occupied that the federal constitution was completed, freed by the efforts of the central government from the vigorous defense of state autonomy that Jalisco under Quintanar had mounted. Jalisco was displaced from its position as leader of the federalist cause, and the vacuum thus left would gradually come to be filled by the more moderate state of Zacatecas in the years to come.[89]

The habit of central government intervention in the affairs of the states, so frequent in both the nineteenth and twentieth centuries, dates from the first moments of the republic. Military interventions were launched against Oaxaca, Puebla, Jalisco, Michoacán, Querétaro, Guanajuato, San Luis Potosí, Zacatecas, and Tabasco. Nine of the nineteen states were the object of military intervention by the central government before the federalist constitution was published. In 1823 and 1824 there were no radical federalist states that had not been objects of central government intervention. Of the ten remaining states, discounting the state of Mexico, which was the base of centralism, all except Yucatán and Veracruz were sparsely populated, poorly organized, and unable to threaten the center meaningfully. Furthermore, every one of these interventions was successful, in the sense that they achieved what the central government set out to achieve. Alone, each state was an easy and largely defenseless target for attack by a central power that, though unable to mobilize very great numbers of troops, could still marshal more than any individual state and could even launch military action on several fronts at once.

As a result of their rigorous military and parliamentary efforts to weaken the states' demands for sovereignty and autonomy, central elites were able to ensure that their interpretation of federalism would triumph, that even within a federal system the particular interests of the *poderes de la Unión* would prevail over regional and local interests. Mexican federalism was moderated to the point that the center could live with it, institutionalizing the possibility that such a weakened federalism might fail and thereby keeping alive the center's dream that outright centralism might someday be created. To seize from triumphant federalism such a substantial degree of power and such potential for further enlargement, even at the moment that the charter of federalism was being produced, was a remarkable accomplishment for the center. From this point on, up to the present day, the two contending impulses of Mexican national history— federalism and centralism—ran parallel to each other. First one was dominant then the other, sometimes for extended periods, but neither one was ever quite able to eliminate the other, engendering a nationhood characterized by a paradox as subtle as it is profound.

CHAPTER SIX

Descent into Politics

The populist, federalist forces, seeing their goal of the attainment of full state sovereignty moderated by the frequent use of military force by the centralist elements, now had the measure of their opponents. Federalists now concentrated on defending their hard-won federalism and bringing their statehood to life. Political affairs, at both the national and the state levels, divided soon after publication of the 1824 constitution along the lines of the two major orders of Freemasonry—the so-called Scottish Rite (Escocés) and York Rite (Yorkino). The Scottish Rite, led by Nicolás Bravo, controlled the government in 1823 and 1824 and remained the dominant voice (though with increasing competition) in 1825 and 1826; it represented the creole elites, the members of the former colonial ruling class who had remained in Mexico, and the Mexico City centralists. In response to the dominance of the Scottish Rite, the York Rite was founded in Mexico in 1825 and quickly came to have lodges in all states and major cities of the country by 1826. The York Rite represented the provinces, the radical populist interests, the people of mixed color and background, and the demand for more widespread participation in decision making. The divisions also represented the split between moderates and radicals within Mexican liberalism in that the vast majority of adherents to the Scottish Rite were also liberals, of the moderate persuasion. From 1826 to 1830 the Yorkinos controlled most of the state governments and by 1827 were dominant in the federal government, and they extracted from their opponents a high price. By 1830 the pendulum would swing sharply against the Yorkinos again, and they would be forced to pay even more.

The Scottish Rite and York Rite were not so much "parties" as they were groupings based on class, economic interest, and differing attitudes toward federalism. Because they tended to focus around personalities, they were extremely tentative and unstable groupings, likely to splinter on the defection of one or several major leaders. Political parties, in the modern sense of the term, did not actually exist during the first federal republic. Mexico came to have government by conspiracy. The two Masonic movements fought hard to influence public opinion and to mobilize their supporters, but they were not publicly accountable, which means that they became instruments for the pursuit of vendettas and revenge based on personal grievance and ideological friction. The entire first presidential administration was clouded, and eventually ruined, by the struggle between the Scottish and York Rite movements. Their struggle for power illustrates the existence of two great visions of the nation, what it was and what it should be, and it was the intensity of those disagreements that destroyed the first republic.

Rejoicing in the miracle of their own political existence, in 1824 and 1825 the states set out to bring their statehood to life, to make it a reality. But the fledgling institutions of the federal system were overwhelmed by the pace and the degree of crisis that confronted them. There was a failure of leadership, a descent into vengeful partisanship, an almost automatic disregard by the central government for the sovereignty of the states, and an immediate malfunction in the electoral processes. Any one of these could be fatal to a state that had proclaimed itself a representative, popular, federal republic.

But the heart of the problem was not federalism. That is, we can distinguish the failure of the first federal republic—the inability of the fledgling institutions of civil government to sink roots deep enough to sustain themselves in a period of intense political and economic crisis—from the idea of federalism as a pact formed between self-governing and self-defining entities. This does not mean, as authoritarians throughout Mexico's subsequent history concluded, that Mexico was ungovernable, either inherently or institutionally, and therefore needed the guidance of an omniscient paternal autocrat or party. It simply means that in the 1820s federalism was not yet sufficiently developed to cope with the numbers of crises it had to face because it had only just been instituted in a country where federalism had not previously existed. We can conclude, as liberals in the 1840s did, that in the first republic federalism did not have a fair chance to prove itself. The spirit of self-determination, the core of the federal idea, was both sound and deep, to the extent indeed that later attempts in Mexico to create systems of government that were not grounded on this spirit always faltered. This is the distillation of Mexican nationhood, the desired objective to which it has returned again and again throughout its almost two hundred years.

When the first federal republic faltered, the regions fell back on caudillism as the most likely guarantee of their survival and as a necessary, if not sufficient (valid, if not optimal), expression of their will to exist. In a country whose history is in its regions, the regionally based military strongman was, as it happened, the only force that could fill the void left by the failure of the civil political institutions. The caudillos were not the cause of the failure of the first republic; they were perhaps its beneficiaries. This, of course, endows caudillism with a historically valid role, something that the historiography, because of the extent to which it has not questioned the late-nineteenth-century view that nationhood cannot exist without order, has been reluctant to concede.

Perhaps if the republic's first president had possessed outstanding political skill the newborn federation might have enjoyed a somewhat easier infancy. That was not the case, however. According to the constitution the president was to be the candidate who received the most votes of the state legislatures in the presidential election, and the runner-up was to become vice president. It was a flaw of the Mexican constitution, but one shared by the first constitutions of many other American countries, that the candidates who scored first and second in the election should become president and vice president insofar as it guaranteed that the two men who headed the federal executive would normally derive from competing political movements.

When the votes of the sixteen state legislatures that participated in the first presidential election were opened and recorded, Guadalupe Victoria received an absolute majority and was thereby elected president. Although Nicolás Bravo polled the second highest total, he did not receive an absolute majority over General Vicente Guerrero. The election for vice president, therefore, went to Congress. Though Bravo and Guerrero were both from the southern regions of the state of Mexico (areas that today are the state of Guerrero), Bravo was a noted centralist and Guerrero a leading radical federalist who was considered by the elites to be an alarming threat, not least because he was the product of mixed Indian and African lineage. Thus, the huge congressional delegation from the state of Mexico, numbering twenty-one and overwhelmingly conservative and centralist, helped swing the congressional election of Bravo as vice president. Many years later, in a brief autobiography, Bravo claimed that it was his intervention in Jalisco that cost him the presidency.[1] Victoria and Bravo took office on 10 October 1824.

Victoria's real name was José Miguel Fernández. During the wars of independence he had adopted the pseudonym "Guadalupe Victoria," combining references to the patriotic image of the Virgin of Guadalupe and victory, surely the most commanding pseudonym a Mexican could invent. As a member of the Supreme Executive Power who was largely uninvolved in its centralizing efforts and as the defender of Veracruz from the Spanish in 1823 and 1824, Victoria had wide popular support. Though considered friendly toward federalism, he was also perhaps the only one of the "old" rebels who had avoided becoming identified with a particular political persuasion. The fact that his politics were not clearly known was his greatest appeal in getting elected; he was a symbol of patriotism and honor. Bravo, on the other hand, as Grand Master of the Scottish Rite Masons, had politics that were not only widely known but that had earned him the strong enmity of some states. His aspiration to supreme leadership was once again thwarted, and he had to settle for the vice presidency.

Unfortunately, however, the political tabula rasa that Victoria presented to the world before his election was, in fact, all there was to his politics. Everybody worried about Victoria's lack of demonstrated political experience. Tomás Murphy in Paris wrote to Michelena in London, "The laws are made; now it is necessary to put them in execution. Will Victoria be incapable of it?" He added cheerily, "Whatever may be the defects attributed to Victoria, I do not consider him capable of conspiring against liberty."[2] He turned out to be so nonassertive in political matters that he remains to this day something of a cipher. The hallmark of his presidency seems to have been his effort to maintain his neutrality in regard to the great issues of the day and to keep a balance between federalists and centralists, or Yorkinos and Escoceses, within his four-man cabinet. Mier wrote of him in 1825, "His favorite plan is to amalgamate the parties."[3] By early 1827 the British minister to Mexico, H. G. Ward, who was known to be close to Victoria, informed his government that the president's refusal to side with either the Yorkinos or Escoceses had cost him the confidence of both parties and guaranteed his presidency would end in disaster.[4] It was a do-nothing presidency in which the partisan spirit that was to continue to tear at the fabric of political life was allowed to grow unchecked. In 1830 Lorenzo de Zavala characterized Victoria as having been "an entirely null personage and the instrument of the men who surrounded him."[5] In four years, he had seven secretaries of relations, eight secretaries of finance, and ten secretaries of war.

In late 1827, when Vice President Bravo rebelled against the government, Victoria's effectiveness had already evaporated. Frequently ill, suffering possibly from hypoglycemia, Victoria allowed affairs of state to drift, failing to fulfill the task he had set for himself of being Mexico's Washington.[6] While some authors emphasize that Victoria was at least the only president for many years to serve out his full four-year term of office, he was also the first who failed to hand over power peacefully to his duly elected successor.

In addition to any weakness of leadership for which Victoria might be criticized, however, there is good reason why it is possible to narrate the history of these turbulent years without the first president of the republic standing at center stage. Whatever his skills and motivations might have been, the first years of the federal republic should not be narrated from the perspective of the federal center. The real initiative in national affairs did not reside with the president. Endowed by the constitution with powers considerably weaker than those of the federal Congress, the president was meant to be the second force in the national government. Furthermore, in a country made up of free, independent, and sovereign states, the standard formula of narrating Mexican history in terms of what the federal government did or did not do is simply the wrong focus. This was a country whose history was being written by its states, not by its federal executive, and even at the federal level Congress should be the center of historians' attention. Victoria's administration appears weak primarily because it was almost entirely reactive; and it was reactive because that is what the 1824 constitution meant the presidency to be. As president, Victoria frequently testified to the benefits of a limited executive with carefully circumscribed powers.[7] Rather than a cause for condemnation, therefore, the fact that Victoria was the only president in the first republic who carefully restrained himself within the constitutional boundaries of presidential action might well be his greatest achievement. José María Tornel, who served as his secretary, was one of the few to rise to the defense of Victoria's reputation: "Neither in life nor in death has entire justice been dispensed to the first president of the nation."[8]

For several years the real activity, the struggle to create and empower functioning federalism, was in the hands of the states. What were the objectives of the states? Jalisco gave a particularly eloquent summary of its aims when it wrote the federal Congress to congratulate it for its adoption of the Acta Constitutiva. In passing the Acta Constitutiva, Jalisco said, Congress had

> consecrated the great principles of social equality that make people happy and opulent. Political liberty will be enjoyed without anguish

and anarchy, civil liberty without confusion or odious distinctions, liberty of the press without restrictions other than those indispensable to refrain licence and defamation, liberty of rights without consideration other than merit and distinguished virtue. . . . From now on merit and genius will be stimulated and compensated because one's own and tutelary Government in each state will distribute justice in the circle of its comprehension without the dangers, uncertainties, and difficulties in which we lay under a distant government that only heard and favored those who drew near its influence.[9]

This statement, of the sort usually dismissed as mere rhetoric, was a precise summary of what the states believed they had achieved in creating federalism. Social equality, political liberty, civil liberty, liberty of the press, civil rights, and laws adopted and administered locally—these were the aspirations of the states, however they might have been expressed and whatever the outcome of the first federalism might have been. They stand in marked contrast to the origins and purposes of the first federal republic as expressed here by Justo Sierra, in the heyday of late-nineteenth-century Positivism (and widely accepted even today by some historians): "Each important city had its political oligarchy, clinging with a death grip to newly won power and determined to compromise with no system except the federalist one, which evinced a strong tendency to separatism." Sierra, however, contradicted himself when he confessed that the 1824 constitution was "the expression of the almost unanimous opinion of the politically-conscious segment of the nation."[10]

As we have seen, much of the literature, which is prepared to grant to the federal government the presumably upright motivation of nation building, remains unwilling to recognize among the states any motive other than the most base and self-serving. Late-nineteenth-century Positivists, such as Justo Sierra, saw the demand for self-determination among the states as an impediment to the imposition of their definitions of order and progress, but historians in our own day should be more discriminating. For a province to aspire to have its "own and tutelary Government," that is, guardianship of its own territory and resources, is not a sordid objective. Even if autonomy meant that local oligarchies gained control over local government, it was still self-government for the regions. It was therefore a substantial step forward compared to the inheritance of the colonial age and no less likely to generate the eventual emergence of democracy than the federalism of the United States that had placed the government of Virginia or South Carolina in the hands of their plantation owners. Hernández Chávez argues that the key to local power relationships in the early republican period was that regional elites derived their influence from their linkages with popular bases in their towns and municipalities.[11] Coatsworth emphasizes that after independence Mexico experienced a genuinely high level of mass political mobilization and rapid social change, based overwhelmingly in the cities and provinces, which "made local governments more democratic than before."[12] It is time to recognize, as Nettie Lee Benson suggests, that the effort of the center to rebuild its weakened hegemony over all aspects of government in the early republic, not the refusal of the states to obey the center, was the more profound source of Mexico's political turmoil.[13]

A multitude of social inequalities undeniably existed within individual states. In Yucatán the oppressed and exploited Maya majority outnumbered the whites and mestizos by three to one, and in Jalisco the landed elites moved immediately under the precepts of dominant liberalism to attempt to gain ownership of traditional communal peasant and Indian lands. The social inequalities in the individual states may have led to various social and political catastrophes, but no amount of direct administration by the center was likely in the early nineteenth century to have done a better job of solving social inequalities; that was not an objective of the center. It is simply inaccurate to assume that state or local governments were less socially enlightened than federal governments in this period.

Early state governments often perceived themselves as well in advance of the center in social and economic thought. The first leaders of Yucatán, for example, represented a mercantile bourgeoisie that was entrepreneurial, bold, and progressive and saw themselves stifled by the center, where they believed power belonged to an alliance representing high clergy, old colonial bureaucrats, former royalist officers, and conservative landowners.[14] In Zacatecas, there was an innovative and liberal state administration that, fueled by a recovery in mining, pursued progressive reforms in education, land use, and banking, including two joint public/private capital ventures to invest in mining and a development bank to buy land and rent it out to farmers.[15] As Hamnett has shown in a study of the principal families of Oaxaca and their adherence to federalism, provincial notables supported federalism for a variety of reasons. But chief among them was their realization that independence from Spain and the fall of the Iturbide monarchy represented the disintegration of centralist bureaucratic absolutism; that the regionalist sentiment had deep cultural, geographic, and economic roots; and that "the doctrine of sovereignty of the states served to legitimize their position" and also "as a doctrine of resistance."[16]

Rural peasants increasingly came to recognize that local autonomy was the source of the defense of their lands against white and mestizo landowners who sought to take it over.[17] Yet paradoxically, the most advanced creole social thought of the day was increasingly hostile to such holdovers from the colonial regime as land ownership by indigenous communities. The liberal philosophy, particularly dedication to the idea of the civic equality of all citizens, provoked most states to regard communal land as incompatible with individual liberty. Hence, laws abolishing communal ownership of land, though they were rarely effective, were passed in 1825 in Chihuahua, Jalisco, and Zacatecas; in 1826 in Chiapas and Veracruz; in 1828 in Puebla and Sonora and Sinaloa; in 1829 in Michoacán; and in 1833 in the state of Mexico. It was not the radicals who supported the maintenance of communal land but rather the reactionaries and archconservatives who argued that the condition of the Indian masses was worsened by independence and legal equality.[18] This debate continued for many decades.

No state was completely happy with the provisions of the Acta Constitutiva or constitution, but all rejoiced at the formal acquisition of internal autonomy. Yucatán, for example, felt it was making particular sacrifices to enter the federal republic because both the Acta Constitutiva and the constitution prohibited a state from establishing its own customs duties, port duties, or tonnage fees, something Yucatán had done since it issued its own Reglamento de Comercio in 1814. Even some of the municipalities in Yucatán had been financed from import and export duties.[19] Yucatán was also severely injured when, in view of Spain's refusal to recognize its independence and the bombardment by Spanish forces of San Juan de Ulúa in Veracruz, the Mexican government declared in 1823 that a state of war existed between Mexico and Spain. This declaration destroyed Yucatán's all-important trade with Cuba. Indeed, throughout most of 1824 Yucatán refused to publish all of the text of the Acta Constitutiva, recognizing only Article 5, which declared the creation of a federal republic. When the constitution appeared, however, Yucatán adhered to it. The termination of Yucatán's trade with Cuba further intensified the ongoing conflict between the city of Mérida, which depended on overseas commerce, and the city of Campeche, which saw its future as dependent on the internal Mexican trade routes. As Antonio López de Santa Anna, who was then serving as general commandant of the state, predicted in 1824 in a remarkable report, this conflict would lead to the later dismemberment of the state of

Yucatán (with the creation of the state of Campeche in 1858 and later the territory of Quintana Roo in 1902).[20]

For Jalisco, the loss of Colima still rankled very deeply, as did the military occupation and overthrow of Governor Quintanar. For some elements in Coahuila, the inability to unify the former Eastern Interior Provinces was a great loss. For Sonora and Sinaloa, Tlaxcala, and others there were serious doubts about the status awarded them at the outset of the federal republic. Nearly all the northern states worried whether they were even viable. Tenenbaum has recently emphasized that the northern states demonstrated substantial loyalty to the Mexican union in the early decades, consistently made large payments to the national treasury, and wanted to participate as parts of the republic.[21] And, in light of later events, it can be said that the mighty state of Mexico lost far more from federalism than any other state. It is worth emphasizing, therefore, that many of the states that formed the federal union did so at considerable cost to themselves, many of them gambled on the belief that integration into the Mexican nation was necessary, and they all had very high stakes at risk. The federal republic saw the states participating with good will and some sacrifice in the simultaneous processes of regional articulation and national integration.

In a book written many years before its publication in 1986, Emilio Rabasa reflected on the essence of the first federal republic. Its real object, he wrote, was to avert the worst evil, falling into a system of absolutism in the guise of a republic. Hence, the essence of the republic was the double separation of powers between the three branches of government—the legislative, executive, and judicial—at both the federal and the state level as well as between the national government and the state governments. Both the Acta Constitutiva and the constitution required that each state, as well as the nation, adopt a republican, representative, and popular form. Thus, the states agreed to await completion of the national constitution before implementing their state constitutions in order to ensure that none would violate the fundamental principles on which the republic was organized. In the late colonial era, Ramos Arizpe and other deputies to the Cortes had complained not so much about Spanish domination of Mexico as about the absolute abandonment of the provinces by the imperial center. Not only did the Spanish Empire do nothing to assist the remote provinces, it did not allow them the means to help themselves in the form of an adequate political system of their own. Thus, it can be no surprise that after independence the real object of the provinces was to institutionalize and practice their political self-sufficiency.[22]

The states proceeded to adopt their individual constitutions. In some states, such as Jalisco, the constitution was virtually complete before the federal constitution was approved, so the state could move quickly to issue it on 18 November 1824. All the other states, except Mexico and Coahuila and Texas, produced their constitutions in 1825. Coahuila and Texas were not well enough organized to write a constitution quickly; their charter was the last to appear, on 11 March 1827. The state of Mexico adopted a provisional organic law in August 1824, but because of the long struggle over whether Mexico City was to be included in the state's territory, it did not complete its formal constitution until 14 February 1827.

For administrative purposes each state divided its territory along lines modeled on the late colonial territorial division of partidos or subdelegados. The state of Mexico created eight prefectures, each with subprefectures corresponding to the former partidos. In Jalisco the twenty-eight colonial partidos became departments, which were in turn part of eight cantons. In Veracruz the terminology was reversed, with twelve cantons subject to four departments, and Querétaro divided the state into six districts. Most states created both a governor and a vice governor. Zacatecas, however, chose to allow rather greater room to executive power and did not establish a vice governor. Most states created a unicameral legislature, but Durango, Jalisco, Oaxaca, Veracruz, and Yucatán established a senate as well. With an elaborate system suitable to a large population, Jalisco had a senate of five members, not as part of the legislative branch but as part of the executive, as a privy council to the governor. The chief political authority of each Jalisco canton was a jefe político named by the governor on the nomination of the senate, while the departments were headed by a director appointed from among the community. The cantonal jefes políticos were granted extensive powers in political, military, and fiscal fields, which would provoke many complaints about their excessive intervention in local political affairs. In the state of Mexico, the district prefects, appointed by the governor, had equally extensive political and economic faculties. The state of Oaxaca, also among the more populous, created a chamber of deputies and a senate as part of its legislature as well as a council of government as part of its executive branch. The state of Veracruz created a bicameral legislature of chamber and senate, with the vice governor and the four senior senators composing a council of government to operate as a permanent commission when the legislature was not in session.

In almost all states, adoption of the state constitution led to a reduction of the number of municipalities that had been created under the Cádiz constitution. Most states decided that the minimum population required for a municipality should be two, three, or four thousand rather than one thousand as decreed in Cádiz.[23] In the state of Mexico, municipalities were limited to capitals of partidos and to settlements with four thousand inhabitants, which cut the number of municipalities by half. Nonetheless, municipalities continued to enjoy considerable autonomy and self-government.[24] As Carmagnani points out, in all these original state constitutions the site of the base sovereignty was the local community, the permanent residents or vecinos, and in each case there was evidence of continuing tension between the community and the elected or appointed authorities. He characterizes the ayuntamiento as "the representative institution of the territorial community."[25] Guerra, too, emphasizes that in the context of the emerging "modern" concept of nationhood as the aggregate of individuals in society, the town or village was the base of the individual citizen's political participation and therefore the fundamental base of nationhood.[26] In their constitutions and legislation every state except Oaxaca declared all towns to be uniformly equal.[27] The ayuntamientos were fundamental as the mechanisms through which the sovereignty of the people was first expressed.

The state constitutions reflected a hierarchy in the delegation of authority, from the people to the ayuntamiento or municipio, from the ayuntamiento to the state congress; and the ayuntamiento was considered to be, as the Zacatecas constitution put it, the political institution in most immediate contact with the citizens. Thus, the constitutions of two states (San Luis Potosí and Nuevo León) decreed that the state governor was to be elected starting with the ayuntamientos. In others he was elected by the state congress (Zacatecas, Chihuahua, Veracruz, Mexico, Puebla, Oaxaca, Tabasco, Chiapas), by the electoral college of the partidos or districts (Sinaloa, Yucatán, Guanajuato, Querétaro, Tamaulipas, Jalisco and Coahuila-Texas), or directly by the state electoral junta (Michoacán).[28] Despite the clear and present danger posed by the opposition of the powerful Mexico City interests, the objective of the states was to retain and institutionalize their self-government.

The response of the states to the continuing threat that centralism posed to their existence clustered around three main issues during the period 1825–27, the first three years of the Victoria presidency. These were, first, the effort of the states to acquire and keep control over independent sources of state revenue; second, the drive to remove Mexico City from the jurisdiction of the state of Mexico in order to weaken both as the key power bases of centralism; and, third, the effort to strike back at the old elites and mobilize the masses through the expulsion of the Spaniards from Mexico. More than simply elements in a radical federalist (Yorkino) partisan political campaign, these were the techniques the federalists adopted in order to gain dominance in national political affairs and to make statehood real.

Probably the most fundamental problem involved in making a federative system work is the issue of dividing revenues between the national level and the state or provincial level. In the colonial era, revenue collection and disbursement had been highly centralized. Federalism obviously required a radically restructured system of collecting and controlling revenues. In early 1824, after the Acta Constitutiva, the provinces faced the daunting task of finding adequate funds for the operation of a host of activities that now devolved upon them. The state of Mexico, for example, found in March 1824 that it had no money in its treasury except a small amount that had been raised by voluntary public subscription, and it petitioned Congress for funds necessary for its expenses until such time as Congress could complete discussions on the subject of how to divide state and national revenues. Congress responded by approving a monthly subsidy to all the states that requested it.[29] This was a short-term measure only, in place from March to October 1824, and obviously highly problematic for the states that had already achieved sovereignty and therefore the right to control their own fiscal affairs. Sovereign entities could not function on monthly subsidies from the national Congress.

Throughout all the congressional debate of March to October 1824 relating to the creation of a federal revenue system, the deputies from the state of Mexico worried out loud about how much federalism was going to cost this richest of Mexican states. The last time anyone had attempted to estimate the relative wealth of the provinces and what each owed to the national government—in an exercise undertaken in the last months of the Iturbide regime in 1822—the province of Mexico, which at the time still included what in 1824 became the separate state of Querétaro, was rated as being more than 3 times as wealthy as the province of Puebla and 278 times richer than Texas, Nuevo Mexico, and the two Californias. It was calculated that the province of Mexico contained nearly a third of the national wealth.[30] The congressional committee drawing up the proposal for the apportionment of sources of income between the states and the federation considered that its purpose was to devise a system in which the national government could manage its own financial system without being required to interfere in the internal affairs of the states.

The final solution was the law adopted by Congress on 4 August 1824. It left to the federal government only the revenues from customs, the tobacco monopoly, the gunpowder and salt monopolies, the mails, the national lottery, the *bienes nacionales* (national property), and the incomes from the federal territories. The decision that the federal government would keep import and export duties had already been included in the Acta Constitutiva.[31] All the other revenue sources passed to the hands of the states—including sales taxes (*alcabalas*), duties on gold and silver, individual contributions (*contribuciones directas*), the government share of the church tithes (*novenos,* or two-ninths of one half of tithes), income taxes leveled on specific civil and ecclesiastical officials, and taxes on pulque and cockfighting. In return, each state was to pay a monthly subsidy to the federal government. This payment, known as the *contingente,* or contingency share, was an assessment calculated on the basis of the estimated wealth of each state.[32]

This meant that the federal government handed over to the states nearly one half (46 percent) of tax collections that in colonial times had belonged to the viceregal government. According to the projections carefully drawn up in 1824, this division of revenue would give the national government 10.6 million pesos in the first year and would provide 7.4 million pesos for the states; the states would then return to the federal government a total assessment of 3.1 million pesos.[33] This permitted the states financial autonomy in return for recognizing the formal supremacy of the federal level in the form of the state assessments. A second law, adopted 17 August 1829, slightly modified the arrangement by requiring the states to contribute 30 percent of their total revenues to the federal government.

When drawn up in 1824, the system for assessing the annual contribution of each state divided the states into five classes based on their estimated wealth. Factors considered in estimating relative wealth included the amount of each state's tax and tithe returns; the condition of its agriculture, commerce, manufacturing, and mining; and the losses it sustained during the struggle for independence. Mexico was the only state placed in the highest of the five classifications, and it was required to contribute at the rate of 6 reales for each of its 1.3 million inhabitants, making a total assessment of 975,000 pesos. Thus, the state of Mexico, with about 21 percent of the national population, would pay 31 percent of the national assessment.

The other assessments provide an interesting view of what Congress, which had only partial data at its disposal, considered the rank of the various states to be by wealth. In the second classification, Jalisco, Zacatecas, San Luis Potosí, and Veracruz were assessed four and a half reales for each of their citizens. Six states—Puebla, Oaxaca, Guanajuato, Michoacán, Querétaro, and Tamaulipas—were in class three, where the assessment was three and a half reales per person. In the fourth class were Chihuahua, Durango, and the territory of Nuevo Mexico. The fifth and poorest class included Yucatán, Coahuila and Texas, Nuevo León, Sonora and Sinaloa, Tabasco, and the territories of Tlaxcala and the Californias. Chiapas was not ranked at the time because it had not yet voted to join the republic.

Both the republic's two wealthiest states, Mexico and Jalisco, protested their assessments. The state of Mexico argued that its assessment was based on statistics dating from the colonial period when it was the capital of the entire viceroyalty instead of only one state in a federation. Jalisco argued that its quota was one-third of the state of Mexico's even though it had only one-fourth the population; but deputies from Mexico countered by pointing out that Jalisco had previously claimed a population larger than that upon which the assessment was based and that its wealth rivaled that of Mexico state.[34] Other states, notably Puebla and Oaxaca, also protested their quotas, but they all found it was difficult to argue that their population was lower than Congress thought because to make that argument successfully meant they would have to give up seats in the Chamber of Deputies.[35] When the law was passed in August 1824, it included two important amendments; one lowered the contributions of each of the states by one-third for the first year so they might have time to establish their own financial systems, and the other authorized the national government to intervene in a state that refused to pay its assessed contribution.

Macune points out that this law, despite ongoing disputes surrounding the amount of assessment, was fundamental to the operation of federalism for the next decade. It breathed life into the self-governing states by granting them guaranteed access to important taxes collected within their territory. With it, "the states became political entities with genuine economic power."[36] Carving out a method that allowed states to retain more of their locally generated tax money provided the most fundamental support for self-government and for federalism.

As it happened, however, only in the first year, 1824, did the states actually meet their assessed payments to the federal government. In every subsequent year the states' contributions fell below their assessed levels as the states contributed less and less to the federal income. In 1824 the states' share payments accounted for 21.7 percent of total federal income; in 1825 it fell to only 9.2 percent and in 1826 and 1827 to 5.8 percent. Thereafter it hovered between 10.1 percent in 1827 and 1828 and 7.4 percent in 1830 and 1831. According to Carmagnani's figures, taken from the federal *Memorias de hacienda,* in 1824 (when all assessments were reduced by one-third) the states paid a total of 2.28 million pesos; thereafter the highest yearly total was 1.4 million in 1828 and 1829.[37]

The federal government was thus forced to finance itself increasingly by borrowing from European banking houses and, by the later 1820s and for several decades thereafter, from internal moneylenders (*agiotistas*). As early as August 1827, the federal government defaulted on its payments to British bondholders. Only seven weeks later, in November 1827, the federal government took up the first of a long series of major internal loans from Mexican moneylenders, the servicing of which would come to paralyze the federal government.[38]

Carmagnani has argued that the political impact of the division of revenue established in 1824 was that it operated to the benefit of the states and severely weakened the federal government, that the chronic fiscal deficits that characterized the federal government throughout the early decades resulted precisely from the fact that the states were able to gain control of the major sources of revenue. He asserted that "not only was the federal state pauperized by the states" but also that the agreement of the states to subsidize the federal government hid a clear intention on their part to impede the functioning of the central power. The federal government, he said, was in effect a state without territory, a state lacking true financial sovereignty.[39]

A federalist of the time would have countered such an interpretation by pointing out that the internal sovereignty of the states meant that to deny them financial autonomy would be a direct contradiction of federalism, that a republic in which the states had no access to independent financial means would hardly have been better able to function anyhow, and that the states' agreement to contribute to the upkeep of the federal government constituted a measure of their willingness to join in the overall process of nation building. One state at least, Zacatecas, wrote into its constitution a provision that it would comply with all the decisions of the federal government regarding the contribution of the states to the general expenses of the federation.[40] Rather than interpret every act of the states as some conspiracy on their part, it seems more appropriate to interpret their actions as efforts designed to bring federalism alive by bringing their own statehood alive. Just as power sharing was critical to the federal system, so was revenue sharing. Only when we presume that the national government had an automatic right to all revenues, that nationhood could not exist without centralized fiscal control, does the revenue-sharing agreement in the first federal republic look like a conspiracy on the part of the states. If, however, we remember federalism's definition of itself as a pact formed between several sovereign entities, then the 1824 revenue law becomes evidence that the states chose freely and of their own accord to participate in nation building. We might contrast this with the tax system that currently exists in Mexico, in which the federal government collects most taxes and redistributes only about 23 percent of the funds to states and municipalities, keeping them dependent on the federal executive.[41]

At present there is no detailed research that traces income levels of the states as compared with the federal government during the first republic. Existing economic history of the period tends to make judgments about "the Mexican economy" using data drawn exclusively from the federal treasury, sometimes altogether failing to notice that there were secondary (state) and tertiary (municipal) levels in the federal republic. Green, however, on the evidence of the annual reports that the states were constitutionally obliged to send to Mexico City, notes that the revenue of the states went up by about 1826, primarily based on the sales tax (alcabala) and the direct contribution. Depending on the state, the alcabala was set at about 8 to 10 percent and was highly regressive from the point of view of the national economy as a whole because goods transported across state borders and sold in several cities were repeatedly taxed. It thus had the effect of being an internal tariff, which tended to discourage the development of both transportation and manufacturing. The direct contribution was at first used to replace the colonial head tax on Indians, but it became so difficult to collect that many states, including Mexico, Guanajuato, Jalisco, Puebla, and Michoacán, gave it up as a lost cause by the late 1820s. Some ceded the tax to the municipalities.[42] Green's impression is that by 1829 the states had begun to experience the same kind of economic decline that the national government was experiencing. The contingente, the annual contribution to the federal treasury, had by then become the major "unbalancing factor" for state budgets because as state revenues declined the bite taken by the annual contribution, which was supposed to be no more than 30 percent, grew to equal 40 or even 50 percent of the income of some states. The states fell behind in their payments until "the contingency debts reached astronomical heights."[43]

Another significant issue in the creation of the first republic was the federalization of the national capital, the separation of Mexico City from the territory of the state of Mexico, and its conversion into a federal district governed by the national Congress. Only weeks after issuing the constitution, Congress voted to convert Mexico City into the Federal District. Because of the vehement resistance of the state of Mexico, however, the decision was not implemented until 11 April 1826.[44]

Almost all the federal countries in the Americas adopted the concept of having a federalized capital city, thereby removing the national capital from the influence of—and from being the power base of—the state or province in which it was located. In Mexico, where the capital city had by far the longest and most profound history of primacy of any American city and where it was, indeed, the source of the name of the country, the federalization stunned the centralists and became a motive, often unspoken, for their desire to create a central republic. This history of rancor is still reflected in the present Mexican constitution (1917), in Article 44, which declares that if the federal government should be moved out of the Federal District, the city will be converted into a state named Estado del Valle de México.

The question of moving the capital had been extensively debated since the Plan of Casa Mata.[45] The first Constituent Congress had discussed a committee report proposing that the newly convoked second Constituent Congress should meet at some location closer to the geographical center of the country. Various deputies and cabinet members, including notably Carlos María de Bustamante and Lucas Alamán, strongly opposed moving the government, while Valentín Gómez Farías and other radical federalists supported it. Congress rejected the proposal, but the question was revived in the second Constituent Congress. The Jalisco caucus in Congress had instructions to support moving the seat of government away from Mexico City. Proposals included one recommending that Congress should create a federal district somewhere in the country to serve as the seat of the national government or, alternatively, that the capital of the state of Mexico should be moved so that Mexico City could be made into the Federal District. Among those cities mentioned as possible choices to become a federal district were Celaya or Salamanca in the state of Guanajuato. But in May 1824 a special committee of Congress proposed that the city of Querétaro be made the national capital. In June 1824 Congress approved the subarticle in the constitution empowering it to establish a federal district, though it did not specify the location.

Deputies from Guanajuato, Zacatecas, and Jalisco strongly supported the choice of Querétaro, arguing that the other states feared that the Mexico City capitalists held too much influence over the national government.

All four members of the federal cabinet, however, appeared before Congress to oppose moving the capital on the grounds of the cost involved. Servando Teresa de Mier, pointing to the District of Columbia in the United States, which in its early years was considered a "swamp," argued that a rural federal district would fail, insisted that it was not even necessary to have a federal city, and agreed with the cabinet's view that the financial power of Mexico City meant that it was the only city that could sustain the costs of a federal government. Leading federalists and centralists staked out opposing sides on the issue.

The matter remained undecided until after promulgation of the constitution. On 18 October 1824, several federalist deputies, led by Lorenzo de Zavala, proposed that Mexico City be declared the Federal District. Four days later, a special congressional committee recommended that the District should have a radius of two leagues from the center of Mexico City's main plaza. This, of course, would force the state of Mexico to move its capital elsewhere because there was already agreement that the seat of the federal government must not be in the capital of any state. As a result, the state of Mexico, charging that it was about to be dismembered, fought back bitterly and with every resource at its disposal. One of the primary points of argument was the claim by some of the states that Mexico City was the property of all the states because it had been built at their expense, which the legislature of Mexico state refuted by insisting that Mexico City had provided the men, the funds, and the tools to settle all of the interior. The state of Mexico insisted that it would never have joined the federation if it had known that the constitution would be interpreted in such a way as to expropriate its state capital, and it charged the national government with bad faith. For the state of Mexico losing the vast assets of Mexico City would be a body blow.

When these statements of the Mexico state legislature were read in a public session of Congress, a passionate debate ensued. Perhaps no other issue involving implementation of the constitution provoked such a clear division between federalists and centralists, between the states and the center. The debate revealed a clear regional split, with most states favoring the federalization of Mexico City while the state of Mexico and the old colonial economic and political center of the country strongly opposed it.[46] Federalists argued that making Mexico City a federal district would free the city from the influence of the state and would add its great wealth to the resources of the federation instead of to the preponderance of one single state. Spokesmen for the state of Mexico retorted that separating the ancient capital from the territory of the state was confiscation. The proposal that Mexico City be declared the Federal District was passed on 30 October, but details were hotly debated for three more weeks after an amendment was proposed that called for the state of Mexico to be indemnified for the loss of its capital. The remaining articles of the bill were passed by 18 November, although Congress agreed to strike a committee to make recommendations about indemnifying the state for its losses, to iron out other details, and to allow the state government to remain in Mexico City until it could prepare a new location and transfer its administrative center there.

Despite passage of the act federalizing Mexico City, the legislature of the state of Mexico continued to resist with great bitterness. In 1825, it appealed directly to President Victoria, to each of the states, and to the new regular Congress, which was installed on 1 January 1825. Victoria, adopting a position of strict neutrality, refused to become involved. Most of the states were indifferent to the appeal, and the new Congress decided against repealing the act. It was not until late 1825 that a committee of the Chamber of Deputies presented a comprehensive plan for implementing the federalization. It proposed that the District be governed as a federal territory entitled on the basis of its population to elect two members to the Chamber of Deputies, that all government revenue collected in the District would go to the federal treasury, and that the state of Mexico would be compensated for its losses by being relieved temporarily of its full annual contribution to the federation. In keeping with the constitution, the Federal District, because it was not a state, would have no senators, would not participate in the election of members of the Supreme Court, and would have no vote in the election of the president of the republic. Almost another year of debate followed, but on 11 April 1826, following votes in both houses of Congress, the law was published that finally implemented creation of the Federal District. With that, Mexico City passed into federal control.

When the borders of the Federal District were drawn up, it consisted of approximately 85 square miles, based on a diameter of four leagues or 10.4 miles, and this area included eighteen outlying towns, some of which the state of Mexico claimed, such as Guadalupe, Tacuba, Tacubaya, Azcapotzalco, Ixtapalapa, Mexicalcingo, Churubusco, and Mixcoac. Dispute over possession of some of these towns continued until the federal republic was dissolved in 1835. Only after the April 1826 transfer of the Federal District did the state of Mexico proceed to approve its state constitution. Though it was still the largest and richest state in the federation, the state of Mexico lost, according to Macune's careful calculation, 73 percent of its state revenues when it lost Mexico City (even though the city had contained less than 30 percent of the state's population). The state ran a deficit in every year after losing the city. Its representation in the Chamber of Deputies, based on an estimated population in 1826 of 920,000, was reduced from twenty-one deputies to twelve. In the remaining years of the first federal republic, the capital of the state of Mexico was moved to Texcoco, then to San Agustín de las Cuevas (Tlalpan), and finally to Toluca.[47]

Yet although the federalization of Mexico City undoubtedly devastated the state of Mexico, extracting from its political domain the country's most economically powerful population and the site of much of its financial, educational, and institutional life, it may not have seriously weakened the city itself. The federalization of Mexico City cost the state of Mexico a great deal; it does not automatically follow, however, that it cost the city of Mexico much at all. That is, although the centralist link between the city and the state was weakened, the city was the real base of centralist interests, and its political power was not erased by its federalization. It might be argued, in fact, that Mexico City was saved from expending its resources and its political efforts in support of the objectives of the state of Mexico and was now free to concentrate on its more important role as the power base of national elites. The ayuntamiento of the city seems to have come to this realization itself, for late in the struggle, in January 1825, the city council actually endorsed the creation of the Federal District, thereby virtually killing any claim that the state of Mexico had over the city.[48] One of the more prescient arguments, from the deputy Cayetano Ibarra, was that the nationalization of Mexico City would centralize the republic by giving the national authorities, in effect, a territory of their own in which they would have a preponderance of power (he intended this as an argument against federalization). Although the city's inhabitants now had only two deputies in Congress (raised to three in 1833), the essential political interests of centralism were still served in countless other ways. The most interesting political impact, which would not have occurred except for the creation of the Federal District, was that the government of the state of Mexico, as Macune shows, would now be forced to stand on the defense of states' sovereignty in an attempt to protect every remaining source of revenue and political power it could.[49] Centralism continued because the people who were centralists were not displaced. But the state of Mexico, shorn of the Federal District, switched from the centralist camp to the federalist camp, at least until the last months of the federal republic.

The third great issue pursued by radical federalists, which rocked the young republic before the end of 1827, was by far the most troubling, not only because of its negative impact on political stability, but because of the peculiar sociopolitical pathology it represents. This was the drive of the Yorkinos and other radicals to expel from Mexico the Spanish-born naturalized citizens living there. I define it as a pathology because it was unique; no other newly independent Spanish American country adopted such a policy, no matter how far-reaching their rejection of Spanish cultural and political traditions might have been in the decades following independence. In Mexico, the direct costs in human suffering for those involved and the economic loss to the nation from the flight of capital, the disruption of trade, and the ruin of families have been extensively investigated by Harold Dana Sims.[50] But what is most important about the mania to expel Mexico's Spaniards, which swept the country in 1826 and 1827, is what it tells us about the structure of Mexican political and social life. Of all the shocks encountered by the first republic, none was more ominous.

What the expulsion of the Spaniards indicates is that early republican Mexico was a society that had no mechanisms in place to prevent or deflect scapegoating, with a political leadership prepared to give in to the worst instincts of demagoguery to achieve political aims and with a rapidly expanding tendency to violence and the use of force in the pursuit of partisan political goals. The rapid recourse to violence played a major role in the malfunction of the first republic and in early Mexico, as elsewhere, was a symptom of the breakdown of civil society. Of course, none of these qualities is unique to Mexico or to the first federal republic; they have been and are encountered in the history of all nations, including some of the most sophisticated, and cannot be considered an exceptional or peculiar characteristic of Mexican history. In a broader sense, however, these were the forces challenging the first federal republic that it was ill equipped to confront. Jesús Reyes Heroles argues that the expulsions need to be understood rather than simply condemned. He argues that although the idea of expulsions clashes with our present-day mentality, we need to recognize that Mexico was torn between the two poles of the lingering colonial order, of which the resident Spaniards were a visible symbol, and the new republican reality and that the expulsions had the objective of impeding the consolidation of an incipient economic, political, and even racial oligarchy. Most important of all, as Reyes Heroles points out, the expulsion of the Spaniards had the effect of raising such fears about the methods and objectives of the Yorkinos who advocated it and made it their political rallying cry that it contributed directly to the neutralization of the Yorkinos as a driving political force.[51]

Popular resentment at the political and economic power of the Spaniards, pejoratively called *gachupines,* dated from the wars of independence and before. In the Plan of Iguala, however, in order to assure the Spaniards' consent to independence, Iturbide had guaranteed security to those who accepted independence and remained in Mexico. This permitted the survival of the Spaniards as a dispersed interest group whose members generally did not seek assimilation. They were an ethnic and cultural minority, visible because of the managerial positions they occupied in trade, agents of encroaching capitalism who were believed to hold more than their fair share of high civil, military, and ecclesiastical positions (though, in fact, they held few positions of political power). A majority of the Spaniards living in Mexico were not wealthy, but they were disproportionately active in mercantile activities and had larger accumulations of coin than most creole or mestizo merchants in a period of scarce specie. Sims suggested that "a substantial source of creole pro-expulsionist sentiment was mercantile rivalry between Mexicans and Spaniards during a period of severe economic decline."[52] The Spaniards were not great in number. Sims estimated that 6,610 Spaniards were still to be found throughout Mexico in 1827. The Spaniard was an appropriate scapegoat for nativists searching for explanations for the economic deterioration that had befallen the country since independence.[53]

Antipathy toward the Spaniards did not originate with the Yorkinos, but the Yorkinos took hold of the anti-Spanish sentiment that existed in all parts of the country and used it as a tool for the political advancement of their goals, as a mechanism for mobilizing mass electoral support. In January 1824, General José María Lobato had led a brief mutiny of the Mexico City guard, demanding the removal from the Supreme Executive Power of the presumed Spanish sympathizers Domínguez and Michelena as well as the removal of all European Spaniards from public office. Congress, amid considerable tension, refused to give in, ordering Lobato and his followers to give up.[54] The mutiny almost immediately began to buckle when on the following day Antonio López de Santa Anna issued a flurry of public statements insisting that, although he had been listed as one of the mutineers, he was loyal to the Congress.[55] Soon after, the mutineers laid down their arms.[56]

In 1824 the second Constituent Congress debated several times the possible removal of Spaniards from office and the expulsion of some of them from the country. A variety of anti-Spanish proposals were brought forward, particularly in April 1824 when the target group was the so-called *capitulados*, those members of the Spanish military who had surrendered in 1821 and remained in Mexico. According to Quinlan, who has reconstructed the events covered in pages of the "actas secretas" of Congress that were ripped out of their bindings, the second Constituent Congress discussed the resident Spaniards on at least seven separate occasions. On two occasions the Constituent Congress voted on the expulsion of the capitulados, and on both occasions the vote tied thirty-four to thirty-four. The tie vote was finally resolved, in favor of the capitulados, by drawing lots.[57]

With the rise of the Yorkino movement, however, politics became more contentious as the York Rite faction appealed directly to the masses in a bid to take political power by electoral means. In the beginning of 1825, General Vicente Guerrero could inform José Mariano Michelena, who had left Mexico City to be minister to England, that public opinion was uniform in its hatred of the Spaniards.[58] By 1826 the York movement had grown so fast that according to Zavala there were 130 lodges throughout the country, while according to Senator José María Alpuche, another leading Yorkino, there were at least 300.[59] The York lodges were not created by the U.S. minister to Mexico, Joel R. Poinsett, as the Escoceses and the legislature of the state of Veracruz alleged, but Poinsett was an active supporter and participant in the York movement.[60] Not only did Poinsett endorse the radical federalism of the Yorkinos, he considered his participation in the York lodges necessary to balance the favor that the British minister H. G. Ward gave to the Scottish Rite movement. In 1826, the York movement created a network of secret societies throughout the country, called the Guadalupes, to work for the expulsion of the Spaniards and a radical seizure of political power.

In late 1825 the Yorkinos began their campaign to gain control of the government. Their first great victory came in September 1825 when, in a well-organized conspiracy, they succeeded in forcing the resignation of Lucas Alamán, the leading conservative, from the ministry of relations. In the months that followed the Yorkinos succeeded in frustrating President Victoria's repeated efforts to maintain a balance in the cabinet between the two factions.[61] By late 1826 the Yorkinos had effective control of the federal cabinet. José Ignacio Esteva (Grand Master of the York Rite) became secretary of finance, while Miguel Ramos Arizpe, acknowledged Yorkino and federalist, was secretary of justice. Manuel Gómez Pedraza, war minister, was considered a federalist leaning toward the Yorkinos, though in fact he belonged to neither Masonic group, and Secretary of Relations Juan José Espinosa de los Monteros was a fervent defender of the federation and therefore acceptable to the Yorkinos.[62]

Using its vast network of lodges and Guadalupe societies, the Yorkinos now mobilized to win the elections for the national and state congresses that would occur in late 1826. Using their own newspapers—primarily *Aguila Mexicana* for the Yorkinos and *El Sol* for the Scottish Rite—the two groups now attacked each other furiously. The Escoceses adopted the technique of attacking Esteva, the Yorkino chief, almost daily in the press. The Yorkinos, for their part, accused centralists and moderate federalists of treason and attempted to associate them with the Spaniards. As the 1826 elections drew near, providing the first opportunity since the adoption of the constitution for either group to gain control of the government, all pretense to an ideological debate between centralists and federalists was abandoned, and the press campaign became an open fight between Escoceses and Yorkinos.[63]

Amid considerable fraud and vote buying, the first, second, and final rounds of the indirect elections occurred in August, September, and October 1826, respectively. The result was the republic's first drastic change of political power, as the Yorkinos swept the elections at both the state and national levels. They gained control of most of the state governments, including the all-important state of Mexico, where the Yorkinos prevented the reelection of a single one of the state's incumbent national deputies or members of the state congress, and they won control of the Chamber of Deputies in the national Congress. Among those states in which new legislatures were being elected, the Scottish Rite retained control of only the legislatures of Puebla and Veracruz. Because it was the state legislatures that elected the president, the Yorkinos assumed that control of a majority of legislatures guaranteed they could elect their candidate as the next president. However, because the outgoing Escocés state legislatures were responsible for the election of new federal senators, the Scottish Rite retained control of the upper chamber.

Costeloe comments that these first national elections in the federal republic were almost completely focused on personalities rather than issues and that the supporters of the Scottish Rite could not speak openly in favor of centralism because federalism was overwhelmingly popular. It is not clear, therefore, whether all Escoceses favored centralism; some perhaps did not, but the Yorkinos invariably accused them of being centralists. On the opposite side of the coin, Stevens has pointed out that federalism and radicalism were not always coterminous, that a leader such as Zavala was a federalist and a radical while governor of the state of Mexico but behaved as a centralist radical when he was minister of finance in 1829. The partisan-inspired crushing of debate on major issues did not augur well for the future of the republic.[64]

In a furious struggle, the outgoing Escocés legislature of the state of Mexico nullified the election of the new Yorkino state legislature. But when the issue was referred to Congress, the federal Senate nullified the state's nullification, and the new Yorkino-dominated Chamber of Deputies endorsed the Senate's decision in January 1827. The sweep was complete when, in March 1827, the Escocés governor of Mexico state, Melchor Múzquiz, resigned without explanation four days before he was to begin his new four-year term. The legislature chose Lorenzo de Zavala, heretofore federal senator for Yucatán and the organizer of the Yorkino effort to carry the state election, as the new governor of the country's most powerful state. Macune points out that these were fundamentally dangerous precedents, because Zavala had used the national Congress to help secure control of a state government for the Yorkinos, a double-edged sword that in the following years would be used against the Yorkinos.[65] Although there had been proposals brought forward in Congress to prohibit secret societies, they had all failed, and although Victoria himself was thought to be considering trying to suppress the Masonic orders, he did not control his own administration by 1827. The liberal York Rite party now dominated, controlling both the national government and most of the state governments from the beginning of 1827 until 1830. The defeated and rapidly fading Scottish Rite would have to resort to drastic action if it were to survive.

Amid the heightened tension that followed the election, and only days after the opening of the new Congress in January 1827, the commandant general of the Federal District uncovered a conspiracy in favor of restoring Spanish imperial rule. It came to his attention when an obscure Spanish friar, Joaquín Arenas, invited him to join the plot. Arenas, considered by some observers to be insane, had published pro-Spanish and reactionary pamphlets.[66] The government immediately reported to the states the existence of a plot to overthrow independence. Because the Yorkino electoral campaign had heated the waters of anti-Spanish sentiment to a boil, the country was ripe for the outbreak of the ugliest manifestations of xenophobia and nativism. In the following months the so-called Arenas conspiracy was used by the Yorkinos to prove the existence of Spanish aggression and the treason of Spaniards living in Mexico and, as a result, the treason of the Escoceses. Tried before a military tribunal, Arenas was executed in June.[67]

In an atmosphere of high alarm, a wave of anti-Spanish sentiment swept the country. Conspiracies were thought to exist in many localities, and prominent peninsulars became the object of wide suspicion. Accusations flew, and when one of the most prominent Spanish-born officers of the army, General Gregorio Arana, was accused and arrested, alarm turned into hysteria amid fears that there existed a military-ecclesiastical conspiracy to destroy independence. In March, following accusations by detained persons, General Pedro Celestino Negrete, the former member of the executive triumvirate, and General José Antonio Echávarri, the leader of Casa Mata (both Spaniards), were arrested. Despite the publication of a plea by Negrete's wife that a public hearing be held so the charges against the two men could be openly contested, a flurry of pamphlets denounced them for unspecified crimes. The pamphleteers assumed they must be guilty of treason against the republic because of their earlier disloyalty to Iturbide in leading the Plan of Casa Mata, a very inconsistent interpretation indeed.[68] When the hysteria eventually died down, no definite proof of treason was found against the three generals. Nonetheless, Arana was found guilty and executed. Both Negrete and Echávarri were absolved in 1828 but were expelled from the country.[69] Sims argues that the vice president, Nicolás Bravo, was implicated by circumstantial evidence at least as much as Negrete and Echávarri, though he was never charged or called as a witness.[70]

The Yorkinos who had whipped up the growing anti-Spanish sentiment in the elections a few months earlier now had a ready-made weapon to raise public sentiment against both the Spaniards and their defenders, the Escoceses. There were immediate proposals in Congress to remove all Spaniards from public office, to expel all Spanish priests, and to expel all Spaniards. Acts of violence began to occur against Spaniards and their property, and several states introduced their own bills to expel Spaniards from public office or from the state. On 10 May Congress passed a law depriving Spaniards of their civil, military, and ecclesiastical offices as long as Spain did not recognize Mexican independence but allowing such persons to retain their full salary. Many of the states passed similar legislation. Radicals, however, were not satisfied and pressed for stronger action.

Bills for the expulsion of the Spaniards were being proposed in various state legislatures, and small uprisings—armed petitions they were called—occurred in various parts of the country demanding stronger anti-Spanish legislation. In the state of Mexico, where Lorenzo de Zavala headed the most important Yorkino state government, there were uprisings in Ajusco, Apan, Toluca, and Acapulco. Although the vice governor of the state, Manuel Reyes Veramendi, was an outspoken supporter of the proposed expulsion, Zavala himself opposed it and spoke out against it, but he was unable to persuade the state legislature. The possibility of the outbreak of fighting between followers of the two Masonic rites in the state of Veracruz, which was the last stronghold of Escocés power by mid-1827, forced President Victoria to send military reinforcements there under the command of Vicente Guerrero to assure that the Escocés governor of that state, Miguel Barragán, and the state legislature controlled by the Escoceses did not launch a rebellion against the Victoria government.[71] Guerrero, the man of color who had risen from the lower social order in the wars of independence and who was the hero of the populists, was already being mentioned by prominent Yorkinos as their candidate to be the republic's second president.

In the overheated political atmosphere of mid-1827, as the states threatened to act on their own to expel the Spaniards, the Escocés press responded by reformulating the centralist arguments against state sovereignty. *El Observador* decried as unconstitutional the view among the states that "federalism is the result of the reunion of many particular governments united in order to make together a single nation." Insisting that "the Mexican nation" existed before Casa Mata and the proclamation of the sovereignty of the states, it argued that the second Constituent Congress in 1823 and 1824 had responded to the demands of the provinces and "in dividing the national territory into states, had created them sovereign and independent in all that which was not reserved in the constitution to the powers of the Union."[72] This directly contradicted the federalist view that the national government possessed only those powers specifically granted to it by the states. *El Observador* also argued that before the Acta Constitutiva the states had no political existence, which meant that the nation, the center, had given legal political being to the states and not the other way around. This was a restatement of the argument against state sovereignty pursued in 1824 by Mier and others, but it was also something of a reformulation because it consciously raised to paramountcy the issues of precedence, of what constituted nationhood, and of possible conflicting claims between the nation and the states to the citizen's loyalty. As the conservative elements in Mexican politics found more and more to fear from the Yorkino menace and responded by formulating a conscious ideology, they began to revise the country's recent history and to generate a historical interpretation about the origin of nationhood that a substantial portion of the historiography, without careful analysis, subsequently accepted as valid.

The state of Jalisco, a center of strident anti-Spanish and profederalist feeling, was the first, on 3 September 1827, to pass a bill expelling all Spaniards from the state, exempting those married to Mexican wives, widows with children, and the ill and infirm. The state of Mexico published a similar law in October, as did Querétaro, followed by Michoacán in November, then Veracruz in December. Similar decrees were adopted in Guanajuato, Coahuila and Texas, and Oaxaca. Some state legislatures, however, rejected proposed expulsion laws. The national Congress suspended some of the state expulsion laws, including those of Jalisco and Mexico, on the grounds that such issues were the jurisdiction of the federal government, but in the end the national Congress could not refuse to act.

Thus, on 20 December 1827, Congress published the first federal expulsion law (there was a second one in 1829). *El Observador* had already predicted that such an act would be "a stain the nation can never wash away."[73] Similar to Jalisco's, it decreed the expulsion within six months of Spaniards from national territory, or until such time as Spain recognized Mexican independence. But the law offered many exceptions, including a provision for the federal government to exempt any Spaniard who was deemed to have given distinguished service to the nation, to their children, and to those persons who provided useful arts and industrial knowledge. In addition, because the law left it to the states to determine which Spaniards were to be expelled and because there was ample room for Spaniards of wealth to win special favor, there were eventually far more exceptions than there were persons expelled. In the end, only 1,779 of the country's 6,610 Spaniards were expelled, while 4,555 specific exemptions were granted. Radical dissatisfaction with the results led to the passage of the second expulsion law in 1829. Nonetheless, the lower-ranking Spaniards among the regular clergy were specifically targeted, and the impact on the clergy was significant. Sims shows that between 1826 and 1828 the regular clergy declined by 17 percent, virtually destroying the hospitals and schools operated by some orders. A renewed outflow of silver and a marked slowdown of exports were also consequences of the expulsion insofar as many of Mexico's most active traders were Spaniards.[74]

The expulsion of the Spaniards, then, is best interpreted as a result of the Yorkino movement's efforts in 1826 and 1827 to find a political platform that would allow it to mobilize the popular masses in the pursuit of Yorkino political power and electoral victory. Moderates, from José Maria Luis Mora on the Escocés side to Francisco García on the Yorkino side, recognized that the fierce partisan struggles of the two Masonic orders were swamping the republic in hysteria and demagoguery, creating a dangerous situation in which some feared a military revolt, while others attempted to foment one. The reigning xenophobia and Hispanophobia was thus a token of the increasing breakdown of civil society and its division into a variety of warring factions motivated both by ideology and the aspiration to power.

The institutions of federalism were in no way to blame for the growing fracturing of society, though the federal republic was already mortally ill and would eventually be unable to withstand the chaos that accompanied the shattering of civil society. The country's division into warring factions did not occur on regional or geographical grounds but on partisan grounds, though it would be natural for a distracted and distraught society to turn inward and concentrate on local and regional issues when the forward movement of national political life lost its momentum and its cohesion. Thus, in years to come, many observers would blame the onset of chaos on federalism, advocating centralism and authoritarianism as the most efficient solutions. The first regular elections for the ordinary constitutional Congress, followed by the expulsion of the Spaniards and the resulting political warfare, saw all persuasions resort to illegal and unconstitutional methods, the use of violence, and pronunciamientos. If this was what congressional and legislative elections brought, what would the election of a new president in 1828 bring? Peaceful government by nonmilitary means, authority mandated by ballot, and the transfer of power through democratic institutional mechanisms were becoming impossible. The infant federal republic stood little chance of surviving to adolescence, even less to maturity.

The Escoceses were rapidly declining in political influence. They had lost much of their public credibility by their indirect but unmistakable defense of the Spaniards throughout 1827. Fearing that the mob and what they viewed as its Jacobin Yorkino political manipulators were now everywhere dominant, some elements within the Scottish Rite movement gave way to panic. In late 1827, as the expulsion laws were being debated in the national Congress, Vice President Nicolás Bravo, Grand Master of the Scottish Rite, began to send out letters and hold meetings with supporters, the result of which was agreement that the only response they could make to the rapid deterioration of Scottish Rite influence and prestige was an armed revolt. For the Escoceses this was a fatal error. And for the republic and the rule of law it was a fatal blow. Bravo's revolt, raised in December 1827, would, in the words of Stanley C. Green, "give official sanction to the end of working republicanism."[75]

The expected Escocés uprising, known as the Montaño rebellion, occurred during the last week of December 1827 and the first week of January 1828. It began on 23 December with the proclamation of a rebellion in the city of Otumba, led by a minor figure, Manuel Montaño, the manager of a hacienda and a retired lieutenant colonel, and consisting of only thirty men. The so-called Plan of Montaño consisted of points that had become cornerstones in the Escocés political program in the preceding months: all secret societies should be prohibited, which would seriously harm the Yorkinos; the federal cabinet should be replaced, meaning Minister of War Gómez Pedraza principally; and the government should expel the U.S. minister, Joel Poinsett, who the Escoceses hated for championing Yorkino radical federalism. According to the deposition later given by Montaño, he had not even seen the plan before it was circulated in Mexico City. The uprising, the second armed revolt against the republic (the first was the Lobato uprising in January 1824) was centered in Tulancingo, in northeast Mexico state, a location chosen because it afforded access to the state of Veracruz where the government was controlled by the Scottish Rite.[76] A simultaneous uprising had been planned in Tlaxcala, but it did not occur. A few days after the appearance of the Plan of Montaño, the two chief Escocés political figures in Mexico City—Francisco Molinos del Campo, senator from the state of Mexico, and Vice President Bravo—rode out to join the rebellion, and Bravo announced that he had taken leadership of the uprising. The Yorkinos, and Victoria himself, assumed that Bravo's real purpose was to overthrow the federalist system and replace it with centralism, and the president once again called on Vicente Guerrero to march out and suppress it.

The rebellion lasted only two weeks. Bravo waited in Tulancingo with a few hundred men, dispatching requests to various officers throughout the country to join his rebellion, apparently having received previous pledges of support. But aid for the rebellion did not materialize. Meanwhile, Guerrero was drawing near with two thousand men. Although Colonel Manuel López de Santa Anna declared his support for the rebellion, his famous brother General Antonio López de Santa Anna, then vice governor of Veracruz and a supporter, it was believed, of the Scottish Rite, rode to the nearby city of Huamantla but decided to offer his services to the government instead of the rebels. The evidence suggests that General Santa Anna would have joined the Bravo rebellion if he had thought it stood a chance of success.

Unable to find further military support, Bravo and the other rebels were captured by Guerrero on 7 January 1828. Apparently unaware of the fall of Bravo, the legislature of Veracruz, in the state capital of Jalapa, called on the federal government to outlaw secret societies, and the governor of Veracruz, Miguel Barragán, rose up against the federal government. When they discovered Bravo had failed, Barragán went into hiding, and the Veracruz legislature withdrew its petition.[77] The state legislature disavowed Barragán, and Santa Anna, as vice governor, became acting governor of Veracruz state. The Yorkino city council of the port of Veracruz opposed Barragán's support of the Montaño rebellion. When the uprising failed, Barragán was captured along with Manuel Santa Anna, both of them having sought refuge at General Santa Anna's hacienda of Manga de Clavo.

In the proceedings against him, Bravo denied that he had plotted to overthrow federalism and replace it with a centralized system and insisted instead that his only purpose was to abolish secret societies and to expel Poinsett. Reflecting on the corrosive influence of the Yorkino armed petitions in support of the expulsion of the Spaniards throughout 1827, Bravo said that because the federal government had not acted to punish those uprisings he believed himself authorized to act with the same impunity to pursue the objectives of the Plan of Montaño.[78] It is evident from Bravo's easy use of such an argument and consistent with the rapid development of a military caste mentality that some leading officers had convinced themselves that members of the army possessed a right to rebel. Indeed, in his short autobiography written in 1845, Bravo, in addition to making very harsh statements about Victoria, said that he revolted in 1827 "using the right of insurrection."[79]

As required by the constitution, Bravo, as vice president, was indicted by a grand jury of the Chamber of Deputies. Despite calls for his execution, when he was tried and found guilty he was sentenced to six years' exile in Chile. Although his loyal supporters claimed to be stunned by the outcome, it is hard to see how they could have expected a more lenient sentence.[80] Unrepentant, Bravo wrote a statement that was published through the efforts of his mother and his wife as he was leaving Mexico City in April 1828 in which he justified his rebellion by accusing the Yorkinos and Joel Poinsett of having turned the republic into their own pri-

vate patrimony, destroying the rule of law, and bankrupting the treasury.[81] By the time he wrote his "Memoria histórica" in 1845, he blamed
Victoria and Esteva for the decline in the affairs of the republic. He and
sixteen others involved in the rebellion sailed from San Blas for South
America in June. One of his children, who was traveling with him, died on
the trip overland. Although ordered to travel to the port of Chiloe in the
far south of the continent, Bravo stopped when he got as far as Guayaquil,
Ecuador.[82] Former Veracruz governor Barragán and General Santa
Anna's brother Manuel were condemned to exile in Guayaquil; Manuel
Santa Anna died on the voyage to South America.[83] The forty-one exiled
generals, colonels, and other officers included the brothers-in-law of
Bravo and Negrete. Among those implicated but not exiled were General
José Morán, ex-marqués de Vivanco, and José Gabriel Armijo, military
commander of San Luis Potosí.[84]

With the presidential election scheduled for 1 September 1828, the fall of
Bravo and a number of other Escocés leaders appeared to guarantee that
the Yorkinos were now secure in their political dominance. The Yorkinos'
choice for their presidential candidate was Vicente Guerrero, who besides
being a hero of both independence and federalism was a man of color
whose standing among the masses was unequaled. As the Scottish Rite
movement disintegrated, the minister of war, Manuel Gómez Pedraza,
was becoming increasingly the candidate of both the moderate Yorkinos
and an emerging new group, known as the Impartials, which consisted of
both Yorkinos alarmed at the extremism and secrecy of their Masonic rite
and Escoceses seeking a new political affiliation. The Yorkino movement
began to divide internally, particularly with the defection to the Impartials
of such distinguished Yorkinos as Ramos Arizpe and Gómez Farías in the
early months of 1828.

The contest for the presidency between Guerrero and Gómez Pedraza
was perceived at the time as symbolizing not only the different political
views but also the immense class and ethnic divisions that the early years
of independence brought to the fore. Juan Suárez y Navarro, a close observer of Mexican affairs who was a supporter of Santa Anna until the
1850s, defined Guerrero as the "son of the people, man of color, caudillo of
the reformist party, of middling knowledge and embarrassing manners"
and said of him, "far from abandoning the indigenous class to which he
belonged, he loved it with all the enthusiasm of one who knew at heart its
pains and its needs." Meanwhile, "the farcical aristocrats that we had and
still have in the country . . . saw in Manuel Gómez Pedraza an old servant

of the king, educated with great care in the school of the viceroys: honorable, active and intelligent, with all the prestige of a life of good antecedents in his beliefs, his aspirations and his interests." Though the Escoceses detested Gómez Pedraza as the minister of war who had presided over the military defeat of Bravo as well as the expulsion of the Spaniards, they preferred him to Guerrero and in August declared their public support for him.[85]

In the end, therefore, the failure of Bravo's rebellion at Tulancingo was significant for the apparently total dominance it gave to the Yorkinos. It marked the fall of the Escoceses as a major influence in the national government, and it marked the triumph of the Yorkinos. But Yorkino dominance would be short-lived, and the Yorkinos' excesses in power would do more to strengthen the forces of centralism, and to provoke the further consolidation of a conservative and antifederalist movement, than even Bravo's achievement of power could have done. Only a year later, in the name of national unity during the invasion of Mexico by a Spanish expeditionary force, General Guerrero decreed on independence day, 16 September 1829, an amnesty for Bravo and the other exiles of the Montaño conspiracy.[86] The greater significance of the Bravo rebellion, however, was that it ruined the aspiration that Victoria had for the federal executive to keep it above partisan squabbles.

All these crises occurred before federal republican institutions were fully in place and functioning, condemning the federal republic to failure at the starting gate. The tremendous struggle over the 1826 election and the debate over the expulsions, as well as the Arenas conspiracy, all occurred before the state of Mexico had even adopted its constitution. The uprising led by the vice president took place when there was still a year left in the first presidential term, and the default on the British loans occurred only a few months later. Three of the qualities most necessary for the creation of successful democratic political institutions—fiscal solvency, recognition of the credibility of the political leadership, and willingness to trust that the political opponents will not misuse their power if allowed to hold high office—had already disappeared. Before all the institutional forms necessary to operate a federal system were in place, the national government was effectively bankrupt, the presidency had lost its credibility, and any simple belief in the ability of elections to settle disputes was swamped in a sea of discord. The foundations were knocked out from under the feet of federalism. How could it have been made to work under these circumstances? In late 1827, Servando Teresa de Mier lay on his deathbed in the National Palace where, as a mark of his distinction and the esteem in which the president held him, he had resided during the presidency of Guadalupe Victoria. The president came to see him and inquired about his health. According to the testimony of Nicolás Bravo, Mier replied, "I go as the republic goes, to my death."[87]

CHAPTER SEVEN

Sovereignty of the People: "A Shoot of a Plant That Has Not Been Cultivated"

The final years of the first federal republic saw the fruition of the great contest that had begun in the war of independence, the struggle to determine whether the ultimate logic of an entirely new political order would emerge in Mexico, and for the first time in any Latin American society, the journey toward a popular government operating in the name of the common man. It occurred in a context rendered chaotic by the highly flawed Yorkino achievement of power, the wholesale abandonment of the constitution, and the loss of a rallying point around which nationhood could be made stronger.

When Vicente Guerrero took office on 1 April 1829 as the second president of the republic he issued a remarkable manifesto that simultaneously expressed both the fatal flaw and the glory of his presidency. The fatal flaw was encapsulated in the sentence with which the statement began, "By the will of God . . . and of my compatriots, I have been constitutionally called to perform the high charge of President of the United Mexican States." That was simply a fiction; every Mexican knew the names of the Yorkino politicians who had put Guerrero in the presidency and who expected to run it in his name. Yet the final two sentences of the twenty-page statement expressed in a few powerful words what Mexicans still see as the glory of this unlettered man who had such aspirations for the well-being of the people: "The people have confided in me their destinies, and I will be everything for the people. One tear less: one ear of corn more: a shoot of a plant that has not been cultivated, that will be the maximum of my happiness."[1]

What was the "shoot of a plant that has not been cultivated" to which Guerrero referred? Guerrero spoke and probably thought in simple naturalistic terms drawn from the experiences of the mestizo and mulatto ranchers and farmers in the Pacific south from whom he derived. Because he represented the coming to power of radical federalism, he was apparently alluding to the promise of a people's government and to the exercise of the will of the people that his presidency represented in his own mind and those of his supporters. Zavala said that Guerrero's followers aspired to establish "absolute equality, despite the present state of society, and democratic liberty, despite the differences in civilization" that existed between Mexicans.[2] As the leading Yorkino newspaper, *Correo de la Federación Mexicana*, phrased it in February 1828, "The Mexican people, under the present institutions that happily reign, ought to be sovereign; by the same principle, the majority of the people ought to govern."[3] The Yorkinos believed their takeover of the presidency represented the beginning of genuine egalitarianism; conservatives, apparently, feared so as well. Many of Guerrero's supporters believed his populist rhetoric suggested his support of sweeping land reform. Guardino judges it "the most radical government to take power in Mexico before 1855."[4]

A fundamentally important transition was emerging, particularly in the way people perceived of the nation and their role in it. Just as the years since independence were characterized by a progression in political empowerment from the center to the state or provincial level, so this process continued within each state down to the level of the municipality. This ever-widening circle of recognition of autonomy had begun with the transition from Iturbide to federalism, and by about 1828 it continued within each state with the impulse toward self-government flowing from state to locality. This was a natural development in that the municipal level—the towns and villages—particularly in the vast rural areas, was the base political community of Mexican organization, representing the individual through the ayuntamiento (in cities and larger towns and cabeceras) or *alcaldías auxiliares* (in villages and smaller jurisdictional divisions such as *rancherías*). It is exemplified in the duality of meaning of the Spanish words *pueblo* (people) and *pueblos* (villages) as used throughout the nineteenth century in what Annino calls "the Mexican politico-constitutional idiom." The pueblos (villages) were, and always had been, the institutional expression and juridical representation of the pueblo (people).[5] They now demanded the same kind of participation, the same kind of autonomy over their own affairs and resources, that the states had demanded in 1823. In the period from late 1828 to late 1829 a particular political tendency found a way to mobilize the citizenship by being expressed at the base level, the pueblos and municipalities.

This tendency, as I have said, was a further widening in the concentric circles of autonomy, a major effort in the direction that Hernández Chávez argues was the dominant thrust of Mexican political life in the nineteenth century as a whole: toward large and flexible autonomies not only for the states but also for the municipalities. The role of the ayuntamientos and the municipalities was both inherent and natural. The growing recognition of the rights of the citizen and the rights of the towns, Hernández Chávez says, imparted a governability to the country by marrying the new constitutional rights with the old system and by linking the old and new forms of politics with the social organization of the community. In addition, the ayuntamiento-municipio was the center of its residents' identity precisely because it did not represent a rupture or destruction of the everyday government of the towns but rather conformed to the traditional modes that dated from the colonial period and before.[6] Here we have, once again, an answer to the charge made by nineteenth-century conservatives that political instability was the result of the adoption of foreign political ideologies and the importation by liberals of exotic institutions, such as federalism, that were out of touch with the country's social and historical reality. The municipio was not a foreign or imported structure but was inherent in the Mexican tradition.

A third concentric circle of sovereignty, sovereignty of the people, was emerging to join the recognized circles of sovereignty of the nation and sovereignty of the states. Thus, what appears to be chaos to the observer who looks only at the stratum of the federal government was to the man on the ground, the citizen, a further expansion of autonomy empowering the vast reaches of the population regardless of ethnicity or prior weakness. It was a further step in the transition from a political structure based on institutions and social estate to one based on the individual. It was a disorderly process, but it constituted the first great attempt in Mexican history to carry to its logical conclusion the principle that the state represents the people. And it was massively resisted by the vested interests—the holders of special privileges, the aristocracy, the well-to-do, the full-time military, the creole heirs of Spanish corporatism—whose political role derived from the colonial heritage. Annino points out that this great struggle, which would continue throughout the nineteenth century, was much stronger than the other struggle that characterizes the century, that between centralism and federalism.[7]

What we are seeing, in fact, is the beginning of the transition by which the principle adopted from the constitution of Cádiz and guardedly restated in the Acta Constitutiva of 1824—that "sovereignty resides radically and essentially in the nation"—was transformed throughout the nineteenth century into the fundamental principle expressed in the 1917 Mexican constitution, that "sovereignty resides essentially and originally in the people," a substantially different idea. Similarly, this period marks the beginning of the transformation from the concept of the 1824 constitution that Mexico was a "representative, popular, federal republic" to the concept of the 1917 constitution that it is a "representative, democratic, federal republic." And although the 1824 constitution was mute on the subject, the role of the municipio as the territorial unit on which the states are based is set forth clearly in Article 115 of the 1917 constitution: "The States will adopt for their internal administration [*régimen interior*] the republican, representative, popular form of government, having the Free Municipality [Municipio Libre] as the base of their territorial division and of their political and administrative organization."

Because of the breakdown of the legally constituted state that had occurred by 1828, a new form of legitimacy and political representation was being born. It was founded on the recognized legitimacy of local notables in each town, region, and state; their role as the spokesmen of their constituents; and the link between them and the mobilized citizenry under arms. The rise of the caudillos in the first third of the nineteenth century is sometimes mistakenly called militarism. As Hernández Chávez argues, however, it was a new form of legitimacy and political representation in which local notables based their legitimate leadership of their communities on their function as members of the ayuntamientos and as officers of the militia. And the rise of the caudillos constituted an indirect sign of the extent to which mobilization had occurred in the wars of independence and the first republic.[8] Although elite gentlemen in the national capital bemoaned the fact, and some historians have tended to repeat their laments, for much of the nineteenth century Mexico could not be governed by the national capital because it refused to be.

Despite the universality with which Guerrero is cited as the man of the people, little is known about his personality and opinions. He said and wrote little about himself, and contemporary observers, both supporters and opponents, appear to have always seen him as a symbol, someone not quite flesh and blood whose mere name conveyed all the meaning that needed to be imparted. Yet the paradox of the image Guerrero used to describe himself—as a shoot of the uncultivated plant of the people's republic—is that, because neither the young plant nor the man would survive very much longer, both remain hard to define. We know too little about Guerrero or about the populist republic he aspired to create to be able to assess either fully. The political and constitutional debates of the first federal republic were giving way to another great clash between the masses and the propertied classes—the next act in the uncompleted revolution that began in 1810 and a further stage in an ongoing drama that weaves throughout modern Mexican history. Guerrero the man remains elusive, overshadowed by the characteristics others attributed to him in his own lifetime and after.

But the imagery was also severely flawed. Guerrero became president as a result of rebellion. The first presidential succession in 1828 marked the definitive breakdown of the constitutional order and in a manner so threatening to the propertied classes that they could be expected to react. Constitutionally, that is, in terms of the original vision of federalism in 1823 and 1824, the republic was adrift. Where there had once appeared to be consensus, by 1828 there was none. Moreover, as a result of the fate of the Guerrero administration in 1830, supporters of autonomy for the states and the pueblos began to turn inward to defend their home state and pueblo, to the extent at least that their meager financial and military resources permitted. The development of regional caudillos received its major impetus from these events. It was not the caudillos who destroyed the first federal republic. It was the breakdown of the first federal republic that created a role for the caudillos to play as individual regions and provinces fell back on the defense of their home territory's self-determination amid the generalized disintegration of civil political order.

In addition, the presidential succession of 1828 provided a major impetus for the organization of a self-conscious centralist conservative coalition between well-to-do sectors of Mexican society. Members of this sector had been slow to organize an assertive defense of their privileges, not so much from lethargy or distaste for getting their hands dirty in the practice of politics, but because it took them some time to recognize the extent to which the disappearance of the former defensive structures that had been provided by the Spanish monarchy and the Iturbide monarchy left them exposed, as a class, to the potential leveling effects of mass politics in a representative federal republic. The men of substance, who began to refer to themselves as hombres de bien, were galvanized by the disorders of 1828 and by Guerrero's seizure of power. The expulsion of the Spaniards, the sweeping Yorkino electoral victories, the destruction of the Escoseses as an organized political group—these had all been warning signs that showed elites how far their position in society had deteriorated. The uprising of Bravo at Tulancingo had reflected the fact that elites were bestirring themselves once again to recapture what they had lost.

By 1830 the elites had regrouped along class lines, with a more ideological focus than in the preceding years and dedicated chiefly to the recovery of their economic influence and the reestablishment of pre-1821 order and social stability. This led many of them to demand a redirection of federalism away from the universal male franchise and toward increased centralized control. Some sense of the hatred of conservatives for the radicals who now took office may be seen in the statement of José Antonio Facio, who was secretary of war in the next government, "Guerrero seated ignorance and evil in the presidential chair."[9] The Guerrero presidency, brief though it was, provoked the reconsolidation of the elites. Conservatives could live with the moderated federalism worked out in the constitution of 1824; they would not stand idly by and watch the rise of a popular system in which the masses influenced or controlled political outcomes. Soon even the liberals drew back from the threat of social leveling, aware as they were that they lived in a multiethnic society in which they were massively outnumbered by the people of color. As Lorenzo de Zavala, the foremost Yorkino radical, pointed out in 1833, of the two hundred thousand voters in the state of Mexico, two-thirds were illiterate, one-half were unclothed, and one-third could not speak the Spanish language.[10] The consensus that had prevailed in 1824 and led to the incorporation of the provinces into the definition of sovereignty now broke down as the masses, activated by the Yorkino political agenda, demanded that they too be included in the vision of nationhood.

The Revolt of the Acordada in December 1828 and Guerrero's assumption of the presidency represented an attempt to expand participatory politics in Mexico that was not dissimilar to the Jacksonian expansion of democracy in the United States that same year. It incorporated some of the same strengths: a military hero as symbol, an essentially rurally based upwelling of demand for political influence, a glorification of the common man, and opposition to the permanent aristocratic officeholding elite. It also shared some of the same weaknesses: a lack of precision in defining goals, a tendency to demagoguery, a revengeful partisanship, and mixed motives on the part of some supporters. There were, of course, many differences, notably that Guerrero did not turn out to be an iron-willed leader like Andrew Jackson and lacked a powerful political machine, such as Jackson's Democratic Party, to sustain him.

In the selection of the second president of the republic, the minister of war, Manuel Gómez Pedraza, the candidate of the Impartials and the Escoceses, won a narrow victory over Vicente Guerrero, the candidate of the Yorkinos, who had been considered the frontrunner. Eighteen of the nineteen state legislatures cast their votes in September 1828 (the state of Durango did not vote). According to the constitution, each state legislature cast two votes, one for president and one for vice president, and those votes were then formally counted and certified in the presence of both chambers of the new Congress in January. Hence, the actual certification of the votes did not occur for five months, although by late September the public knew for whom the legislatures had voted. Because the votes for president and vice president were counted as a single pool, the final tally was Manuel Gómez Pedraza, 11; Vicente Guerrero, 9; Anastasio Bustamante, 6; Melchor Múzquiz, 2; Ignacio Rayón, 2; Juan Ignacio Godoy, 2; Luis de Cortázar, 1; Valentín Gómez Farías, 1; José Ignacio Esteva, 1; and Lorenzo de Zavala, 1. Two states, Michoacán and Tabasco, voted for both Gómez Pedraza and Guerrero.[11] On the basis of total votes, therefore, Gómez Pedraza should have become president, and Guerrero should have become vice president.

The narrow victory of Gómez Pedraza was a result of the fear of Yorkino radicalism felt by many individuals among the propertied classes. The Yorkinos, who had expected their candidate to become the new president, felt that the election had been stolen from them. Although it had appeared in the first half of 1828 as if Guerrero was going to win the presidency easily, the defection of the so-called Impartials by June showed that a campaign to stop Guerrero from achieving the presidency was underway. Supported by many former Yorkinos and strong federalists, notably Ramos Arizpe, Juan de Dios Cañedo, Esteva, Gómez Farías, and Francisco García, Gómez Pedraza also appeared to have the support of President Victoria.[12] Guerrero meanwhile was strongly supported by the governors of about half the states, including José María Tornel, governor of the Federal District; Antonio López de Santa Anna, interim governor of Veracruz; and, most notably, Lorenzo de Zavala, governor of the state of Mexico. Even before the voting was over, Santa Anna began an uprising in the name of Guerrero.[13]

The uprising eventually resulted in the so-called Acordada rebellion, and it brought to the presidency the foremost living hero of the wars of independence. Years later, in his autobiography, Santa Anna still referred to Guerrero simply as "the patriot of the people."[14] Guerrero was universally perceived as a man of absolute probity and simple decency and as a symbol of the Mexican masses. Guillermo Prieto, in his *Memorias*, remembered the day in his childhood when he met Guerrero in his uncle's house. He spoke of Guerrero's "inexpressible gentleness," remembering the way this simple mulatto hero had conferred gravely with the children of the house about their toys and amusements and concluding, "Near him, one felt the goodness of his soul and he had certain characteristics of an unsophisticated rancher that were really charming."[15] Tornel said Guerrero possessed "the incontestable power of genius."[16]

But the old elite and their allies were terrified of the Jacobins; feared the reforms advocated by the political handlers of "el Negro Guerrero"; and hated Guerrero for his dark skin, country mannerisms, and lack of polish.[17] Most contemporary sources agreed that the Guerrero regime was weak and vacillating and made too many concessions to its opponents, most notably granting amnesty to General Bravo who would later lead the forces hunting down Guerrero in the south. Suárez y Navarro wrote that Guerrero's fatal weakness was that he was "kind by temperament." Mora wrote that the Guerrero presidency was in a period of crisis and the government was too deeply weakened by its preoccupations to survive on a day-to-day basis.[18] Most significantly, Zavala, the man who made Guerrero president, said that he was characterized by "a mildness that has degenerated into a true weakness."[19]

The manner by which Guerrero came to office cost him the support of most moderates, including federalists, who might otherwise have sustained him. Indeed, as Costeloe argues, the seizure of the presidency by the radical wing of the Yorkinos revealed the division among the Yorkinos themselves; the disintegration of the Yorkinos as a cohesive movement; and the first emergence of the tripartite division among conservatives, moderate liberals, and radical liberals that would continue to characterize Mexican politics well into the era of the Reforma.[20] Reyes Heroles dubbed the two wings that emerged among the liberals in 1828 as the "democratic" (radical) wing and the "enlightened" (moderate) wing.[21] The parties were now more clearly divided according to the social aspirations and backgrounds of their members, which meant that political divisions formed simply on the basis of the secret Masonic societies were now largely irrelevant. This does not mean, of course, that Freemasonry ceased to play a role in Mexican political life, only that it became less apparent and less founded on the simple dichotomy of York and Scottish rites.[22] Overall, the tendency to ignore the constitution was universal, partic-

ularly given the extent to which the right to armed petition, to pronunciamiento, had become the norm since 1826.

On 12 September 1828, Santa Anna began his rebellion in support of
Guerrero.[23] As acting governor of the state of Veracruz he had failed to
convince the state legislature to vote for Guerrero, whereupon he organized protests in several municipalities against the legislature for casting
its electoral vote for Gómez Pedraza. The legislature replied by removing
him from the governorship, he responded by resigning the governorship,
and having carefully organized support and material ahead of time he led
eight hundred troops in seizing the important fortress of Perote near the
state capital of Jalapa. The paradox, of course, is that Santa Anna had previously been thought to be a supporter of the Escoceses but after the Tulancingo rebellion had converted to what appeared to be the winning Yorkino movement. Declaring that Guerrero's election as president was the
will of the people and their choice had been nullified by the self-serving
politicians, Santa Anna's plan, issued at Perote, demanded annulment of
the election of Gómez Pedraza, a new law of expulsion for Spaniards, the
declaration of Guerrero as president, and the annulment of the vote of
those state legislatures that had gone to Gómez Pedraza.[24]

Besieged in Perote by a much larger army of the federal government,
Santa Anna's rebellion seemed destined to fail. As a result, he and his
forces slipped out of the fortress and moved to the city of Oaxaca, where
they established their headquarters in a monastery and were again besieged by federal forces. The federal Congress removed from office such
prominent Guerrero supporters as Tornel, governor of the Federal District, and on 25 October passed a law prohibiting all secret societies, which
meant the Yorkinos. Santa Anna's rebellion was seconded by militia units
on the Costa Grande, led by Juan Alvarez and Isidro Montes de Oca.
Alvarez, making his first appearance on the national scene, led his troops
to Cuernavaca, in the vicinity of Mexico City, and explicitly based his
movement on the support of the rural masses.[25] Meanwhile, Zavala, governor of the state of Mexico and the most prominent supporter of Guerrero, was accused in the federal Senate of complicity in the rebellion and
was ordered detained. Rather than fall into the hands of President-elect
Gómez Pedraza, Zavala fled into the mountains. After nearly a month, he
secretly entered Mexico City to organize his own rebellion against the
government.[26]

On 30 November 1828, two and a half months after Santa Anna's initial
uprising, Zavala unleashed a rebellion in the heart of the capital city. His

supporters seized the Acordada, the federal government's arms depository. José María Lobato, the leader of the radical federalist and anti-Spanish rebellion of 1824, led the rebel troops in the Acordada. According to Gómez Pedraza's own later testimony, the federal government was paralyzed by the strife between President Victoria and his cabinet. Amid the exchange of bombardment between the rebels in the Acordada and government forces in the National Palace, Guerrero arrived on 2 December to join the rebels in the Acordada.

At that point, for reasons he did not explain, Gómez Pedraza abandoned the fight and on the morning of 3 December left the city. Fleeing to Guadalajara, on 27 December he renounced the presidency and left the country for Europe without his wife and family. In November 1830, Gómez Pedraza issued an appeal to Congress in which he stated that he had freely abandoned the field because he believed his absence would calm discord. He added that President Victoria and members of the cabinet "are witnesses of my advance resolution not to accept in any case or circumstance the presidency of the republic" but did not explain further what he meant by that other than to insist that he had not been forced out by the Acordada rebellion.[27] Sims suggests an alternative explanation for Gómez Pedraza's hasty flight from Mexico City. He argues that the president-elect went to Guadalajara in the hopes that the commander there, General Joaquín Parres, could protect him. The Guerrerist and anti-Spanish rebellion led by Juan José Codallos, however, which began in Querétaro but spread to Guanajuato and then to Guadalajara, forced Gómez Pedraza to renounce the presidency completely.[28]

Without defenders and with the majority of members of Congress and the cabinet in hiding, President Guadalupe Victoria was left virtually alone. When a white flag was run up over the Acordada on 4 December, Victoria ordered a cease-fire, which allowed the rebels to spread throughout the city and capture principal points. When Lobato gained control of the plaza in front of the palace, Victoria went out to speak to Lobato from the balcony, asking "Will I be safe if I come down?" The president then rode with Lobato to the Acordada to confer with Zavala and Guerrero, an event that at the time was considered the ultimate humiliation for the first president of the republic.[29]

Mexico City now experienced the closest thing to anarchy it had encountered in 136 years, since the great riot of 1692. Never having been attacked during the wars of independence, the capital had been, as Van Young phrases it, an "island in the storm," relatively untouched even as it presided over a country engulfed in social violence.[30] Now it lived through what according to all accounts was its worst hour, the Parián Riot, which more than any other single event galvanized propertied elites to a reborn conservatism.

A mob, described as beggars, *léperos*, escaped prisoners, soldiers, and the poor, rioted through the city's main market, the Parián, a collection of hundreds of shops located in the main square (the Zócalo) in front of the National Palace, where they looted and burned the shops and warehouses owned by the city's major creole and Spanish businessmen. Carlos María de Bustamante, who despised Zavala, charged that the governor of the state of Mexico had for weeks been buying the support of bandits and highwaymen throughout the state in order to unleash them on the good citizens of Mexico City.[31] What Zavala had actually done was to distribute arms to militiamen throughout the state in anticipation of a possible clash with the regular army.[32] Goods valued between 2 and 3 million pesos were pillaged, the fires burned for ten to twelve hours, and at least a thousand persons lost their livelihoods.[33] Even storerooms in the National Palace were looted. The mob was dispersed in the evening after an army troop with a cannon arrived at the Zócalo.

On 4 and 5 December President Victoria was entirely abandoned by the members of his government and Congress, left alone to preside over the wreckage of his administration. Tornel hints that Victoria, completely powerless, may have expected the victorious rebels to overthrow him; but Zavala made the point that the victorious side gave command to President Victoria at the moment of their triumph, allowed the government to function, and did not overthrow the Senate or Chamber of Deputies.[34] In a triumphant statement on 5 December, Zavala and Lobato celebrated their victory, exulting, "The president . . . enjoys the inexplicable pleasure of seeing himself surrounded by his true friends."[35] There were also rebellions against the federal government in Puebla and Querétaro, the first opposed to the Yorkino capture of the presidency and the second in favor of it.[36] Victoria's presidency had completely disintegrated.

After four years of popular, representative federalism in a context of remarkably widespread male franchise, a truly outspoken press, relentless xenophobia directed at Spaniards, and extreme political tension, the Parián Riot violently reminded elites of the potential costs of mobilizing the masses in pursuit of partisan objectives. For the well-to-do, the most terrifying aspect of the riot was that all civil authority disappeared, even if it was only for the afternoon and evening of 4 December. From their own writings, it is clear that even such stalwart Yorkinos as Zavala and Anastacio Zerecero were repelled by this uprising of the poor. At the other extreme, such conservative authors as Carlos María de Bustamante and Francisco Ibar (author of various pamphlets published from January to August 1829 and collected in a publication called *Muerte política de la república mexicana*) were provoked to extreme statements of hysteria. The specter of anarchy and class war and the dangers of mass mobilization loomed larger in the minds of the national elite than at any time since the Hidalgo rebellion, but because they occurred on the streets where the elites lived their impact was more immediate. Throughout the nineteenth century, both liberal and conservative parties would be characterized by an enduring social conservatism. Arrom summarizes, "The riot, though just one episode in one city, was a pivotal event in dampening the democratic idealism of early independent Mexico."[37]

Guerra points out yet another level of the impact of the Parián Riot. Mexico had proclaimed itself a representative republic, but the idea of representation was modified by the fact that the universal male suffrage was exercised indirectly, that is, the masses participated only in the first of the three stages of voting. The exercise of universal suffrage was contained within the institutional boundaries first set out in the Spanish constitution of 1812, creating a representative republic in which the government belonged to the elite. But when the masses, as represented by the urban mob in the Parián, attempted to exercise direct influence on the political system without intermediaries, changing the makeup of the government, elites of both conservative and liberal persuasion recognized the danger and determined to prevent the logic of representativeness from putting the social order itself in danger.[38] It is necessary to remember that in the Mexican first federal republic "the people" were not sovereign; it was the nation and the states that shared sovereignty, while representative institutions exercised that sovereignty in the name of the people. Thus, in Guerra's terminology, the first federal republic would be considered a transitional system, midway between a system based on institutional or corporate power and one based on the individual. From the viewpoint of urban elites, a good deal of retrenchment was now necessary, and it would occur by the end of 1829. Two very similar riots of the plebeian elements occurred in the city of Puebla within days of the Parián Riot, one on 12 December and one on 25 December, provoking the same fears of social dissolution.[39]

In the days following the riot, Tornel was restored to the governorship of the Federal District, and according to his own self-congratulatory account he slowly brought order to the city.[40] Guerrero was appointed minister of war for a few days, replacing Gómez Pedraza. Although the legislatures or officials in at least seven states—Veracruz, Puebla, Querétaro, Jalisco, Zacatecas, San Luis Potosí, and Yucatán—appeared unwilling to accept the outcome of the Acordada revolt, which they saw as little more than a barracks coup, the departure of Gómez Pedraza meant Guerrero would become president. Yet the cost of the Acordada revolt was that it assured that Guerrero would come to the presidency with remarkably little political support. Even such strong federalist states as Zacatecas and Jalisco did not support him. The military commanders of Jalisco, Puebla, Querétaro, and Guanajuato would continue to support Gómez Pedraza even after he was in exile. Though the Yorkinos had presented Guerrero as the great symbol of the federalist cause, the degree to which he was an avowed populist meant he would have to govern without the support of the most federalist states. Justo Sierra's judgment is that "General Guerrero's administration was born dead."[41]

On 12 January 1829 the Chamber of Deputies, which had begun the new legislative term at the beginning of the month, designated Guerrero president and Anastasio Bustamante vice president. This meant that all the votes for Gómez Pedraza, which had come from nine states placing him first and two states placing him second, had to be voided, the greatest breach yet of the constitution. As Costeloe puts it, "The repudiation of the votes legally emitted by the states which had opted for Gómez Pedraza constituted the negation of the essence of the federal system."[42]

Guerrero had won the undying enmity of the privileged as well as the suspicion of all moderate federalists and constitutionalists. The Parián Riot burned itself into the memories of the central elites, who had previously been remarkably insulated from the direct impact of political anarchy and its resulting terror. No single event so clearly illustrates the close links between central elites and the capital city, for the response of the hombres de bien and the aristocracy to the Parián Riot was disproportional. In a country long troubled by violence, much of the urban elite had their first direct taste of it, and the conservative tendency of many men of property received a major impetus. In addition to the dislike of the privileged, despite the fact that Guerrero promoted a number of officers to the rank of general, a majority of army general officers did not support him either. Finally, while he may have had the support of the masses, as Green puts it, "his working-class constituency could support him in a civil war but not in Congress or the state legislatures."[43] Guerrero was thus placed in an untenable position because he was imposed by arms in a coup manufactured by the radicals. Because the Mexican presidency was constitutionally quite weak, Guerrero would be the virtual tool of his cabinet, in which his secretary of finance, Zavala, was the dominant figure. Yet although Zavala was a radical federalist, he did not support those elements of Guerrero's program that appealed most to the masses, such as its populism, protectionism, and support for a second law to expel the Spaniards.[44]

One important element in the sense of drift that set in after 1828 amid the chaos that characterized politics was the absence for the first time since independence of a figure in whom the nation could vest its aspirations. There were only three real heroes of the independence movement left whose reputations were based on the constancy of their devotion to the struggle for independence: Bravo, Victoria, and Guerrero. All three had now had their images irretrievably clouded. The conservative centralism of Bravo had made him anathema to federalists since 1823, while his bad judgment worried conservatives. Victoria's image was ruined by his presidency. Carlos María de Bustamante had been assiduously at work since 1825 accusing him of every fault, and the Acordada revolt now reduced him to an object of pity whose presidency was universally judged a failure. And Guerrero's public image, far more complex because it was grounded in his appeal to the poor and people of color, became that of an innocent marionette manipulated by his radical handlers, as much an object of pity as Victoria. The elites did not want Guerrero to be perceived as the symbol of the nation's ethical and civic virtues, even if later generations perceived him that way. The exquisite paradox of Guerrero's weakness in his brief eight months as president was summarized by Tornel, "The Yorkinos congratulated themselves on a triumph that was their defeat, on having overcome their enemies in a war whose outcome effectively served to dissipate all illusions."[45] In what appeared to be a moment of unparalleled triumph, Guerrero came to office as the Yorkino movement was disintegrating. What is more, there were no heroes left, only a painful emptiness at the heart of nation building.

There was, however, one emerging hero, a man who saw in the political events he had helped precipitate at the end of 1828 his long-sought opportunity to acquire national influence. He emerged from the Acordada revolt possessed of substantial moral authority, which would be greatly enhanced a short time later by his involvement in the military response to the invasion of a Spanish expeditionary force. The defeat of Spanish General Isidro Barradas in Tamaulipas in September 1829 is often said to be the

cause of Santa Anna's rapid rise to national prominence. But it actually began in the first months of 1829 when he was hailed, at least by his supporters, as the great voice of the people's will who, alone and valiantly, pronounced against Gómez Pedraza's election. Santa Anna was seen, and not
without substance, as second only to Guerrero as the defender of federalism and the friend of democracy. Furthermore, his home base in the state
of Veracruz was now complete in that by 1829 his zone of political influence on the east coast ran from La Antigua to Alvarado and on the east-
west axis from Veracruz city through Jalapa to Perote.[46] His domination
of both the coast and the interior road running from the port of Veracruz
to Mexico City meant that he could control the republic's major import/
export trade route and the single largest source of federal government revenues, the Veracruz customs house. He would now have to be consulted
on any important issue affecting the national destiny. An anonymous
pamphlet breathlessly recounted his achievements in resisting the tyranny
of the aristocratic party: "A guardian divinity, a single man, with his ac-
customed valor, freed us from such evils."[47] Santa Anna had at last found
the perfect métier. The new Congress so completely adhered to the four
demands of Santa Anna's Plan of Perote that, in addition to annulling Gómez Pedraza's election and replacing him with Guerrero, it also passed the
second law expelling Spaniards from Mexico. The anti-Spanish feeling,
Sims says, was the "cardinal point" of the popular movement.[48]

The practical issue in which Guerrero's administration showed its
championing of the common man was its support of high tariffs against
the import of cheap European textiles. Many of the lower and lower middle classes depended on the domestic textile industry, as did incipient in-
dustrialists and cotton producers. Their plight had grown increasingly
desperate in the rush to free foreign trade after independence. The discontent of artisans played a significant role in the Yorkino victory. Thus, one
of Guerrero's first acts in office was to raise tariffs on imported textiles.[49]
This was a serious blow to the import merchants of Mexico City and Veracruz (though supported by the cotton producers of Veracruz for whom
Santa Anna spoke). Though his tariff increases were later overturned, the
issue of the protective tariff illustrates that a profound dispute over strate-
gies for economic development underscored the struggle for power.

In the brief life of the Guerrero administration, the undoubted high
point was the defeat of the Spanish expeditionary force sent by the government of Ferdinand VII to regain what Madrid still considered the rebellious viceroyalty of New Spain.[50] Although the Mexican government

received ample warning, having known since January 1829 that a Spanish expedition was assembling in Cuba to invade Mexico, the assault was expected to occur on the south coast between Veracruz and Campeche. As late as a week before the Spanish landing, the conservative press in Mexico City was denying that Spain planned such an invasion, insisting that the radicals were merely trying to spread public hatred of the Spaniards in Mexico. When the force of thirty-five hundred men under the command of General Isidro Barradas landed on the beaches at Cabo Rojo near Tampico in the last days of July 1829 and then marched into Tamaulipas, the government in Mexico City was ill prepared to defend the northern coast of the republic. General Felipe de la Garza, commandant general of Tamaulipas, skirmished with the invaders but was unable to stop them, while General Manuel Mier y Terán in Matamoros marched his forces to the scene; his contribution would be to keep the Spaniards hemmed in at Tampico.[51]

Although other troops were being raised in San Luis Potosí and elsewhere, the major response came from Santa Anna, newly restored as acting governor of Veracruz. In a display of remarkable energy that reflected in turn the high level of support he enjoyed in his home state, he organized a force of sixteen hundred men in less than a week, extracted pledges of money to supply them with arms and food, and commandeered merchant ships in the harbor to transport his infantry by sea, while his cavalry marched overland. As was his custom, Santa Anna called not only upon his wide group of supporters to join the civic militia but even on his own employees and field hands. In this case, for example, we have specific evidence that he recruited a number of employees from the sugar hacienda of Zapotal owned by his wife, Inés García.[52] Santa Anna moved this force to engage the enemy at Tampico just across the Pánuco River, on the border between Veracruz state and Tamaulipas. Nearly defeated in his first major engagement with the Spanish, Santa Anna's army was allowed to retreat because Barradas's intention was not to conquer Mexico with his small expedition but rather to provide the rallying point for what Spain expected would be a general uprising among Mexicans. The Spaniards who had been expelled from Mexico and who had settled in Cuba or had made it back to Spain had convinced Madrid that the Mexican masses hated their rulers and would rise up against them in support of the restoration of colonial rule.

The Spanish forces barricaded themselves inside Tampico to await the expected uprising of the Mexican people, which never occurred. Meanwhile, the Spanish soldiers, hungry, demoralized, and besieged by mosquitoes, began to contract yellow fever. One writer noted that disease and hunger left only 20 percent of the Spanish soldiers able to stand but that Santa Anna pressed an attack on Tampico on 9 September in order to gain glory.[53] In addition, a hurricane devastated the coast from 9 to 11 September. On 11 September the Spanish surrendered unconditionally. Commenting on the Spanish surrender, Santa Anna remarked in his autobiography, "When fortune smiles on Santa Anna, she smiles fully!"[54] For the rest of his long and active life he was known, first and foremost, as the "Victor of Tampico." Even so, he left Tampico for Veracruz a few days later, leaving everything in the hands of his second in command, Mier y Terán.[55] Taken prisoner, the Spaniards succumbed rapidly to disease. Finally, in November and December, 1,792 survivors of the original 3,500 Spanish troops, only half the expedition, were embarked for transport to Cuba.

Outside of any individual or group glory to be gained from defending the republic from a foreign invasion—and many Mexicans at the time thought that Mier y Terán and other officers merited as much of the glory as Santa Anna—the ultimate meaning of the defeat of the Barradas expedition is that it put an end to any lingering doubts that may have existed among the Spanish exiles or among discontented elements in the country about the existence of Mexican nationhood. All elements rallied to the defense of the nation, and only a year and a half after the ill-fated Arenas uprising not a single movement in favor of restoring Spanish rule occurred. Even the centralists, who had long downplayed the fears of a Spanish invasion, mobilized their efforts in a patriotic fervor. One telling example of the way in which the Spanish invasion brought about the final coalescence of the idea of Mexican identity, and for which we have specific historical evidence, occurred in the municipio of Tlacotalpan, state of Veracruz, where the local people, primarily mestizos, had always defined themselves socially as "españoles." Under threat of conquest by Spanish troops and participating fully in defense of their homes, they were forced to affirm their identity as "mexicanos."[56] Even in 1824 when the Spaniards still controlled San Juan de Ulúa in Veracruz harbor, the threat they posed had always served as a uniting force for the Mexicans. But standing up to and defeating the invasion of their expeditionary force, for a country so recently freed from Spanish colonialism, was considered by many to be the consolidation of independence. From that moment, as Díaz puts it, the Mexican nation acquired a greater sense of its capacity as an independent country and of the possibilities for defending itself. In the development of national identity, the moment was galvanizing. It was of such importance that from that rich gold-bearing vein Santa Anna extracted decades of military and political prestige.[57]

After a bitter three-week debate in Congress, President Guerrero on 25 August was granted the special war powers (*facultades extraordinarias*) allowed by the constitution. This effectively suspended the constitution, allowing Guerrero to rule by decree until he fell from the presidency on 18 December. Several state legislatures also granted extraordinary powers to their governors. One of the many decrees of Guerrero during the time he held special powers was his abolition of slavery on 15 September, although at the request of the government in San Antonio he suspended application of the decree in Texas.[58] Zavala, as minister of finance, imposed sweeping emergency taxes. Before the Spanish invasion he had created a direct levy, often seen as a radical income tax. During the invasion he decreed further taxes in a largely ineffective attempt to overcome the government's insolvency. Most of the hostile response toward the government's decrees was aimed at Zavala because his policy was seen as representing a sudden switch in fiscal policy from a reliance on customs revenues as the main source of federal income to the direct taxation of the propertied classes.

No sooner had the threat of Spanish invasion been overcome than the Guerrero administration began to disintegrate. The legislature of the state of Mexico revoked the permission it had given Zavala to take leave of his office of governor and join the Guerrero cabinet. He resigned from the cabinet in the face of strong resistance from many states to his tax decrees, which they perceived as federal intervention in state finances. But the Mexico state legislature then refused to return the governor's office to him. Meanwhile, José María Bocanegra, secretary of external relations, finally acceded to the many complaints about the political involvement of Joel R. Poinsett and asked the U.S. government to withdraw him as its minister to Mexico. The political significance of the Yorkino administration having to request the withdrawal of its most devoted supporter was lost on no one. The Guerrero presidency was on its last legs.

A special reserve army had been located at Jalapa during the Spanish invasion in case an expected second wave of Spanish forces landed on the Veracruz coast. This army, under the command of Vice President Anastasio Bustamante, became the center of conspiracy against Guerrero, and on 4 December 1829 it issued the Plan of Jalapa. Among the leaders of the uprising were Bravo, Barragán, and Bustamante's private secretary Colonel José Antonio Facio, each of whom had been exiled following the Montaño rebellion but had only recently returned from exile thanks to Guerrero's clemency. After a brief period of hesitation, Bustamante agreed to take leadership of the uprising. Although the Plan of Jalapa only called for the government to surrender its extraordinary war powers and remove "those public officials against whom public opinion had been expressed" (an odd, ambiguous phrase little noticed at first but the purpose of which later became clear), Guerrero and everyone else understood that the plan was directed at him. The rebellious troops shouted "Long live centralism" and "Death to the negro Guerrero."[59] Alamán, though not directly involved with the military uprising, was the figure to whom the participants looked for a program, and the rebels, many of whom were centralists, aimed at a general restructuring of the federal government. The Plan of Jalapa declared its support for the federalist system, but it was widely recognized that this was a ruse, that the leaders of the Jalapa uprising advocated a centralist republic but felt that an outright call for the overthrow of federalism would provoke too much resistance. Santa Anna was invited to assume the leadership of the movement jointly with Bustamante, but he refused and declared that the Jalapa rebels were hiding their real objectives.

After gathering an army personally loyal to him, Guerrero left Mexico City. On the night of 22 December 1829, General Luis Quintanar occupied the capital in the name of the Plan of Jalapa. On 25 December Guerrero gave up the presidency, declaring he would leave it to Congress to decide who should be president. With an escort of fifty loyal men under the command of Colonel Francisco Victoria, brother of the former president, Guerrero retired to his hacienda, Tierra Colorada, near Tixtla, the base of his zone of caudillist influence.

Bustamante assumed the executive power as vice president in the absence of the president on 31 December 1829.[60] In his first manifesto Bustamante promised to reanimate federalism and protect the sovereignty of the pueblo.[61] However, a new liberal periodical that had just begun publishing, *El Atleta*, declared that the Jalapa uprising aspired to destroy the principles of federalism, equality, rights of the individual, and sovereignty of the states.[62] The next months would show not only that the periodical was correct but to what lengths the conservatives would go to eliminate the political role of the common man and grassroots political communities for which Guerrero and the Yorkinos stood.

Throughout January 1830 the dedication of the Bustamante administration to eliminating the radicals in the government became clear. Bustamante's cabinet consisted of centralists and Escoceses, among whom the
two most significant were Lucas Alamán, once again serving as secretary
of interior and exterior affairs, and José Antonio Facio, secretary of war.
In addition, Rafael Mangino, who as a member of Congress in 1824 had
opposed sovereignty for the states, became secretary of the treasury, and
José Ignacio Espinosa, who had spoken in Congress in favor of centralizing the civil power, became secretary of justice. Bustamante had been an
ardent federalist in his days as commander of Jalisco, was still reputed by
army officers to be one, and continued to be very ambivalent on many issues. For these reasons and because the Mexican political system was characterized by a constitutionally weak chief executive, Alamán was undoubtedly the driving force of the administration, even more than Zavala
had been in the Guerrero administration. Many historians, therefore, refer to the Bustamante government as "the Alamán administration."

Bustamante's position as vice president meant it was not possible to in-
validate Guerrero's election as president. As a result, the Senate passed an
act declaring that Guerrero was "morally impeded" from governing. The
Chamber of Deputies, following Andrés Quintana Roo's demand to
know what "morally impeded" meant, approved the act but suppressed
the word *morally*, judging that Guerrero's poor health prevented him
from fulfilling the duties of president.[63] Because Guerrero had, in effect,
given up, there was little the states could do. Governor José Salgado of
Michoacán, however, informed the central government that his state
would keep its civic militias at the ready "to conserve its internal peace
and, in all cases, its political existence." The Michoacán state legislature
declared that because events had moved on without them, their only options were to accept Bustamante or see a civil war break out. In a striking
statement, it declared that it was Mexico's misfortune that the revolution
begun in 1810 had not yet concluded.[64]

Given the outright centralist preferences of the Bustamante government, several important pro-Guerrero or Yorkino officeholders resigned
in order to get out of the way of the foreseeable assaults to come. These
included Esteva, governor of the Federal District, and Santa Anna, who
resigned all his offices in the state of Veracruz. As soon as Santa Anna, the
foremost defender of Guerrero and the radical liberals, made it clear he
would not take up arms to oppose the new government, Alamán initiated
a campaign to induce his agents in all parts of the country to launch formal

complaints against pro-Guerrero or Yorkino governors and state legislatures in order to put into effect the article of the Plan of Jalapa that called for the removal of public officials who were opposed by "public opinion."[65] In addition, the commandantes generales frequently acted to organize the assault against the governors and legislatures. A petition would be sent to the federal Congress requesting the removal of those officeholders and the restoration of the previous incumbent or the calling of new elections. Governor José Salgado of Michoacán was a particular target of the new federal government. Alamán wrote to Mariano Michelena, his agent in Michoacán who he had just named commandant general there, reminding him that because it was difficult to legalize some of the efforts being attempted to overthrow the state governments, he should concentrate on getting supporters in Morelia to "make motions that will help us and fortify us. The revolution cannot be stationary, and everything that has its origin in the capital will not be well received in all the states."[66]

In this way, Alamán launched an organized purge of the Yorkinos who controlled most of the state governments. It constituted the most serious assault launched by a central government thus far against the principles of federalism. Petitions for the removal of Yorkino officeholders had to be approved by the federal Congress, in which the Senate, dominated by conservatives, strongly supported Alamán and the Chamber of Deputies was divided between Escoceses and Yorkinos. This was no problem because Articles 58 to 60 of the constitution required that if a proposal was rejected by one chamber of Congress it could be considered a second time by the chamber where it originated. And if it passed by a two-thirds majority, the measure would become law unless it was specifically rejected by two-thirds of the members of the chamber that had opposed it. In this way, the central government brought about the overthrow of Yorkino state governments throughout the country. In all, Alamán engineered the deposition of all or part of the state legislatures in eleven states, and several of the governors too. The state legislatures were deposed in Jalisco, Michoacán, Querétaro, Durango, Tamaulipas, Tabasco, Oaxaca, Puebla, Veracruz, Chiapas, and Mexico.[67]

The firestorm unleashed by the federal government upon the sovereignty of the states seriously weakened federation. Alamán's purpose, however, was not openly to revoke or rewrite the constitution or to eliminate the federal system because conservatives realized that federalism by 1830 was sustained by a network of individual interests and loyalties throughout the country that was too extensive and too deep to ignore. Alamán knew that a full-scale assault on federalism would be opposed by too many forces within the country. Better to pursue the original antifederalist option from 1823, to create the system Servando Teresa de Mier had called "federal in name and central in reality." Thus, the Plan of Jalapa was always referred to by the government and its supporters as a pronouncement "for the reestablishment of constitutional order" and "for the consolidation of the republic."

The real objects of attack, in Costeloe's words, were "those states in which radicals or representatives of the lower democracy occupied office."[68] The purpose was to eliminate genuine state sovereignty by sweeping out of office those governors and legislatures that represented the masses. As Reyes Heroles puts it, "The Bustamante government did not touch de jure federalism, but it practiced a de facto centralism." In his first ministerial report to Congress in February 1830, Alamán insisted it was the Yorkinos who, through the manipulation of their secret association, had centralized the government. It had always been Alamán's contention that the state legislatures, which he dismissively called "congresitos," served merely as instruments of local oligarchies, an argument that much of the historiography has repeated.[69] As Costeloe phrases it, "Those states in which representatives of the masses [*baja democracia*] or radicals held office were the object of attack. . . . They were replaced by individuals whose political ideas were not necessarily uniform, but all were hombres de bien with the same interests as the ruling classes in the capital."[70] The Bustamante government's official periodical, a daily entitled *Registro Oficial*, which began publishing on 22 January 1830 and was controlled by Alamán, declared in October 1830 precisely what the significance of these events was in the eyes of the government: "This is not, nor has it ever been, a war of opinions; it does not deal with systems nor even with persons; it is a war of civilization against barbarism, of property against thieves, of order against anarchy."[71]

One of the main techniques Alamán used in his campaign to overthrow the state governments was to provoke elements of the civic militias to revolt against those governments. In Michoacán, for example, while street demonstrations sponsored by Michelena and other supporters of the Plan of Jalapa attempted to overthrow the state legislature, governor, civil service, and ayuntamientos, four of the six corps of the civic militia refused to accept orders from Governor Salgado when he tried to avoid the outbreak of fighting.[72]

On 17 February, the federal Senate approved the nullification of the Yorkino state legislature of Puebla, and the state governor resigned. The legislature of the state of Mexico was deposed after the civil authorities of various towns pronounced against it in early March. In Oaxaca the federal Senate voted to nullify the state legislature, and the arrival of the new commandant general persuaded the governor to resign and the deputies to disperse. In Guadalajara, a group of armed men took over the legislative building and forced the Jalisco state congress to declare that the seated assembly was merely preliminary to the convocation of a new state congress.[73]

Amid the general assault on state sovereignty, Michoacán under Governor José Salgado and San Luis Potosí under Governor Vicente Romero moved to resurrect the idea of a coalition between the states of the northwest for the defense of federalism.[74] In Guanajuato, Luis de Cortázar, commandant general since 1827 and scion of one of the richest noble families in the Bajío, was emerging as caudillo. A moderate federalist and supporter of Gómez Pedraza, Cortázar would dominate Guanajuato until his death in 1840.[75] On 13 January 1830 the legislature of San Luis Potosí declared that if the federal institutions were attacked the states of San Luis Potosí and Guanajuato would proceed to joint action in defense of federalism. Michoacán joined, and by the middle of February seven states had expressed their support.[76] On 13 March San Luis Potosí called for a meeting of the participating states in the city of León, where they would pursue constitutional reforms designed to guarantee state sovereignty and force the resignation of Alamán and Facio. Meanwhile, Governor Salgado mobilized his troops under the command of Juan José Codallos. But the federal government's agent, Michelena, had already done his work so well that both the local garrison in Morelia and the city council demanded the governor's resignation. On 20 February the federal Senate declared Salgado's election null. Salgado made a final desperate attempt to save himself by marching to Zamora, where he hoped to raise an army and receive aid from Governor Romero of San Luis Potosí. After two weeks of struggle with federal troops, Salgado was captured and jailed. Though sentenced to death, Salgado managed to escape.[77] Alamán had urged that Salgado not be executed because he feared it would provoke the Chamber of Deputies to break completely with the administration.[78]

Nevertheless, the Bustamante government launched a massive assault against its opponents in Congress that would lead to the arrest and deposition of many deputies, notably the two outspoken Yorkinos José María Alpuche and Anastasio Zerecero, both of whom were condemned to exile. On 24 March mass arrests were made in Mexico City for a supposed conspiracy against the government. Mariano Zerecero, brother of the deputy Anastasio Zerecero, was shot. Lorenzo de Zavala fled the country after charges were brought against him. Meanwhile, the two leading federalist periodicals, Zavala's *Correo de la Federación Mexicana* and *El Atleta*, were driven out of existence. There was no opposition periodical left in Mexico City for nearly a year.

In an effort to prevent the states from defending themselves with their own military forces, the government attempted to suppress the civic militias. The attack on the civic militias began with Melchor Múzquiz, governor of the state of Mexico who had replaced the fallen Zavala, proposing a reform in the functioning of the civic militia. Múzquiz argued that the civic militias had become real military forces that duplicated the function of the army and the active militias and that their officers, chosen by the militia members themselves, lacked the skill to command them effectively. In addition, he charged that the civic militia, consisting of citizens recruited in each locality, was converting Mexico into a nation of soldiers at an insupportable fiscal and political cost. He concluded by proposing that the civic militias be placed under the control of the regular army or dissolved.[79] Thus, in the name of maintaining the civilian nature of Mexican politics, reducing costs, and professionalizing the command structure, the centralists proposed to eliminate the institution that the states had at their disposal for the defense of federalism. Spokesmen for the states, however, easily saw through the hidden motives behind the proposal and refused to accede to it. The 1832 rebellion that brought down the Bustamante regime would be based on the civic militias in the states.

The assault launched by the central government on the states and on supporters of federalism was the most extreme organized campaign of government persecution of political opponents since independence. In many individual cases it was heavy-handed and brutal, representing a major escalation in the risks of political participation. It was now very dangerous to be on the opposing side in politics. One illustrative example was the offensive the government launched against one of Mexico's most distinguished liberals, Andrés Quintana Roo, president of the Chamber of Deputies in 1830. After the arrests of Deputies Alpuche and Zerecero, the only outspoken opponents of the Bustamante regime in Congress were members of a small group consisting of Quintana Roo, fellow deputy Juan de Dios Cañedo, and Senators Antonio Pacheco Leal and Manuel Crecencio Rejón.[80] Quintana Roo had brought to Congress an accusation against Minister of War Facio demanding his resignation. In January 1831 he began publication of a short-lived federalist periodical, *El Feder-*

alista Mexicano, which frequently proclaimed the Bustamante regime to be illegitimate and terrorist. Quintana Roo's wife, Leona Vicario, was the most famous woman in Mexico, the heroine of the wars of independence who Congress had awarded a valuable hacienda for her wartime work as a messenger between supporters of independence in the capital and the Morelos army. The legislature of Coahuila and Texas voted twice in 1827 to change the name of its capital city to "Leona Vicario."

On the night of 2 February 1831, four military officers attempted to destroy the press that printed Quintana Roo's newspaper but failing to do so went to his house with the apparent intent of assaulting him. Leona Vicario told them her husband was not present, and after a tense night she went in person to the National Palace to protest to Vice President Bustamante the threat of violence against her husband. Bustamante called in Felipe Codallos, commandant general of the capital. Codallos crudely told Leona that the purpose of the officers' visit was to bring such a federalist to account for his opposition to the government and that "it had become indispensable to answer such writers with blows." Stunned by such a brutal reply in the presence of the chief of state, Leona replied that it proved "that we should consider [civil] society dissolved, leaving each person obliged to defend himself" and said to Bustamante, "you are not the Sultan of Constantinople but the chief of a free republic; you should not permit the law to be made into a joke in your presence by a functionary such as Codallos." Insulted, Leona said she had only come to ask the vice president if she could count on his protection or if she had to defend herself "as in the state of nature," to which Bustamante replied that she was safe while in his house but that he could not answer for what happened outside it.[81]

There followed a furious round of attack and counterattack in the press, with *El Federalista* on Leona's side and *El Sol* and *Registro Oficial* on the government's side, which proved that there were a few individuals the regime could not intimidate. When even Alamán waded into this extraordinary public attack on a woman of the highest stature by attempting to disparage Leona's wartime services in the *Registro Oficial*, she wrote him a stinging rebuke: "What do you find strange or ridiculous about a woman loving her patria and giving it what services she can?"[82] In her published responses to Alamán Leona repeated her statement to Bustamante that when society was reduced to a state of nature all existing legitimacy was dissolved, an idea Bustamante had defended in 1823 when he was commandant of Jalisco. Such was her despair that Leona confessed to one of her children in a letter in June that she had considered fleeing to the United

States. "While there are officers [in control of government], we can have no other government than a cruel despotism shielded with the name of a republic."[83] Her exertions did not guarantee her husband's safety either. On 23 April 1831 *El Federalista* closed down because of heavy fines imposed on it by the government, and in January 1832 Quintana Roo went into hiding to escape an attempt by the government to assassinate him.

Other high-ranking opponents of the regime in Mexico City were subjected to similar harassment and intimidation by the government throughout 1830 and 1831. In January 1831 Deputy Juan de Dios Cañedo brought to the Chamber of Deputies a discussion on the subject of the legitimacy of Bustamante's power and pressed the effort to have Facio removed from office for having employed methods of terror. Cañedo and Quintana Roo argued that Gómez Pedraza was the legitimate president, and this point of view was sustained in the Senate by Pacheco Leal. In response Pacheco Leal was attacked and beaten senseless on the street by a group of thirty officers. Viewed by many as the leader of the opposition in Congress, Cañedo feared for his life and as a result accepted appointment as minister to South America. Manuel Crecencio Rejón ceased publication of a short-lived periodical, *El Tribuno del Pueblo Mexicano*, after the newspaper's offices were ransacked by soldiers, and Rejón was subsequently attacked as he left the Congress building by officers with drawn sabers. When Congress demanded an explanation of this attack on the parliamentary immunity of a member, Alamán appeared in person before Congress to say that Rejón's senatorial immunity had not been violated "because the soldiers assaulted Rejón the writer, not Rejón the senator." Vicente Rocafuerte, who had published pamphlets critical of the government, charged that Alamán had a secret fund of one hundred thousand pesos that he used to terrorize journalists and destroy freedom of the press. He was indicted on charges that his "Essay on Religious Toleration" was seditious, although the jury acquitted him.[84] Even Carlos María de Bustamante, a conservative who had criticized Facio but not Bustamante, saw the government subsidy of his newspaper, *Voz de la Patria*, withdrawn, forcing him to suspend publication.

When Vicente Rocafuerte began publication in December 1831 of a major new antigovernment periodical, *El Fénix de la Libertad*, he was charged with violating press laws, and the newspaper was heavily and frequently fined. *El Fénix* managed to survive, at one point posting a court-ordered surety bond of the enormous sum of twenty thousand pesos, made possible by the backing of its wealthy supporters and the group of Congress members leading the resistance to the government. It would be the foremost voice of the opposition in 1832. However, the well-known journalist Pablo Villavicencio, editor of the clandestine *El Duende*, did not fare as well. Villavicencio, known by his pseudonym, El Payo del Rosario, was charged with sedition, jailed, and exiled from Mexico City. When Villavicencio did not cease distributing *El Duende* in the city, the government sent soldiers to destroy his press; he fled with his equipment to Veracruz. In March 1831 the sale of periodicals from outside the city was banned in the capital.[85]

In response to the centralist agenda of the Bustamante regime, a series of uprisings erupted in 1830. In Puebla a revolt broke out that was led by Francisco Victoria, brother of the former president, who was soon defeated and captured. Juan Nepomuceno Rosains, a hero of independence and a federal deputy, was arrested as a presumed conspirator with Victoria even though no definitive evidence against him could be produced. Both men were tried by military court and executed, to the great anger of Guadalupe Victoria and his friends. Other relatively short-lived rebellions in support of Guerrero occurred in San Luis Potosí (an uprising of the civic militia under José Márquez) and in Morelia (under José María Méndez and Gregorio Mier).

The real danger for the Bustamante government, however, came in the southern Pacific coastal regions where central government control had always been tenuous. Juan José Codallos rose up in the south of Michoacán and published a plan on 10 March 1830 calling for restoration of the legislatures and governors that had been deposed, for Congress to determine who would be president, and for the states to form a league and declare a provisional government if none of these provisions were met. Codallos was the brother of Felipe, commandant general of Mexico City and a Bustamante stalwart.

The Codallos uprising was followed soon after by the uprising of Guerrero himself. In mid-March 1830 Guerrero left the security of his hacienda and moved to the mountains near Acapulco where, in conjunction with Juan Alvarez, caudillo of the Tierra Caliente coast; Gordiano Guzmán, caudillo of southern Michoacán and southern Jalisco; and Isidro Montes de Oca, he began the uprising that stretched from the Costa Grande of Acapulco to Zacatula and was known as the "war of the south." The program of Alvarez's uprising called for new elections for president and vice president, guarantees for the retention of federalism, and restoration of the sovereignty of the states. The government sent Generals Nicolás Bravo and José Gabriel Armijo to oppose this southern rebellion.

Two points stand out about this wave of rebellions aimed at protecting the essential principles of federalism and state sovereignty from the Bustamante government's organized assault on them. One is that, as had been seen in Mexico since 1823, as long as states acted independently or in disorganized conjunction with a few other states the military power of the federal government continued to be sufficient to contain them. The central government could always respond fast enough on both the military and the political fronts to disrupt the much more ponderous process by which various states attempted to confer between themselves with the objective of reaching an accord for joint action. And this was certainly true when both the state governors and the legislatures were under separate but coordinated attack. This is the principle that Alamán might be said to have discovered in 1823, and it would remain a distinct factor in Mexican affairs in the nineteenth and twentieth centuries. A full-blown exercise of genuine states' rights remained a difficult prospect in Mexico.

The second significant fact about the 1830 rebellions is that they saw the first full-fledged attempt to appeal to the sovereignty of the base political communities and the people. The uprising of Guerrero, Alvarez, and other caudillos of the south represented, as Guardino puts it, an "alliance between segments of Mexico's impoverished rural majority and provincial elites [which] was the worst nightmare of the Mexico City–based dominant class."[86] Annino points out that since 1821 it had become necessary to obtain the support of some provinces and ayuntamientos in order to achieve national political power. This was the origin of that new political prototype, the pronunciamiento, which continued to play a fundamental role throughout the nineteenth century. By 1830, the new source of political authority, autonomy of the towns as the base political communities, had become sufficiently ingrained and customary that in his insurrection against the Bustamante government Guerrero openly appealed to the "sovereignty of the towns."[87] Indeed, we might say that the war of the south in 1830 and 1831 was the first war of the caudillos, for it pitted the leading caudillos of the west-central coast—Guerrero himself, Alvarez, Guzmán—against the central government. Jaime Olveda argues that as the protectors of the exploited Indians and mulattoes these caudillos had no option but to raise a peasant revolt in order to try and strengthen the political situation of their followers and lessen their exploitation.[88]

A new source of Mexican political legitimacy had emerged. During the victorious progress of the Trigarante Army in 1821, Iturbide constantly sought the help of the ayuntamientos, both large and small, and independence was possible because of an alliance between the army and the constitutional ayuntamientos. The Plan of Casa Mata swept the country on the strength of pronouncements of support from provincial deputations and ayuntamientos. The revolt of the provinces that established federalism was also a series of pronouncements by provinces and cities, supported by the smaller towns. The Yorkinos' "armed petitions" throughout 1826 and 1827 demanding the expulsion of the Spaniards were yet further expressions of the will of the people by way of their subnational and subregional political voices. Such regional caudillos as Santa Anna (who in this phase was the darling of the liberals) or Alvarez (the perennial power in Guerrero right up to the Reforma), and several others, were by 1830 an established fact. In this light, they can be seen as perhaps the major force of subnational autonomy and self-determination, fighting partly for their own wealth and power certainly, but partly also for the clearly expressed needs of their constituents when such needs were blatantly ignored, as they often were, by superior governments.

The phenomenon we are witnessing was, in fact, the emerging mode of Mexican political action of the nineteenth century. It was a constant thread in the political history of the first and subsequent republics as the pronunciamiento became the instrument by which the people were heard. To countless individuals participating in such events, the local pronunciamiento must have seemed like a ray of hope, a means to bring about desired change, a way to express the peoples' will, and not, as the historical literature universally views it, a cynical exercise in destabilization. As with disintegration, destabilization is in the eye of the beholder.

But for many liberals, as well as for the conservatives, the Guerrero presidency, with its promise of equality for the masses, had been a frightening glimpse into the abyss. Many prominent liberals, such as José María Luis Mora, joined Alamán's conservatives to praise Bustamante as "the protector of the constitution and the laws." In his periodical, *El Observador*, which ceased appearing in early 1828 but resumed publication in 1830 after Bustamante took power, Mora called for the establishment of property qualifications for voting in both state and local elections. He particularly attacked the doctrines of sovereignty of the people and supremacy of "the general will," arguing that only society's most educated and experienced men, people with property to lose, should govern the nation. In a long essay in *El Observador* in 1830 he argued that members of the true or natural "aristocracy," "the men most outstanding for their virtue, talent, learning, and valor," should have control of the government. Mora had long been on the conservative wing of Mexican liberalism, but as for many others among the gentlemen the specter of uncontrolled democracy raised in the Guerrero presidency was for him genuinely frightening.[89] He wrote in *El Observador*, "Everything is unequal in this world. There are no two beings perfectly equal."[90] Alamán, for his part, entirely endorsed such views, arguing in his 1830 ministerial report to Congress that the masses now so dominated voting that men of property and education had been all but excluded from election, while offices went to people who possessed nothing but aspired to everything. He insisted that property and education qualifications were the only foundations for a truly liberal system.[91]

Even Zavala, the foremost Yorkino, came to question popular sovereignty after his experience in the Guerrero government. By 1831 he was urging property qualifications for voters in order to prevent political control from falling into the hands of intriguers and demagogues. In 1833 he wrote, "In reality there is not nor can there be democracy" in a society as ill educated and subject to demagoguery as the Mexican society.[92] A similar shift to the right had occurred in the politics of many persons who had played prominent roles in the creation of federalism, such as Michelena, Quintanar, and Anastasio Bustamante himself. Thus, a major transformation of creole liberal thought had occurred as a result of Mexico's brief flirtation with mass political participation in the Guerrero presidency. As Hale puts it, "The sociological reality of Mexico made 'equality' and 'democracy' abstract terms, terms that could mean juridical equality in the face of corporate privilege, but not popular political participation."[93]

Thus, the war of the south launched by Guerrero and Alvarez and the various uprisings in support of their cause took on the appearance of an incipient civil war, particularly given the intensity of the feeling on both sides and the substantial armies involved. The supporters of Guerrero were fighting for a vaguely defined peoples' democracy and the overthrow of the usurper Bustamante; the government fought, according to its self-proclaimed objectives, for civilization and order. This was the utterly classic dichotomy of nineteenth-century Mexico.

The rebellion of the civic militia of San Luis Potosí was quickly defeated by the federal commandant general of that state, and so was the uprising in Morelia. Their leaders were summarily executed. In the south, however, a war raged. José Gabriel Armijo's forces, operating near the port of Acapulco, laid waste to fields, burned down villages, and killed any Indian who they encountered with a rifle in hand. When Armijo attacked Alvarez near Texca, however, he was defeated and brutally killed by villagers while attempting to flee on foot.[94] Nicolás Bravo, overall commander of government forces in the south, promised to avenge Armijo's murder.[95] Acapulco fell to Guerrero, although in December 1830 the attempt by Codallos and Guzmán to take Morelia failed.

As the anonymous author of *Dos años en México* pointed out, if the states of Zacatecas and Jalisco, as well as San Luis Potosí, had been able at this critical juncture to make common cause with Guerrero and Alvarez the usurper Bustamante might well have been overthrown. As usual, however, there were many factors preventing a genuine military coalition between the states. Not least of these was that Zacatecas and Jalisco still supported the legal claim of Gómez Pedraza to the presidency and did not favor the restoration of Guerrero; these states were now emerging as the leaders of the moderate federalist forces, while the southern caudillos emerged as the voice of the masses.[96] Meanwhile, Santa Anna, who was the linchpin of any military rebellion, did not want to see Gómez Pedraza in power, had chosen not to oppose Bustamante, and had retired to his Veracruz hacienda, where in June 1830 he wrote, referring to his retirement, "I would not change my [way of life] for any title on earth."[97]

When after a year and a half in exile Gómez Pedraza arrived at the port of Veracruz in October 1830 protesting he only wished to join his family again, he was immediately expelled from the country by order of Bustamante and Facio. Many members of the Chamber of Deputies and Senate, among them Andrés Quintana Roo, protested this violation of Gómez Pedraza's rights as a Mexican citizen.[98] As a result of Alamán's machinations to overthrow the state legislatures and governors, most of the states were now in the hands of Bustamante supporters. When the congressional elections were held to select the members of the Chamber of Deputies for 1831 and 1832, the supporters of the government won most of the seats, with a substantial number of clergy gaining election. Elections to the Senate, which were in the hands of the state legislatures, naturally favored the Alamán party as well.

Meanwhile, the war in the south became the final contest between the two classic military protagonists of the early Mexican republic representing the two opposing poles of politics and social attitude, Guerrero and Bravo. The two contenders controlled the two different zones of what would later be the state of Guerrero. Guerrero himself, with the support of Alvarez, controlled the Costa Grande and Tierra Caliente coastline, a region of extensive ethnic mingling in which the overwhelming majority of people were mixed native and black. Bravo, a caudillo too, controlled

the cooler mountainous inland centers of Tixtla, Chilapa, and Chilpancingo, an area where whites, blacks, and mestizos were almost equal in
number and whites were politically dominant.[99] Guerrero was the great
patron of the Yorkinos, Bravo the great patron of the Escoceses. Guardino
found that the regions controlled by Guerrero had a high incidence of
participation in the insurrections for independence and high levels of support for federalism, while those controlled by Bravo had low insurgent
mobilization in the 1810–20 period, had far fewer autonomous municipalities, and were far more centralist.[100] This was, therefore, a struggle
with ideological and social implications, both regionally and nationally.
Guerrero and Bravo were natural enemies in their home region, while on
the national level they stood for two different visions of Mexico.

Guerrero and his followers in the rebellion made frequent appeals to the
concept of sovereignty of the people, and they saw themselves as spokesmen for the common man, particularly of the peasant and indigenous
population, against the tyranny of the well-to-do and the creole propri-
etors. The peasant radicalism Guerrero represented was perceived by the
government in Mexico City as a profound threat. Minister of War Facio,
in his *Memoria* to Congress on 24 January 1831, declared, "[Guerrero] disseminated his agents throughout the republic in order to raise the pueblos
in insurrection and to take up arms against the government on the fraudu-
lent claim that it had fallen into the hands of the Spaniards. . . . He raised
the indigenous pueblos using the depraved means of offering them the
properties of the Mexicans who opposed him, and attempting to excite in
them the most barbarous, inhuman, and ferocious hatreds."[101] The government told Congress that the rebellion in the south attacked property
and individual security, the very cement of society.[102] In the publication in
which he later defended his actions and those of the Bustamante cabinet,
Facio insisted that the war in the south threatened a genuine civil war and
that "Guerrero and his followers rose up in 1830 for the same causes and
with the same objective that they had rebelled in 1828; the rebellion of the
south was the continuation of the mutiny of the Acordada."[103]

Whether this appeal to the common man could have brought victory
to Guerrero's rebellion cannot be known. In February 1831 the uprising in
the south came to a sudden end with perhaps the most shocking single
event in the history of the first federal republic: the capture of Guerrero in
Acapulco through an act of betrayal and his execution a month later. Annino writes, "The assassination of Guerrero was also an intent on the part
of the Alamán group to crush the political autonomy of the pueblos."[104]

The outline of events leading to Guerrero's death are fairly simple, though the debate over them continues to this day. An Italian merchant ship's captain, Francisco Picaluga, whose vessel, the *Colombo*, was anchored in Acapulco harbor (controlled at the time by Guerrero), went to Mexico City and proposed to Minister of War Facio that he would place his ship at the service of the federal government for the sum of fifty thousand pesos. The cabinet met and, with the approval of the vice president, accepted the proposal. Returning to Acapulco, Picaluga invited Guerrero aboard his ship for a meal. Thinking Picaluga was a friend, Guerrero came aboard with two or three aides on 14 January 1831, and Picaluga, during a jovial lunch, took his guests captive, set sail from the harbor, and delivered Guerrero to federal troops in the port of Huatulco.

As soon as Guerrero's capture became known, many voices were raised in his defense. As early as 5 February, *El Federalista Mexicano* exposed the government's payment of fifty thousand pesos to Picaluga; on 7 February the state of Zacatecas warned the central government not to impose the death penalty on Guerrero; and on 15 February the state of Jalisco did the same.[105] Nonetheless, after being transported to the city of Oaxaca Guerrero was quickly condemned to death by a court-martial under provisions of the court-martial law passed by the Constituent Congress on 27 September 1823. He was executed by firing squad in Cuilapam on 14 February 1831. Guerrero was buried in the local church, but in 1833 after the Bustamante regime was overthrown his remains were transferred with full honors to the cathedral of Oaxaca, and in 1842 they were moved to Mexico City.[106] Although many states and municipalities sent the government their pro forma congratulations on the capture of Guerrero, there is no doubt that many Mexicans were stunned to hear of the death of "the martyr of Cuilapam" and "Patriarch of Independence." As early as 19 February *El Federalista Mexicano* dubbed his death "judicial murder" and "assassination," arguing that because he had only been suspended from the exercise of the presidency he was still covered by its protection and should not have been tried by a military court.[107]

Following the execution of its leader, the rebellion of the south quickly faltered. The federal government redoubled its efforts to eliminate the followers of the "hero of the South." Juan Alvarez now inherited the mantle of Morelos and Guerrero as defender of the peasant and common man. The central government offered an amnesty, but when Codallos, Salgado, Gordiano Guzmán, and others met on 2 April 1831 they announced their intention to continue the resistance. Lacking a figure of genuine national appeal to lead them, however, the rebellion began to wind down. Alvarez entered into negotiations with Bravo and, after receiving assurances of the security of his followers, reached an accord on 14 April and put down his arms. Guzmán did the same in May. All the dissidents from Acapulco to Colima had now given up with the exception of Juan José Codallos. Two days after the final accord was signed with Guzmán, Codallos was apprehended and shot in Michoacán.[108]

Supporters of Guerrero quickly dubbed the federal cabinet as the "picaluganos" and Guerrero's capture and death as "the picalugada."[109] The members of the cabinet, especially Alamán and Facio, spent the rest of their lives defending themselves from the charge that they were responsible for the ultimate betrayal in the history of the first republic, that is, that they had arranged not just for the service of Picaluga's ship but specifically for his capture of Guerrero. The entire Bustamante cabinet was brought before a grand jury of Congress in 1833 on charges of ordering Guerrero's murder and other crimes. Alamán and Facio both published extensive defenses of their roles in the affair.[110] Radicals and supporters of Guerrero never forgave the Bustamante government; the death of Guerrero was seen as the deepest national wound. Because, in fact, all the leaders of the southern rebellion who fell into the government's hands, including Codallos, Victoria, Márquez, and several others, were executed, one thing was abundantly clear. Rebellions and pronouncements in the name of the masses were treated differently from those that occurred in the name of creoles and their agendas.

There never has been a final independent judgment on the question of whether the death of Guerrero was a case of judicial murder ordered by the Bustamante government. After the fall of the Bustamante regime and the return to power of the liberals, within days of the beginning of the Gómez Farías administration in April 1833, a highly partisan and radical Chamber of Deputies sat as a grand jury to consider petitions brought against all four members of Bustamante's cabinet: Alamán, Facio, Rafael Mangino, and José Ignacio Espinosa. The petitions against them were brought by Juan Alvarez, caudillo of the south, and Deputy José Antonio Barragán.[111] After hastily considering what evidence could be mobilized, the Chamber on 24 April 1833 found adequate grounds for bringing criminal charges against Alamán, Facio, and Espinosa but not against Mangino, who was thought to have been the only member of the cabinet who voted against Guerrero's death.

That charges were not brought against Anastasio Bustamante indicates that he was considered by liberals to have been something of a figurehead at the top of an Alamán administration. Bustamante never wrote or spoke of the matter for the rest of his life. During the grand jury proceedings Alamán went into hiding for fifteen months, while Facio fled permanently to Europe. When in April 1834 Santa Anna finally assumed the presidency to which he had been elected the year before, having converted to the side of the centralist conservatives, he began a campaign to restore Alamán's reputation. Ultimately, the Supreme Court in March 1835 completely exonerated Alamán and Espinosa.[112] Neither of these two judgments, one guilty and one not guilty, was independent of partisan passions, however. The guilty verdict was the result of a radical Congress, and the not guilty verdict came from the Supreme Court after the abandonment of federalism.

In terms of historical evidence, the two key pieces of testimony against the cabinet are contradictory and of dubious validity. One was José Antonio Mejía's statement that he had given Guerrero's widow a letter from Bustamante to Santa Anna in which Bustamante said that the cabinet had met and voted three to one to execute Guerrero. Because there was never any substantiation of this claim, however, from Bustamante, Santa Anna, or Guerrero's widow, it remains unproved. When asked to give evidence about the matter during the 1833 grand jury proceedings, Bustamante refused.[113] All four cabinet members insisted there was no such meeting: Alamán said that Bustamante contemplated expelling Guerrero from the country; Facio said the cabinet only discussed a possible amnesty for Guerrero; Espinosa said there was no such meeting, or if there was, he was not present; and Mangino said he did not participate in such a meeting. The other item of evidence came from the mid-nineteenth-century liberal statesman José María Lafragua, who in an article published in 1854 described a conversation he had with José María Tornel, who spoke with Alamán as he lay on his deathbed in 1853. Alamán told Tornel, "The vote on the business of General Guerrero was the following: Facio and Espinosa for death; Mangino and I for exile in South America; the vice president of the Republic decided it."[114] Lafragua conceded, however, that such hearsay evidence was inadequate for a court of law. Suárez y Navarro, writing his history in 1850, testified that he had been given full access to the archive of the ministry of war and that, although he could find no document clearly linking the government to the death of Guerrero, the papers relating to the event had been intentionally mutilated.[115]

The defeat of the rebellion in the south was not the end of the demand for autonomy at the base political level, nor the end of a national role for such caudillos as Alvarez. In fact, it was only the beginning of both tendencies. The period from 1830 to 1833 saw the emergence of Mexico's first full-fledged caudillos: Nicolás Bravo and Juan Alvarez controlling upland and coastal zones of the south, Santa Anna in full control of the two axes of Veracruz, Gordiano Guzmán in Michoacán, Antonio de León in Oaxaca, and Luis de Cortázar in Guanajuato. Neither did the end of the war in the south guarantee the security of the Bustamante regime under Alamán's dominant influence, now carrying the burden of a special infamy. It did, however, mark the emergence of the tripartite split between radical, moderate, and conservative political persuasions; the definitive disappearance of the political role of the Masonic lodges; and the emergence of a self-conscious and aggressive conservative political ideology that was at the moment in control of the federal government and most of the state governments. Not coincidentally, state sovereignty and the constitution were virtually dead, run over by the new coalition that had formed between the elites, whatever their political persuasion, in the face of the perceived threat of mass populist participation. As the spirit of a peoples' democracy gradually emerged, so did the resistance to it by hombres de bien. Mexican politics had taken on the form they would display for the next several decades. In light of what the federal republic was meant by its creators to be, however, the first federal republic was entering its death throes.

CHAPTER EIGHT

The War of 1832 and Stalemate

The excesses of the administration of Vice President Anastasio Bustamante in its pursuit of political order and the growing fears that the central government intended an overall attack against the states to destroy
federalism led in 1832 to what may properly be considered Mexico's first
civil war, the greatest convulsion of violence between independence in 1821
and the revolution of Ayutla in 1855. Throughout its nearly three years in
power, the Bustamante government was considered by radicals and moderates to be tyrannous. The reality of Mexican federalism was no longer in
harmony with the ideals expressed in 1823 and 1824, and the federal republic was collapsing.

In the capital, the opposition against Bustamante and his chief minister
Lucas Alamán was led by outspoken critics in Congress, namely, Antonio
Pacheco Leal, Manuel Crecencio Rejón and Andrés Quintana Roo, as
well as by Vicente Rocafuerte, editor of *El Fénix de la Libertad*, Juan
Rodríguez Puebla, and Mariano Riva Palacio, Guerrero's son-in-law.
Among the states, Jalisco was the first to make a definitive break with the
Bustamante regime. In November 1831, the commandant general of Jalisco, Ignacio Inclán, ordered the arrest and execution of Juan Brambillas,
printer of the state of Jalisco's publications, for pamphlets critical of the
federal government. Although Brambillas was eventually released, many
moderates were convinced that they had to act to defend state sovereignty. The state legislature fled from Guadalajara to the city of Lagos,
and Governor Anastasio Cañedo appealed to other states to assist Jalisco.
Zacatecas, Guanajuato, and San Luis Potosí, fearing that the Bustamante
regime intended to destroy state sovereignty, pledged their support of Jalisco. Zacatecas, under Governor Francisco García, now had the best-
equipped state militia in the republic; with a state population of three

hundred thousand, Zacatecas had a civic militia of twenty thousand men. Federalist civilian politicians, including Valentín Gómez Farías of Zacatecas and Governor Sebastián Camacho of Veracruz, made a calculated decision to invite a number of regular military officers to support a revolt against the government. The primary fear of the civilians was that the military would take over any revolt, and to limit this danger the leaders of the revolt eventually insisted that its primary aim was to place Manuel Gómez Pedraza in the presidency, to which he was legally elected in 1828.[1]

Fearing that the growing discontent of the officers in Veracruz might provoke rebellion, Minister of War José Antonio Facio ordered changes in the military command there. This provoked Colonel Pedro Landero to issue the Plan of Veracruz on 2 January 1832, which declared that the government's oppression threatened the federation. The Plan of Veracruz called for changes in the government and invited General Antonio López de Santa Anna to assume command of the uprising.[2]

Santa Anna, federalist stalwart in waiting, took the leadership of the uprising but favored a moderate approach. He initially wrote Bustamante demanding merely that the government rescind the changes in the military command of Veracruz and, because Alamán and Facio had compromised the good faith and patriotism of the vice president, that the cabinet should be replaced. To make up a new cabinet, Santa Anna proposed Governor Camacho for secretary of interior and exterior affairs; Gómez Farías for justice; Melchor Múzquiz, governor of Mexico state, for war; and Governor García of Zacatecas for finance.[3] This was unacceptable to the civilian supporters of the uprising in the capital, who refused to consider a solution that would allow Bustamante to remain in office. The complaints of opponents had thus far been directed overwhelmingly against Facio and Alamán; the most frequently heard argument was that Bustamante was the captive of despotic ministers. Now, however, the civilians responsible for the uprising enlarged the circle of complaint to include Bustamante. By April, *El Duende*, attempting to increase public anger at the vice president, pointed out that since independence three men had usurped the national executive—Iturbide, Guerrero, and Bustamante—and given that the first two had died before firing squads as retribution, what then of Bustamante?[4] Nonetheless, Bustamante does not seem to have been as widely hated by the government's opponents as were Facio and Alamán.

Thus, in February 1832, Santa Anna, with some reluctance, launched the armed conflict. This was one of the leading examples of the way in which supposedly military rebellions in nineteenth-century Mexico were often started by civilians but carried out by officers. To judge from an assertion in *El Duende*, some of the rebels in Veracruz believed that an outbreak of cholera had just begun in the port city and would protect them from the federal army marching to confront them.[5] In fact, however, the great cholera epidemic that swept much of the republic in the following year did not reach Mexico until 1833, and it entered the country through Tampico, with Veracruz one of the last cities reached by the contagion. The fact that the fear of cholera was being manipulated for political or military gain, debilitating civil and military authorities in some locations, combined with the fact that various leaders of the revolt pursued different objectives helps explain why this rebellion went on for almost the entire year and would not terminate until December 1832. Although the federal army hesitated several weeks, it pressed on toward the coast and defeated Santa Anna on 3 March at Tolomé. Though Colonel Pedro Landero was killed in the battle, Santa Anna declared his intention to keep fighting.[6] The government's army, however, abandoned its siege of the city of Veracruz.

The state of Tamaulipas joined the rebellion when General Francisco Moctezuma took to the field against the government. Not only did this give renewed life to the rebellion, but it cut off the federal government from its two major sources of revenue: the customs duties from the ports of Veracruz and Tampico, which were now diverted by the rebels. One source reported that the Veracruz customs house had four hundred thousand pesos on hand in cash and over a million pesos in credits due when Santa Anna took control of it and that Santa Anna made efforts to collect the notes. The source also reported that the country's second most important port, Tampico, had a million pesos in credits.[7] As new opposition to the government appeared in many states, Bustamante dispatched two major armies to the east, but on 13 May General Moctezuma struck a major blow when he defeated the federal army at Tampico.

The opposition pressed its demand that only the departure of Bustamante from the executive and his replacement with Gómez Pedraza could end the revolt and restore constitutional legitimacy to the government. As the fortunes of the regime began to falter, Bustamante sought negotiations, and in May the cabinet offered its resignation. But the opposition would not settle for anything short of the fall of the government as Santa Anna's forces marched inland and Moctezuma advanced to San Luis Potosí. Bustamante responded by removing Alamán, Facio, and Espinosa from the cabinet, but the opposition leaders who Bustamante invited to take their places refused his offer. In July the government of Jalisco issued a decree recognizing Gómez Pedraza as the legitimate president and declaring the Bustamante administration an "intrusive government." Zacatecas, one of the most prosperous states in these years owing to the rapid recovery of its mining industry to preindependence levels of output by 1828, launched its militia against the federal government.[8] In the south, Juan Alvarez, Gordiano Gúzman, and the other amnestied rebel leaders of 1830 pronounced against the government.

Increasingly desperate, the government unleashed something close to a reign of terror on its opponents in the capital throughout July and August 1832. As Rejón and Quintana Roo went into hiding, the government arrested Rocafuerte on 12 July. Hundreds of citizens were detained. A sister of Santa Anna's was beaten when she attended Sunday Mass on 1 August, then she was imprisoned and held incommunicado. Jalisco, Zacatecas, and Durango had now joined Veracruz and Tamaulipas in open revolt, while Puebla was on the verge of joining them. General Moctezuma occupied San Luis Potosí. As Bustamante moved to take personal command of the federal armies in the field, uniformed guards and secret police roamed the capital arresting hundreds of suspects. The police received orders to shoot on sight the principal leaders of the opposition, Rejón, Quintana Roo, Pacheco Leál, Rocafuerte, and Pablo Villavicencio, the editor of *El Duende*. The police discovered and killed Villavicencio, but the others, protected by friends, managed to escape by constantly moving about, sleeping in different houses every night.

Both sides in the civil war of 1832 made direct appeals to ayuntamientos in an attempt to gain the legitimacy provided by municipal pronouncements of support. The government sent agents throughout the states of Mexico, Jalisco, Oaxaca, and Michoacán, gaining thirty-four acts of adhesion from as many ayuntamientos. The opposition under Santa Anna did the same, with Santa Anna declaring himself to be the "mediator of the general will." Both sides sought the new legitimacy provided since the war of the south in 1830 by seeking the support of towns and ayuntamientos. Thus, in the midst of political crisis, communities continued negotiating the terms of their political alliances with superior authorities in order to assure themselves the maximum of autonomy.[9] The social and political protest thus unleashed never really abated. Hernández Chávez suggests, for example, that one sign of this was the frequent replacement of state governors by state legislatures acting on petition from ayuntamientos.[10]

Stevens shows that between 1825 and 1855 the average duration of state governors was eight months. In only three of the states—Durango, Zacatecas, and Aguascalientes—were there fewer than twenty governors in those thirty years; but in eleven states—Oaxaca, Puebla, Michoacán, Querétaro, Sonora, Tamaulipas, Jalisco, Chihuahua, San Luis Potosí, Tabasco, and Sinaloa—there were from thirty to fifty governors in that same period.[11]

In the midst of the war of 1832 the election for the new president of the republic was scheduled to take place on 1 September. This corresponded with the period when the war was reaching its highest level, and the election was perhaps the most important casualty of the fighting. The political standing of many of the possible candidates was clouded, whether they came from the opposition or from the government side. Many of the state legislatures had been usurped; others were in open rebellion. Intense political struggles over control of the legislatures and the governors offices raged in several states.

General Manuel Mier y Terán, former minister of war and current commandant of federal armies in the four northeastern states, emerged as the only figure whose reputation was not besmirched by the political struggle. This was because, although his political background suggested he was something of a conservative, he had avoided political entanglements in the three previous years and had concentrated on defending Texas and Tamaulipas from absorption by foreign interests either in the form of the Anglo-American colonists in Texas or the Spanish invaders in Tamaulipas. In 1832 he emerged as the preferred presidential candidate for a remarkable coalition that was forming between the moderates, former Escoceses, and many former Yorkinos as well. He was an appointee of the Bustamante government whose political leanings were conservative but federalist (though Tornel said he was a liberal republican but not a federalist), a close personal friend of Alamán and Facio, but with close contacts among the government's opponents, especially Governor García of Zacatecas. He thought the only solution to the political crisis was for Bustamante to resign so that the president of the Supreme Court and two other individuals could hold a provisional presidency, as required by Article 97 of the constitution.[12] Florstedt has judged Mier y Terán as being simply too indecisive to have developed a clear political position: "He never did what he could have done, because he avoided political controversies in all ways possible."[13]

Nonetheless, moderate liberals, chief among them Mora, actively promoted the candidacy of Mier y Terán. When Mora took it upon himself to conduct a poll of the state legislatures, he found that twelve of them favored Mier y Terán for president, which would have guaranteed his election. Mora presented what he said was Mier y Terán's political program, which consisted of abolition of judicial privileges for the military and clergy, gradual confiscation of church property, and abolition of the federal commandancies general.[14] The leading conservatives, meanwhile, leaned toward Bravo as their candidate.

But Mier y Terán suffered from deep depression brought about by ill health, the war of 1832, and what he saw as the inevitable loss of Texas to the Anglo-Americans. He did not want to be president, or at least was extremely reluctant, and wrote Mora, "If I were president I would commit perhaps greater errors than those of Alamán as minister, but I do not have either his knowledge or his business experience."[15] At the end of June 1832, he went to the town of Padilla in Tamaulipas, the very place where Iturbide had been executed, and selected for his living quarters the same rooms that Iturbide had occupied. On 2 July he paced through the town and stood contemplating the tomb of Iturbide for more than an hour. He then wrote a letter to his friend Lucas Alamán:

> A great and respectable Mexican nation, a nation of which we have dreamed and for which we have labored so long, can never emerge from the many disasters which have overtaken it. . . . My soul is burdened with weariness. I am an unhappy man, and unhappy people should not live on earth. . . . The spirit is uncomfortable, it commands me to set it free, and it is necessary to obey.

The next morning, 3 July, he put his sword against a stone behind the ruined church of San Antonio de Padilla, where Iturbide was buried, and placing the point against his heart fell on the sword. In acknowledgment of the symbolic role of Iturbide as the only leader who had united independent Mexico, Mier y Terán left directions that he was to be buried in the same tomb as the former emperor, with his body literally touching the bones of Iturbide.[16] Interestingly, in 1838 General Anastasio Bustamante, in his second term as president, had the remains of Iturbide transferred to Mexico City, though the remains of Mier y Terán stayed in Padilla. Just before his own death in 1853, Bustamante ordered that his heart should be buried with the remains of Iturbide in the cathedral in Mexico City.[17]

The death of Mier y Terán broke the unlikely alliance of moderates and radicals that had been forming around his candidacy. The more conservative elements turned to the candidacy of Bravo, while the more liberal elements began to insist that the election for president that was to be held on

1 September would be invalid on the grounds that most state legislatures had been imposed by the central government. When the voting occurred, six states then in rebellion—Zacatecas, Jalisco, Durango, San Luis Potosí, Tamaulipas, and Tabasco—refused to take part. Among the twelve states that voted, Bravo received seven votes and the remainder were divided between four others, an insufficient number to elect under any circumstances.[18] The vote was never certified by Congress because by the end of the year the Treaty of Zavaleta nullified it and called for a new presidential election.

On 18 September 1832, in the Battle of Gallinero near San Miguel Allende, Bustamante's forces won a crushing victory against Moctezuma, who was commanding a joint force that included the civic militias of Zacatecas and Tamaulipas. With at least a thousand killed on the rebel side, this defeat was a severe blow to Zacatecas, and it effectively destroyed the coalition between the states of the northwest. It also cost the regular army many of its professional officers. It did not end the war, however. With Santa Anna advancing on Mexico City from the east, García from the north, and Alvarez from the south, the government had lost control of the country. Following the well-established pattern, the opposition forces encircled Mexico City. At the end of September Santa Anna defeated Facio near the city of Puebla, which left Mexico City unprotected, and on 5 October he took Puebla. As the Bustamante regime in Puebla crumbled, the hated police chief of the state government was captured and murdered by the people, his body mutilated.[19] The government declared that Mexico City was in a state of siege as Santa Anna's four thousand troops drew near. Meanwhile, Gómez Pedraza, brought from New Orleans at the request of Santa Anna, returned from exile on 6 November, and he immediately issued public statements proposing an amnesty for all participants in the war and new elections for president. On 5 December, Bustamante's forces met Santa Anna's in an indecisive battle, after which Bustamante sued for peace and proposed new elections for state legislatures and thereafter for Congress and chief executive. The U.S. minister, Anthony Butler, reported on 12 December that the fate of the government was sealed and the constitution was at an end, destroyed not only by the repeated violations committed upon it but also by its failure to complete the most important obligation of electing the next president and Congress.[20]

Exhaustion prevailed on all sides. Bustamante and the centralists who pursued what they interpreted as order and civilization were defeated and could not retain power. At the same time, however, the victorious forces of state sovereignty and federalism were hopelessly divided between moderates and radicals, and their leader was now Santa Anna, a figure many of the federalists distrusted intensely. The uprising had increasingly stood on the platform that only Gómez Pedraza's assumption of the presidency could restore constitutional legitimacy. Thus, though it was in many ways utterly absurd in that by December 1832 there were less than four months left until the presidential term would expire on 1 April 1833, there was nothing to do but honor Gómez Pedraza's rights to the presidency, to which he had been legally elected four very long years before.

That Gómez Pedraza's possession of the presidency would not settle anything became clear in a remarkable series of letters between Gómez Pedraza in Veracruz and Governor Sebastian Camacho in Jalapa. The letters suggest not only how complex the political situation had become but also how acutely conscious the political elites were of the overshadowing presence of the common people. Immediately upon his arrival in Veracruz Gómez Pedraza wrote Camacho to tell him that the first commission Santa Anna had sent to him, urging his return to Mexico, had failed to convince him. But when Santa Anna sent a second commission to him, carrying news of the spontaneous declaration of various state legislatures in his support and acclaiming him as the only constitutional president of the republic, Gómez Pedraza had realized it was possible to contribute to the settlement of the civil war and had therefore decided to return to Mexico. Camacho replied, however, warning him that he was perhaps not fully informed of the situation in Mexico and that there were many obstacles threatening the objective he desired of restoring peace. Having read the periodicals and other background information Camacho sent him, Gómez Pedraza replied, saying he was offended by the tone of Camacho's letter, which sounded as if Camacho did not trust his motives for returning. All the U.S. newspapers had urged him to return, and he had come to believe that if he refused to answer the call the destruction of the nation would be attributed to him; he believed it was the moment to act decisively. To this, Camacho told Gómez Pedraza that his presence was not the magic force that would bring tranquillity: "You believe, as far as I can tell, that this is a fight for liberty against despotism, and that power and wealth figure on one side as combatants with the masses on the other." But it was not that simple, Camacho argued, because if the struggle were simply between elites and masses the masses, possessing overwhelming numbers, would have won by now. The reason they had not won yet was because the masses could only be moved by the efforts of others; they did not rise up spontaneously on their own account. What was certain, he said, was that now in 1832 there would be a president imposed by the same means as in 1828, by *bayonetazos*. The placing of Gómez Pedraza in the presidency, in other words, would be the result of force, not the law, because the constitution prescribed the election by Congress of either a provisional or a substitute president following the resignation or removal of the incumbent. This was the reason, Camacho insisted, that those persons who had fought to put Gómez Pedraza in the presidency in 1828 were now lukewarm about his taking the office. In other words, by 1832 very different political forces were at work to place him in the presidency, and Camacho thought he should be aware of that fact. Gómez Pedraza replied that Camacho was wrong to say that the people were not interested in the revolt; the people were slow in adopting political views, but when they did they defended them with tenacity, as they had defended independence itself. The series of letters concluded with both men pledging their respect for each other, despite their differing opinions on the presidency.[21]

In this interesting exchange of views, Camacho was correct, as the Treaty of Zavaleta, signed the next month, would indicate. Gómez Pedraza had been called home to answer the invitation of the people to restore the constitution. But, to a great extent, the constitution was now irrelevant because both Guerrero and Bustamante had seized presidential power in contradiction to the constitution. Nor were the people on their way to gaining, for placing Gómez Pedraza in the presidency was simply the device used by one element of the elite to oppose the Bustamante regime, which was supported by another element of the elite. What Gómez Pedraza apparently failed to notice was that he had made himself virtually an instrument of Santa Anna's ambitions.

Luis de Cortázar, who had emerged from the war as the undisputed caudillo of Guanajuato through his skill at playing the two sides off against each other, acted as an intermediary and opened negotiations between Bustamante and Gómez Pedraza.[22] To arrive at the peace settlement, Bustamante and his leading officers met with Santa Anna, Gómez Pedraza, Ramos Arizpe, and other leading federalists at the hacienda of Zavaleta near Puebla. On 23 December 1832 they reached an agreement, the so-called Treaty of Zavaleta, by which Gómez Pedraza assumed the presidency, military officers from both sides of the war were promoted, and new elections for Congress and the state legislatures were scheduled to be held before 15 February and for president and vice president on 1 March 1833. Congress, which had rejected such an agreement when it was first proposed, was threatened if it refused to recognize Gómez Pedraza as president. Although civilians had participated in writing the Treaty of Zavaleta, only officers and one representative of each army corps signed it.[23] When Gómez Pedraza, Santa Anna, and Bustamante entered Mexico City together on 3 January 1833, it was Santa Anna who was the dominant power.

Thus, the peace was signed without the direct involvement of the civilians in Mexico City and in Congress who had launched the opposition to Bustamante and who had turned to the military officers to lead the rebellion. The settlement of this essentially civilian issue was almost entirely the work of military officers. Santa Anna, who in 1828 had risen up to prevent Gómez Pedraza from gaining the presidency, now brought him to the presidency, precisely because it guaranteed his own occupancy of the office in a few months. More than that, the struggle for power since 1830 had also been characterized by the mobilization of many indigenous towns and ayuntamientos, which threatened the equilibrium between the ruling elites fighting among themselves for control.[24] The Treaty of Zavaleta ended this danger by reasserting the dominance of the elites. As Reynaldo Sordo Cedeño puts it, "Analysis of the Treaty of Zavaleta leaves no doubt of its praetorian nature. The army made itself the restorer of constitutional order, breaking all the dispositions of the constitution."[25] Zavaleta was the compact that brought together the reconsolidated elites under the tutelage of the military officers to dictate the form of government without interference from the masses.

Thus, the winner in this struggle was not the constitution, not the states, and not even federalism. The winner was Santa Anna. Not so much diabolical as cynical and politically ambiguous, Santa Anna was no longer one of several major figures; he was now the indispensable man. He received almost all the credit for overthrowing the authoritarian Bustamante regime, he was overwhelmingly popular, and the presidential elections were three months overdue. It was the point at which, though federalism appeared victorious, it was actually breathing its last because the Treaty of Zavaleta was not designed to reactivate or assure a federalism now mortally weakened by the decimation of the civic militias in almost a year of warfare. Although the Treaty of Zavaleta theoretically restored constitutional legality, it did nothing to guarantee adherence to the constitution. Costeloe argues that the Treaty of Zavaleta became, in effect, the constitutional charter of the nation. Vázquez confirms that, although the states had won the victory, the Treaty of Zavaleta was essentially military, and it supplanted the constitutional order when it annulled the presidential election of 1832.[26]

The war of 1832 was the great watershed in the history of early republican Mexico, although the historical literature in general treats it only briefly. Its consequences were massive; but perhaps of greatest importance was that it left a Mexico exhausted in spirit and pessimistic about the future. It separated the bright hopes that prevailed earlier from the sense of almost formless chaos that followed. It was the first really destructive internecine conflict, and it left all participants painfully aware that their hopes for a prosperous and peaceful republic were lost. It was the point at which the election for president became so irrelevant that it was nullified. It was also the point at which the contest between the civic militias and the regular army took center stage in that state sovereignty could not survive without civic militias. In the process, Mexicans realized that whoever controlled the instruments of force would determine the political future, reducing the constitution to little more than an instrument to be manipulated. The substantial loss of life in the various battles decimated both the regular army and the militias, but future political life would be dominated by an endless series of shifting alliances between officers and civilian politicians, which is often incorrectly dubbed militarism but was actually a symbiotic link between civilian politicians and military officers.[27] This is what conservatives and later generations of historians blamed federalism for and what they blamed caudillism for, but neither was the cause of it. Rather, federalism was the victim of this emergence of praetorian politics, and caudillism was its beneficiary.

The war of 1832 saw the institutionalization of the caudillos. Santa Anna, the most ambitious of them, had gained control of the customs revenues of Veracruz for a year, and in a classic ploy he financed his rise to national power on the basis of the federal government's own receipts. As he drew close to achieving the presidency, he was well on the way to augmenting his well-grounded regional clientele by building a national clientele that would be with him for the next two and a half decades. Other caudillos consolidated their control over their regions. In Guanajuato, Luis de Cortázar outmanuevered his various opponents, both liberal and conservative, to achieve undisputed control of the state.[28] In the south, the turmoil there had resulted in a fragile and altogether surprising alliance between Juan Alvarez and Nicolás Bravo. For months Alvarez had invited Bravo to join with him in opposing the Bustamante government, and on 12 September they issued a statement declaring that "all the towns of the South . . . are united now, forming a single voice to defend their interests and present and future rights against the aspirantism of tyrants." Above all else, their pact, signed in Tixtla on 18 December, served to guarantee their respective zones of influence in the south. This was the case despite the fact that Alvarez would continue as the country's most radical caudillo and Bravo as its most conservative one. Bravo's opposition to the beloved Guerrero had made him the enemy of the masses and the friend of the well-to-do.[29] Although some caudillos, such as Alvarez, offered the people restitution of their lands and waters, all the caudillos depended on the dual pillars of electoral influence and military influence.[30] And it was not ideology that determined a caudillo's success in consolidating his zone of influence, for Alvarez was a radical, Bravo a conservative, and Cortázar a moderate federalist with aristocratic roots. And Santa Anna, who had dubbed himself the mediator of the national will, lived up to the term by becoming the weather vane that revolved atop the national edifice.

Caudillism and state sovereignty, or regional autonomy, were now so intimately linked that they were inextricable and virtually identical, for the caudillos were the only guarantee that such autonomy could survive. Most of the caudillos who were in place by 1832 held their power as long as they lived; Juan Alvarez even passed his on to his son. By 1835 other caudillos, all of whom combined the zeal for federalism with local issues, included José Urrea in areas of Sonora, Sinaloa, and Durango; Pedro Lemus in Nuevo León and Coahuila; Antonio Canales across the Bravo River in Tamaulipas, Nuevo León, and Coahuila; and Santiago Méndez in Yucatán.[31]

Whatever the course of caudillism might have been in later decades, in the early 1830s the phenomenon of caudillism arose because of a conjunction of factors: the urge to defend state and local autonomy from centralist attacks, the legacy from the wars of independence of military forces based in the regions, and the rapid growth of local civic militias. The profound legitimacy of regional and state autonomy, to which all of Mexican history then and now has resonated, spread its mantle over the caudillos. In the defense of their own people in the states and regions, the caudillos had not only a critical but a legitimate role to play. Certainly the federal republic had signally failed to defend the people in their states and regions, and between 1828 and 1832 it had become irrelevant to them. As Annino has said, the caudillos "guaranteed the territorial basis of creole intermediate power."[32]

In the elections, which were held on 1 March 1833 in keeping with the Treaty of Zavaleta, Santa Anna was elected president and Gómez Farías vice president. They were both federalist liberals, although Gómez Farías was more radical than Santa Anna. Continuing the habit that would characterize his life, Santa Anna immediately sought the restoration of his health by retiring to his hacienda of Manga de Clavo, leaving Gómez Farías to act as chief executive in his place. Although the seat of the national government was Mexico City, Santa Anna was the first Mexican president to have the luxury of being able to abandon it without fear because his domain in Veracruz permitted him to withstand any attack against him.[33] He did have genuine health problems, but his habit of frequently abandoning the presidency and retiring to his hacienda reflected both his desire to avoid losing political support at times of controversy, particularly when he foresaw the need to make decisions the army might not like, and his need to protect his support base at home.[34] Like Anastasio Bustamante, Santa Anna was characterized as much by ambiguity as by anything else, which probably helps account for the longevity of influence of both men. At all times, he was protecting the two props of his political support, the army and his Veracruz base. His frequent retirements, which seem to have mystified some historians, were really very logical from Santa Anna's point of view and no doubt an important element in his long survival as the dominant political figure between 1833 and 1855. No other general in these decades had the same sort of political clientele; no other general had the same capacity to mobilize the army and realize significant political alliances with civilian leaders.

In Santa Anna's absence, Vice President Gómez Farías and the new Congress, dominated by radicals, then launched a program of reform that significantly threatened the property and privileges of the church as well as the untouchable status of the military officers.[35] Gómez Farías attempted to abolish the clergy's immunity from civil prosecution (the fuero) and to submit the military commandants general to the governments of the states in which they operated, while simultaneously strengthening the civic militias on which the states depended for the protection of their sovereignty. These reforms did not become effective, however, because they caused officers and clergy to forge a new alliance to defend their threatened privileges, and they in turn convinced Santa Anna to reclaim the presidency and attempt to pressure Congress to revoke the reform laws.[36] Santa Anna remained a federalist, but if he sat idly by while the army was threatened he would have no chance of political survival. When Congress began debating a proposed law on the provision of curacies in the church—the most delicate issue because it implied acceptance of the transfer of the former royal patronage over the church to the government of the republic—Santa Anna again retired to Manga de Clavo in December 1833, still unwilling to run the political risks inherent in such a controversial issue. Santa Anna's role was unique, as Justo Sierra has pointed out, because he was in the peculiar position of being simultaneously the figurehead of a radical regime and the person to whom all the antiprogressive elements looked for protection.[37]

In the first months of 1834 the reformist struggle intensified, and in April Santa Anna returned to the capital as the savior of religion. He had decided where his future prospects lay. When Congress attempted to proceed with the reforms, Santa Anna announced that he would not recognize the legality of its enactments. Gómez Farías then resigned the vice presidency and left the country, bringing to an end the first great attempt in Mexican history to reform the church and the army. When on 25 May 1834 the military garrison of Cuernavaca pronounced against Congress, the state legislatures, and the reformers, Santa Anna took over the leadership of the movement. Congress and most of the state legislatures were dissolved. Although the more moderate federalist states, such as Durango and Zacatecas, acquiesced in the Plan of Cuernavaca, other radical states opposed it. The central government repressed those states, including San Luis Potosí, Michoacán, Yucatán, Puebla, and Jalisco, in a series of military campaigns during the months of June, July, and August 1834.[38] Santa Anna governed alone for the rest of the year.

Santa Anna was still a federalist, however, in spite of the almost universal call for the overthrow of federalism and the establishment of a centralist system. He favored reforming the constitution of 1824. He convoked elections for the new Congress, which would be dominated by centralists when it began to meet in January 1835. When Santa Anna, unable to work with a centralist Congress, attempted to renounce the presidency, Congress refused, although it granted him permission once again to retire to Manga de Clavo. Congress then nullified the reform laws passed in 1833 and 1834. Overturning the legislation to strengthen the civic militias, it proposed new legislation that gave to the national Congress and not to the state legislatures the right to determine which forces would be assigned to each state and territory based on their population and circumstances. The civic militia was fused with the active militias into a single organization and placed under command of army officers. The states knew their ruin was drawing near.[39]

Santa Anna once again took command of the government, by now convinced that it was impossible to resist the spread of centralist sentiment. It appears that it was at this point, in April 1835, that he abandoned his long devotion to federalism and placed himself at the head of the centralist movement. José María Tornel, his most intimate adviser who held cabinet posts under him more frequently than any other person, was heard to remark on 12 April "that the most persuasive proof that could be given that the federal system no longer suited the nation was that now not even [Santa Anna] himself wanted it."[40] Torn by a year of agonizing personal debate and seeing his own political dominance threatened, Santa Anna converted. He did not engineer the end of the federal republic, as most of the historiography argues, but with political realism he reluctantly acceded to it; an opportunist no doubt, but more the prey than the predator.

Because central government control of the civic militias was the most fundamental of all threats to federalism, the states of Zacatecas, Jalisco, San Luis Potosí, and Guanajuato formed another coalition to defend their sovereignty. Santa Anna, whose position depended on his having turned the army into his foremost national client group, argued that the civic militias must submit to the command of the regular army to avoid becoming a torment to society at large.[41] To implement this policy required defeating the civic militia of Zacatecas, under the command of former governor Francisco García, on the battlefield, which occurred on 11 May 1835 when Santa Anna personally led the government's forces against the Zacatecas militia. To punish Zacatecas, the region of Aguascalientes was removed from the state and converted into a territory, which effectively ruined Zacatecas for decades to come.[42] In many ways the sacrificial lamb, Zacatecas fulfilled its destiny in the first federal republic by becoming its final defender and paid such a high price in men, treasure, and territory that it would never again recapture the stature it had in the late 1820s as Mexico's most important state.

With the defeat of Zacatecas, there remained no major obstacles to the overthrow of the federal republic and its replacement with a central republic. The first federal republic, long on its deathbed, expired finally in May 1835. On his return trip from Zacatecas to Manga de Clavo, Santa Anna stopped long enough to confer with leading politicians at Tacubaya. In the discussions the idea prevailed that the Congress should be converted into a constituent congress to draft the transformation in the government system. The centralists needed the approval of Santa Anna and the votes of the *santanistas* in Congress, and they received such support when on 14 September 1835 the two chambers of Congress were joined into a single chamber and declared a constituent congress. A total of eighteen months were spent dismantling the federal institutions and enacting, on 30 December 1836, the new constitution, the so-called Constitución de las Siete Leyes. The Siete Leyes established a complex unitary form of government that removed all political and financial autonomy from the states and reduced them to the status of departments and restricted the franchise to persons with economic qualifications. Only persons with annual incomes of more than one hundred pesos could vote, which disenfranchised the vast majority. Furthermore, most of the municipalities were abolished. The Siete Leyes was largely the work of Manuel Sánchez de Tagle, Lucas Alamán, and Carlos María de Bustamante in the Chamber of Deputies and was adopted after Santa Anna had been taken prisoner in Texas.

The change to centralism provided the pretext for the Anglo-American settlers in Texas to rise up and declare independence from Mexico. Santa Anna's leadership of the Mexican armies in Texas, his defeat at San Jacinto in April 1836, and his subsequent trip to Washington to plead his case, cost him the presidency. By the time he returned to the country in 1837, centralists had turned to General Anastasio Bustamante as their more appropriate and natural leader. Santa Anna claimed that the fact that federalism was abolished during his absence from the country meant that it was not his doing.[43]

What killed the first federal republic in Mexico? Michael Costeloe argues that there was in 1835 a genuine widespread public sentiment, based in the disillusionment of the eleven years of federalism, that blamed all the country's ills on the federal system. In 1835 the press and leading conservative writers and politicians relentlessly pursued the argument that federalism was a foreign import unsuited to the Mexican scene. Conservatives carefully presented the intellectual and political case for the abandonment of federalism in an organized propaganda campaign that seems to have convinced many historians as well as many Mexican hombres de bien. In this campaign the most common argument was that the "frenzy of provincialism" and uncontrolled aspirations to public employment lay at the heart of the federalist urge, that the existence of separate state governments and their administrative machinery was excessively costly, that the effect of federalism had been the breakdown of law and order and the standards of civilized political conduct, that liberalism had weakened the church and public morals, and that the colonial era had been a time of harmony and social peace. Artificially stimulated by conservative political interests and such periodicals as the centralist *El Sol*, the campaign to discredit federalism was successful. Ironically, one of the techniques used to pressure Santa Anna into choosing centralism was a campaign organized from Mexico City that induced four hundred seemingly spontaneous pronunciamientos in favor of centralism from towns and ayuntamientos throughout the country. As Costeloe puts it, "What Alamán and his colleagues in the 1835 Congress sought was to centralize power in their own social class throughout the country." Centralism was in the air, and the word *federalism* had lost its once magical appeal.[44] Sordo Cedeño confirms that federalism was so damaged by its own excesses that the "party of order" was now dominant in all parts of the country, that not even the federalists questioned the need to reform the system, and that the attitude of Zacatecas had settled the issue. When Zacatecas opted to fight and then lost, the general government and Santa Anna were at the mercy of the centralists, and the federalists had nothing further to offer.[45]

At the heart of the campaign to overthrow federalism, what conservatives most feared in the institutions of federalism was the premise of equality that Guerrero and his followers had contributed. Over and over again, the complaint from the men of property was that liberal extremists preached a "chimerical equality," that the sansculottes threatened law and order and had destroyed the values of earlier times. This profound bias against the poor, the indigenous peasants, and the urban proletariat, in which the common folk became not just an inconvenience to elites but a threat to civilization, underscored almost all nineteenth-century historical writing, by both Mexicans and foreigners. Although Stevens calls it "more a political prejudice than a sociological fact," modern-day historians must always be aware of the great distortions it may have caused in the documents and eyewitness accounts.[46] At the same time, the centralists insisted, the Guerrero government had threatened law and order, while the Gómez Farías administration had even threatened religion. The civic militias had upset public order and threatened administrative chaos.

The argument was grounded mainly on the false assumption that the social disorder of the day had resulted from federalism and that the rise of the common people happened because of federalism. Therefore, the elimination of federalism would constitute a solution to the country's social divisions and the deterioration of civil society. Even stalwart federalists had been frightened and disillusioned by the threat of popular sovereignty. In June 1835, Andrés Quintana Roo issued a public statement defending a decision he had made as a member of the Supreme Court of Justice, which encapsulated the attitude of both liberals and conservatives on the great social issue that federalism had ultimately raised, sovereignty of the people. He declared that the people could do nothing by themselves, they could only be governed by the constituted authorities; sovereignty of the people was a metaphysical abstraction; the people's right to constitute a government themselves extended only as far as the right to participate in elections; when acting directly the people were guided by feelings rather than thought and would become a mob.[47] Thus, the first federal republic came to an end with the social issue that would dominate the next century of Mexican history first and foremost: was the people's direct exercise of sovereignty a desirable or even an attainable goal?

The central republic, however, failed as surely as the first federal republic. The deficiency of the conservative centralists was their inability to propose an acceptable alternative to federalism. When the central republic eliminated both state and municipal autonomy, the result was a rapid mobilization in the north, west, and center-north to defend those autonomies, in which large numbers of cities and towns adhered to the appeal to restore the constitution of 1824.[48] Almost as soon as the central republic was created, support for centralism evaporated as regional governing interests demanded the return of financial autonomy. Throughout the decade of the central republic, 1835 to 1846, Vázquez argues that there was not a single moment in which the federalists were not the majority, but at no point in that decade were they able to overcome their internal division between moderates, led by Gómez Pedraza, and radicals, led by Gómez Farías.[49] The conversion to a central republic only served to highlight for the former sovereign states the fact that their regions possessed a distinct cultural and political consciousness that had been translated into alternatives of social life and of specific historical development.[50] The devotion to individual and group self-determinism, which was the primary principle of federalism in the first republic, had already emerged as the essence of Mexican nationhood and national identity and the idea to which Mexicans would return again and again. There continued to be a frequently unstated sense among Mexicans that at its deepest and most meaningful level their nationhood was really about the right to self-definition and self-determination on both the regional and the individual level, about social justice and equality. In 1846, amid the crisis of war with the United States, the constitution of 1824 was restored.

There are two existing arguments in the literature of Latin American federalism that do not apply to Mexico. One is the argument, seen frequently in Venezuelan history, that federalism was merely a ploy to guarantee caudillos and local landowners their power, a political structure to uphold neofeudalism.[51] In Mexico, federalism was the means to unite the dis-united, to create union and thereby forge nationhood in a vast and multi-cultural country whose political precedents derived primarily from colonialism. As such, it was a profoundly sensible solution to real political and administrative problems, and therefore it had enduring appeal. The other main argument, drawn from Colombian history, is that federalism was a system that granted power to the states in order thereby to deny power to the municipal level.[52] Although political conflicts between states and municipalities, and between primary and secondary towns, certainly existed in Mexico, the evidence in Mexico is that state autonomy and municipal autonomy went hand in hand; the linkage between local notables that occurred in the ayuntamientos, militias, and state legislatures meant that there was significant similarity of purpose on the subnational and local levels; and the indigenous communities relished municipal autonomism within federalism as the primary instrumentality for defending their land and water rights. It is true that one of the institutional weaknesses of the first republic was the inability of Congress to function as a device for resolving disputes between states and between states and municipalities, something that by the Porfiriato it was able to do. But the founders of the first republic quite correctly believed that the object of federalism was to strengthen the power of the states as the best guarantee against tyranny from the central government.

By 1835 the warring forces of Mexican political life had fought to a stalemate. This impasse may have been rooted in the contradiction between the political liberalism of the first republic and the traditional social structures inherited from colonialism that prevailed in the first decades after independence, but it was not the result of the adoption of federalism. The radicalism of a Guerrero or a Gómez Farías and the conservatism of an Alamán or an Anastasio Bustamante produced a kind of stasis in which neither achieved clear victory, in which neither a powerful dictatorship nor a solid civilian regime could emerge. The areas of major political disagreement between conservatives, moderates, and radicals included such fundamental issues as state organization, methods of social control, state intervention in the economy, church-state relations, and attitudes toward the colonial experience.[53] Early-nineteenth-century Mexican leaders had political ideals and principles that were not mere affectations disguising a bid for power. It is precisely because no school of thought, no ideological force, decisively carried the field in nineteenth-century Mexico that unanimity and consensus were not possible. Abandoning the simplistic tendency to blame the caudillos for everything or, more to the point, attempting to account for and distinguish between the caudillos, we must reject the "caudillo thesis" as an explanation for Mexican instability in the early decades. This allows us to overcome the historiography's dependence on "caudillism, chaos, and backwardness" as explanations for Mexico's nineteenth-century troubles, replacing that outmoded formula with "stalemate."

Mexico's history can only be understood by incorporating the full diversity of players. This brings us back to the quotation by Thomas C. Cochran with which this book began about the interplay between national history and regional or state history in a federal republic.[54] If it was true of the United States, it is certainly true of Mexico that the historical literature has been characterized by an excessive focus on the primary role of the central government in Mexico's historical development. This has placed the historiography on a false footing, orienting it almost entirely toward a central government whose annals form only part of the history of the Mexican nation, for without the states and municipalities there was no nation. Local and state autonomy, rather than serving as an obstacle to the forging of a nation-state, was its base. And, as was seen briefly at the time of the 1829 Spanish invasion and as would become clear at later points in the nineteenth century, local and state autonomy was also the source of the nation's survival.[55]

An important reason for the great significance of these years in Mexican history is that in the brief period of only twenty years, from 1810 to about 1830, Mexicans experienced a succession of sovereignties—from an absolute king in Spain, to a concept of the nation's sovereignty after 1812, to a struggle over possession of sovereignty between Iturbide and the Congress, to a definition of dual sovereignty of the nation and the states, and finally to the first expressions of the ideal of the sovereignty of the people. This process requires from us a very different interpretation of what the first years of Mexican republican nationhood meant.

Pedro Pérez Herrero has written that if we want to understand the early republican period in Mexico we have to revise the nineteenth-century liberal discourse that equated "order" with "progress" and "disorder" with "crisis." And if we want to understand the processes of decentralization, federalization, democratization, and modernization that are underway in Mexico today, we have to begin with a revision of the origin of the Mexican nation-state and the foundations of national identity, which occurred in the early republican period.[56] The Positivist historiography of the end of the nineteenth century constructed the myth of the stage of "anarchy" and "backwardness by disorder" because it justified the achievements of Porfirian "order and progress."[57] This approach relates closely to another widespread thesis, which originated with Bolívar, Alamán, and other centralists, that the caudillos betrayed independence. The first half of the nineteenth century, in both Mexico and other Latin American countries, came to be seen by elites as characterized by "anarchy," "militarism," and "caudillism."[58]

The "disorder thesis" of nineteenth-century Mexican history has exercised a compelling influence on the historiography. This is mainly because it has been so easy to ascribe the collapse of the first republic, as well as the political and economic failures of much of nineteenth-century Mexico, to "disorder," so easy, that is, to embrace uncritically Alamán's 1830 concept of the "war of order against anarchy." Literally any inadequacy or dysfunction can be attributed to "disorder," and practically any political agenda can be strengthened by appeals to "order." But the historian must ask: whose order and whose disorder are we discussing; at whose cost and to whose benefit was order achieved? The "disorder thesis" is wrong because it focuses on the wrong things. It focuses on the center, it ignores the states and regions, and it discounts or dismisses the common people. It assumes nationhood before it existed; it assumes that the process of creating a nation was disintegration; and it assumes that the definition of nationhood came exclusively in the form of a political existence granted by the center to the regions.

The recent work by Peter Guardino on the state of Guerrero in the early republic is a major step toward redefining what was at stake shortly after independence. In the nineteenth century Guerrero was overwhelmingly characterized by small farmers and ranchers and the legacy of the colonial repúblicas de indios (a form of communal self-government for Indian villages). It was also the most radical region of the country, the home of two of early republican Mexico's most influential revolutionaries, Vicente Guerrero and Juan Alvarez, and the constant champion of radical federalism. After the judicial murder of Vicente Guerrero in 1831, the farmers, ranchers, and muleteers of the region followed Juan Alvarez, one of Mexico's classic caudillos, in an endless series of uprisings and pronunciamientos against the central government. What the traditional historiography and the central elites always saw as formless chaos and mindless resistance to the civilizing dictates of Mexico City, Guardino shows was a profound struggle for local autonomy, municipal self-government, democratic inclusion, and ultimately a populist form of federalism that was incorporated into Mexican liberalism in the Reforma of 1855 and after.[59]

My argument has been that in the first federal republic, what the traditional historiography called "disorder" and "crisis" was, in fact, the struggle for progress, particularly for social justice, in a context of provincial self-determination; the birth of a new and more fulfilling structure of nationhood; and the expression of a movement characterized by the construction of new political institutions and definitions of being more in accord with the existing characteristics of the country and its people. The Mexican nation-state as well as the Mexican national identity were and are unique products of the Mexican soil. If rejecting the rule of the center and its traditional elites constituted political disorder, then political disorder, by its very nature, was the route to social, economic, and political progress. Politically volatile it may have been, but its object was not to eliminate the long-term cohesion of the nation. Quite the contrary, although the history of the first federal republic is neither simple nor untroubled, its object was to forge a Mexican nation, one based on union, not uniformity, and one that recognized that the absence of uniformity did not mean the absence of nationhood. The enduring self-government that resulted from regional and provincial autonomy has been a prominent component of the struggle for democracy in Mexico.[60] This is why federalism established a legacy that has endured for nearly two hundred years. Provincehood and nationhood were not opposed but were two sides of the same coin.

Ultimately, my argument is that federalism remains not only the fundamental cement of Mexican nationhood but the instrument by which that nationhood was forged. Because there is nothing supernatural about nations or about history, Mexico, like all nations, was not so much "imagined" or "invented" as it was forged, that is, formed together out of the preexisting parts, the mosaic of identities and regions, that made it up. It was "constituted" or brought into being over a long period of time by the effort of the millions of men and women who composed it.

That work began with the first federal republic but is not yet concluded. The fact that nationhood is a constantly evolving process requiring continued effort was soberly articulated by President Ernesto Zedillo in his first annual state-of-the-nation address on 1 September 1995:

> The federalist ideal has deep roots in our history, roots entwined with our first aspirations for independence and the original struggle for national sovereignty. The organization of the Republic as a federation inspired heroic acts and demanded the finest talents of great

Mexicans. We must recognize that a century and a half later, the reality of our federalism is not yet in harmony with that ideal, with those deeds, with those Mexicans. To a great extent, the states and municipalities—and the men and women who live in them—continue suffering the consequences of centralism.[61]

Thus, as Mexicans look toward the great political transition underway in their nation in the last decade of the twentieth century, the demand for a renewed federalism of genuine substance is increasingly heard. We can paraphrase Cerutti and González to say that although the Mexico of the 1990s seems very distant from the one that preoccupied Lucas Alamán and Vicente Guerrero in 1830, part of what we hear in their encounter suggests that the regional imperative continues not only to live but even threatens to return to its past of autonomism and rebellion. The ideal to which President Zedillo referred may be summarized in the words Cerutti and González used to explain the attitude toward national organization that came to prevail by the 1860s in the north of Mexico: "If it was certain that a central power had to exist, it had to be characterized by its discretion, by admitting the importance and weight of the forces of the interior of the country, and by recognizing not only the rights [of the provinces] but the necessity that resources generated by those same provinces remain with them."[62]

Mexico's national historical process is the history of the integration of diverse regional societies, and the explanatory key to this process is the identification of the dynamic of interrelationships. The processes of national integration and regional self-determination are unavoidably entwined, particularizing and harmonizing, occurring simultaneously, neither having meaning without the other.[63] Thus, the argument of this book is that the Mexican nation was created by the actions of its constituent parts; the states created the nation, not the other way around. The first formulation of Mexican nationhood, in the first federal republic, was based on a principle of genuine power sharing between the center and the provinces and regions. As Mexicans look to the beginning of the twenty-first century, the ideals of 1823 and 1824, upon which national identity was founded, and the institutional and constitutional structures forged at the birth of Mexican nationhood offer precedents as well as warnings for possible alternative formulations for the renewal and enhancement of both federalism and nationhood.

NOTES

ABBREVIATIONS

AGI   Archivo General de Indias, Seville
AGN   Archivo General de la Nación, Mexico City
AHN   Archivo Histórico Nacional, Madrid
BNAH   Biblioteca Nacional de Antropología e Historia Eusebio Dávalos Hurtado, Instituto Nacional de Antropología e Historia, Mexico City
BLAC   Nettie Lee Benson Latin American Collection, University of Texas at Austin

I. "FRAGMENTS AVERSE TO INTEGRATION"

1. Thomas C. Cochran, "The Social Sciences and the Problem of Historical Synthesis," in *The Varieties of History: From Voltaire to the Present*, ed. Fritz R. Stern (New York: Meridian, 1956), 351–52.
2. Aspásia Camargo, "La federación sometida: Nacionalismo desarrollista e inestabilidad democrática," in *Federalismos latinoamericanos: México/Brasil/Argentina*, ed. Marcello Carmagnani (Mexico City: El Colegio de México/Fondo de Cultura Económica, 1993), 300. Unless otherwise noted, all translations are my own.
3. Constitución de los Estados Unidos Mexicanos, 1917, Title 2, Article 40.
4. Carmagnani, "El federalismo," 10.
5. Mörner, *Region and State*, 6.
6. Filippi, *Instituciones e ideologías*, 92–93, 188–89.
7. Romano, "Algunas consideraciones."
8. Guerra, "Introducción," 13.
9. Pietschmann, "Estado colonial," 429.
10. Malamud, "Acerca del concepto."
11. Garza, "Una visión historiográfica."
12. Van Young, "The Raw and the Cooked," 78, 94.
13. Otero, *Consideraciones*, 127.

14. Brading, *The First America*, 674.
15. *The Economist* (London), 19 October 1861, cited in Salvucci, Salvucci, and Cohen, "The Politics of Protection."
16. Lorenzo Meyer, "El estado mexicano contemporáneo," *Historia Mexicana* 23, no. 4 (abril–junio 1974): 722–52.
17. Florescano, *Memory, Myth, and Time*, 221–22, 227.
18. Richard Warren, "The Construction of Independence Day, 1821--1864" (paper presented at "Culture, Power, and Politics in Nineteenth-Century Mexico: A Conference in Memory of Dr. Nettie Lee Benson," University of Texas at Austin, 15–16 April 1994).
19. For an interesting preliminary discussion of this issue, see Gortari Rabiela, "El territorio."
20. Cerutti, "Monterrey and Its *Ambito*," 146.
21. Bartra, *The Cage of Melancholy*, 1.
22. Lomnitz-Adler, *Exits from the Labyrinth*, 248.
23. Acta Constitutiva de la Federación Mexicana, Mexico City, 31 January 1824, BLAC.
24. Knight, "Peasants into Patriots."
25. Benson, *The Provincial Deputation*, 21.
26. Carmagnani, "Del territorio," 221.
27. Hernández Chávez, *La tradición republicana*, 17.
28. For example, see Arnold, *Bureaucracy and Bureaucrats*; Hamnett, *Roots of Insurgency*.
29. Costeloe, *The Central Republic*, 3. John H. Coatsworth also wishes to emphasize discontinuity, looking at the nineteenth century at large; see his "Los orígenes sociales."
30. Agustín de Iturbide, *Memoria de Livorno*, 27 September 1823, BLAC, Hernández y Dávalos Collection. I used the handwritten, draft English translation by Iturbide's British friend Michael Joseph Quin.
31. Mora cited in Hale, *Mexican Liberalism*, 113–14.
32. Peter Gerhard, referring to the historical geography before the Conquest, emphasizes, "There were varying degrees of independence among these native states. . . . The largest empire, the famed Triple Alliance. . . , controlled much of the [central] area. . . . Within this complex were countless quite autonomous states. . . . Rivals of the Triple Alliance, Michoacán and Tototépec (on the Pacific coast), and perhaps Metztitlan, were smaller empires. . . . Other areas . . . seem to have been composed of numerous small states loosely united through dynastic ties or in military federations but generally without a dominant leader. Elsewhere, the political map of Mexico in 1519 was divided into fragments, each little kingdom often surrounded by hostile neighbors." Gerhard, *A Guide to the Historical Geography of New Spain*, rev. ed. (Norman: University of Oklahoma Press, 1993), 4–5.

33. Paz, *Labyrinth of Solitude*, 127, 149.
34. Zepeda, "La nación," 498.
35. Bernstein, "Regionalism in the National History of Mexico," 389.
36. González, "Patriotismo y matriotismo," 480, 487.
37. Lomnitz-Adler, *Exits from the Labyrinth*; see page 306 for the definition of *fetish*.
38. Rubin, "Decentering the Regime," 118.
39. Van Young, "Are Regions Good to Think?"
40. Benjamin, "Regionalizing the Revolution," 327–28.
41. González, "Patriotismo y matriotismo," 477.
42. Tenenbaum, "Streetwise History." The classic historical study of the impact of cultural uniformity through education in modern Mexico is Vázquez de Knauth, *Nacionalismo y educación en México*.
43. Bartra, *The Cage of Melancholy*, 167.
44. Héctor Aguilar Camín and Lorenzo Meyer, *In the Shadow of the Mexican Revolution: Contemporary Mexican History, 1910–1989*, trans. Luis Alberto Fierro (Austin: University of Texas Press, 1993), 261.
45. Bartra, *The Cage of Melancholy*, 174–75.
46. Bartra, *The Cage of Melancholy*, 175.
47. Van Young, "The State as Vampire."
48. Monsiváis, "Just over That Hill."
49. Carmagnani, "El federalismo," 414.
50. Bartra, *The Cage of Melancholy*, 175.
51. Vázquez, "De la difícil constitución," 12.
52. González, "Patriotismo y matriotismo."
53. Zepeda, "La nación," 516.
54. Carmagnani, "Territorios, provincias," 65.
55. Coatsworth, "Los orígenes sociales," 219.
56. Burns, *The Poverty of Progress*; see also Burns, *Patriarch and Folk*.
57. Paz, *Labyrinth of Solitude*, 119.
58. Filippi, *Instituciones e ideologías*, 22.
59. Stevens, "Autonomists, Nativists," 262.
60. Jesús Reyes Heroles, "La constitución de 1824 es fruto de una ideología liberal, madura, y realista," in *Crónicas* 2:1027.
61. Stevens, *Origins of Instability*, 47–48, 110–15. This point is also made by Hale, "The Reconstruction of Nineteenth Century Politics."
62. Coatsworth, "The Decline of the Mexican Economy," 29.
63. Costeloe, *The Central Republic*, 25, 151.
64. Benson, *Mexico and the Spanish Cortes*, 208–9.
65. Cerutti, "Monterrey and Its *Ambito*," 147.
66. Pérez Herrero, " 'Crecimiento' colonial," 2:94. A very different article but one that arrives at the same conclusion is Pérez Herrero, "El México borbónico."

67. Carmagnani, "Territorialidad y federalismo."
68. Carmagnani, "Territorios, provincias," 71.
69. Florescano, "El poder," 225.
70. Siemens, *Between the Summit and the Sea*, xvii. Siemens's book is a remarkable study of the impact of the tropical lowlands of Veracruz on nineteenth-century foreign visitors that clearly establishes how what they encountered in the narrow coastal fringe colored their thinking about all the rest of Mexico.
71. Costeloe, "Federalism to Centralism."
72. González Oropeza, "Características iniciales."
73. Quoted in Quintanilla, *El nacionalismo*, 69.
74. Hamnett, "Between Bourbon Reforms," 59.
75. Brading, *The First America*, 642.
76. In the past fifty years, every president has removed some state governors from office. Miguel Alemán and Carlos Salinas de Gortari hold the records for removing the largest number of governors, twelve for Alemán, fifteen for Salinas (ten of whom were simply removed from office plus five others called to high positions in the central administration). Rogelio Hernández Rodríguez, "Inestabilidad política y presidencialismo en México," *Mexican Studies/Estudios Mexicanos* 10, no. 1 (winter 1994): 187–216.
77. Carmagnani, "El federalismo."
78. Rubin, "Decentering the Regime," 86, 90.
79. Zepeda, "La nación," 516.
80. Carmagnani, "El federalismo."
81. Filippi, *Instituciones e ideologías*, 194, 204–6.
82. Reyes Heroles, "La constitución de 1824," 1032.
83. Reyes Heroles, "La constitución de 1824," 1029.
84. Mario Cerutti, *Economía de guerra y poder regional en el siglo XIX* (Monterrey: Archivo General del Estado de Nuevo León, 1983); Cerutti and González Maíz, "Autonomía regional."
85. Carmagnani, "El federalismo," 413.
86. Ortega Noriega, "Hacia la regionalización."
87. The Ortega quotations in this and the preceding paragraph are drawn from his "Hacia la regionalización," 14, 17–18. For Angel Bassols Batalla, see such books as his *La división económica regional de México* (Mexico City: UNAM, 1967) and *México: Formación de regiones económicas. Influencias, factores y sistemas* (Mexico City: UNAM, 1979).

2. THE IMPULSE TO PROVINCEHOOD

1. Thomson, *Puebla de los Angeles*, 1.
2. Tutino, *From Insurrection*, 218–22.
3. Hamnett, "Between Bourbon Reforms," 48.
4. Guerra, "Identidades e independencia," 103.

5. Carmagnani, "Del territorio," 2:221.
6. Van Young, "The State as Vampire," 355–56.
7. Guerra, "Identidades e independencia."
8. Zepeda, "La nación," 499.
9. Florescano, "El poder."
10. Tenenbaum, "Streetwise History," 136, 141.
11. For a brief history of the intendancies, see Rees Jones, *El despotismo.*
12. Hamnett, "Absolutismo ilustrado."
13. Ortega Noriega, "Hacia la regionalización," 19.
14. Hamnett, "Between Bourbon Reforms," 45.
15. See Anna, *Spain and the Loss of America.*
16. Pantoja, *Idea de soberanía*, 73–78.
17. Jiménez Codinach, *La Gran Bretaña.*
18. Jiménez Codinach, "Confédération Napoléonnie"; Jiménez Codinach, "Veracruz, almacén."
19. The handwritten original of the decree is in AHN, Estado 54.
20. Council of Regency to Spanish America, León, 14 February 1810, AGI, Ultramar 795.
21. See Anna, "Spain and the Breakdown."
22. "Junta Superior de Cádiz da cuenta a la América . . ." in Juan E. Hernández y Dávalos, ed., *Colección de documentos para la historia de la Guerra de Independencia de México*, 6 vols. (Mexico City: José María Sandoval, 1877–1882), 2:22–27.
23. Gabriel H. Lovett, *Napoleon and the Birth of Modern Spain*, 2 vols. (New York: New York University Press, 1965), 1:343–45.
24. Michael P. Costeloe, "Spain and the Spanish American Wars of Independence: The *Comisión de Reemplazos*, 1811–1820," *Journal of Latin American Studies* 13, no.2 (November 1981): 223–37; Costeloe, "Spain and the Latin American Wars of Independence: The Free Trade Controversy, 1810–1820," *Hispanic American Historical Review* 61, no. 2 (May 1981): 209–34.
25. Thomson, "Traditional and Modern Manufacturing," 84.
26. Thomson, *Puebla de los Ángeles*, 197.
27. Smith, "The Institution of the Consulado"; Smith, "The Puebla Consulado."
28. "Oficio que la N.C. dirigio al Exmo. Sr. Virrey sobre que durante la ausencia del Señor D. Fernando VII goviene estos dominios Su Excellencia," 19 July 1808, Archivo de la Ciudad de México, Historia, en general, vol. 2254, no. 34; and identical phrasing in "Testimonio de las representaciones que esta N. Ciudad presentó al Exmo. Sr. D. José de Iturrigaray, promoviendo . . . la conservación y defensa del Reyno," AHN, Consejos 21081.
29. For "Hispanic American municipalism," see Filippi, *Instituciones e Ideologías*, 93.
30. Royal Accord, 6 September 1808, AHN, Estado 58, E.

31. Luis Villoro, *El proceso ideológico de la revolución de independencia*, 37–38 (Mexico City: Universidad Nacional Autónoma de México, 1967).

32. Brading, *Origins*, 43; see also Margaret E. Crahan, "Spanish and American Counterpoint: Problems and Possibilities in Spanish Colonial Administrative History," in *New Approaches to Latin American History*, ed. Richard Graham and Peter H. Smith, 36–70 (Austin: University of Texas Press, 1974); and Annino, "Some Reflections."

33. Hamnett, "Absolutismo ilustrado," 107.

34. For the most thorough treatment of the American deputies, among whom the Mexicans were the most numerous, see Rieu-Millan, *Los diputados*.

35. Anna, *Spain and the Loss of America*, 67–69; see also James F. King, "The Colored Castes and American Representation in the Cortes of Cádiz," *Hispanic American Historical Review* 33, no. 1 (February 1953): 33–64.

36. Anna, *Spain and the Loss of America*, 70–71.

37. Brading, *The First America*, 542–45.

38. Pantoja, *Idea de soberanía*, 80–82.

39. Guerra, *Modernidad e independencias*, 341–46.

40. Anna, *Spain and the Loss of America*, 79–81; W. Woodrow Anderson, "Reform as a Means to Quell Revolution," in Benson, *Mexico and the Spanish Cortes*, 185–207.

41. "Representación de la diputación americana en las Cortes," 1 August 1811, AGN, Impresos oficiales, vol. 60, no. 44; Anna, *Spain and the Loss of America*.

42. Easily available copies of the constitution of 1812 are in Hernández y Dávalos, *Colección de documentos*, 4:50–95; and Tena Ramírez, *Leyes fundamentales*, 59–104.

43. Benson, *La diputación provincial*, 21; see also David T. Garza, "Mexican Constitutional Expression in the Cortes of Cádiz," in Benson, *Mexico and the Spanish Cortes*, 56.

44. Stevens, "Autonomists, Nativists," 258.

45. Benson, *The Provincial Deputation*, 6, 9–22.

46. Benson, *The Provincial Deputation*, 21.

47. Carmagnani, "Territorios, provincias," 58.

48. Guedea, "The First Popular Elections"; Nettie Lee Benson, "The Contested Mexican Election of 1812," *Hispanic American Historical Review* 26, no. 3 (August 1946): 336–50.

49. Archer, "La Causa Buena," 96.

50. Archer, "Politicization of the Army," 21, 26.

51. Hamnett, *Roots of Insurgency*, 178–79; Hamnett, "Factores regionales."

52. Tecpan was the embryo of what in 1849 would be the state of Guerrero, as well as a part of the state of Morelos. O'Gorman, *Historia de las divisiones*, 32–34.

53. Garza, "La transición," 28.

54. Pérez Herrero, "El México borbónico," 142–43, 145.

55. For comparison, there are approximately twenty-four hundred municipios in Mexico today.
56. Hernández Chávez, *La tradición republicana*, 23–25.
57. Rugeley, *Men of Audacity*, chaps. 2 and 3.
58. Jaime E. Rodríguez O., "The Creation of the Mexican State" (paper presented at "Culture, Power, and Politics in Nineteenth Century Mexico: A Conference in Memory of Dr. Nettie Lee Benson," University of Texas at Austin, 15–16 April 1994).
59. Annino, "Otras naciones," 235, 237.
60. Hernández Chávez, "La Guardia Nacional," 207–8.
61. Annino, "Some Reflections," 41.
62. Hamnett, "Factores regionales," 305.
63. Archer, "Insurrection—Reaction," 90.
64. The following paragraphs are taken from Benson, *The Provincial Deputation*, 23–46.
65. Anna, *The Mexican Empire*, 20–21; Garza, "La transición."
66. This is a point emphasized by Stevens, "Autonomists, Nativists." See also Guedea, *En busca*; Guedea, "Las sociedades"; and Benson, *The Provincial Deputation*.
67. Apodaca to Minister of Ultramar, Mexico City, 29 May 1821, AGI, Mexico 1680.
68. Timothy E. Anna, "Francisco Novella and the Last Stand of the Royal Army in New Spain," *Hispanic American Historical Review* 51, no. 1 (February 1971): 92–110.
69. Benson, *The Provincial Deputation*, 47–60.
70. García Quintanilla, "En busca," 100.
71. Wortman, "Legitimidad política."

3. "WITHOUT TEARS AND WITHOUT LAMENTATIONS"
1. See Anna, *The Mexican Empire*.
2. Iturbide, *Memoria de Livorno*.
3. Iturbide to Apodaca, Iguala, 24 February 1821, AGI, Mexico 1680.
4. Iturbide, *Memoria de Livorno*.
5. Carlos María Bustamante, "Manifiesto histórico á las naciones y pueblos del Anáhuac, leído en la sesión pública del Soberano Congreso de 15 de abril de 1823," Mexico City, 1823, BLAC, Alamán Papers; Poinsett, *The Present Political State*, 25.
6. Hamnett, "The Economic and Social Dimension."
7. For economic data see TePaske, "The Financial Disintegration."
8. Coatsworth, "The Decline of the Mexican Economy," 28.
9. Vázquez, "El federalismo mexicano."
10. Alamán, *Historia*, 1:379. In addition to his treatment of the massacre at the Alhóndiga in his *Historia*, Alamán wrote a longer, more detailed account of the

event, probably a draft of that section of his book, which is preserved as a manuscript in BLAC. This manuscript account is much more moving.

11. Hale, *Mexican Liberalism*, 19–27.
12. Annino and Filippi, "Las formas del poder."
13. González Navarro, "La venganza."
14. Guardino, *Peasants*, 6.
15. González Navarro, "Tipología del conservadurismo."
16. Di Tella, *National Popular Politics*, viii, 4.
17. Costeloe, *The Central Republic*, 16–23.
18. Hamnett, *Roots of Insurgency*, 82–83.
19. The most complete and most accurate study of the provenance of the Plan of Iguala is Rodríguez, "The Transition."
20. Archer, "Where Did All the Royalists Go?"
21. "Resumen histórico de los acontecimientos de N. Esp., dado al Exmo. Sr. Capitán General de la Ysla de Cuba y su ejército por el Ten. Coronel de Navarra Expedicionario (Vicente Bausá)," Havana, 18 December 1821, AGI, Mexico 1680.
22. "Representación del Exmo. Ayuntamiento de Méjico al comandante accidental de armas, Francisco Novella," 2 September 1821, AGN, Impresos oficiales, vol. 60, no. 103.
23. Regency to Iturbide, Mexico City, 22 February 1822, BLAC, Hernández y Dávalos Collection; Iturbide to Regency, Mexico City, 7 December 1821, BNAH, T-3, 35, Colección Antigua.
24. Apodaca to Minister of Ultramar, Guanabacoa, Cuba, 17 November 1821, AGI, Mexico 1680.
25. Ocampo, *Las ideas*.
26. Among works by Christon I. Archer, see particularly, "Politicization of the Army"; "To Serve the King: Military Recruitment in Late Colonial Mexico," *Hispanic American Historical Review* 55, no. 2 (May 1975): 226–50; "La Causa Buena"; "The Army of New Spain and the Wars of Independence," *Hispanic American Historical Review* 61, no. 4 (November 1981): 705–20; and "The Militarization of Mexican Politics."
27. See Guedea, *En busca*.
28. Guedea, *En busca*, 7–8.
29. Rodríguez, "The Transition," 131.
30. Salvucci, "La parte más difícil."
31. Vázquez, "El ejército."
32. Anna, *The Mexican Empire*, chap. 1; Anna, "The Rule of Agustín de Iturbide"; Anna, "The Iturbide Interregnum"; Anna, "Iturbide, Congress, and Constitutional Monarchy"; and Anna, "Modelos de continuidad y ruptura, Nueva España y Capitania General de Guatemala," in vol. 5 of *Historia General de America Latina*, ed. Germán Carrera Damas and John V. Lombardi (UNESCO, forthcoming).

33. "Plan de la independencia de Mexico proclamada y jurada en el pueblo de Iguala en los días 1 y 2 de marzo de 1821," AGN, Impresos oficiales, vol. 60, no 62; Tena Ramírez, *Leyes fundamentales*, 113–16.
34. Servando Teresa de Mier, "Memoria político-instructiva, enviada desde Filadelfia en agosto de 1821 a los gefes independientes del Anáhuac," Mexico City, 1822, BLAC, García Collection.
35. Report in Mier's handwriting, n.d., BLAC, García Collection.
36. Van Young, "Quetzalcóatl, King Ferdinand"; and Van Young, "Who Was That Masked Man."
37. William Spence Robertson, *Iturbide of Mexico* (Durham NC: Duke University Press, 1952), 3–9.
38. Di Tella, "Ciclos políticos."
39. Vázquez, "Un viejo tema," 622.
40. Ocampo, *Las ideas*, 171.
41. Iturbide to Apodaca, Iguala, 24 February 1821, AGI, Mexico 1680.
42. "Resumen histórico de los acontecimientos de Nueva España, dado al Exmo. Sr. Capitan General de la Ysla de Cuba y su ejercito por el Ten. Coronel de Navarra expedicionario (Vicente Bausá)," Havana, 18 December 1821, AGI, Mexico 1680.
43. O'Donojú to Minister of Ultramar, Villa de Córdoba, 31 August 1821, AGI, Mexico 1680.
44. David A. Brading, "El jansenismo español y la caída de la monarquía católica en México," in *Interpretaciones del siglo xviii mexicano: El impacto de las reformas borbónicas*, ed. Josefina Zoraida Vázquez (Mexico City: Nueva Imagen, 1992) 187–215.
45. Iturbide, "Breve manifiesto del que subscribe," Mexico City, 1821, in California State Library, *Catalogue*, 229–32.
46. Luis Villoro, "The Ideological Currents of the Epoch of Independence," in *Major Trends in Mexican Philosophy*, ed. Mario de la Cueva et al. (South Bend IN: University of Notre Dame Press, 1966), 185–219.
47. Wortman, "Legitimidad política."
48. Ocampo, *Las ideas*, 228–29.
49. Brading, *Origins*.
50. Anna, *The Mexican Empire*.
51. Ocampo, *Las ideas*, 13–36.
52. This includes Presidents Bustamante, Barragán, Herrera, Paredes, Arista, and Santa Anna. Only the first two presidents, Guadalupe Victoria and Vicente Guerrero, had stalwartly fought for independence. Brading, *Origins*, 67.
53. "Estado que manifiesta los Diputados proprietarios y suplentes que se han de nombrar para el Congreso constituyente del Imperio Mexicano," Mexico City, 1821, BLAC, W. B. Stephens Collection.
54. Decree of Sovereign Junta, Mexico City, 17 November 1821, BNAH, T-3, 35, Colección Antigua.

55. Alamán, *Historia*, 5:259, 315, 317, 320.
56. Elections of deputies, AGN, Gobernación, Legajo II, exps. 25 and 26.
57. Iturbide to Congress, Mexico City, 22 October 1822, AGN, Gobernación, Legajo 10 (1), exp. II; Zavala, *Ensayo crítico*, 2:102–3.
58. "Proyecto de reforma del congreso, propuesto por el diputado Don Lorenzo de Zavala," Mexico City, 1822, BLAC, García Collection.
59. Villoro, "The Ideological Currents."
60. *Gaceta Imperial de Mexico*, 2 March 1822.
61. Zavala, *Ensayo crítico*, 1:107, 132.
62. Bocanegra, *Memorias*, 1:38–39.
63. Anna, *The Mexican Empire*, 61–78.
64. Zavala, *Ensayo crítico*, 1:121; Francisco Bulnes, *La guerra de independencia: Hidalgo-Iturbide* (Mexico City: Talleres de "El Diablo," 1910), 349.
65. Iturbide, *Memoria de Livorno*.
66. Unsigned letter in code to Mier, n. d., n. p., BLAC, García Collection.
67. Bravo Ugarte, *Historia de México*, 141.
68. Bocanegra, *Memorias*, 1:2; Zavala, *Ensayo crítico*, 1:141.
69. Reply of Emperor to Congress, Mexico City, 22 October 1822, AGN, Gobernación, Legajo 10 (1), exp. II.
70. Iturbide, *Memoria de Livorno*.

4. "THE MEXICAN NATION IS COMPOSED OF THE PROVINCES"

1. Guerra, "Identidades e independencia."
2. "Manifiesto que hace la diputación provincial del Estado libre de Xalisco," Guadalajara, 21 June 1823, in Santoscoy, *Canón cronológico*, 95–109.
3. For a summary of requests that Cortes deputies made in the period 1812–14, see Anna, *Spain and the Loss of America*, 85–93.
4. González Esparza, "Patriotismo vs. nación," 10.
5. Sergio de la Peña, "Visión global de los orígenes de la estadística," in *La estadística económica en México: Los orígenes*, by Sergio de la Peña and James W. Wilkie (Mexico City: Siglo Veintiuno Editores, 1994), 1–126.
6. González Esparza, "Patriotismo vs. nación."
7. Mónica Quijada, "Que Nación? Dinámicas y dicotomías de la nación en el imaginario hispanoamericano del siglo XIX," *Imaginar la Nación, Cuadernos de Historia Latinoamericana* (AHILA) (1994): 15–51.
8. "Acta Constitutiva de la federación mexicana," Mexico City, 31 January 1824, BLAC.
9. Guerra points out that the same approach characterized the creation of other Latin American federal republics. For example, the 1811 Venezuelan constitution was issued in the name of "We, the people of the states of Venezuela" and the 1811 constitution of New Granada in the name of "We the representatives of the provinces of New Granada." Guerra, "Identidades e independencia," 126.

10. Population figures from Green, *The Mexican Republic*, 54–55. Green lists population figures drawn from reports of the individual states and territories.

11. Macune, "The Expropriation of Mexico City."

12. Macune, "The Expropriation of Mexico City."

13. Rabasa, *El pensamiento político*, 100.

14. Olveda, *Gordiano Guzmán*, 118.

15. Alamán, *Historia*, 5:427–29; Santa Anna, *The Eagle*, 16.

16. Alamán, *Historia*, 5:436.

17. "Plan del pronunciamiento en Veracruz y reformas que se le hicieron," Veracruz, 2 and 6 December 1822, BLAC, Hernández y Dávalos Collection.

18. *Gaceta del gobierno imperial de Mexico*, 12 and 14 December 1822.

19. Bustamante, *Diario histórico*, 1:95, 127; Leonard D. Parrish, "The Life of Nicolás Bravo, Mexican Patriot (1786–1854)" (Ph.D. diss., University of Texas, Austin, 1951), 104.

20. Proclamation of Guerrero and Bravo, Chilapa, 13 January 1823, in Bustamante, *Diario histórico*, 1:131; Bravo to Brigadier Francisco Antonio Berdejo, Chilapa, 13 January 1823, BNAH, T-2, 10, Colección Antigua.

21. Echávarri to Ramón Rayón, Campo de Casa Mata, 1 February 1823, BNAH, T-2, 10, Colección Antigua.

22. Acta de Casa Mata, Cuartel General de Casa Mata, 1 February 1823, BNAH, T-1, 10, Colección Antigua.

23. Benson, "The Plan of Casa Mata."

24. Castro Morales, *El federalismo*, 73–74.

25. Zavala, *Ensayo crítico*, 1:157–58; Iturbide, *Memoria de Livorno*.

26. Hamnett, "Factores regionales," 310.

27. Alamán, *Historia*, 5:449.

28. Bravo Ugarte, *Historia de México*, 153.

29. Provincial Deputation of Mexico to Emperor, Mexico City, 1 March 1823, BNAH, Colección Bustamante, vol. 17, no. 4.

30. Macune, "Conflictos entre el gobierno"; "Justicia de la nación para reclamar Congreso," Mexico City, 1823, BNAH, Colección Bustamante, vol. 17, no. 7.

31. García Quintanilla, "En busca."

32. Vega, "La opción federalista."

33. Manifesto of provincial deputation of Guadalajara, 12 March 1823, cited in Hamnett, "Factores regionales," 307; the manifesto is published in Muría, *El federalismo*, 33–37.

34. Decree of Iturbide, Ixtapaluca, 4 March 1823, BNAH, T-3, 36, ColecciónAntigua.

35. Anna, *The Mexican Empire*, 173, 186.

36. The text of the note is in Bustamante, *Continuación del cuadro histórico*, 2:114–15.

37. Alamán, *Historia*, 5:467–69.

38. Rabasa, *El Pensamiento político*, 127.

39. Benson, *The Provincial Deputation*, 65–66.

40. Bravo Ugarte, *Historia de México*, 157.

41. Benson, "Plan of Casa Mata"; Benson, *The Provincial Deputation*, 78–81.

42. Rodríguez, "Formation of the Federal Republic." It is very difficult to keep track of membership in Mexican cabinets or Congresses during the unstable first decades, but two sources provide detailed lists: *Diccionario Porrúa*, 1:853–61 (for cabinets in the years 1821–36); and Moreno Valle, 872–80 (for Executive) and 893–909 (for members of the legislature) in the years 1821–35.

43. Zavala, *Ensayo crítico*, 1:178.

44. Alamán, *Historia*, 5:470–72; Zavala, *Ensayo crítico*, 1:170.

45. "Dictamen de la comisión especial de convocatoria para un nuevo congreso," Mexico City, 12 April 1823, BLAC, Hernández y Dávalos Collection.

46. Barragán, *Introducción al federalismo*, 124–25.

47. "Resolución de la provincia de Guadalajara, y sucesos ocurridos en la misma," *Aguila Mexicana*, 22 May 1823.

48. Rodríguez, "Formation of the Federal Republic."

49. Annino, "Otras naciones," 47–48; Plan of Veracruz in Jiménez Codinach, *Planes*, 1:139.

50. Rodríguez, "Formation of the Federal Republic," 316–28, n. 23.

51. Stevens, "Autonomists, Nativists," 261–62.

52. Lucas Alamán to the Jefes políticos of the provinces, Mexico City, 17 June 1821, AGN, Gobernación, Legajo 21, exp. 37.

53. Circular of Alamán to authorities of Oaxaca, Mexico City, 11 June 1823, AGN, Gobernación, Legajo 21, exp. 39.

54. *El Sol*, 3 July 1823.

55. Vázquez, "Los pronunciamientos."

56. The poll of municipalities in Guadalajara province has been reprinted in a modern publication; see *Voto general de los pueblos*.

57. Lira, "Mier y la Constitución de México."

58. Servando Teresa de Mier, "Discurso que el dia 13 de diciembre del presente año de 1823 pronuncio . . . sobre el articulo 5 del Acta Constitutiva," Mexico City, 1823, BLAC.

59. *Voto general de los pueblos*, passim.

60. Guardino, "Barbarism or Republican Law?" 190. See also Guardino, *Peasants*, 81–98.

61. Ortega Noriega, "Hacia la regionalización."

62. For the significance of the deputation's words, see Benson, *The Provincial Deputation*, 94–96.

63. Pérez Verdía, *Historia particular*, 1:278.

64. "Reglamento para el gobierno provisional del estado de Zacatecas," 12 July 1823, BLAC, Hernández y Dávalos Collection.

65. Guardino, *Peasants*, 90.

66. Di Tella, "Ciclos políticos," 115. See also Santoni, "A Fear of the People."
67. For a brief, and incomplete, schematic summary of the mass press in this period, see Bravo Ugarte, *Periodistas y periodicos*, 43–51.
68. Guerra, *Modernidad e independencias*.
69. Costeloe, *The Central Republic*, 12.
70. Daniel A. Morales-Gómez, *The State, Corporatist Politics, and Educational Policy Making in Mexico* (New York: Praeger, 1990), 13.
71. Costeloe, *The Central Republic*, 12.
72. Major finding aids for these pamphlet collections include the following: for the Lafragua Collection, Moreno Valle, *Catálogo de la Colección Lafragua*; for the Benson Latin American Collection, Carlos Eduardo Castañeda and Jack Autrey Dabbs, eds., *Independent Mexico in Documents: Independence, Empire, and Republic: A Calendar of the Juan E. Hernández y Dávalos Manuscript Collection* (Mexico City: Editorial Jus, 1954); and for the Sutro Collection, California State Library, *Catalogue* and *Supplement*.
73. Di Tella, "Ciclos políticos," 122.
74. "Manifiesto que hace la diputación provincial del Estado libre de Xalisco," Guadalajara, 21 June 1823, in Santoscoy, *Canón cronológico*, 95–109.
75. Rabasa, *El Pensamiento político*, 119.
76. Olveda, *La política de Jalisco*, 21; Muría, *Historia de Jalisco*, 2:446.
77. Rabasa, *El Pensamiento político*, 120–24.
78. Manifesto of provincial deputation of Guadalajara, 12 March 1823, in Muría, *El federalismo*, 34–36.
79. Tena Ramírez, *Derecho constitucional mexicano*, 112–13.
80. Prisciliano Sánchez, "Pacto Federal de Anáhuac," Mexico City, 28 July 1823, published in Sánchez, *Memoria sobre el estado*, 53–74.
81. Anastasio Bustamante to Miguel Barragán, Zapotlán el Grande, 28 November 1823, BLAC, Hernández y Dávalos Collection.
82. "El Supremo Poder Ejecutivo a la Nación," Mexico City, Palacio Nacional, June 1823, in BLAC, Hernández y Dávalos Collection.
83. Benson, *The Provincial Deputation*, 13–118.
84. Rodríguez, "Formation of the Federal Republic," 326.
85. Rodríguez, "Formation of the Federal Republic," 327.
86. "Sesiones celebradas en la Villa de Lagos," Lagos, 1823, BLAC; Olveda, *La política de Jalisco*, 26. The most careful treatment of the Lagos meeting, which did not actually result in a treaty (despite the fact that many sources say it did), is in Benson, *The Provincial Deputation*, 103–5.
87. Muría, *El federalismo*, 58.
88. Act of Ayuntamiento of Colima, Colima, 20 June 1823, AGN, Gobernación 12, exp. 22; Quintanar to Brizuela, Guadalajara, 2 July 1823, and "Instrucción dada por el gobierno de este estado a los eclesiasticos comisionados que marcharen a Colima," Guadalajara, 4 July 1823, in Pérez Verdía, *Historia particular*, 2:270–76.

89. Statement of provincial deputation of Michoacán, Valladolid, 3 July 1823, AGN, Gobernación 12, exp. 22.
90. Muría, *Historia de Jalisco*, 2:448–49.
91. Dalton, *Oaxaca*, 2:30–32, 34; Hamnett, "Oaxaca."
92. Bustamante, *Diario histórico*, 1:426.
93. Dalton, *Oaxaca*, 2:49–57.
94. On the jurisdictions of Acayucan and Tehuantepec, see Decree of Congress, Mexico City, 14 October 1823, AGN, Gobernación, Legajo 21, exp. 16.
95. Pérez Betancourt and Ruz Menéndez, 1:325–27; *El Sol*, 1 February 1824.
96. Bocanegra, *Memorias*, 1:216–18.
97. Quinlan, "Issues and Factions."
98. Constitution of 1824, in Tena Ramírez, *Leyes fundamentales*, 161.

5. MODERATED FEDERALISM

1. Hamnett, "Factores regionales," 314.
2. Barragán, *Introducción al federalismo*, 296.
3. Barragán, *Introducción al federalismo*, 181–87.
4. Barragán, *Introducción al federalismo*, 196–97.
5. Quinlan, "Issues and Factions." See also the discussion in Reyes Heroles, *El liberalismo mexicano*, 1:385–410.
6. Barragán, *Introducción al federalismo*, 192–95. The Jalisco statement is printed in Muría, *El federalismo*, 56–60.
7. I am citing the final Acta Constitutiva, 31 January 1824, BLAC.
8. Barragán, *Introducción al federalismo*, 195.
9. Quinlan, "Issues and Factions."
10. The members of Congress, based on those given in the Acta Constitutiva, are listed in Moreno Valle, *Catálogo de la Colección Lafragua*, 896–97.
11. Barragán, *Introducción al federalismo*, 187; Rodríguez, "The Constitution of 1824." It is important not to confuse the wording of the 1824 Acta Constitutiva with the wording contained in the present Mexican Constitution of 1917, Article 39: "Sovereignty resides essentially and originally in the people."
12. Mier, "Discurso . . . sobre el articulo 5," Mexico City, 1823, BLAC.
13. Reyes Heroles, *El liberalismo mexicano*, 1:398–410.
14. Barragán, *Introducción al federalismo*, 197–200.
15. Reyes Heroles, *El liberalismo mexicano*, 1:417.
16. Reyes Heroles, *El liberalismo mexicano*, 1:412.
17. Annino, "Otras naciones."
18. Annino, "Some Reflections."
19. Krauze, *Siglo de caudillos*, 43–45.
20. "Dictamen de la comisión de Constitución del Congreso del Estado sobre el Acta Constitutiva," Guadalajara, 13 December 1823, in Muría, *El federalismo*, 61–65.

21. Quinlan, "Issues and Factions"; Rodríguez, "The Constitution of 1824."
22. Barragán, *Introducción al federalismo*, 202–5; Reyes Heroles, *El liberalismo mexicano*, 1:410–17.
23. Quinlan, "Issues and Factions."
24. Barragán, *Introducción al federalismo*, 183, 190.
25. Barragán, *Introducción al federalismo*, 207–8.
26. Recent collections of documents relating to debates over these two fundamental enactments are *Crónicas: Acta Constitutiva* (Mexico City: Cámara de Diputados, 1974), and *Crónicas: Constitución Federal de 1824*. Published to honor the 150th anniversary of the constitution, these volumes are organized in such a manner as to make them practically impossible to use.
27. Quinlan, "Issues and Factions," 191.
28. *El Sol*, 21 January, 22 January 1824.
29. Barragán, *Introducción al federalismo*, 304–5; Quinlan, "Issues and Factions."
30. "El Congreso constituyente a los habitantes de la federación," Mexico City, 31 January 1824, in "Acta Constitutiva de la federación Mexicana," BLAC.
31. Archivo General de la Nación, *Guía General* (Mexico City: AGN, 1990), 489.
32. Barragán, *Introducción al federalismo*, 298.
33. Decree of Congress, Mexico City, 11 September 1823, AGN, Gobernación, Legajo 1662. This Legajo is not divided into *expedientes*.
34. Green, *The Mexican Republic*, 82.
35. For a brief summary of the development of the army and militias, see Ortiz Escamilla, "Las fuerzas militares."
36. Hamnett, "Partidos políticos," 574.
37. Brading, *Origins*, 68.
38. *El Sol*, 25 July 1824. As commandant general, Santa Anna wrote the first major report detailing the growing rivalry between Mérida and Campeche for control of the development of Yucatán, but he was unable to resolve the issues that would later lead Campeche to separate statehood.
39. Congress of Michoacán to President, Valladolid, 21 July 1825, AGN, Gobernación 31, exp. 22.
40. Brading, *Origins*, 68.
41. Vázquez, "El federalismo mexicano."
42. Ortiz, "Las fuerzas militares"; Decree of Congress, Mexico City, 29 December 1827, AGN, Gobernación, Legajo 68, exp. 1.
43. Vázquez, "El ejército."
44. Arturo Arnáiz y Freg, prologue to Lucas Alamán, *Semblanzas e Ideario* (Mexico City: Ediciones de la Universidad Nacional Autonoma, 1939), xx.
45. Alamán quoted in González Navarro, *El pensamiento político de Lucas Alamán*, 120.
46. Hale, "Liberalismo mexicano," 461.
47. Hamnett, "Oaxaca," 69.

284   *Notes to Pages 160–166*

48. Castro Morales, *El federalismo*, 136.
49. Hamnett, "Factores regionales."
50. Castro Morales, *El federalismo*, 148–49; *El Sol*, 7 January 1824.
51. "El general Guerrero a los habitantes de la provincia de Puebla," Puebla, 6 January 1824, *El Sol*, 14 January 1824.
52. *El Sol*, 9 July 1824.
53. Reyes Heroles, *El liberalismo mexicano*, 1:417–27.
54. Quinlan, "Issues and Factions," 177.
55. Barragán, *Introducción al federalismo*, 268.
56. Quoted in *Primer Centenario*, 359.
57. Hamnett, "Oaxaca." Hamnett has reiterated to me his view that the constitution of 1824 prohibited agreements among the states; Hamnett, personal communication, 24 July 1995. He argues that the phrasing of this passage in the constitution is ambiguous in that it could have been interpreted to mean that states could apply for a posteriori congressional approval of transactions they had already made concerning their territorial limits, which would be contradictory. He believes the entire section is not dependent for its meaning on the final phrase that reads "si la transacción fuere sobre arreglo de limites."

On the other hand, Vázquez, in one article, interpreted the constitution as I do, as not prohibiting coalitions between the states; see Vázquez, "El federalismo mexicano." In another article, however, she appeared to accept the opposite interpretation: Vázquez, "Political Plans."

Acknowledging this complexity, the present Mexican constitution (1917) separates the two issues and contains unambiguous wording on the matter. Article 46 says, "The states can arrange among themselves, by friendly agreement, their respective limits; but such arrangements cannot go into effect without the approval of the Congress of the Union," while Article 117 says, "The States cannot, in any case, (1.) celebrate an alliance, treaty, or coalition with another State or with foreign powers."

58. For the sake of comparison, I primarily use a copy of the constitution published in 1824: "Constitución Federal de los Estados-Unidos Mexicanos, Sancionada por el Congreso General Constituyente, el 4 de octubre de 1824" (Mexico City: Imprenta del Supremo Gobierno de los Estados-Unidos Mexicanos, 1824), BLAC. Many other copies are readily available, for example, *Cronicas: Constitución federal de 1824*, 1:81–109; Tena Ramírez, *Leyes fundamentales*, 168–95.
59. Arnold, "La administración"; and Arnold, "Reflections on Conflict."
60. Reyes Heroles, *El liberalismo mexicano*, 2:6, 11.
61. Camp, "La cuestión Chiapaneca"; *El Sol*, 3 October 1824.
62. Miguel Ramos Arizpe, "Informe a los ayuntamientos y pueblos de Coahuila," Mexico City, 8 May 1824, in *Coahuila*, comp. Enríquez Terrazas and Rodríguez García, 75–82.

63. Enríquez Terrazas and Rodríguez García, *Coahuila*, 96–97.

64. *El Sol*, 21 January 1824; documentation involving the status of Tlaxcala is in AGN, Gobernación 12-A, exp. 3, although important items have been removed from the *expediente*.

65. See O'Gorman, *Historia de las divisiones*, 55–74.

66. Sánchez Luna, "Francisco García Salinas."

67. Quinlan, "Issues and Factions," 193.

68. "Dictamen de la comisión extraordinaria encargada de consultar las providencias que deban dictarse para asegurar la tranquilidad pública" (Mexico City, 6 April 1824), BLAC, Hernández y Dávalos Collection; the proposal is also in Mateos, *Historia parlamentaria*, 2:752–62.

69. The debates are in *El Sol*, 21, 23, 24 April, 1 May 1824. The discussion, as it appears in *El Sol*, is not well focused and appears to shift from the issue of the directorship to the issue of a single president by 1 May. Possibly this shift took place as a result of the daily afternoon closed sessions, which were not reported in the press.

70. *El Sol*, 16 July 1824.

71. Pérez Verdía, *Historia particular*, 2:285.

72. Sánchez to Gómez Farías, Guadalajara, 22 May 1824, BLAC, Gómez Farías Papers.

73. Sánchez to Gómez Farías, Guadalajara, 21 May 1824, BLAC, Gómez Farías Papers.

74. Unsigned statement, undated, begins "Se han vertido diferentes especies contra las provincias . . . ," BLAC, Gómez Farías Papers.

75. Muría, *Historia de Jalisco*, 2:452–43.

76. Jaime Olveda Legaspi, "El Iturbidismo en Jalisco," Cuadernos de los Centros, no. 9 (n.p.: INAH, Dirección de Centros Regionales, 1974).

77. Bocanegra, *Memorias*, 1:305; *Crónicas de Constitución*, 1:381.

78. Anastasio Bustamante to Gómez Farías, Guadalajara, 27 February 1824, BLAC, Gómez Farías Papers.

79. Bustamante, *Continuación del cuadro histórico*, 2:213; *Crónicas de constitución*, 1:381–84; Bocanegra, *Memorias*, 1:302.

80. Bustamante, *Continuación del cuadro histórico*, 2:213–15; Quinlan, "Issues and Factions."

81. Muría, *Historia de Jalisco*, 2:454.

82. This accord is published in Jiménez Codinach, *Planes*, 1:191.

83. Suárez y Navarro, *Historia de México*, 64.

84. Santoscoy, *Canón cronológico*, 171–73.

85. Pérez Verdía, *Historia particular*, 2:284.

86. "Manifiesto que el Vice-Gobernador del Estado Libre de Jalisco dirige a sus conciudadanos," Guadalajara, 5 July 1824, AGN, Gobernación, Legajo 61-A, exp. 16.

87. Muría, *Historia de Jalisco*, 2:455.
88. Decree of State of Jalisco, Guadalajara, 25 January 1825, AGN, Gobernación, Legajo 22, exp. 19.
89. Vega, "La opción federalista."

6. DESCENT INTO POLITICS

1. Nicolás Bravo, "Memoria histórica en cuya relación de grandes sucesos se manifiesta los importantes servicios que hizo a la república el Exmo. Sr. General . . . D. Nicolás Bravo," Mexico City, 1845, BLAC, García Collection.
2. Tomás Murphy to José Mariano Michelena, Paris, 22 November 1824, BLAC, Hernández y Dávalos Collection.
3. Mier to José Mariano Michelena, Mexico City, 26 March 1825, BLAC, Hernández y Dávalos Collection.
4. Sims, *La Reconquista*, 55.
5. Lorenzo Zavala, "Juicio imparcial sobre los acontecimientos de México en 1828 y 1829," New York, 1830, BLAC.
6. Flaccus, "Guadalupe Victoria."
7. As he did in his speech to the closing of the second Constituent Congress, 24 December 1824, *Primer centenario de la constitución de 1824*, 344–48.
8. Tornel, *Breve reseña*, 24.
9. Congress of Jalisco to National Congress, Guadalajara, 16 February 1824, in *Libro de Actas del Honorable Congreso del Estado de Jalisco*, 83–87.
10. Sierra, *Political Evolution*, 186, 190.
11. Hernández Chávez, *La tradición republicana*, 30.
12. Coatsworth, "Las orígenes sociales," 218.
13. Benson, *Mexico and the Spanish Cortes*, 209.
14. Pérez Betancourt and Ruz Menéndez, *Yucatán*, 1:321.
15. Vega, "La opción federalista."
16. Hamnett, "Oaxaca," 55.
17. Guardino, "Barbarism or Republican Law?"
18. Stevens, *Origins of Instability*, 39–42.
19. According to Fernando Valle, deputy for Yucatán, *El Sol*, 10 January 1824.
20. García Quintanilla, "En busca." See also Patch, "The Bourbon Reforms."
21. Tenenbaum, "The Making of a Fait Accompli."
22. Rabasa, *El Pensamiento político*, 122–23.
23. Baranda and García, *Estado de Mexico*, 1:126–38; Muría, *Breve historia de Jalisco*, 221–23; Blazquez Domínguez, *Veracruz*, 1:280–83; Landa Fonseca, *Querétaro*, 1:132–36; Dalton, *Oaxaca*, 2:110–11. The only source I know of that contains all the state constitutions, but difficult to use, is Galván Rivera, *Colección de constituciones*.
24. Guardino, "Barbarism or Republican Law?"
25. Carmagnani, "Territorios, provincias," 64.

26. Guerra, *Modernidad e independencias.*

27. Stevens, *Origins of Instability*, 39 n. 52.

28. Carmagnani, "Del territorio."

29. Macune, *El Estado de México*, 68–70.

30. Macune, *El Estado de México*, 62.

31. As Ramos Arizpe made clear in debates on the Acta Constitutiva, *El Sol*, 10 January 1824.

32. Macune, *El Estado de México*, 76.

33. Tenenbaum, *Politics of Penury*, 22–23. The Mexican peso was the equivalent of the U.S. dollar.

34. Macune, *El Estado de México*, 75, 79–80. Macune is the only author to give a thorough discussion of this fundamental legislation. See *El Sol*, 4 July 1824.

35. *El Sol*, 10 July 1824.

36. Macune, *El Estado de México*, 81.

37. Carmagnani, "Finanzas y estado."

38. Tenenbaum, *Politics of Penury*, 22–40.

39. Carmagnani, "Finanzas y estado," 287.

40. Vega, "La opción federalista."

41. "Economic crisis worsens financial problems of Mexican States," mexico2000 [electronic news list], 15 August 1995 [cited 25 August 1995], available from mexico2000@mep-d.org.

42. Guardino, *Peasants*, 90–91.

43. Green, *The Mexican Republic*, 153–54.

44. Only one author, Charles W. Macune Jr., has dealt in detail with this important issue. See Macune, *El estado de México*; Macune, "A Test of Federalism: Political, Economic, and Ecclesiastical Relations between the State of Mexico and the Mexican Nation, 1823–1835" (Ph.D. diss., University of Texas at Austin, 1970); Macune, "Conflictos"; and Macune, "The Expropriation of Mexico City." Another modern author, Gerald L. McGowan, considers aspects of it from a position of advocacy: McGowan, *El Distrito Federal*; and McGowan, *El Estado del Valle.*

45. The following discussion comes from Macune, *El estado de México*, 24–39.

46. Quinlan, "Issues and Factions."

47. See Macune, *El estado de México*, 40–58.

48. Macune, *El estado de México*, 33.

49. Macune, *El Estado de México*, 156.

50. Sims, *La expulsión*; Sims, *Descolonización en México*; Sims, *Expulsion of Mexico's Spaniards.* See also Sims, "Los exiliados españoles." For an earlier and less detailed study of the expulsions, see Flores Caballero, *La contrarevolución.*

51. Reyes Heroles, *El liberalismo mexicano*, 2:63–64, 70.

52. Sims, *Expulsion of Mexico's Spaniards*, 18–19.

53. Sims, *La expulsión*, 33–39.

54. Plan, José María Lobato, Mexico City, 23 January 1824; Decree of Supremo Poder Ejecutivo, Mexico City, 24 January 1824; both in BLAC.

55. "Breve Manifiesto del General Antonio López de Santa Anna a sus compatriotas," Mexico City, 25 January 1824, BLAC; *El Sol*, 26 January, 28 January 1824.

56. "El verdadero grito de la razon, o sea proclama de ciudadano brigadier José María Lobato a los mejicanos," 29 January 1824, BLAC, Hernández y Dávalos Collection.

57. Quinlan, "Issues and Factions."

58. For Guerrero's abolition of slavery, see Guerrero to Michelena, Hacienda de la Compañía, 25 January 1825, BLAC, Hernández y Dávalos Collection.

59. Sims, *La expulsión*, 25.

60. Poinsett replied to the charge that he had created York lodges by publishing a pamphlet on 4 July 1827: "Exposición de la conducta política de los Estados Unidos, para con las nuevas republicas de América," Mexico City, 1827.

61. Costeloe, *La primera república federal*, 64–67.

62. On Gómez Pedraza's relation to the Masonic groups, see Costeloe, *La primera república federal*, 119. Costeloe quotes *El Amigo del Pueblo* (15 August 1827): "If [Gómez Pedraza] is a Yorkino, he is a good Yorkino, and if he is an Escocés, he is a good Escocés."

63. Costeloe, *La primera república federal*, 72–78.

64. Costeloe, *La primera república federal*, 85–86; Stevens, *Origins of Instability*, 42–43.

65. Macune, *El estado de México*, 156–60.

66. Arenas, Joaquín de, "Frayle contra frayle a cara descubierta," Mexico City, 1823, in California State Library, *Catalogue*, 386–91.

67. The details were published in pamphlet form as "Ejecución de justicia en el religioso dieguino Fr. Joaquin de Arenas," Mexico City, 1827, BLAC.

68. "Complicidad de cinco senadores en el crimen de Negrete," Mexico City, 1827; "Virtudes y gracias de los traidores Fray Echávarri y Fray Negrete," Mexico City, 1827; "Visperas de los editores del Sol para festejarse en Acapulco y Perote," Mexico City, 1827; "Los malvados se descubren cuando menos se imaginan," Mexico City, 27 March 1827, all in BLAC.

69. Costeloe, *La primera república federal*, 90–98.

70. Sims, *Reconquista de México*, 42.

71. This discussion comes from Costeloe, *La primera república federal*, 98–113.

72. "Censura Publica, Sistema Federal," *El Observador de la República Mexicana*, vol. 1, no. 10, 18 August 1827.

73. *El Observador de la República Mexicana*, vol. 1, no. 11, 12 September 1827.

74. Sims, *Expulsion of Mexico's Spaniards*, 36–40.

75. Green, *The Mexican Republic*, 149.

76. Green, *The Mexican Republic*, 148.

77. Costeloe, *La primera república federal*, 140–47.
78. "Espediente instructivo, formado por la seccion del Gran Jurado de la Cámara de Representantes, sobre la acusacion . . . contra el vice-presidente de la república D. Nicolás Bravo," Mexico City, 1828, BLAC.
79. Bravo, "Memoria histórica," BLAC, García Collection.
80. "Destierro del Escmo. Sr. Vice-Presidente de la República D. Nicolás Bravo y Socios," Mexico City, 15 April 1828, BLAC.
81. "Manifiesto del Exmo. Señor D. Nicolás Bravo," Mexico City, 20 April 1828, BLAC. Also in BNAH, Colección Bustamante 21.
82. Bravo, "Memoria histórica," BLAC, García Collection; Bravo to Carlos María Bustamante, Guayaquil, 24 July 1828, BLAC, Hernández y Davalos Collection.
83. Blazquez Domínguez, *Veracruz*, 1:322–25.
84. Sims, *La Expulsión*, 270–73.
85. Suárez y Navarro, *Historia de México*, 1:99.
86. Decree of Guerrero, Mexico City, 16 September 1829, AGN, Gobernación, Legajo 87, exp. 1.
87. Bravo, "Memoria histórica," BLAC, García Collection. A description of the ceremony in which Mier was given the viaticum in the palace, at the hands of Miguel Ramos Arizpe, who was then minister of justice, is in *El Sol*, 17 November 1827. Mier died on 3 December 1827.

7. SOVEREIGNTY OF THE PEOPLE

1. "Manifiesto del ciudadano Vicente Guerrero, segundo presidente de los Estados-Unidos Mexicanos a sus compatriotas," Mexico City: 1 April 1829, BLAC.
2. Zavala, *Ensayo crítico*, 2:101.
3. *Correo de la Federación Mexicana*, 8 February 1828, in Costeloe, *La primera república federal*, 161.
4. Guardino, *Peasants*, 123–24, 127–28.
5. Annino, "Otras naciones," 253.
6. Hernández Chávez, *La tradición republicana*, 35–37.
7. Annino, "Otras naciones."
8. Hernández Chávez, "La Guardia Nacional."
9. José Antonio Facio, "Memoria que sobre los sucesos del tiempo de su ministerio, y sobre la causa intentada contra los cuatro ministros del Exmo. Sr. Vice-President D. Anastasio Bustamante, presenta a los mejicanos. . ." (Paris: Imprenta de Moquet y Cia., 1835), 107.
10. Green, *The Mexican Republic*, 175.
11. I prefer the full accounting of the vote given by Bocanegra, *Memorias*, 1:505–6, because it makes it clear that each state cast two ballots. Compare to Costeloe, *La primera república federal*, 182; Green, *The Mexican Republic*, 159.
12. Tornel, *Breve reseña*, 310.

13. Green, *The Mexican Republic*, 154–59.
14. Santa Anna, *The Eagle*, 20.
15. Prieto, *Memorias de mis tiempos*, 38–39.
16. Tornel, *Breve reseña*, 313.
17. "Para que viva la patria que muera el negro Guerrero," Mexico City, 1830, BLAC.
18. Suárez y Navarro, *Historia de México*, 1:164, 176; Mora, *Obras sueltas*, II.
19. Zavala, "Juicio imparcial."
20. Costeloe, *La primera república federal*, 183–87.
21. See the review of Reyes Heroles by Hale, "Liberalismo mexicano," 456–63.
22. Bastian, "Una ausencia notoria."
23. The following narrative is from Costeloe, *La primera república federal*, 189–206.
24. Trens, *Historia de Veracruz*, 1:209–10.
25. Guardino, *Peasants*, 125–26.
26. Lorenzo de Zavala, "Manifiesto del gobernador del estado de Mexico," Tlalpam, 20 January 1829, BLAC.
27. Manuel Gómez Pedraza, "Ciudadanos Diputados," New Orleans, 10 November 1830, BLAC, Hernández y Dávalos Collection.
28. Sims, *Expulsion of Mexico's Spaniards*, 53–54.
29. For the president's ride with Lobato to the Acordada, see *Voz de la Patria*, 8 July 1829; Sims, *Expulsion of Mexico's Spaniards*, 48–50.
30. Van Young, "Islands in the Storm."
31. Bustamante, *Continuación del cuadro histórico*, 3:208–9.
32. Guardino, *Peasants*, 126.
33. Arrom, "Popular Politics in Mexico City"; Costeloe, *La primera república federal*, 206–7; Bustamante, *Continuación del cuadro histórico*, 3:207; Alamán, *Historia*, 5:529.
34. Tornel, *Breve reseña*, 395; Zavala, "Juicio imparcial."
35. "Mejicanos," Lorenzo de Zavala and José María Lobato, Mexico City, 5 December 1828, BLAC, Hernández y Dávalos Collection.
36. Tornel, *Breve reseña*, 415–22.
37. Arrom, "Popular Politics in Mexico City."
38. Guerra, *Modernidad e independencias*, 368–69.
39. Thomson, *Puebla de los Angeles*, 207–8.
40. Tornel, *Breve reseña*, 401; Tornel, "Manifestación del C. José María Tornel," Mexico City, 10 May 1833, BLAC; Bustamante, *Continuación del cuadro histórico*, 3:210.
41. Sierra, *Political Evolution*, 195.
42. Costeloe, *La primera república federal*, 210.
43. Green, *The Mexican Republic*, 164.
44. Guardino, *Peasants*, 127.
45. Tornel, *Breve reseña*, 394.
46. Díaz, *Caudillos y caciques*, 64.

47. "Pronunciamiento de Perote por el General Antonio López de Sta. Anna y sucesos de su campaña," Mexico City, 1829, BLAC.

48. Sims, *Expulsion of Mexico's Spaniards*, 44.

49. Potash, *Mexican Government*, 12–33.

50. The following discussion is from Sims, *La reconquista*; Miguel A. Sánchez Lamego, *La invasión española de 1829* (Mexico City: Editorial Jus, 1971); and Green, *The Mexican Republic*, 167–70.

51. Morton, *Terán and Texas*, 86.

52. Lozano y Nathal, "Tlacotalpan."

53. *Dos años en México*, 6–7. The anonymous author was a Spanish liberal who, although in Havana at the time of the invasion, lived in Mexico briefly before and after the Spanish expedition. His book, published in 1838 in Spain and reprinted in Mexico in 1840, has a number of insights.

54. Santa Anna, *The Eagle*, 24.

55. Morton, *Terán and Texas*, 91.

56. Lozano y Nathal, "Tlacotalpan," 1:329–43.

57. Díaz, *Caudillos y caciques*, 343.

58. Decree of Guerrero, Mexico City, 15 September 1829, AGN, Gobernación, Legajo 87, exp. 1.

59. Unsigned note to Guerrero, Jalapa, 6 December 1829, AGN, Gobernación, Legajo 72, exp. 1.

60. Costeloe, *La primera república federal*, 243–47; Green, *The Mexican Republic*, 170–74.

61. "Manifiesto que el vicepresidente de la república mexicana dirige a la nación," Mexico City, 4 January 1830, BLAC, García Collection.

62. *El Atleta*, 31 December 1829.

63. The relevant documents are printed in Bocanegra, *Memorias*, 2:228–34.

64. José Salgado to Secretary of Relations, Morelia, 5 January 1830; Statement of Congress of Michoacán, Morelia, 4 January 1830, both in AGN, Gobernación, Legajo 90, exp. 1.

65. Costeloe, *La primera república federal*, 255–67.

66. Alamán to Michelena, Mexico City, 19 January 1830, BLAC, Hernández y Dávalos Collection.

67. Zavala, *Ensayo crítico*, 1:506.

68. Costeloe, *La primera república federal*, 280.

69. For Alamán's contention, see Reyes Heroles, *El liberalismo mexicano*, 2:156–58.

70. Costeloe, *La primera república federal*, 280–81.

71. Quoted in Costeloe, *La primera república federal*, 274.

72. José Salgado to Secretary of Relations, Morelia, 8 January, 9 January, and 18 January 1830, all in AGN, Gobernación, Legajo 90, exp. 1.

73. Costeloe, *La primera república federal*, 258–60.

74. The following chronology is from Costeloe, *La primera república federal*, 260–70.

75. Serrano, "Luis de Cortazar."

76. Decree of government of San Luis Potosí, 25 January 1830, AGN, Gobernación 67, exp. 1.

77. Unsigned letter to Carlos María de Bustamante, reporting the trial and escape of Salgado, Morelia, 20 August 1830, BNAH, Colección Bustamante 23.

78. Alamán to Michelena, Mexico City, 16 August 1830, BLAC, Hernández y Dávalos Collection.

79. Costeloe, *La primera república federal*, 300–301; Ortiz, "Las fuerzas militares."

80. Rodríguez, "Oposición a Bustamante"; Rodríguez, "Origins of the 1832 Rebellion."

81. Genaro García, *Leona Vicario, Heroina insurgente*, facsimile (Mexico City: Editorial Innovación, 1979), 138–43; Leona Vicario's full account of the incident and the government's defense are in *El Sol*, 6, 7, 8 February 1831, and *El federalista mexicano*, 5, 9 February 1831; *Registro Oficial*, 9, 10 February 1831.

82. García, *Leona Vicario*, 142, 187–89.

83. Leona Vicario to "mi hijito," Mexico City, 15 June 1831, BLAC, García Collection.

84. Rodríguez, "Origins of the 1832 Rebellion," 151.

85. Rodríguez, "Oposición a Bustamante"; Rodríguez, "Origins of the 1832 Rebellion."

86. Guardino, *Peasants*, 131.

87. Annino, "Otras naciones," 250.

88. Olveda, *Gordiano Guzmán*, 104–5.

89. Hale, *Mexican Liberalism*, 95–105.

90. *El Observador de la República Mexicana*, 8 September 1830.

91. Alamán, "Memoria, 1830," 13.

92. Zavala, "Memoria de la gestión de gobierno del estado de México durante el año de 1833" (Toluca, 1833), 2–4.

93. Hale, *Mexican Liberalism*, 124.

94. Suárez y Navarro, *Historia de México*, 1:214.

95. Díaz, *Caudillos y caciques*, 108–10.

96. *Dos años en México*, 21–22.

97. Santa Anna to Sebastian Camacho, Manga de Clavo, 17 June 1830, BLAC, Alamán Papers.

98. Andrés Quintana Roo, "Copia de una protesta presentada a la Camara de Diputados contra la resolución del ministro de Guerra, José Antonio Facio, no permitiendo la entrada del Gral. Manuel Gómez Pedraza, a su regreso de Burdeos," Mexico City, 20 October 1830, BLAC, Gómez Farías Papers; Gómez Pedraza, "Ciudadanos Diputados," New Orleans, 10 November 1830, BLAC; see also the statement in Congress of Antonio Pacheco Leal, *El federalista mexicano*, 9 February 1831.

99. Díaz, *Caudillos y caciques*, 94–96.
100. Guardino, *Peasants*, 95–96.
101. Quoted in Díaz, *Caudillos y caciques*, 110.
102. *El Federalista Mexicano*, 15 January 1831.
103. Facio, "Memoria," 16, 116.
104. Annino, "Otras naciones," 250.
105. *El Federalista Mexicano*, 5, 16 February; 2, 6, 9 April 1831.
106. For Guerrero's 1833 burial, see "El soberano estado de Oaxaca, Al Ciudadano, Al General, El benemérito de la patria, el grado heroico, Vicente Guerrero, Con los amigos, Con los enemigos . . . ," Oaxaca, 1833.
107. *El Federalista Mexicano*, 19 February 1831.
108. Olveda, *Guzmán*, 140–45.
109. *Dos años en México*, 32.
110. Facio's defense primarily appeared in his "Memoria" of 1835; Alamán's appeared in his "Defensa del ex-ministro de relaciones D. Lucas Alamán en la causa formada contra él y contra los Ex-ministros de Guerra y Justicia. . . ," Mexico City, 1834.
111. "Proceso instructivo formada por la sección del gran jurado de la Cámara de Diputados del Congreso General, en averiguación de los delitos de que fueron acusados los ex-ministros D. Lucas Alamán, D. Rafael Mangino, D. José Antonio Facio y D. José Ignacio Espinosa," Mexico City, 1833.
112. Green, *The Mexican Republic*, 230–31.
113. Sordo Cedeño, *El congreso*, 26.
114. José María Lafragua, "El General Don Vicente Guerrero," in *Hombres Ilustres Mexicanos*, vol. 4 (Mexico City: I. Cumplido, 1874), 297–378. The article was originally published in the *Diccionario Universal de Historia y Geografía* (1855), vol. 3, 738–63.
115. Suárez y Navarro, *Historia de México*, 1:227–28.

8. THE WAR OF 1832 AND STALEMATE

1. The following narrative comes from Rodríguez, "Origins of the 1832 Rebellion"; Rodríguez, "Oposición a Bustamante"; and Vázquez, "Los pronunciamientos."
2. "Plan de Veracruz," *El Fénix de la Libertad*, 11 January 1832.
3. Santa Anna to Bustamante, Veracruz, 4 January 1832, BLAC, Riva Palacio Collection.
4. *El Duende*, 23 April 1832.
5. *El Duende*, 15 February 1832.
6. *El Duende*, 10 March 1832.
7. *Dos años en México*, 54, 65.
8. Vega, "La Opción federalista."
9. Annino, "Otras naciones."

10. Hernández Chávez, *La tradición republicana*, 41.
11. Stevens, "Riot, Rebellion."
12. Vázquez, "Los pronunciamientos."
13. Florstedt, "Mora contra Bustamante," 33.
14. Morton, *Terán and Texas*, 171; Florstedt, "Mora contra Bustamante."
15. Florstedt, "Mora contra Bustamante," 36.
16. Morton, *Terán and Texas*, 176–83. Morton cites the letter to Alamán, from the Hospital de Jesús Collection in the AGN. Details of the burial and the later opening of the tomb to move the remains of Iturbide are in Noriega, *Funestos recuerdos*.
17. Francisco Castellanos, *El trueno, gloria y martirio de Agustín de Iturbide* (Mexico City: Editorial Diana, 1982), 210.
18. Costeloe, *La primera república federal*, 342. Anastasio Bustamante received the vote of Querétaro, which argued that he was not barred from succeeding to the presidency because he had only been vice president. Two states, Nuevo León and Coahuila and Texas, voted for Francisco García.
19. Thomson, *Puebla de los Angeles*, 210–11.
20. Anthony Butler to Edward Livingston, Mexico City, 12 December 1832, BLAC, Justin H. Smith Papers.
21. Correspondence of Manuel Gómez Pedraza and Sebastian Camacho: Gómez Pedraza to Camacho, Veracruz, 6, 9, 12 November 1832; Camacho to Gómez Pedraza, Jalapa, 8, 11, 17 November 1832. These letters were given to José María Gutiérrez Estrada on 22 November 1832, who gave them to Carlos María de Bustamante, BNAH, Colección Bustamante 26.
22. Serrano, "Luis de Cortázar."
23. "Convenio celebrado entre las divisiones al mando de los Ecsmos. Señores D. Anastasio Bustamante y D. Antonio López de Santa Anna," Hacienda de Zavaleta, 23 December 1832, BLAC, Santa Anna Papers.
24. Annino, "Otras naciones."
25. Sordo Cedeño, *El congreso*, 19–20.
26. Costeloe, *La primera república federal*, 347; Vázquez, "Los pronunciamientos."
27. On the loss of life, see Vázquez, "El ejército," 321.
28. Serrano, "Luis de Cortázar."
29. Díaz, *Caudillos y caciques*, 118–19, 338–39.
30. Hernández Chávez, "La Guardia Nacional."
31. Vázquez, "La crisis."
32. Annino, "Some Reflections," 41.
33. Vázquez, "El federalismo mexicano."
34. Samponaro, "La alianza."
35. See Sordo Cedeño, *El congreso*, 24–59.
36. The following narrative comes from Sordo Cedeño, "Santa Anna."

37. Sierra, *Political Evolution*, 208.
38. Sordo Cedeño, *El congreso*, 61–80.
39. Vázquez, "La crisis."
40. Quoted in Sordo Cedeño, "Santa Anna," 291.
41. Ortiz Escamilla, "Las fuerzas militares."
42. Vázquez, "El federalismo mexicano."
43. Sordo Cedeño, "Santa Anna."
44. Costeloe, "Federalism to Centralism," 181; Costeloe, *The Central Republic*, 39–45, 57–62.
45. Sordo Cedeño, *El congreso*, 181.
46. For Stevens's quotation, see his *Origins of Instability*, 36.
47. "Defensa del voto del ciudadano Andrés Quintana Roo, sobre el pronunciamiento de esta capital," Mexico City, 23 June 1835, cited in Sordo Cedeño, *El congreso*, 177.
48. Marcello Carmagnani, "El federalismo liberal mexicano," in *Federalismos latinoamericanos*, ed. Marcello Carmagnani, 135–79; Ortiz Escamilla, "El pronunciamiento federalista."
49. Vázquez, "La crisis."
50. Urías Horcasitas, "Conciencia regional."
51. Filippi, *Instituciones e ideologías*, 194.
52. Richard Stoller, "Dialectics of Federalism in Socorro, Colombia, 1810–1870" (paper presented at Conference on Latin American History meeting, San Francisco, 6–9 January 1994).
53. Stevens, *Origins of Instability*, 110, 115.
54. Cochran, "The Social Sciences," 351–52.
55. Cerutti and González Maíz, "Autonomía regional."
56. Pérez Herrero, " 'Crecimiento' colonial."
57. Garza, "Una visión historiografica," 39.
58. Annino, "Some Reflections."
59. Guardino, *Peasants*.
60. Rubin, "Decentering the Regime."
61. Ernesto Zedillo, State of the Nation Address, 1 September 1995, *La Jornada*, 2 September 1995.
62. Cerutti and González Maíz, "Autonomía regional," 560.
63. Ortega Noriega, "Hacia la regionalización."

SELECTED BIBLIOGRAPHY

The archival material, not repeated here but listed fully in the notes, came primarily from the Archivo General de la Nación in Mexico City, the Biblioteca Nacional de Antropología e Historia Eusebio Dávalos Hurtado in Mexico City, and the Nettie Lee Benson Latin American Collection at the University of Texas at Austin. Published sources not shown here are listed in the notes.

The appearance since 1989 of many publications on the early republic, long the forgotten era of Mexican history, is a significant development in the historiography. Mexicans are in the process of reconsidering the first years of their nation's existence. Therefore, this bibliography emphasizes the most recent works.

Acta constitutiva de la federación mexicana. Mexico City: Imprenta del Supremo Gobierno en Palacio, 1824.

Actas del congreso constituyente del estado libre de México. 10 vols. Mexico City: Imprenta a cargo de Martín Rivera, 1824–31.

Actas del Congreso Constituyente Mexicano. 4 vols. Mexico City: Alejandro Valdés, 1822–23.

Aguirre Costilla, Virgilio. *Primeros ensayos constitucionales del México independiente.* Mexico City: Facultad de derecho de la UNAM, Seminario de derecho constitucional, 1962.

Alamán, Lucas. *Documentos diversos (inéditos y muy raros).* Compiled by Rafael Aguayo Spencer. 4 vols. Mexico City: Editorial Jus, 1945–47.

———. *Historia de Méjico desde los primeros movimientos que prepararon su independencia en el año de 1808 hasta la época presente.* 5 vols. 1849–52. Reprint, Mexico City: Editorial Jus, 1942.

Aldana Rendón, Mario. "La privatización de los terrenos comunales en Jalisco: Los primeros pasos, 1821–1833." In *Los lugares y los tiempos: Ensayos sobre las estructuras regionales del siglo XIX en México,* ed. Alejandra García Quintanilla and Abel Juárez, 50–82. Mexico City: Editorial Nuestro Tiempo, 1989.

Anderson, Rodney D. *Guadalajara a la consumación de su independencia: Estudio de su población según los padrones de 1821–1822*. Guadalajara: Gobierno de Jalisco, 1983.

———. "Race and Social Stratification: A Comparison of Working-Class Spaniards, Indians, and Castas in Guadalajara, Mexico in 1821." *Hispanic American Historical Review* 68, no. 2 (May 1988): 209–43.

Anna, Timothy E. "Demystifying Early Nineteenth-Century Mexico." *Mexican Studies* 9, no. 1 (winter 1993): 119–37.

———. *The Fall of the Royal Government in Mexico City*. Lincoln: University of Nebraska Press, 1978.

———. "The Independence of Mexico and Central America." In *The Cambridge History of Latin America*, vol. 3, ed. Leslie Bethell, 51–94. Cambridge: Cambridge University Press, 1985.

———. "Inventing Mexico: Provincehood and Nationhood after Independence." *Bulletin of Latin American Research* 15, no. 1 (January 1996): 7–17.

———. "Iturbide, Congress, and Constitutional Monarchy in Mexico." In *The Political Economy of Spanish America in the Age of Revolution, 1750–1850*, ed. Kenneth J. Andrien and Lyman L. Johnson, 17–38. Albuquerque: University of New Mexico Press, 1994.

———. "The Iturbide Interregnum." In *The Independence of Mexico and the Creation of the New Nation*, ed. Jaime E. Rodríguez O., 185–99. Los Angeles: UCLA Latin American Center, 1989.

———. *The Mexican Empire of Iturbide*. Lincoln: University of Nebraska Press, 1990.

———. "The Rule of Agustín de Iturbide: A Reappraisal." *Journal of Latin American Studies* 17, no. 1 (May 1985): 79–110.

———. "Spain and the Breakdown of the Imperial Ethos: The Problem of Equality." *Hispanic American Historical Review* 62, no. 2 (May 1982): 254–72.

———. *Spain and the Loss of America*. Lincoln: University of Nebraska Press, 1983.

Annino, Antonio. "Otras naciones: Sincretismo político en el México decimonónico." *Imaginar la nación: Cuadernos de historia Latinoamericana*, no. 2 (1994): 215–55.

———. "Some Reflections on Spanish American Constitutional and Political History." *Itinerario* 19, no. 2 (1995): 26–47.

Annino, Antonio, and Alberto Filippi. "Las formas del poder: Proyecto político y efectividad." In *America Latina: Dallo stato coloniale allo stato nazione*, 2 vols., ed. Antonio Annino et al., 2:415–26. Milan: Franco Angeli, 1987.

Annino, Antonio, et al., eds. *América Latina: Dallo stato coloniale allo stato nazione*. 2 vols. Milan: Franco Angeli, 1987.

Archer, Christon I. "'La Causa Buena': The Counterinsurgency Army of New Spain and the Ten Years' War." In *The Independence of Mexico and the Creation of the New Nation*, ed. Jaime E. Rodríguez O., 85–108. Los Angeles: UCLA Latin American Center, 1989.

————. "Insurrection—Reaction—Revolution—Fragmentation: Reconstructing the Choreography of Meltdown in New Spain during the Independence Era." *Mexican Studies* 10, no. 1 (winter 1994): 63–98.

————. "The Militarization of Mexican Politics: The Role of the Army, 1815–1821." In *Five Centuries of Mexican History*, 2 vols., ed. Virginia Guedea and Jaime E. Rodríguez O., 1:285–302. Mexico City: Instituto de Investigaciones Dr. José María Luis Mora/University of California, Irvine, 1992.

————. "Politicization of the Army of New Spain during the War of Independence, 1810–1821." In *The Evolution of the Mexican Political System*, ed. Jaime E. Rodríguez O., 17–43. Wimington DE: SR Books, 1993.

————. "Where Did All the Royalists Go? New Light on the Military Collapse of New Spain, 1810–1822." In *The Mexican and Mexican American Experience in the Nineteenth Century*, ed. Jaime E. Rodríguez O., 24–43. Tempe AZ: Bilingual Press, 1989.

Arnaiz y Freg, Arturo. "El Dr. José María Luis Mora, 1794–1850." *Memoria de la Academia Mexicana de la Historia* 25, no. 4 (1966): 405–525.

Arnold, Linda. "La administración, la ajudicación y la política en la rama judicial en México, 1825 a 1835." In *Memoria del IV Congreso de historia del derecho mexicano (1986)*, 2 vols., ed. Beatriz Bernal, 59–69. Mexico City: UNAM, 1988.

————. *Bureaucracy and Bureaucrats in Mexico City, 1742–1835*. Tucson: University of Arizona Press, 1988.

————. "Reflections on Conflict, Politics, and Jurisprudence: The Federal District vs. the State of Mexico, 1833–1851." Paper presented at the Eighth Congress of Mexican and North American Historians, San Diego, October 1990.

Arrom, Silvia. "Popular Politics in Mexico City: The Parián Riot, 1828." *Hispanic American Historical Review* 68, no. 2 (May 1988): 245–68.

————. *The Women of Mexico City, 1790–1857*. Stanford CA: Stanford University Press, 1985.

Baranda, Marta, and Lía García, comps. *Estado de México: Textos de su historia*. 2 vols. Mexico City: Instituto de Investigaciones Dr. José María Luis Mora, 1987.

Barker, Nancy Nichols. *The French Experience in Mexico, 1821–1861: A History of Constant Misunderstanding*. Chapel Hill: University of North Carolina Press, 1979.

Barragán Barragán, José. *Introducción al federalismo (la formación de los poderes en 1824)*. Mexico City: Universidad Nacional Autónoma de México, 1978.

————. "La legislación gaditana como derecho patrio." In *Memoria del II Congreso de historia del derecho mexicano (1980)*, ed. José Luis Soberanes Fernández, 377–92. Mexico City: Universidad Nacional Autónoma de México, 1981.

————. *Principios sobre el federalismo mexicano: 1824*. Mexico City: Departamento del Distrito Federal, 1984.

Bartra, Roger. *The Cage of Melancholy: Identity and Metamorphosis in the Mexican Character*, trans. Christopher J. Hall. New Brunswick NJ: Rutgers University Press, 1992.

Bastian, Jean-Pierre. "Una ausencia notoria: La francmasonería en la historiografía mexicanista." *Historia Mexicana* 44, no. 3 (enero–marzo 1995): 439–60.

Baur, John E. "The Evolution of a Mexican Foreign Trade Policy, 1821–1828." *The Americas* 19, no. 3 (January 1963): 225–61.

Bazant, Jan. *Alienation of Church Wealth in Mexico*. New York: Cambridge University Press, 1971.

———. *Antonio Haro y Tamariz y sus aventuras políticas, 1811–1869*. Mexico City: El Colegio de México, 1985.

———. "Evolución de la industria textil poblana (1554–1845)." *Historia Mexicana* 13, no. 4 (abril–junio 1964): 473–516.

———. *Historia de la deuda exterior de México (1823–1946)*. Mexico City: El Colegio de México, 1968.

———. "Industria algodonera poblana de 1800–1843 en números." *Historia Mexicana* 14, no. 1 (julio–septiembre 1964): 131–43.

Benjamin, Thomas. "Regionalizing the Revolution: The Many Mexicos in Revolutionary Historiography." In *Provinces of the Revolution: Essays on Regional Mexican History, 1910–1929*, ed. Thomas Benjamin and Mark Wasserman, 319–57. Albuquerque: University of New Mexico Press, 1990.

Benson, Nettie Lee. *La diputación provincial y el federalismo mexicano*. Mexico City: El Colegio de México, 1955.

———. "The Plan of Casa Mata." *Hispanic American Historical Review* 25, no. 1 (February 1945): 45–56.

———. *The Provincial Deputation in Mexico: Harbinger of Provincial Autonomy, Independence, and Federalism*. Austin: University of Texas Press, 1992.

———. "Servando Teresa de Mier, Federalist." *Hispanic American Historical Review* 28 (1948): 514–25.

———. "Territorial Integrity in Mexican Politics, 1821–1833." In *The Independence of Mexico and the Creation of the New Nation*, ed. Jaime E. Rodríguez O., 275–307. Los Angeles: UCLA Latin American Center, 1989.

Benson, Nettie Lee, ed. *Mexico and the Spanish Cortes, 1810–1822: Eight Essays*. Austin: University of Texas Press, 1966.

Bernecker, Walther L. "Comercio y comerciantes extranjeros en las primeras décadas de la independencia mexicana." In *América Latina en la época de Simón Bolívar: La formación de las economías nacionales y los intereses europeos, 1800–1850*, ed. Reinhard Liehr, 87–114. Berlin: Colloquium Verlag, 1989.

Bernstein, Harry. "Regionalism in the National History of Mexico." *Acta Americana* 2 (October–December 1944): 305–14. Reprinted in *Latin American History: Essays in Its Study and Teaching, 1898–1965*, 2 vols., ed. Howard F. Cline, 1:389–94. Austin: University of Texas Press, 1967.

Bertola, Elisabetta, Marcello Carmagnani, and Paolo Riguzzi. "Federación y estados: Espacios políticos y relaciones de poder en México (Siglo XIX)." In *Región e historia en México (1700–1850): Métodos de análisis regional*, ed. Pedro Pérez

Herrero, 237–59. Mexico City: Instituto de Investigaciones Dr. José María Luis Mora/Universidad Autónoma Metropolitana, 1991.

Blazquez Dominguez, Carmen, ed. *Veracruz: Textos de su historia*. 2 vols. Mexico City: Instituto de Investigaciones Dr. José María Luis Mora, 1988.

Bocanegra, José María. *Memorias para la historia de México independiente, 1822–46*. 2 vols. Mexico City: Imprenta del Gobierno Federal, 1892–97.

Booker, Jackie R. *Veracruz Merchants, 1770–1829: A Mercantile Elite in Late Bourbon and Early Independent Mexico*. Boulder CO: Westview, 1992.

Brading, D. A. "Creole Nationalism and Mexican Liberalism." *Journal of Interamerican Studies and World Affairs* 15 (May 1973): 139–90.

———. *The First America: The Spanish Monarchy, Creole Patriots, and the Liberal State, 1492–1867*. Cambridge: Cambridge University Press, 1991.

———. *The Origins of Mexican Nationalism*. Cambridge: Cambridge University Press, 1985.

———. "El patriotismo liberal y la Reforma Mexicana." In *El nacionalismo en México*, ed. Cecilia Noriega Elío, 179–204. Zamora: El Colegio de Michoacán, 1992.

Bravo Ugarte, José. *Historia de México: Independencia, caracterización política e integración social*. 2d ed., rev. Mexico City: Editorial Jus, 1953.

———. "Independencia de las Provincias Unidas del Centro de América y adhesión definitiva de Chiapas a México." *Memorias de la Academia Mexicana de la Historia* 14, no. 1 (enero–marzo 1955): 43–48.

———. *Periodistas y periódicos mexicanas (hasta 1935, selección)*. Mexico City: Editorial Jus, 1966.

Bulnes, Francisco. *Las grandes mentiras de nuestra historia: La nación y el ejército en las guerras extranjeras*. 1904. Reprint, Mexico City: Consejo Nacional Para La Cultura y Las Artes, 1991.

Burns, E. Bradford. *Patriarch and Folk: The Emergence of Nicaragua, 1798–1858*. Cambridge: Harvard University Press, 1991.

———. *The Poverty of Progress: Latin America in the Nineteenth Century*. Berkeley and Los Angeles: University of California Press, 1980.

Bustamante, Carlos María de. *Continuacion del cuadro histórico: Historia del emperador D. Agustín de Iturbide hasta su muerte, y sus consecuencias, establecimiento de la república popular federal*. Vol. 6 of the original *Cuadro histórico*. Mexico City: Imprenta de I. Cumplido, 1846.

———. *Diario histórico de México*. 2 vols. Mexico City: Instituto Nacional de Antropología e Historia, 1980–81.

Calderón, Francisco. "El pensamiento económico de Lucas Alamán." *Historia Mexicana* 34, no. 3 (enero–marzo 1985): 435–59.

California State Library, Sutro Branch. *Catalogue of the Mexican Pamphlets in the Sutro Collection, 1623–1888*. San Francisco: California State Library, 1939.

———. *Supplement to the Catalogue of the Mexican Pamphlets in the Sutro Collection (1800–1828)*. San Francisco: California State Library, 1941.

Calvillo, Manuel, general coordinator. *La consumación de la independencia y la instauración de la república federal, 1820–1824.* 2 vols. Mexico City: Departamento del Distrito Federal, 1974. (This title may also be listed as *La república federal mexicana: Gestación y nacimiento. Obra conmemorativa de la fundación de la república federal y de la creación del distrito federal en 1824.*)

Camp, Roderic A. "La cuestión Chiapaneca: Revisión de una polémica territorial." *Historia Mexicana* 24, no. 4 (abril–junio 1975): 579–606.

Carmagnani, Marcello. "Del territorio a la región: Líneas de un proceso en la primera mitad del siglo XIX." In *Cincuenta años de historia en México,* 2 vols., ed. Alicia Hernández Chávez and Manuel Miño Grijalva, 2:221–41. Mexico City: Centro de Estudios Históricos, El Colegio de México, 1991.

——. "El federalismo, historia de una forma de gobierno." In *Federalismos latinoamericanos: México/Brasil/Argentina,* ed. Marcello Carmagnani, 397–416. Mexico City: El Colegio de México/Fondo de Cultura Económica, 1993.

——. "Finanzas y estado en Mexico, 1820–1880." *Ibero-Amerikanisches Archiv* 9, no. 3/4 (1983): 279–317.

——. "Territorialidad y federalismo en la formación del estado mexicano." In *Problemas de la formación del estado y de la nación en Hispanoamérica,* ed. Inge Buisson et al., 289–304. Cologne: Bohlau Verlag, 1984.

——. "Territorios, provincias y estados: Las transformaciones de los espacios políticos en México, 1750–1850." In *La fundación del estado mexicano, 1821–1855,* ed. Josefina Zoraida Vázquez, 39–73. Mexico City: Nueva Imagen: 1994.

Carrion, Antonio. *Historia de la ciudad de Puebla de los Angeles.* 2d ed. 2 vols. Puebla: Editorial José M. Cajica, 1970.

Castañeda, Carmen. "La formación de la élite en Guadalajara, 1792–1821." In *Elite, clases sociales y rebelión en Guadalajara y Jalisco, siglos XVIII y XIX,* ed. Carmen Castañeda, 17–57. Guadalajara: El Colegio de Jalisco, 1988.

Castro Morales, Efraín. *El federalismo en Puebla.* Puebla: Gobierno del Estado de Puebla, 1987.

Cerutti, Mario. "Monterrey and Its *Ambito Regional,* 1850–1910: Historical Context and Methodological Recommendations." In *Mexico's Regions: Comparative History and Development,* ed. Eric Van Young, 145–65. San Diego: Center for U.S.-Mexican Studies, University of California, San Diego, 1992.

Cerutti, Mario, and Rocío González Maíz. "Autonomía regional y estado nacional a mediados del siglo XIX: Santiago Vidaurri y el liberalismo 'de la frontera' (1846–1867)." In *El nacionalismo en México,* ed. Cecilia Noriega Elío, 551–61. Zamora: El Colegio de Michoacán, 1992.

Coahuila, Estado de. *Miguel Ramos Arizpe: El federalismo, y otros temas.* Coahuila: Gobierno del Estado, 1988.

Coatsworth, John H. "The Decline of the Mexican Economy, 1800–1860." In *América Latina en la época de Simón Bolívar: La formación de las economías nacionales y los intereses económicas europeos, 1800–1850,* ed. Reinhard Liehr, 27–53. Berlin: Colloquium Verlag, 1989.

———. "Obstacles to Economic Growth in Nineteenth Century Mexico." *American Historical Review* 83, no. 1 (February 1978): 80–100.

———. "Los orígenes sociales del autoritarismo en México." In *Los orígenes del atraso: Nueve ensayos de historia económica de México en los siglos XVIII y XIX*, 209–37. Mexico City: Alianza Editorial Mexicana, 1990.

Connaughton, Brian. *Ideología y sociedad en Guadalajara (1788–1853)*. Mexico City: Consejo Nacional para la Cultura y las Artes, 1992.

Costeloe, Michael P. "The Administration, Collection, and Distribution of Tithes in the Archbishopric of Mexico, 1800–1860." *The Americas* 23, no. 1 (July 1966): 3–27.

———. *The Central Republic in Mexico, 1835–1846: "Hombres de bien" in the Age of Santa Anna*. Cambridge: Cambridge University Press, 1993.

———. *Church and State in Independent Mexico: A Study of the Patronage Debate, 1821–1857*. London: Royal Historical Society, 1978.

———. *Church Wealth in Mexico: A Study of the "Juzgado de Capellanías" in the Archbishopric of Mexico, 1800–1856*. Cambridge: Cambridge University Press, 1967.

———. "Federalism to Centralism in Mexico: The Conservative Case for Change, 1834–1835." *The Americas* 45, no. 2 (October 1988): 173–85.

———. "Hombres de bien in the Age of Santa Anna." In *Mexico in the Age of Democratic Revolutions, 1750–1850*, ed. Jaime E. Rodríguez O., 243–57. Boulder CO: Lynne Rienner, 1994.

———. *La primera república federal de México (1824–1835): Un estudio de los partidos políticos en el México independiente*. Translated by Manuel Fernández Gasalla. Mexico City: Fondo de Cultura Económica, 1975.

———. "Santa Anna and the Gómez Farías Administration in Mexico, 1833–1834." *The Americas* 31, no. 1 (July 1974): 18–50.

Crónicas: Constitución federal de 1824. 2 vols. Mexico City: Secretaría de Gobernación, 1974.

Cue Cánovas, Agustín. *El federalismo mexicano*. Mexico City: Libro Mex, 1960.

———. *Historia social y económica de México (1521–1854)*. 3d ed. Mexico City: Editorial F. Trillas, 1963.

Cuevas, Luis G. *Porvenir de México*. N.d. Reprint, Mexico City: Editorial Jus, 1954.

Dalton, Margarita, comp. *Oaxaca: Textos de su historia*. 2 vols. Mexico City: Instituto de Investigaciones Dr. José María Luis Mora, 1990.

Davies, Keith A. "Tendencias demográficas urbanas durante el siglo XIX en México." *Historia Mexicana* 21, no. 3 (enero–marzo 1972): 481–524.

Deans-Smith, Susan. "State Enterprise, Work, and Workers in Mexico: The Case of the Tobacco Monopoly, 1750–1850." In *The Political Economy of Spanish America in the Age of Revolution, 1750–1850*, ed. Kenneth J. Andrien and Lyman L. Johnson, 63–93. Albuquerque: University of New Mexico Press, 1994.

DeVolder, Arthur L. *Guadalupe Victoria: His Role in Mexican Independence*. Albuquerque NM: Artcraft, 1978.

Díaz Díaz, Fernando. *Caudillos y caciques: Antonio López de Santa Anna y Juan Alvarez.* Mexico City: El Colegio de México, 1972.

Díaz y Díaz, Martín. "Las relaciones de propiedad en el proceso de constitución nacional." In *El nacionalismo en México,* ed. Cecilia Noriega Elío, 519–49. Zamora: El Colegio de Michoacán, 1992.

Diccionario Porrúa de historia, biografía y geografía de México. 3d ed., corrected and augmented. 2 vols. Mexico City: Editorial Porrúa, 1976.

Di Tella, Torcuato S. "Ciclos políticos en la primera mitad del siglo XIX." In *La fundación del estado mexicano, 1821–1855,* ed. Josefina Zoraida Vázquez, III–33. Mexico City: Nueva Imagen, 1994.

———. "The Dangerous Classes in Early Nineteenth Century Mexico." *Journal of Latin American Studies* 5, no. 1 (May 1973): 79–105.

———. "Las huelgas en la minería mexicana, 1826–1828." *Desarrolo Económico* 26 (enero–marzo 1987): 579–608.

———. *National Popular Politics in Early Independent Mexico, 1820–1847.* Albuquerque: University of New Mexico Press, 1996.

Dos años en México: O memorias críticas sobre los principales sucesos de la república de los Estados-Unidos Mexicanos, desde la invasión de Barradas hasta la declaración del Puerto de Tampico contra el Gobierno del General Bustamante, escritos por un español. Valencia, 1838. Reprint, Mexico City: José Uribe, 1840.

Dublán, Manuel, and José María Lozano, eds. *Legislación mexicana: O colección completa de las disposiciones legislativas expedidas desde la independencia de la república.* 34 vols. Mexico City: Imprenta del Comercio, 1876–1914.

Echanove Trujillo, Carlos A. *La vida pasional e inquieta de don Crecencio Rejón.* Mexico City: El Colegio de México, 1941.

Enríquez Terrazas, Eduardo, and Martha Rodríguez García, comps. *Coahuila: Textos de su historia.* Mexico City: Instituto de Investigaciones Dr. José María Luis Mora, 1989.

Escobar, Manuel María. "Campaña de Tampico de Tamaulipas, año de 1829." *Historia Mexicana* 9, no. 1 (julio–septiembre 1959): 44–96.

Estep, Raymond. *Lorenzo de Zavala: Profeta del liberalismo mexicano.* Translated by Carlos E. Echanove Trujillo. Mexico City: Libreria de M. Porrúa, 1952.

Falcón, Ramona. "Poderes y razones de las jefaturas políticas: Coahuila en el primer siglo de vida independiente." In *The Evolution of the Mexican Political System,* ed. Jaime E. Rodríguez O., 137–62. Wilmington DE: SR Books, 1993.

Fernández de Córdoba, Joaquín. *Pablo de Villavicencio: El payo del Rosario, escritor sinaloense precursor de la reforma en México.* Mexico City: El Libro Perfecto, 1949.

Filippi, Alberto. *Instituciones e ideologías en la independencia hispanoamericana.* Buenos Aires: Alianza Editorial, 1988.

Flaccus, Elmer W. "Guadalupe Victoria: His Personality as a Cause of His Failure." *The Americas* 23, no. 3 (January 1967): 297–311.

Flores Caballero, Romeo. *La contra-revolución en la independencia: Los españoles en la vida política, social, y económica de México (1804–1838)*. Mexico City: El Colegio de México, 1969.

———. "Del libre cambio al proteccionismo." *Historia Mexicana* 19, no. 4 (abril–julio 1970): 492–512.

———. *Protección y libre cambio: El debate entre 1821 y 1836*. Mexico City: Banco Nacional de Comercio Exterior, 1971.

Florescano, Enrique. *Memory, Myth, and Time in Mexico: From the Aztecs to Independence*. Translated by Albert G. Bork and Kathryn R. Bork. Austin: University of Texas Press, 1994.

———. *El nuevo pasado mexicano*. Mexico City: Cal y Arena, 1991.

———. "El poder y la lucha por el poder en la historiografía Mexicana." *Nova Americana* 3 (1980): 199–238.

———. "El problema agrario en los últimos años del virreinato, 1800–1821." *Historia Mexicana* 20, no. 4 (abril–junio 1971): 477–510.

Florescano, Enrique, and Isabel Gil Sánchez, comps. *Descripciones económicas regionales de Nueva España*. 2 vols. Mexico City: Instituto Nacional de Antropología e Historia, 1976.

Florstedt, Robert F. "Mora contra Bustamante." *Historia Mexicana* 12, no. 1 (julio–septiembre 1962): 26–51.

———. "Mora y la génesis del liberalismo burgués." *Historia Mexicana* 11, no. 2 (octubre–diciembre 1961): 207–23.

Fowler, Will. "Valentín Gómez Farías: Perceptions of Radicalism in Independent Mexico, 1821–1847." *Bulletin of Latin American Research* 15, no. 1 (January 1996): 39–62.

Gallardo, Miguel Angel, comp. *Cuatro constituciones federales de Centro América y las constituciones políticas de El Salvador*. San Salvador: Tip. La Unión, 1945.

Galván Rivera, Mariano, comp. *Colección de constituciones de los Estados Unidos Mexicanos*. Facsimile of 1928 edition. Mexico City: Miguel Angel Porrúa, 1988.

Gamas Torruco, José. *El federalismo mexicano*. Mexico City: Sep Setentas, 1975.

García Cubas, Antonio. *Atlas geográfico, estadística e histórico mexicano*. Mexico City: Imprenta J.M. Fernández de Lara, 1858.

García Quintanilla, Alejandra. "En busca de la prosperidad y la riqueza: Yucatán a la hora de la independencia." In *Los lugares y los tiempos: Ensayos sobre las estructuras regionales del siglo XIX en México*, ed. Alejandra García Quintanilla and Abel Juárez, 83–108. Mexico City: Editorial Nuestro Tiempo, 1989.

García Quintanilla, Alejandra, and Abel Juárez, eds. *Los lugares y los tiempos: Ensayos sobre las estructuras regionales del siglo XIX en México*. Mexico City: Editorial Nuestro Tiempo, 1989.

Garza, Luis Alberto de la. "La transición del imperio a la república o la participación indiscriminada (1821–1823)." *Estudios de historia moderna y contemporánea de México* 11 (1988): 21–57.

————. "Una visión historiografica erronea: La idea de nacionalidad." In *Evolución del estado mexicano: Tomo 1, Formación, 1810–1910*, 21–54. Mexico City: Ediciones El Caballito, 1986.

Garza Guajardo, Celso, comp. *Nuevo León: Textos de su historia*. 2 vols. Mexico City: Instituto de Investigaciones Dr. José María Luis Mora, 1989.

Gaxiola, Francisco Javier. *Gobernantes del Estado de México: Múzquiz-Zavala-Olaguirre*. Facsimile of 1899 edition. Mexico City: Biblioteca Enciclopédica del Estado de México, 1975.

Gayón Córdova, María. *Condiciones de vida y de trabajo en la ciudad de México en el siglo XIX*. Mexico City: Instituto Nacional de Antropología e Historia, 1988.

González, María del Refugio, ed. *La formación del estado mexicano*. Mexico City: Editorial Porrúa, 1984.

————. "Ilustrados, regalistas y liberales." In *The Independence of Mexico and the Creation of the New Nation*, ed. Jaime E. Rodríguez O., 247–63. Los Angeles: UCLA Latin American Center, 1989.

————. "El pensamiento de los conservadores mexicanos." In *The Mexican and Mexican American Experience in the Nineteenth Century*, ed. Jaime E. Rodríguez O., 55–67. Tempe AZ: Bilingual Press, 1989.

González Angulo, Jorge. "Los gremios de artesanos y la estructura urbana." In *Ciudad de México: Ensayo de construcción de una historia*, ed. Alejandra Moreno Toscano, 25–36. Mexico City: SEP/INAH, 1978.

González de la Vara, Martín. "La política del federalismo en Nuevo México, 1821–1836." *Historia Mexicana* 36, no. 1 (julio–septiembre 1986): 49–80.

González Esparza, Victor M. "Patriotismo vs. nación: Nueva Galicia y los orígenes del estado nacional en México." Paper presented at IX Congreso de Historiadores Canadienses, Mexicanos y de los Estados Unidos, Mexico City, October 1994.

González Navarro, Moisés. "La independencia, el yorkinato y la libertad." In *Extremos de México: Homenaje a don Daniel Cosío Villegas*, 151–80. Mexico City: El Colegio de México, 1971.

————. *El pensamiento político de Lucas Alamán*. Mexico City: El Colegio de México, 1952.

————. "Tipología del conservadurismo mexicano." In *La revolución francesa en México*, ed. Solange Alberro, Alicia Hernández Chávez, and Elías Trabulse, 215–34. Mexico City: El Colegio de México, 1991.

————. "Tipología del liberalismo mexicano." *Historia Mexicana* 32, no. 2 (octubre–diciembre 1982): 198–225.

————. "La venganza del sur." *Historia Mexicana* 21, no. 4 (abril–junio 1972): 677–92.

González Oropeza, Manuel. "Características iniciales del federalismo mexicano (1823–1837)." In *El nacionalismo en México*, ed. Cecilia Noriega Elío, 413–32. Zamora: El Colegio de Michoacán, 1992.

————. *El Federalismo*. Mexico City: Universidad Nacional Autónoma de México, 1995.

González Pedrero, Enrique. *La ronda de los contrarios*. Vol. 1 of *País de un solo hombre: El México de Santa Anna*. Mexico City: Fondo de Cultura Económica, 1993.

González y González, Luis. "Patriotismo y matriotismo: Cara y Cruz de México." In *El nacionalismo en México*, ed. Cecilia Noriega Elío, 477–95. Zamora: El Colegio de Michoacán, 1992.

Gortari Rabiela, Hira de. "El federalismo en la construcción de los estados." In *Mexico in the Age of Democratic Revolutions, 1750–1850*, ed. Jaime E. Rodríguez O., 209–22. Boulder CO: Lynne Rienner, 1994.

———. "La minería durante la guerra de independencia y los primeros años del México independiente, 1810–1824." In *The Independence of Mexico and the Creation of the New Nation*, ed. Jaime E. Rodríguez O., 129–61. Los Angeles: UCLA Latin American Center, 1989.

———. "Realidad ecónomica y proyectos políticos: Los primeros años del México independiente." In *El nacionalismo en México*, ed. Cecilia Noriega Elío, 163–78. Zamora: El Colegio de Michoacán, 1992.

———. "El territorio y las identidades en la construcción de la nación." In *Cincuenta años de historia en México*, 2 vols., ed. Alicia Hernández Chávez and Manuel Miño Grijalva, 2:199–220. Mexico City: Centro de Estudios Históricos, El Colegio de México, 1991.

Green, Stanley C. *The Mexican Republic: The First Decade, 1823–1832*. Pittsburgh: University of Pittsburgh Press, 1987.

Guardino, Peter. "Barbarism or Republican Law? Guerrero's Peasants and National Politics, 1820–1846." *Hispanic American Historical Review* 75, no. 2 (May 1995): 185–213.

———. *Peasants, Politics, and the Formation of Mexico's National State: Guerrero, 1800–1857*. Stanford CA: Stanford University Press, 1996.

Guardino, Peter, and Charles Walker. "The State, Society, and Politics in Peru and Mexico in the Late Colonial and Early Republican Periods." *Latin American Perspectives* 19, no. 2 (spring 1992): 10–43.

Guedea, Virginia. *En busca de un gobierno alterno: Los guadalupes de México*. Mexico City: Universidad Nacional Autónoma de México, 1992.

———. "The First Popular Elections in Mexico City, 1812–1813." In *The Evolution of the Mexican Political System*, ed. Jaime E. Rodríguez O., 45–69. Wilmington DE: SR Books, 1993.

———. "El pueblo de México y la política capitalina, 1808–1812." *Mexican Studies* 10, no. 1 (winter 1994): 27–61.

———. "Las sociedades secretas durante el movimiento de independencia." In *The Independence of Mexico and the Creation of the New Nation*, ed. Jaime E. Rodríguez O., 45–62. Los Angeles: UCLA Latin American Center, 1989.

Guerra, Francois-Xavier. "Identidades e independencia: La excepción americana." *Imaginar la nación: Cuadernos de Historia Latinoamericana*, no. 2 (1994): 93–134.

———. "Introducción: Epifanías de la Nación." *Imaginar la nación: Cuadernos de Historia Latinoamericana*, no. 2 (1994): 7–14.

————. *Modernidad e independencias: Ensayos sobre las revoluciones hispánicas.* Mexico City: Editorial Mapfre/Fondo de Cultura Económica, 1993.

————. "The Spanish-American Tradition of Representation and Its European Roots." *Journal of Latin American Studies* 26, no. 1 (February 1994): 1–35.

Hale, Charles A. "Alamán, Antuñano, y la continuidad del liberalismo." *Historia Mexicana* 11, no. 2 (octubre–diciembre 1961): 224–45.

————. "José María Luis Mora and the Structure of Mexican Liberalism." *Hispanic American Historical Review* 45, no. 2 (May 1965): 196–227.

————. "Liberalismo mexicano." *Historia Mexicana* 12, no. 3 (enero–marzo 1963): 456–63.

————. *Mexican Liberalism in the Age of Mora, 1821–1853.* New Haven: Yale University Press, 1968.

————. "The Reconstruction of Nineteenth Century Politics in Spanish America: A Case for the History of Ideas." *Latin American Research Review* 8 (summer 1973): 53–73.

————. *The Transformation of Liberalism in Late-Nineteenth-Century Mexico.* Princeton: Princeton University Press, 1989.

Hamill, Hugh M., Jr. "Caudillismo and Independence: A Symbiosis?" In *The Independence of Mexico and the Creation of the New Nation,* ed. Jaime E. Rodríguez O., 163–74. Los Angeles: UCLA Latin American Center, 1989.

Hamnett, Brian R. "Absolutismo ilustrado y crísis multidimensional en el periodo colonial tardío, 1760–1808." In *Interpretaciones del siglo XVIII mexicano: El Impacto de las reformas borbónicas,* ed. Josefina Zoraida Vázquez, 67–108. Mexico City: Nueva Imagen, 1992.

————. "Anastacio Bustamante y la guerra de independencia—1810–1821." *Historia Mexicana* 28, no. 4 (abril–junio 1979): 515–45.

————. "Between Bourbon Reforms and Liberal Reforma: The Political Economy of a Mexican Province—Oaxaca, 1750–1850." In *The Political Economy of Spanish America in the Age of Revolution, 1750–1850,* ed. Kenneth J. Andrien and Lyman L. Johnson, 39–62. Albuquerque: University of New Mexico Press, 1994.

————. "The Economic and Social Dimension of the Revolution of Independence in Mexico, 1800–1824." *Ibero-Amerikanisches Archiv* 6, no. 1 (1980): 1–27.

————. "Faccionalismo, constitución y poder personal en la política mexicana, 1821–1854: Un ensayo interpretativo." In *La fundación del estado mexicano, 1821–1855,* ed. Josefina Zoraida Vázquez, 75–109. Mexico City: Nueva Imagen, 1994.

————. "Factores regionales en la desintegración del regimen colonial en la Nueva España: El federalismo de 1823–1824." In *Problemas de la formación del estado y de la nación en Hispanoamérica,* ed. Inge Buisson et al., 305–17. Cologne: Bohlau Verlag, 1984.

————. *Juárez.* London: Longman, 1994.

————. "Oaxaca: Las principales familias y el federalismo de 1823." In *Lecturas históricas del Estado de Oaxaca,* Colección Regiones de México, vol. 3, ed. María

Angeles Romero Frizzi, 51–69. Mexico City: Instituto Nacional de Antropología e Historia, 1990.

———. "Partidos políticos mexicanos e intervención militar, 1823–1855." In *América Latina: Dallo stato coloniale allo state nazione*, 2 vols., ed. Antonio Annino, 2:573–91. Milan: Franco Angeli, 1987.

———. *Roots of Insurgency: Mexican Regions, 1750–1824.* Cambridge: Cambridge University Press, 1986.

———. "Social Structure and Regional Elites in Late Colonial Mexico, 1750–1824." Glasgow: University of Glasgow, Occasional Papers, 1984.

Harris, Charles H. *A Mexican Family Empire: The Latifundio of the Sánchez Navarros, 1765–1867.* Austin: University of Texas Press, 1975.

Heath, Hilarie J. "British Merchant Houses in Mexico, 1821–1860: Conforming Business Practices and Ethics." *Hispanic American Historical Review* 73, no. 2 (May 1993): 261–90.

Hernández Chávez, Alicia. "La Guardia Nacional y mobilización política de los pueblos." In *Patterns of Contention in Mexican History*, ed. Jaime E. Rodríguez O., 207–25. Wilmington DE: SR Books, 1992.

———. *La tradición republicana del buen gobierno.* Mexico City: El Colegio de México/Fondo de Cultura Económica, 1993.

Hernández Chávez, Alicia, and Manuel Miño Grijalva, eds. *Cincuenta años de historia en México.* 2 vols. Mexico City: Centro de Estudios Históricos, El Colegio de México, 1991.

Herrejón Peredo, Carlos, ed. *La independencia según Ignacio Rayón.* Mexico City: Secretaría de Educación Pública, 1985.

Herrera Canales, Inés. *El comercio exterior de México—1821–1875.* Mexico City: El Colegio de México, 1977.

Hutchinson, C. A. *Valentín Gómez Farías: La vida de un republicano.* Guadalajara: Gobierno de Jalisco, 1983.

Jiménez Codinach, Guadalupe. "Confédération Napoléonnie: El desempeño de los conspiradores militares y las sociedades secretas en la Independencia de México." *Historia Mexicana* 38, no. 1 (julio–septiembre 1988): 43–68.

———. *La Gran Bretaña y la Independencia de México, 1808–1821.* Mexico City: Fondo de Cultura Económica, 1991.

———. "Veracruz, almacén de plata en el Atlántico: La Casa Gordon y Murphy, 1805–1824." *Historia Mexicana* 38, no. 2 (octubre–diciembre 1988): 325–53.

Jiménez Codinach, Guadalupe, coordinator. *Planes políticas de la nación mexicana,* vol. 1 (1808–1830). Mexico City: Senado de la República, 1987.

Jones, Oakah L., Jr. *Santa Anna.* New York: Twayne, 1968.

Kahle, Günter. *Militär und Staatsbildung in den Anfangen der Unabhängigkeit Mexicos.* Cologne: Bohlau Verlag, 1969.

Kenyon, Gordon. "Mexican Influence in Central America, 1821–1823." *Hispanic American Historical Review* 41, no. 2 (May 1961): 175–205.

Knight, Alan. "Peasants into Patriots: Thoughts on the Making of the Mexican Nation." *Mexican Studies* 10, no. 1 (winter 1994): 135–61.

Krauze, Enrique. *Siglo de caudillos: Biografía política de México (1810–1910)*. Mexico City: Tusquets Editores, 1994.

Landa Fonseca, Cecilia, comp. *Querétaro: Textos de su historia*. 2 vols. Mexico City: Instituto de Investigaciones Dr. José María Luis Mora, 1988.

Landázuri Benítez, Gisela, and Verónica Vázquez Mantecón. *Azúcar y Estado, 1750–1880*. Mexico City: Fondo de Cultura Económica, 1988.

Libro de Actas del Honorable Congreso del Estado de Jalisco (1 de enero-31 de mayo de 1824). Guadalajara: Poderes de Jalisco, 1975.

Lindley, Richard B. *Haciendas and Economic Development: Guadalajara, Mexico, at Independence*. Austin: University of Texas Press, 1983.

Lira, Andrés. *Comunidades indígenas frente a la ciudad de México: Tenochtitlan y Tlatelolco, sus pueblos y barrios: 1812–1919*. Zamora: El Colegio de México/El Colegio de Michoacán, 1983.

Lira González, Andrés. "Mier y la Constitución de México." In *Mexico in the Age of Democratic Revolutions, 1750–1850*, ed. Jaime E. Rodríguez O., 161–76. Boulder CO: Lynne Rienner, 1994.

Lomnitz-Adler, Claudio. *Exits from the Labyrinth: Culture and Ideology in the Mexican National Space*. Berkeley and Los Angeles: University of California Press, 1992.

Lozano y Nathal, Gema. "Tlacotalpan: Los riesgos de su frontera con el mar." In *Five Centuries of Mexican History*, 2 vols., ed. Virginia Guedea and Jaime E. Rodríguez O., 1:329–43. Mexico City: Instituto de Investigaciones Dr. José María Luis Mora/University of California, Irvine, 1992.

Macune, Charles W., Jr. "Conflictos entre el gobierno nacional y el estado de México—1823–1835." *Historia Mexicana* 26, no. 2 (octubre–diciembre 1976): 216–37.

———. *El Estado de México y la Federación Mexicana*. Mexico City: Fondo de Cultura Económica, 1978.

———. "The Expropriation of Mexico City—Regional Antipathy in Newly Independent Mexico." *Proceedings of the Pacific Coast Council on Latin American Studies* 2 (1973): 117–42.

———. "The Impact of Federalism on Mexican Church-State Relations, 1824–1835: The Case of the State of Mexico." *The Americas* 40, no. 4 (April 1984): 505–29.

Magaña Esquivel, Antonio. *Guerrero: El heroe del sur*. Mexico City: Ediciones Xochitl, 1946.

Malamud, Carlos D. "Acerca del concepto de 'Estado colonial' en la América hispana." *Revista de Occidente* 116 (enero 1991): 114–27.

Mallon, Florencia E. "Peasants and State Formation in Nineteenth-Century Mexico: Morelos, 1848–1858." *Political Power and Social Theory* 7 (1988): 1–54.

Marichal, Carlos. *A Century of Debt Crises in Latin America: From Independence to the Great Depression, 1820–1930*. Princeton: Princeton University Press, 1989.

Márquez, Enrique, comp. *San Luis Potosí: Textos de su historia*. Mexico City: Instituto de Investigaciones Dr. José María Luis Mora, 1986.

Mateos, Juan Antonio, ed. *Historia parlamentaria de los congresos mexicanos de 1821 a 1857*. 25 vols. Mexico City: S. Reyes, 1877–1912.

Mayo, John. "Imperialismo de libre comercio e imperio informal en la costa oeste de México durante la época de Santa Anna." *Historia Mexicana* 40, no. 4 (abril–junio 1991): 673–96.

McGowan, Gerald L. *El Distrito Federal de dos leguas: Ó como el Estado de México perdió su capital*. Zinacantepec: El Colegio Mexiquense, 1991.

McGowan, Gerald L., comp. *El Estado del Valle de México, 1824–1917*. Zinacantepec: El Colegio Mexiquense, 1991.

Mecham, J. Lloyd. "Mexican Federalism—Fact or Fiction?" *The Annals of the American Academy of Political and Social Science* 108 (March 1940): 24–38.

———. "The Origins of Federalism in Mexico." *Hispanic American Historical Review* 18, no. 2 (May 1938): 164–82.

Meyer, Jean. *Problemas campesinos y revueltas agrarias, 1821–1910*. Mexico City: Sep Setentas, 1973.

Meyer Cosío, Rosa María. "Empresarios, crédito y especulación (1820–1850)." In *Banca y poder en México (1800–1925)*, ed. Leonor Ludlow and Carlos Marichal, 99–117. Mexico City: Editorial Grijalbo, 1986.

Mills, Elizabeth Hoel. *Don Valentín Gómez Farías y el desarrollo de sus idea políticas*. Mexico City: Universidad Nacional Autónoma de México, 1957.

Miranda Marrón, Manuel. *Vida y escritas del héroe insurgente: Lic. D. Andrés Quintana Roo*. Mexico City: Imprenta de la Secretaría de Fomento, 1910.

Monsiváis, Carlos. "'Just over That Hill': Notes on Centralism and Regional Cultures." In *Mexico's Regions: Comparative History and Development*, ed. Eric Van Young, 247–54. San Diego: Center for U.S.-Mexican Studies, University of California, San Diego, 1992.

Mora, José María Luis. *México y sus revoluciones*. 3 vols. 1813. Reprint, Mexico City: Fondo de Cultura Económica/Instituto Cultural Helénico, 1986.

———. *Obras sueltas*. 2d ed. Mexico City: Editorial Porrúa, 1963.

Moreno Toscano, Alejandra. "Cambios en los patrones de urbanización en México, 1810–1910." *Historia Mexicana* 22, no. 2 (octubre–diciembre 1972): 160–87.

———. "El paisaje rural y las ciudades: Dos perspectivas de la geografía histórica." *Historia Mexicana* 21, no. 2 (octubre–diciembre 1971): 242–68.

Moreno Toscano, Alejandra, and Carlos Aguirre Anaya. "Migrations to Mexico City in the Nineteenth Century: Research Approaches." *Journal of Interamerican Studies and World Affairs* 17, no. 1 (February 1975): 27–42.

Moreno Valle, Lucina, ed. *Catálogo de la Colección Lafragua de la Biblioteca Nacional de México, 1821–1853*. Mexico City: Instituto de Investigaciones Bibliográficas, 1975.

Mörner, Magnus. *Region and State in Latin America's Past*. Baltimore: Johns Hopkins University Press, 1993.

312   *Selected Bibliography*

Morton, Ohland. *Terán and Texas: A Chapter in Texas-Mexican Relations.* Austin: Texas State Historical Association, 1948.

Muría, José María. *Breve historia de Jalisco.* Guadalajara: Universidad de Guadalajara, 1988.

———. *El federalismo en Jalisco (1823).* Mexico City: Instituto Nacional de Antropología e Historia, 1973.

Muría, José María, ed. *Historia de Jalisco.* 4 vols. Guadalajara: Gobierno de Jalisco, 1981.

Muría, José María, Cándido Galvan, and Angélica Peregrina, comps. *Jalisco en la conciencia nacional.* 2 vols. Guadalajara: Gobierno del Estado de Jalisco/Instituto de Investigaciones Dr. José María Luis Mora, 1987.

Muro, Luis, comp. *Historia parlamentaria mexicana: Sesiones secretas, 1821–1824.* Mexico City: Instituto de Investigaciones Legislativas, Cámara de Diputados, 1982.

———. "Relación de las fechas de las sesiones secretas de los cuerpos legislativos mexicanos (1821–1824) cuyas actos no aparecen en el libro manuscrito original." *Historia Mexicana* 32, no. 3 (enero–marzo 1984): 459–62.

Noriega, Alfonso. *El pensamiento conservador y el conservadurismo mexicano.* Mexico City: Instituto de Investigaciones Jurídicas, Universidad Nacional Autónoma de México, 1972.

Noriega, José María Díaz. *Funestos recuerdos del libertador de México: Exhumación y autenticidad de sus respetables restos.* Mexico City: Imprenta de J.M. Lara, 1860.

Noriega Elío, Cecilia, ed. *El nacionalismo en México: VIII Coloquio de antropología e historia regionales.* Zamora: El Colegio de Michoacán, 1992.

Ocampo, Javier. *Las ideas de un día: El pueblo mexicano ante la consumación de su independencia.* Mexico City: El Colegio de México, 1969.

O'Gorman, Edmundo. *Historia de las divisiones territoriales de México.* 5th ed. Mexico City: Editorial Porrúa, 1979.

Olavarría y Ferrari, Enrique. *México independiente, 1821–1855.* Vol. 4 of *México á través de los siglos,* ed. Vicente Riva Palacio. Mexico City: Ballescá y Compañía, 1888–89.

Olveda, Jaime, ed. *Cartas a Gómez Farías.* Guadalajara: Gobierno del Estado de Jalisco, 1990.

———. *Gordiano Guzmán: Un cacique del siglo XIX.* Mexico City: SEP/INAH, 1980.

———. *La política de Jalisco durante la primera época federal.* Guadalajara: Poderes de Jalisco, 1976.

Ortega, Sergio, and Edgardo López Mañón, comps. *Sinaloa: Textos de su historia.* 2 vols. Mexico City: Instituto de Investigaciones Dr. José María Luis Mora, 1987.

Ortega Noriega, Sergio. "Hacia la regionalización de la historia de México." *Estudios de historia moderna y contemporánea de México,* no. 8 (1980): 9–21.

Ortiz de Ayala, Tadeo. *Mexico considerado como nación independiente y libre.* 2 vols. Burdeos, 1832. Reprint, Guadalajara: Ediciones I.T.G., 1952.

Ortiz Escamilla, Juan. "Las fuerzas militares y el proyecto de estado en México, 1767–1835." In *Cincuenta años de historia en México*, 2 vols., ed. Alicia Hernández Chávez and Manuel Miño Grijalva, 2:261–82. Mexico City: Centro de Estudios Históricos, El Colegio de México, 1991.

————. "El pronunciamiento federalista de Gordiano Guzmán, 1837–1842." *Historia Mexicana* 38, no. 2 (octubre–diciembre 1988): 241–82.

Otero, Mariano. "Consideraciones sobre la situación política y social de la república mexicana en el año de 1844." 1848. Reprinted in *Obras*, 2 vols., 1:95–140, Mexico City: Editorial Porrúa, 1967.

————. "Ensayo sobre el verdadero estado de la cuestión social y política que se agita en la República Mexicana." 1842. Reprinted in *Obras*, 2 vols., 1:3–94. Mexico City: Editorial Porrúa, 1967.

Pantoja Morán, David. *La idea de soberanía en el constitucionalismo latinoamericano.* Mexico City: Universidad Nacional Autónoma de México, 1973.

Parcero, María de la Luz. *Lorenzo de Zavala: Fuente y origen de la reforma liberal en México.* Mexico City: Instituto Nacional de Antropología e Historia, 1969.

Patch, Robert W. "The Bourbon Reforms, City Councils, and the Struggle for Power in Yucatán, 1770–1796." In *Mexico in the Age of Democratic Revolutions, 1750–1850*, ed. Jaime E. Rodríguez O., 57–70. Boulder CO: Lynne Rienner, 1994.

Paz, Octavio. *The Labyrinth of Solitude: Life and Thought in Mexico.* Translated by Lysander Kemp. New York: Grove, 1961.

Pérez Betancourt, Antonio, and Rodolfo Ruz Menéndez, comps. *Yucatán: Textos de su historia*, 2 vols., coordinated by José Luis Sierra. Mexico City: Instituto Mora, 1988.

Pérez Herrero, Pedro. "'Crecimiento' colonial vs. 'crisis' nacional en México, 1765–1854: Notas a un modelo explicativo." In *Five Centuries of Mexican History*, 2 vols., ed. Virginia Guedea and Jaime E. Rodríguez O., 2:81–105. Mexico City: Instituto Dr. José María Luis Mora/University of California, Irvine, 1992.

————. "El México borbónico: Un 'éxito' fracasado?" In *Interpretaciones del siglo XVIII mexicano: El impacto de las reformas borbónicas*, ed. Josefina Zoraida Vázquez, 109–51. Mexico City: Nueva Imagen, 1992.

————. "Regional Conformation in Mexico, 1700–1850: Models and Hypotheses." In *Mexico's Regions: Comparative History and Development*, ed. Eric Van Young, 117–44. San Diego: Center for U.S.-Mexican Studies, University of California, San Diego, 1992.

Pérez Herrero, Pedro, ed. *Región e historia en México (1700–1850): Métodos de análisis regional.* Mexico City: Instituto de Investigaciones Dr. José María Luis Mora/Universidad Autónoma Metropolitana, 1991.

Pérez Verdía, Luis. *Biografía del Excmo. Sr. Don Prisciliano Sánchez: Primer Gobernador Constitucional del Estado de Jalisco.* Guadalajara: Tipografía de Banda, 1881.

————. *Historia particular del estado de Jalisco.* 2 vols. 1910. Reprint, Guadalajara: Gobierno de Jalisco, 1951.

314 *Selected Bibliography*

Pietschmann, Horst. "Estado colonial y mentalidad social: El ejercicio del poder frente a distintos sistemas de valores, siglo XVIII." In *América Latina: Dallo stato coloniale allo stato nazione*, 2 vols., ed. Antonio Annino, 2:427–47. Milan: Franco Angeli, 1987.

Piñera Ramírez, David. *El nacimiento de Jalisco y la gestación del federalismo mexicano*. Guadalajara: Poderes de Jalisco, 1974.

Poinsett, Joel Roberts. *Notes on Mexico made in the Autumn of 1822*. Reprint, New York: Frederick R. Praeger, 1969.

———. *The Present Political State of Mexico*. Edited by L. Smith Lee. Salisbury NC: Documentary Publications, 1976.

Potash, Robert A. *Mexican Government and Industrial Development in the Early Republic: The Banco de Avío*. Amherst: University of Massachusetts Press, 1983.

Prieto, Guillermo. *Memorias de mis tiempos (de 1840 a 1853)*. Puebla: Editorial José M. Cajica Jr., 1970.

Primer centenario de la constitución de 1824: Obra conmemorativa. Mexico City: Cámara de Senadores, 1924.

Quijada, Mónica. "Que Nación? Dinámicas y dicotomías de la nación en el imaginario hispanoamericano del siglo XIX." *Imaginar la nación: Cuadernos de Historia Latinoamericana*, no. 2 (1994): 15–51.

Quinlan, David M. "Issues and Factions in the Constituent Congress, 1823–1824." In *Mexico in the Age of Democratic Revolutions, 1750–1850*, ed. Jaime E. Rodríguez O., 177–207. Boulder CO: Lynne Rienner, 1994.

Quintanilla Obregón, Lourdes. *El nacionalismo de Lucas Alamán*. Guanajuato: Gobierno del Estado de Guanajuato, 1991.

———. "El nacionalismo de Lucas Alamán." In *El nacionalismo en México*, ed. Cecilia Noriega Elío, 377–86. Zamora: El Colegio de Michoacán, 1992.

Rabasa, Emilio. *El pensamiento político del constituyente de 1824 (Integración y realización)*. Mexico City: Universidad Nacional Autónoma de México, 1986.

Radding de Murrieta, Cynthia, and Juan José Gracida Romo. *Sonora: Una historia compartida*. 3 vols. Mexico City: Instituto de Investigaciones Dr. José María Luis Mora, 1989.

Rees Jones, Ricardo. *El despotismo ilustrado y los intendentes de Nueva España*. Mexico City: Universidad Nacional Autónoma de México, 1979.

Reina, Leticia. *Las rebeliones campesinas en México (1819–1906)*. 4th ed. Mexico City: Siglo Veintiuno Editores, 1988.

Reyes Heroles, Jesús. *El liberalismo mexicano*. 3 vols. 1957. Reprint, Mexico City: Fondo de Cultura Económica, 1974.

Rieu-Millan, Marie Laure. *Los diputados americanos en las Cortes de Cádiz (Igualdad o independencia)*. Madrid: Consejo Superior de Investigaciones Científicas, 1990.

Rocafuerte, Vicente. *Rocafuerte y el periodismo en México*. Vol. 9 of *Colección Rocafuerte*, ed. Neptalí Zúñiga. Quito: Talleres Gráficas Nacionales, 1947.

———. *Rocafuerte y las ideas políticas de México*. Vol. 8 of *Colección Rocafuerte*, ed. Neptalí Zúñiga. Quito: Talleres Gráficas Nacionales, 1947.

Rodríguez O., Jaime E. "La Constitución de 1824 y la formación del Estado mexicano." *Historia Mexicana* 40, no. 3 (enero–marzo 1991): 507–35.

———. "The Constitution of 1824 and the Formation of the Mexican State." In *The Evolution of the Mexican Political System*, ed. Jaime E. Rodríguez O., 71–90. Wilmington DE: SR Books, 1993.

———. *Down from Colonialism: Mexico's Nineteenth Century Crisis.* Chicano Studies Research Center Publications, no. 3. Los Angeles: University of California, 1983.

———. *The Emergence of Spanish America: Vicente Rocafuerte and Spanish Americanism, 1808–1832.* Berkeley and Los Angeles: University of California Press, 1975.

———. "The Formation of the Federal Republic." In *Five Centuries of Mexican History*, 2 vols., ed. Virginia Guedea and Jaime E. Rodríguez O., 1:316–38. Mexico City: Instituto de Investigaciones Dr. José María Luis Mora/University of California, Irvine, 1992.

———. "La independencia de la América Española: Una reinterpretación." *Historia Mexicana* 42, no. 3 (enero–marzo 1993): 571–620.

———. "Mexico's First Foreign Loans." In *The Independence of Mexico and the Creation of the New Nation*, ed. Jaime E. Rodríguez O., 215–35. Los Angeles: UCLA Latin American Center, 1989.

———. "Oposición a Bustamante." *Historia Mexicana* 20, no. 2 (octubre–diciembre 1970): 199–234.

———. "The Origins of the 1832 Rebellion." In *Patterns of Contention in Mexican History*, ed. Jaime. E. Rodríguez O., 145–62. Wilmington DE: SR Books, 1992.

———. "The Struggle for the Nation: The First Centralist-Federalist Conflict in Mexico, 1822–1824." *The Americas* 49, no. 1 (July 1992): 1–22.

———. "The Transition from Colony to Nation: New Spain, 1820–1821." In *Mexico in the Age of Democratic Revolutions, 1750–1850*, ed. Jaime E. Rodríguez O., 97–132. Boulder CO: Lynne Rienner, 1994.

Rodríguez O., Jaime E., ed. *The Evolution of the Mexican Political System.* Wilmington DE: SR Books, 1993.

———. *The Independence of Mexico and the Creation of the New Nation.* Los Angeles: UCLA Latin American Center, 1989.

———. *Mexico in the Age of Democratic Revolutions, 1750–1850.* Boulder CO: Lynne Rienner, 1994.

———. *Patterns of Contention in Mexican History.* Wilmington DE: SR Books, 1992.

———. *Servando Teresa de Mier, Obras Completas: La formación de un republicano.* Mexico City: Universidad Nacional Autónoma de México, 1988.

Romano, Ruggiero. "Algunas consideraciones alrededor de Nación: Estado (y Libertad) en Europa y América centro-meridional." In *América Latina: Dallo stato coloniale allo stato nazione*, 2 vols., ed. Antonio Annino, 1:1–21. Milan: Franco Angeli, 1987.

Romero Flores, Jesús. *Historia de Michoacán.* 2 vols. Mexico City: Imprenta "Claridad," 1946.

Rosenzweig, Fernando, Rosaura Hernández, María Teresa Jarquín, and Manuel Miño Grijalva. *Breve historia del estado de México.* Mexico City: El Colegio Mexiquense, 1987.

Rubin, Jeffrey W. "Decentering the Regime: Culture and Regional Politics in Mexico." *Latin American Research Review* 31, no. 3 (1996): 85–126.

Rugeley, Terry. "Men of Audacity: Yucatán's Maya Peasantry and the Origins of the Caste War, 1800–1847." Manuscript submitted for publication.

Salvucci, Richard J. "'La parte más difícil': Recent Works on Nineteenth-Century Mexican History." *Latin American Research Review* 28, no. 1 (1993): 102–10.

————. *Textiles and Capitalism in Mexico: An Economic History of the Obrajes, 1539– 1840.* Princeton: Princeton University Press, 1987.

Salvucci, Richard J., Linda K. Salvucci, and Aslán Cohen. "The Politics of Protection: Interpreting Commercial Policy in Late Bourbon and Early National Mexico." In *The Political Economy of Spanish America in the Age of Revolution, 1750–1850,* ed. Kenneth J. Andrien and Lyman L. Johnson, 95–114. Albuquerque: University of New Mexico Press, 1994.

Samponaro, Frank N. "La alianza de Santa Anna y los federalistas, 1832–1834: Su formación y desintegración." *Historia Mexicana* 30, no. 3 (enero–marzo 1981): 358–90.

————. "Santa Anna and the Abortive Anti-federalist Revolt of 1833 in Mexico." *The Americas* 40, no. 1 (July 1983): 95–107.

Sánchez, Prisciliano. *Memoria sobre el estado actual de la administración pública del estado de Jalisco leída por el C. Gobernador Prisciliano Sánchez (1826): Seguida del Pacto federal de Anahuac.* Guadalajara: Poderes de Jalisco, 1974.

Sánchez-Arcilla Bernal, José. "La aportación de los diputados de la Nueva España a las Cortes de Cádiz: Mariano Mendiola." In *Memoria del IV Congreso de historia del derecho mexicano (1986),* 2 vols., ed. Beatriz Bernal, 2:961–87. Mexico City: Universidad Nacional Autónoma de México, 1988.

Sánchez Lamego, Miguel A. "El Colegio Militar y el motín de la Acordada." *Historia Mexicana* 10, no. 3 (enero–marzo 1961): 425–38.

Sánchez Luna, Gabriela. "Francisco García Salinas: Gobernador de Zacatecas (1828–1834)." In *Memoria del IV Congreso de historia del derecho mexicano (1986),* 2 vols., ed. Beatriz Bernal, 2:989–1001. Mexico City: Universidad Nacional Autónoma de México, 1988.

San Juan Victoria, Carlos. "Las utopías oligárquicas conocen sus límites (1821– 1834)." In *La formación del estado mexicano,* ed. María del Refugio González, 89– 120. Mexico City: Editorial Porrúa, 1984.

Santa Anna, Antonio López de. *The Eagle: The Autobiography of Santa Anna.* Edited by Ann Fears Crawford. Austin TX: Pemberton, 1967.

————. *Mi historia militar y política (1810–1874).* Vol. 2 of *Documentos ineditos o muy raros para la historia de México,* ed. Genaro García. Mexico City: Libreria de la Vda. de Ch. Bouret, 1905.

Santoni, Pedro. "A Fear of the People: The Civic Militia of Mexico in 1845." *Hispanic American Historical Review* 68, no. 2 (May 1988): 269–88.

Santoscoy, Alberto. *Canón cronológico razonado de los gobernantes de Jalisco: Desde la consumación de la independencia mexicana.* Guadalajara: Imprenta del "Diario de Jalisco," 1890.

Sepúlveda, César. "Historia y problemas de los límites de México: 1. La frontera Norte." *Historia Mexicana* 8, no. 1 (julio–septiembre 1958): 1–34.

———. "Historia y problemas de los límites de México: 2. La frontera Sur." *Historia Mexicana* 8, no. 2 (octubre–diciembre 1958): 145–74.

Serrano O., José Antonio. "El ascenso de un caudillo en Guanajuato: Luis de Cortázar, 1827–1832." *Historia Mexicana* 43, no. 1 (julio–septiembre 1993): 49–80.

Siemens, Alfred H. *Between the Summit and the Sea: Central Veracruz in the Nineteenth Century.* Vancouver: University of British Columbia Press, 1990.

Sierra, Catalina. *El nacimiento de México.* Mexico City: Universidad Nacional Autónoma de México, 1960.

Sierra, Justo. *The Political Evolution of the Mexican People.* Translated by Charles Ramsdell, notes by Edmundo O'Gorman. Austin: University of Texas Press, 1969.

Sims, Harold D. *Descolonización en México: El Conflicto entre mexicanos y españoles (1821–1831).* Mexico City: Fondo de Cultura Económica, 1982.

———. "Los exiliados españoles en México en 1829." *Historia Mexicana* 31, no. 3 (enero–marzo 1981): 390–414.

———. *La expulsión de los Españoles de México (1821–1828).* Mexico City: Fondo de Cultura Económica, 1974.

———. *The Expulsion of Mexico's Spaniards, 1821–1836.* Pittsburgh: University of Pittsburgh Press, 1990.

———. *La reconquista de México: La historia de los atentados españoles, 1821–1830.* Mexico City: Fondo de Cultura Económica, 1984.

Smith, Robert S. "The Institution of the Consulado in New Spain." *Hispanic American Historical Review* 24, no. 1 (February 1944): 62–83.

———. "The Puebla Consulado, 1821–1824." *Revista de historia de América* 21 (1946): 19–28.

Sordo Cedeño, Reynaldo. *El congreso en la primera república centralista.* Mexico City: El Colegio de México/Instituto Tecnológico Autónomo de México, 1993.

———. "El congreso y la formación del Estado-nación en México, 1821–1855." In *La fundación del estado mexicano, 1821–1855,* ed. Josefina Zoraida Vázquez, 135–78. Mexico City: Nueva Imagen, 1994.

———. "Santa Anna y la república centralista de las siete leyes." In *Cincuenta años de historia en México,* 2 vols., ed. Alicia Hernández Chávez and Manuel Miño Grijalva, 2:283–98. Mexico City: Centro de Estudios Históricos, El Colegio de México, 1991.

Sprague, William Forrest. *Vicente Guerrero, Mexican Liberator: A Study in Patriotism.* Chicago: R.R. Donnelley, 1939.

Staples, Anne. "Clerics as Politicians: Church, State, and Political Power in Independent Mexico." In *Mexico in the Age of Democratic Revolutions, 1750–1850*, ed. Jaime E. Rodríguez O., 223–41. Boulder CO: Lynne Rienner, 1994.

———. *La iglesia en la primera república federal mexicana (1824–1835)*. Mexico City: Editorial Sep Setentas, 1976.

———. "Secularización: Estado e iglesia en tiempos de Gómez Farías." *Estudios de historia moderna y contemporánea de México* 10 (1986): 109–23.

Stevens, Donald Fithian. "Autonomists, Nativists, Republicans, and Monarchists: Conspiracy and Political History in Nineteenth-Century Mexico." *Mexican Studies* 10, no. 1 (winter 1994): 247–66.

———. "Economic Fluctuations and Political Instability in Early Republican Mexico." *Journal of Interdisciplinary History* 16, no. 4 (spring 1986): 645–65.

———. *Origins of Instability in Early Republican Mexico*. Durham NC: Duke University Press, 1991.

———. "Riot, Rebellion, and Instability in Nineteenth-Century Mexico. In *Five Centuries of Mexican History*, 2 vols., ed. Virginia Guedea and Jaime E. Rodríguez O., 1:344–54. San Diego: Instituto de Investigaciones Dr. José María Luis Mora/University of California, Irvine, 1992.

Suárez y Navarro, Juan. *Historia de México y del general Antonio López de Santa Anna*. 2 vols. Mexico City: Imprenta de I. Cumplido, 1850–51.

Tanck Estrada, Dorothy. *La educación ilustrada (1786–1836)*. Mexico City: El Colegio de México, 1977.

Tayloe, Edward Thornton. *Mexico, 1825–1828: The Journal and Correspondence of Edward Thornton Tayloe*. Edited by C. Harvey Gardiner. Chapel Hill: University of North Carolina Press, 1959.

Tena Ramírez, Felipe. *Derecho constitucional mexicano*. 18th ed. Mexico City: Editorial Porrúa, 1981.

———. *Leyes fundamentales de México, 1808–1975*. 6th ed., rev. Mexico City: Editorial Porrúa, 1975.

Tenenbaum, Barbara. "Banqueros sin bancos: El papel de los agiotistas en México (1826–1854)." In *Banca y poder en México (1800–1925)*, ed. Leonor Ludlow and Carlos Marichal, 75–97. Mexico City: Editorial Grijalbo, 1986.

———. "The Chicken and the Egg: Reflections on the Mexican Military, 1821–1846." In *Five Centuries of Mexican History*, 2 vols., ed. Virginia Guedea and Jaime E. Rodríguez O., 1:355–70. Mexico City: Instituto de Investigaciones Dr. José María Luis Mora/University of California, Irvine, 1992.

———. "The Making of a Fait Accompli: Mexico and the Provincias Internas, 1776–1846." In *The Evolution of the Mexican Political System*, ed. Jaime E. Rodríguez O., 91–115. Wilmington DE: SR Books, 1993.

———. "Merchants, Money, and Mischief: The British in Mexico, 1821–1862." *The Americas* 35, no. 3 (January 1979): 317–40.

———. *The Politics of Penury: Debts and Taxes in Mexico, 1821–1856*. Albuquerque: University of New Mexico Press, 1986.

————. "Streetwise History: The Paseo de la Reforma and the Porfirian State, 1876–1910." In *Rituals of Rule, Rituals of Resistance: Public Celebrations and Popular Culture in Mexico*, ed. William H. Beezley, Cheryl English Martin, and William E. French, 127–50. Wilmington DE: SR Books, 1994.

————. "Taxation and Tyranny: Public Finance during the Iturbide Regime, 1821–1823." In *The Independence of Mexico and the Creation of the New Nation*, ed. Jaime E. Rodríguez O., 201–13. Los Angeles: UCLA Latin American Center, 1989.

TePaske, John Jay. "The Financial Disintegration of the Royal Government of Mexico during the Epoch of Independence." In *The Independence of Mexico and the Creation of the New Nation*, ed. Jaime E. Rodríguez O., 63–83. Los Angeles: UCLA Latin American Center, 1989.

Thomson, Guy P. C. *Puebla de los Angeles: Industry and Society in a Mexican City, 1700–1850.* Boulder CO: Westview, 1989.

————. "Traditional and Modern Manufacturing in Mexico, 1821–1850." In *América Latina en la época de Simón Bolívar: La formación de las economías nacionales y los intereses europeos, 1800–1850*, ed. Reinhard Liehr, 55–85. Berlin: Colloquium Verlag, 1989.

Tornel, José María. *Breve reseña de los acontecimientos mas notables de la nación mexicana desde el año de 1821 hasta nuestros dias.* Mexico City: Imprenta de Cumplido, 1852.

Torres Bautista, Mariano. "Estado-nación y legitimidad, misma búsqueda, mismas ficciones." In *Espacio y perfiles: Historia regional mexicana del siglo XIX*, ed. Carlos Contreras Cruz, 213–21. Puebla: Universidad Autónoma de Puebla, 1989.

Torre Villar, Ernesto de la. "El origen del estado mexicano." In *Problemas de la formación del estado y de la nación en hispanoamérica*, ed. Inge Buisson et al., 127–42. Cologne: Bohlau Verlag, 1984.

Trens, Manuel B. *Historia de Chiapas: Desde los tiempos más remotos hasta la caída del segundo imperio.* 2d ed. Mexico City: Talleres Gráficos de la Nación, 1957.

————. *Historia de Veracruz.* 6 vols. Jalapa: Enriquez, 1948.

Trueba, Alfonso. *Nicolás Bravo: El mexicano que perdonó.* Mexico City: Editorial Jus, 1976.

Tutino, John. *From Insurrection to Revolution in Mexico: Social Bases of Agrarian Violence, 1750–1940.* Princeton: Princeton University Press, 1986.

Urías Horcasitas, Beatriz. "Conciencia regional y poder central: Ensayo sobre el pensamiento separatista yucateco en la primera mitad del siglo diecinueve." *Estudios de historia moderna y contemporánea de México* II (1988): 59–83.

————. "El pensamiento económico moderno en el México independiente." In *The Independence of Mexico and the Creation of the New Nation*, ed. Jaime E. Rodríguez O., 265–74. Los Angeles: UCLA Latin American Center, 1989.

Valadés, José C. *Alamán: Estadista e historiador.* Mexico City: José Porrúa e Hijos, 1938.

————. *México, Santa Anna, y la guerra de Texas.* Mexico City: Editores Mexicanos Unidos, 1965.

—. *Orígenes de la república mexicana: La aurora constitucional.* Mexico City: Editores Mexicanos Unidos, 1972.

Valle, Rafael Hiliodoro, ed. *La anexión de Centroamerica a México.* Vols. 4, 5, and 6 of Archivo Histórico Diplomatica Mexicano. Mexico City: Secretaría de Relaciones Exteriores, 1945, 1946, 1949.

Van Young, Eric. "Are Regions Good to Think?" In *Mexico's Regions: Comparative History and Development,* ed. Eric Van Young, 1–36. San Diego: Center for U.S.-Mexican Studies, University of California, San Diego, 1992.

—. *La crisis del orden colonial: Estructura agraria y rebelión popular en la Nueva España, 1750–1821.* Mexico City: Alianza Editorial, 1991.

—. *Hacienda and Market in Eighteenth-Century Mexico: The Rural Economy of the Guadalajara Region, 1675–1820.* Berkeley and Los Angeles: University of California Press, 1981.

—. "Islands in the Storm: Quiet Cities and Violent Countrysides in the Mexican Independence Era." *Past and Present* 118 (February 1988): 130–55.

—. "Quetzalcóatl, King Ferdinand, and Ignacio Allende Go to the Seashore: Or Messianism and Mystical Kingship in Mexico, 1800–1821." In *The Independence of Mexico and the Creation of the New Nation,* ed. Jaime E. Rodríguez O., 109–27. Los Angeles: UCLA Latin American Center, 1989.

—. "The Raw and the Cooked: Elite and Popular Ideology in Mexico, 1800–1821." In *The Middle Period in Latin America: Values and Attitudes in the Seventeenth-Nineteenth Centuries,* ed. Mark D. Szuchman, 75–102. Boulder CO: Lynne Rienner, 1989.

—. "The State as Vampire—Hegemonic Projects, Public Ritual, and Popular Culture in Mexico, 1600–1990." In *Rituals of Rule, Rituals of Resistance: Public Celebrations and Popular Culture in Mexico,* ed. William H. Beezley, Cheryl English Martin, and William E. French, 343–74. Wilmington DE: SR Books, 1994.

—. "Who Was That Masked Man, Anyway? Popular Symbols and Ideology in the Mexican Wars of Independence." Rocky Mountain Council on Latin American Studies, Annual Meeting, *Proceedings* 1:18–35. Las Cruces, New Mexico, 1984.

Van Young, Eric, ed. *Mexico's Regions: Comparative History and Development.* San Diego: Center for U.S.-Mexican Studies, University of California, San Diego, 1992.

Vázquez, Josefina Zoraida. "La crisis y los partidos políticos, 1833–1846." In *América Latina: Dallo stato coloniale allo stato nazione,* 2 vols., ed. Antonio Annino, 2:557–72. Milan: Franco Angeli, 1987.

—. "De la difícil constitución de un Estado: México, 1821–1854." In *La fundación del estado mexicano, 1821–1855,* ed. Josefina Zoraida Vázquez, 9–37. Mexico City: Nueva Imagen, 1994.

—. *Don Antonio López de Santa Anna: Mito y enigma.* Mexico City: Condumex, 1987.

————. "El ejército: Un dilema del gobierno Mexicano (1841–1864)." In *Problemas de la formación del estado y de la nación en Hispanoamérica*, ed. Inge Buisson et al., 319–38. Cologne: Bohlau Verlag, 1984.

————. "El federalismo mexicano: 1823–1847." In *Federalismos latinoamericanos: México/Brasil/Argentina*, ed. Marcello Carmagnani, 15–50. Mexico City: El Colegio de México/Fondo de Cultura Económica, 1993.

————. "Iglesia, ejército y centralismo." *Historia Mexicana* 39, no. 1 (julio–septiembre 1989): 205–34.

————. *Mexicanos y norteamericanos ante la guerra del 47.* Mexico City: Secretaría de Educación Pública, 1972.

————. "Political Plans and Collaboration between Civilians and the Military, 1821–1846." *Bulletin of Latin American Research* 15, no. 1 (January 1996): 19–38.

————. "Los pronunciamientos de 1832: Aspirantismo político e ideología." In *Patterns of Contention in Mexican History*, ed. Jaime E. Rodríguez O., 163–86. Wilmington DE: SR Books, 1992.

————. "Un viejo tema: El federalismo y el centralismo." *Historia Mexicana* 42, no. 3 (enero–marzo 1993): 621–31.

Vázquez, Josefina Zoraida, ed. *De la rebelión de Texas a la guerra del 47.* Mexico City: Nueva Imagen, 1994.

————. *La fundación del estado mexicano, 1821–1855.* Mexico City: Nueva Imagen, 1994.

————. *Interpretaciones del siglo XVIII mexicano: El impacto de las reformas borbónicas.* Mexico City: Nueva Imagen, 1992.

————. *Planes políticos de la nación mexicana, vols. 2 and 3.* Mexico City: Senado de la República, 1987.

Vázquez, Josefina Zoraida, and Lorenzo Meyer. *México frente a Estados Unidos (Un ensayo histórico, 1776–1988).* 2d ed. Mexico City: Fondo de Cultura Económica, 1989.

Vázquez de Knauth, Josefina. *Nacionalismo y educación en México.* 2d ed. Mexico City: El Colegio de México, 1975.

Vega, Mercedes de. "La opción federalista en Zacatecas, 1820–1835." In *Cincuenta años de historia de México*, 2 vols., ed. Alicia Hernández Chávez and Manuel Miño Grijalva, 2:243–59. Mexico City: Centro de Estudios Históricos, El Colegio de México, 1991.

Velázquez, Gustavo G. *La diputación del Estado de México en el supremo congreso constituyente de 1823: Notas Biográficas.* Toluca: Gobierno del Estado de México, 1977.

Velázquez, Primo Feliciano. *Historia de San Luis Potosí.* 4 vols. Mexico City: Sociedad Mexicana de Geografía y Estadística, 1947–48.

Victoria, Guadalupe. *Discursos y manifiestos.* Presentación por Salvador Reyes Nevares. Mexico City: Partido Revolucionario Institucional, 1976.

Villalpando César, José Manuel. "La evolución histórico-jurídico de la guardia nacional en México." In *Memoria del IV Congreso de historia del derecho mexicano* (*1986*), 2 vols., ed. Beatriz Bernal, 1:1117–62. Mexico City: Universidad Nacional Autónoma de México, 1988.

Voss, Stuart F. *On the Periphery of Nineteenth-Century Mexico: Sonora and Sinaloa, 1810–1877.* Tucson: University of Arizona Press, 1982.

Voto general de los pueblos de la provincia libre de Xalisco denominada hasta ahora de Guadalajara sobre constituir su forma de gobierno en república federal. 1824. Reprint, Guadalajara: Poderes de Jalisco, 1973.

Walker, David W. *Kinship, Business, and Politics: The Martínez del Río Family in Mexico, 1823–1867.* Austin: University of Texas Press, 1986.

Ward, Henry George. *Mexico in 1827.* 2d ed. London: Colburn, 1829.

Weber, David J. *The Mexican Frontier, 1821–1846: The American Southwest under Mexico.* Albuquerque: University of New Mexico Press, 1982.

———. "Mexico's Far Northern Frontier, 1821–1854: Historiography Askew." *The Western Historical Quarterly* 7, no. 3 (July 1976): 279–93.

Wortman, Miles. "Legitimidad política y regionalismo—El Imperio Mexicano y Centroamérica." *Historia Mexicana* 26, no. 2 (octubre–diciembre 1976): 238–62.

Yáñez, Agustín. *Santa Anna: Espectro de una sociedad.* Mexico City: Océano, 1982.

Zavala, Lorenzo de. *Ensayo crítico de las revoluciones de México desde 1808 hasta 1830.* Vol. 2 of *Obras.* Paris, 1831–32. Reprint, Mexico City: Editorial Porrúa, 1969.

Zepeda Patterson, Jorge. "La nación vs. las regiones." In *El nacionalismo en México*, ed. Cecilia Noriega Elío, 497–517. Zamora: El Colegio de Michoacán, 1992.

Zorrilla, Juan Fidel, Maribel Miró Flaquer, and Octavio Herrera Pérez, comps. *Tamaulipas: Textos de su historia, 1810–1921.* 2 vols. Mexico City: Instituto de Investigaciones Dr. José María Luis Mora, 1990.

INDEX

Gómez Pedraza, Manuel (*cont.*)
  252, 253, 254, 255; as secretary of
  war, 205; and Yorkinos, 198–99;
  mentioned, 249
Grito de Dolores, 51
Guadalajara: on federalism, 121–23;
  and formation of federal republic,
  120; provincial deputation of, 129.
  See also Nueva Galicia; Jalisco
Guadalupes: in War of Independence,
  80; as Yorkino society, 198
Guatemala, II, 12, 38, 56, 57. *See also*
  Central America
Guerrero (state), II, 123
Guerrero, Vicente: as candidate for
  president, 202, 207–8, 216; death
  of, 241–42; and 1824 election, 178;
  and expulsion of Spaniards, 198;
  image of, 223; and Montaño rebellion, 205–6; and Plan of Iguala, 69,
  82; presidency of, 210–11, 215, 217,
  222–23, 224–25, 227, 228; and
  Puebla, 160, 161; rebels against Iturbide, 105; and Supreme Executive
  Power, 112, 152; and war of the
  south, 236, 240–41
Guridi y Alcocer, José Miguel, 55, 143
Guzmán, Gordiano: as caudillo of
  Michoacán, 245; as federalist, 103;
  and war of the south, 236, 243, 249

Herrera, José Joaquin, 113, 140, 171
Hidalgo, Miguel, 7, 50–51, 60, 73
Historia Antigua de México (Clavijero),
  39
Honduras, 12, 72
Huarte, Ramón, 83, 107
Humboldt, Alexander von, 45, 100

Ibar, Francisco, 221
Ibarra, Cayetano, 195

identity: creole, 39–40; national, 15, 18,
  21, 36, 40, 87–88, 99–101; provincial, 10
Impartials, 207
intendancies, xi, II, 38, 41
Internal Provinces of the East, II, 56, 57
Internal Provinces of the West, II, 56,
  57
Isabel (of Castile), 36, 37
Isla de Términos, 137
Iturbide, Agustín de: abdication of, x,
  108; and Constituent Congress, 91,
  93, 94; as emperor, 94–96; on independence, 73–74; and the
  masses, 83; on monarchy, 86–87;
  and Plan of Iguala, 78, 82–83; and
  provinces, 89; and Puebla, 48; and
  Spaniards, 87; Veracruz uprising
  against, 103–5; mentioned, 7, 13–14,
  35, 68–69, 83–84, 85
Iturrigaray, José de, 49, 50

Jalisco: and Acta Constitutiva, 147–48,
  180–81; and expulsion of Spaniards,
  203; and Guerrero's death, 242; in-
  vasions of, 133–36, 172–74; and
  Iturbidism, 169–72; population of,
  102; and provinces, 60; state constitution of, 167, 185
Juan Carlos (king of Spain), 37
Juárez, Benito, 155
Junta Central, 43, 45
Junta of Puebla, 109

Lafragua, José María, 244
Lagos conferences, 135
Landero, Pedro, 247, 248
Lemus, Pedro, 257
León, Antonio de, 136–37, 157, 245
Lobato, José María, 197, 219
Louis XVIII (king of France), 66
Luaces, Domingo, 69

Zacatecas (*cont.*)
  federalism, 124, 134, 174, 182, 260;
  and Guerrero's death, 242; state
  constitution of, 190
Zavala, Lorenzo de: and Acordada revolt, 218–19, 220, 221; in Congress,
  137; and expulsion of Spaniards, 202;
  flees Mexico, 233; governor of Mexico state, 200; on Guerrero, 211; and
  popular sovereignty, 239; as secretary of finance, 223, 227; and Victoria, 179; mentioned, 68, 93, 94, 112
Zavaleta, Treaty of, 254, 255
Zedillo, Ernesto, 267–68
Zerecero, Anastacio, 221, 232
Zerecero, Mariano, 232–33